Söyüngül C.......... ..

THE LAND DRENCHED IN TEARS

"Kökte yultuz yaltiridir tün qara bolghan sayi,
  Yadima tengrim töshedir bextim qara bolghan sayi."
"The stars brightened the sky as the darkness spread;
  My Lord lightens my heart amidst the clouds and darkness of my fate."

Abdulla Toqay

Translated from the Uyghur by Rahima Mahmut

HERTFORDSHIRE PRESS

HERTFORDSHIRE PRESS

Published & Printed in UK
Hertfordshire Press Ltd © 2018
e-mail: publisher@hertfordshirepress.com
www.hertfordshirepress.com

THE LAND DRENCHED IN TEARS
Söyüngül Chanisheff ©

English

Translated from the Uyghur by Rahima Mahmut
Edited by Iskandar Ding, Gareth Stamp
Design by Alexandra Rey

British Library Catalogue in Publication Data
A catalogue record for this book is available from the British Library
Library of Congress in Publication Data
A catalogue record for this book has been requested

ISBN: 978-1-910886-38-0

Supported using public funding by
ARTS COUNCIL
ENGLAND

This book has been selected to receive financial assistance from English PEN's Writers in Translation programme supported by Arts Council England. English PEN exists to promote literature and its understanding, uphold writers' freedoms around the world, campaign against the persecution and imprisonment of writers for stating their views, and promote the friendly co-operation of writers and free exchange of ideas.

Each year, a dedicated committee of professionals selects books that are translated into English from a wide variety of foreign languages. We award grants to UK publishers to help translate and champion these titles. Our aim is to celebrate books of outstanding literary quality from all over the world.

www.englishpen.org

CONTENTS

Söyüngül Chanisheff - photo was taken in 1963, in the city of Urumchi, East Turkistan, while studying at Medical University

FROM AUTHOR

I would like to acknowledge and thank the endless hard work and effort that has been given by Rahima Mahmut for her translation of my biography, The Land Drenched in Tears. Without her assistance and tireless work in translating my book, the world would not have had the chance to know all that has occurred in East Turkistan, and all the suffering that many ethnic minorities in China, such as Uyghurs, Tatars, Uzbeks, Kazakhs etc. have endured for many years and continues to face even to this day. It has been a dream of mine to write my biography and let the world in to see the true historical events through my eyes, and Rahima has had the tough task of translating all this, which she has done so well. I am grateful to her and her helpers who have made my dream become a reality.

Söyüngül Chanisheff
8 August 2016
Adelaide, Australia

TRANSLATOR'S ACKNOWLEDGEMENT

I would like to thank the author, Söyüngül Chanisheff in giving me the honour of translating this heart-wrenching story of her life. She is the source of inspiration and role model for me in overcoming my own difficulties in the journey of exile as a human rights defender for my people, country and family. I also would like to thank my son, Zulfukar, for giving me strength, support and understanding. Above all my heartfelt gratitude goes out to my dear friends John Ramsey and Adeeba Yakub who tirelessly offered their support in perfecting the translation, without them all of this would not have been possible. Finally, I am very grateful for my friend Iskandar Ding for his excellent editing and additions of the footnotes.

Rahima Mahmut

NOTE ON TRANSLITERATION

In this book, we have adopted the Uyghur Latin Alphabet to transliterate Uyghur words, names, and toponyms. As a result, some names may not appear in the same way as they usually do in other texts (e.g. Ürümchi and not Urumqi, Chöchek and not Qoqak, Seypidin Ezizi and not Saifuddin Azizi), the only exceptions being the three historical cities of Kashgar, Yarkand, and Khotan, where the 'historical' transliteration has been preferred. Chinese names are uniformly transliterated with the pinyin system, except in the widely accepted case of Chiang Kai-shek, where the Wade-Giles transliteration has been kept. Dungan (Hui) names, if given in Arabic, are transliterated according to the conventional Romanisation of Arabic names, or in pinyin, if given in Chinese. Names in other languages, such as Russian, are transliterated according to international conventions. Words and names in other languages, which do not apparently have a standardised way of transliteration, are transliterated with the Uyghur Latin Alphabet according to their pronunciation in Uyghur.

PRONUNCIATION GUIDE TO CERTAIN LETTERS

In Uyghur:
j: like 'j' in English 'John'
zh: like 'j' in French 'Jean', or 'g' in French 'rouge'
gh: like 'r' in French 'rouge'
q: a 'deep, throaty k'
x: like 'ch' in Scottish Gaelic 'loch'
é: a narrow 'e' sound, like 'é' in French 'été'
ö: like in German and Turkish
ü: like in German and Turkish, or the 'u' in French 'tu'

In Chinese:
c: like 'ts' in English 'eats'
zh: like 'j' in English 'John', but with the tip of the tongue curled
q: like 'ch' in English 'cheese'
x: like 'sh' in English 'sheep'

FROM UNIVERSITY TO IMPRISONMENT

Prison

The prison van I was travelling in turned the corner into a very narrow side street. 'Do you know where this place is?' asked Mr Turdi, pointing at the tall gates in front of them. It was obvious from the first glance that it was a prison, surrounded by a three-metre high wall with watchtowers on the corners. I observed two heavily armed guards in each tower holding their weapons as if they were ready for war, while other guards patrolled the walls.

'Surely you know where you are by now?' said Mr Turdi as the van came to a stop near the prison gate blowing its horn. A smaller black painted door creaked open and two armed policemen emerged to stand at either side of the doorway. 'Wait here in the van' ordered Mr Turdi, as he got out and went inside the prison. As I sat waiting, I gazed around before looking into the prison yard through the doorway to see people working in pairs carrying baskets of earth. I thought they must be prisoners. I stared at them as they moved around. I noticed that they looked at the van sympathetically and whispered to each other.

Mr Turdi quickly returned. 'Get out now and stand here until we are allowed to enter.' He told the driver to unload my cases at the prison gate and leave. While we were waiting, Mr Turdi commiserated with me. 'You could have had a wonderful life, like a beautiful young rose, but you didn't nurture it.'

I listened to him, but my eyes were fixed on what was happening within the prison yard. The prisoners were dark-skinned from having worked under the scorching sun for long hours; they looked frail and exhausted. Their clothes were nothing more than multi-coloured patched rags. They reminded me of lost souls as they stumbled around with their heavy loads. As I exchanged glances with the prisoners, I could not help wondering whom these people were, why they were here, and how long they had been enduring this hardship. My heart ached for them. The scene of the Chinese guards pacing back and forth along the walls, watching the prisoners from ethnic minorities carrying out hard manual labour, was a stark reminder of injustices that we were facing everywhere at all times. Was such hardship to be written in our destiny?

I waited for Mr Turdi to finish speaking before asking, 'How can I tell my family that I have been arrested? Is it possible to write them letters from here?'

'That should be the least of your worries at the moment. I imagine the whole city knows of your arrest by now, not only your parents.' Mr Turdi replied coldly.

'Have you informed my family?' I enquired.

'No, I haven't. Don't you think they know by now? Perhaps the news has even spread throughout Xinjiang. No doubt during the next several days, your case will be discussed by various government organisations.' I gaped at Mr Turdi. 'What's the matter? Why are you looking so shocked?' he asked.

'Me shocked! Nothing surprises me any more! There are always things for people to examine, even small insignificant student matters.' I laughed.

'To you it may seem simple, but to others it isn't. And that's why you've ended up here, the No.1 Provincial top security prison. So, do you still consider your involvement to be trivial?' He was becoming more agitated.

'Demanding independence isn't a crime, it's everyone's right.' I protested. 'It's against the law when you try to split a country by promoting separatism.' Mr Turdi said.

'That's interesting.' I laughed.

Mr Turdi pointed at the prisoners and asked, 'Tell me the truth, what do you see? Do you recognise anyone there?'

'No one.' I said as I started to walk forward.

Mr Turdi looked at me in shock, 'Where are you going? You students are disgraceful. If you carry on behaving like this you will put me in a very difficult situation.' He grabbed my sleeve to stop me, as I glanced through the doorway and saw my friend Sajide, waving and smiling at me. 'Oh!' I exclaimed, 'Sajide is here as well!'

'Didn't you expect to find Sajide imprisoned here? Ok, let's go. Aren't you scared of entering a place like this?' Mr Turdi enquired.

'There's nothing for me to be scared of here, to me it's just another school.'

We walked into the prison and turned right towards an office where an old Chinese man and Police Investigator Ömerjan were sitting at a table.

As I entered, Ömerjan looked at me with a smile and delivered a scathing indictment of my current situation, 'Ah, so your dream has come true. Are you happy now that you have achieved what you wanted?'

I looked at him with disgust, 'My aim in life is not to end up in here, despite your aim of locking up anyone who dares to speak their mind. You should be happy today since *your* dream has been fulfilled.'

'Oh, so you are still acting with bravado. Don't realise where you are, do you? This is a place where tigers are transformed into mice.' The threat in Ömerjan's voice was clear.

'You know she was amused by seeing Sajide waving to her earlier. You wouldn't believe how happy they both looked to see each other.' Mr Turdi added.

The Chinese man began filling out the official prison documentation.

After it was done, Ömerjan and Mr Turdi stood up saying: 'We're leaving now. So if you wish to say anything, you had better say it now because you won't see us again.'

'No thank you. I have nothing to say, nor do I require anything from you.' I replied. They laughed as they left.

A small Chinese man entered and walked up to me; he ran a full body check on me, then searched through my pockets. Afterwards he ordered me to collect my belongings and follow him. When I went outside to collect them, I noticed two men, one was a tall, dark-eyed, and had bushy eyebrows, the other was slim and was wearing a Galifi Shalwar. His colleague was an old man of medium stature with blue eyes and a long thin greyish beard. His appearance was typical of an ethnic Tatar. They were carrying a basket balanced between two poles between them as they passed me by.

The tall man looked at me with pain in his eyes, 'Sister, what has brought you here? Oh, don't worry.' His simple words carried much sadness and touched me deeply. My experiences since arriving had been like a game and hadn't affected me. However, these quietly spoken words were different and made me realise that my life was about to take a harsh and dangerous turn, one from which there would be no coming back. As I stared, I heard someone shouting: 'Mr Ötkür and Semet Abliz please bring those tools here.' I now knew their names. They glanced at me in parting, and said to me, 'It didn't matter sister, the days will pass by, just be patient and strong.' These words of comfort made me feel better.

After my belongings had been searched, I picked up my cases and slowly followed the Chinese man into the prison complex, thinking that this was to be my final peaceful carefree moment. I wanted to hold onto it as long as I could.

The man stopped in front of the prison hall doors. The clock above the door read 3 pm. This is how I know the exact time I was incarcerated. We entered the dark hall lit by a round window in the high arched circular ceiling. From the hall there were five corridors leading off in different directions. Hanging from the ceiling in the centre of the hall were circular security mirrors, which allowed armed Chinese guards to watch all five corridors.

I was escorted to a corridor on the right. As I walked into the corridor, I saw further doors off the corridor that I guessed must lead to cells. I thought there must be about two to three women per cell. The man who was carrying my bedding stopped at the second door on the right, cell number three.

The man unlocked and opened the cell door. I was shocked when I looked inside to see a dank, dirty room, thick with dust and layers of cobwebs. It stank of human sweat, urine and excrement. The only furniture was a filthy wooden sleeping platform, a broom, and a cement cupboard, built into the wall of the room. As I entered, the bile rose in my throat and I retched. I wanted to vomit.

The man followed me in and put my bedding onto the sleeping platform. I stood in the centre of the cell and stared at the filthy walls, ceiling, and the small dust-covered metal-framed window near the top of one wall. Only on hearing the clunk of the metal door and the key turning in the lock did I realise that I was now alone. I was appalled by the implications of being in this dreadful place – what would happen to me? What was happening to me now? 'This can't be real!' I thought in denial, 'It's a nightmare, that's all.' I shook my head hard; telling myself to wake up, wake up! Nothing changed and the awful truth began to sink in: this was not a nightmare.

I was now in prison and this was to be my room. I decided that if this was to be my home, I would start by cleaning it. I opened my case, took out a headscarf to cover my hair, and rolled up my sleeves. I took the brush and began sweeping the ceiling and walls free of cobwebs and dust, working from top to bottom. The dust made me sneeze continuously. I left the wooden platform and floor until last. Through watering eyes, I swept the pile of dirt into the furthest corner of the room. Then I turned to the wall unit. I cleaned it out, still sneezing, and stacked my cups, plates, a bowl and other small belongings in it. Finally, I unpacked my rose-petal woollen rug, the rug that I had bought in the market with my father when I was ten. I spread it across the wooden platform and placed my bedding against the wall.

I hadn't stopped sneezing from all the dust and the smell, and the sound echoed round the cell. A prison guard, who was patrolling along the corridor outside, slid the food slot in the door open –

'What's happened? Why are you sneezing so much?' He burst out laughing when I stuttered my answer, in between sneezes, that the dust had irritated my nostrils and throat, and that I couldn't help it. The guard left the food slot open for at least thirty minutes but it made no difference. I didn't stop sneezing for quite a while.

Since I had nothing else to do, I sat down to rest. I quickly became bored, and tried to sleep, but my mind was churning furiously. I got up and paced backwards and forwards, singing, in a vain attempt to distract myself, only failing to allay my restless boredom. I looked around at the walls noticing for the first time that there were messages written on them. Curious to read them, I moved closer to the wall. The messages told of darkness, love, sickness, the pain of hunger, and cried out for freedom or death. One verse stood out and remains etched in my mind forever,

'One can never understand without experiencing it, one can not die if death doesn't come to him.' The name Mirza Ahmet was signed below the verse.

Reading this name reminded me of what my friend Abliz had told me: 'There are many good men out there like Mirza Ahmet and Mirzahit who have been arrested in Ghulja, accused of being nationalist and sent for re-education in hard labour camp.' This made me wonder if they had been kept here, in this very cell and I reflected on where they might be now.

I remembered what Ibray from Chöchek had said, 'Is there any other mad man in this world more crazier than me? Having brought myself to this security prison I pounded on the gates and shouted: 'I am a criminal, arrest me'! Two guards emerged through the gates to find me drunk so they dragged me to the main road telling me to go home. However I repeatedly returned to the gate shouting: 'I am a criminal as I have travelled here with false documents, arrest me now'! I awoke the next day to find myself in this cell and fifteen months later I am still here. You will not find anyone else in this prison like me." His story lightened my mood and I laughed.

I had been informed that use of the toilet would be at 4 o'clock and dinner would be at 5 o'clock. I felt my sense of time slipping. Hadn't an hour already passed? Why does time pass so slowly? It felt like it was getting darker and seemed as if I had been alone for hours. Never having been isolated from people in the past, I had always found it difficult to deal with loneliness. If one hour was passing so slowly, what would a day, months or years in this place feel like? I briskly told myself that I might get used to it after a few days, and felt better as I looked out through the dusty window at the shining sun and blue sky.

I walked over to the door, hoping to find a crack or peep-hole that would allow me to see into the corridor. As I scrutinised the door, I realised that it was covered with a sheet of metal. After a long painful search I managed to find a small hole from which I could see the corridor, and the opposite cell, No.22. I gazed out for a long time but saw nothing, so I returned to sit on the wooden platform.

The silence was broken by the sound of keys turning and doors opening. I knew then that it was 4 o'clock. I wondered if the toilets were outside of the building as I heard heavy footsteps approaching. Although I knew my door would be opened, the sound of the key turning and the bang of the door opening made me jump and my heart beat faster. I walked into the corridor to be escorted to the toilet, which was at the end of the corridor. Two armed guards escorted two prisoners at a time to the toilet and both the toilet and the prisoner's cell were searched every time.

It wasn't long afterwards that the food slot was opened and a Chinese man appeared, shouting, 'Did you arrive today? Do you have your own bowl?' I passed my bowl to him, which he returned, filled with red bean soup. Having little appetite I only managed two spoonfuls before pushing the bowl aside. I told myself that everything to keep me occupied had been done – now there was nothing left for me to do until tomorrow morning.'

The light that came on at that moment was the size of a tiny glow-worm, and only bright enough to light up the area of a small round grape. It barely lit the cell at all. In the dimness, the cell looked gloomy and sad and I began to feel depressed. Quite suddenly the sound of a voice singing came to my ears. The voice was filled with love, which was both painfully moving and beautiful in reminding me that I was not alone. The sounds of singing increased as other prisoners joined in; they sang songs of pain and suffering. It was as though all the prison cells were rising into the sky through the poignant lyrics sung by these hapless souls. The prison guards ran from one cell to another, trying to stop the song of the prisoners, but none of the singers took any notice. I immersed myself in the moment until it faded away. Then the cell once again took on the chill of a haunted town.

Feeling restless and saddened, I moved closer to the wall and reflected upon what had happened to me and where we had gone wrong. We had had so many dreams and ambitions, look where I was now! The dimness of the light bulb made me think of the words spoken by our head teacher, Ms Rizwan, 'You must achieve a good standard of education, be successful and happy in the future as you are the hopes of our country.' She had always encouraged me to work harder and praised me for achievements. The events of our high school graduation ceremony flashed before my eyes.

It was June 1957, in Hang Ching Hall in Ürümchi. The Hall was a stunning building made even more attractive by all the flower decorations and bunting hung throughout. I was very emotional as I stood on the stage being presented with my diploma by Ms Rizwan, while the national anthem of East Turkistan was being played. For me, the moment represented my achievements over the last ten years. Ms Rizwan congratulated me and smiled as she shook my hand and wished me success in the future. Then, all the other teachers on the stage shook my hand in congratulation. The Hall, which could hold 800 people, was filled to capacity with students, in traditional dress, celebrating our achievements. Everyone was in a joyful mood.

This was the culmination of my school years and I never forgot the feeling that day of flying among the stars. To me, all the courses I had undertaken were only the beginning to unveiling the mysteries of the world around me. I dreamt of becoming a writer or a poet with my pen as a sword to fight against the injustices of the world. In my writings, I wished to praise the bravery of my people and tell the world of my ideas about the future of East Turkistan.

Other times, I dreamt of becoming a doctor to save the sick and dying. I even imagined seeking a cure for death so that we all could live forever. I also wanted to become a teacher, so that I could educate the future generations who would go on to become the most successful people in the world. In my heart and mind I was very indecisive as I fantasised about my many possible and brilliant career paths. As humans, what don't we desire? What is our fate? Only God knows what is to be our future.

The 'Thought Reform Movement'

In September 1957, when I returned from my summer vacation I found out that I had been accepted into the Xinjiang Medical Institute, to which all my belongings had already been sent. There were a hundred and twenty-five students accepted from all over Xinjiang, of whom six of us were from my High School. I quickly made many new friends and got to know most people.

Two days after arriving at University the nationwide 'Thought Reform Movement' was implemented by the Chinese government. Everyone from teachers, doctors, nurses, workers and cadres and students were ordered to attend. It was a mobilising movement for the ethnic groups except Chinese. This meant that all Chinese, including teachers, students and other staff, could go about their daily tasks uninterrupted. The ethos of this meeting was to 'Let a hundred flowers bloom and a hundred schools of thought contend'. It called upon individuals to openly express their opinions of the communist regime. The government would make public sector reforms according to people's opinions, we were told. We were divided into small, medium, or large groups and encouraged to open up and sing, as our opinions would be used to 'improve the lives of the people in the future!

We were forced to attend these meetings everyday. At the beginning the discussions were only concerned with minor issues, however these innocuous talks gradually moved into more dangerous areas such as whether Xinjiang should become an independent state, or whether the people of Xinjiang should be given their own rights with regard to the wealth and resources of the region.

At this point in our discussions, the students from our year brought a copy of a written Chinese People's Constitutional document which had been drawn up at the First Communist Parties Congress in which Mao had stated, 'Xinjiang has ample space and rich resources, therefore it is reason enough for it to be added as a part of the Republic.'

The students pointed Mao's words out with some denouncing his view, 'He says that our land was added to the Republic because of its wealth, and that's the only reason they have their eyes on our country.' The debate became more and more heated as the students boldly expressed their opinions. 'In Mao's words he stated that we were a Republic, so why is it that Xinjiang is referred to as a province rather than an independent Republic?' The majority of students argued that Xinjiang should be an independent republic, one in which we could retain and control our own wealth, choose our own coat of arms and flag, and make our own laws, regulations and policies.

These ideals of self-rule in Xinjiang were widely supported by the students, teachers and the University cadres, and became the centre of many fervent debates across the university as the days passed. Those who failed to participate in the exchanges had their photographs taken and displayed on the University walls to shame them, with accusations that they were against the separatist movement. This forced everyone to speak out regardless of their true beliefs. I personally felt that it was important to speak out, although I was nervous about doing so in a public forum.

I pushed myself to express my thoughts and stood up, 'When in Year 4 at Tatar school we had a history lesson where we studied a book called "A Brief History of East Turkistan Up to 1912", published in Tashkent in 1949. In this text, the author argued that the land of Xinjiang had always belonged to the Uyghur people, and that the land within the Great Walls of China belonged to the Chinese people. Therefore the Chinese people should leave Xinjiang and return the land back to its rightful owners.

'Since the Chinese arrived in Xinjiang, there has been a rise in street–crime, and in night–time muggings and murders, which have been committed by Chinese criminals. This anti-social behaviour is disturbing the peaceful lives of the native peoples and if it continues, the consequences for this country will be disastrous.' My spoken opinions gave confidence to other students who came forward to express similar opinions. These meetings turned into interesting passionate discussions amongst all the students in the hope of establishing an Independent Republic of Xinjiang.

A few months later all those who had voiced their truthful opinions were branded as rightist, native nationalists, or were branded as having rightist sympathies and were then subjected to criticisms. Public struggle meetings were implemented and were held daily in the university hall for students, teachers and staff alike. Those who had been branded were ordered to stand on the stage in front of everyone to be humiliated; they were interrogated and forced to confess their wrongdoings.

Before they could speak, some pro-government students would jump in front of them and shout pro-government slogans and accusations of being traitors while poking their fingers into the faces and eyes of those branded. Everyone in the hall was made to shout out policy slogans and those who didn't were dragged onto the stage and beaten for sympathising with criminals. The meeting hall was always filled with thick acrid smoke from the constant smokers. It made my eyes red and itchy and I coughed constantly. These endless public struggle meetings lasted for hours and were mental torture, as we had no power or control over the situation.

Amongst those targeted in the public struggle meetings was Tursun Qasimov who worked as an interpreter in the university head office. He was constantly tortured and humiliated, both in and out of the meetings, for three months. One morning he failed to turn up and we waited three hours before he was dragged to the hall by pro-government activists. He had had a bowl-shaped haircut and looked so ridiculous that everyone laughed.

Qasimov was a slim, tall, strong and muscular man with distinctive grey eyes and a friendly, talkative personality. So his new haircut was totally out of character and you couldn't help but laugh. He was pulled by his collar, punched and pushed before being interrogated. First he was questioned about his hair-style, to which he replied, 'This was the style of the last Chinese Emperor, I thought by adopting this style, I might be cleared from being branded a nationalist and a target of the regime.' This provoked his tormentors to beat him even more aggressively.

Abdukerim, a doctor from Ghulja who was here for further training, was also targeted. He was one of a number of mature students who had worked for the East Turkistan Army, some of them during the Three Districts Revolution.[1] Abdukerim was a short and sturdy man with a calm disposition. They demanded he divulge the nature of his relationship with the Mayor of Ghulja City. He was interrogated and tortured for four days. On the fifth day rumours spread that Abdukerim had committed suicide. We were all called to a meeting early that morning to be told that it was true.

This was followed by criticism of him for over two hours. We were ordered to write slogans against Abdukerim that were soon posted on the University walls. He was denounced as a class enemy, a people's enemy, a traitor, a reactionary, a rightist, and against the revolution. Sadly his life had ended with all of these labels. Four of his former army colleagues transported his body on a wheel cart to the Green Mountain and buried him amongst the Dungan Muslims.[2] The poor man had come with big ambitions to further his knowledge and profession, but he now lay alone on top of the Green Mountain. I pray that God shall bless him in paradise, and that red flowers shall cover his grave.

During this period, numerous doctors, students and cadres, including some of my classmates, were denounced. Since most of the students supported the idea of an independent Xinjiang, it was impossible to label them all. I was also criticized for my opinions in these meetings.

---

1   *The scholarly name adopted by many for the political movement that lead to the establishment of the East Turkistan Republic of 1944-1949 in Ghulja, also referred to as the 'Second East Turkistan Republic' to distinguish it from the Islamic Republic of East Turkistan (1933-1934) in Kashgar, which is also known as the 'First East Turkistan Republic'. The 'three districts' refer to Ili, Tarbagatay and Altay, in the north today's Xinjiang, which formed the core territory of the republic.*

2   *Chinese-speaking Muslims of mixed Persian, Arab, and Chinese descent, referred to by the Chinese as 'Hui', and by the Uyghurs as 'Tunggan'.*

The 'Iron Refining Movement'[3]

In April 1958, all the students were sent to Nanshan and ordered to dig out the Youth River Canal for a month. It was spring and the open fields around the mountains were always windy and cold. We didn't have any warm clothes, so were forced to cope with the ever-present wind, whilst working like donkeys. In July, we were moved to another area of Nanshan to thresh wheat. Then in August we were sent to work on the railway in Seyapul for one and a half months under extreme weather conditions, from scorching sun to severe storms.

In October, we were transported by truck to Shiao Leng Ku, a place a hundred kilometres south of Ürümchi, where we were to dig out iron ore. On the final part of our journey we drove through mountain valleys with wheat-fields and streams of clear bubbling water lined by fig trees. Our destination was not so welcoming. We arrived in a barren, rocky valley, and stopped in front of some low mud huts beside the road, the only buildings in this desolate place. Getting off the trucks, I saw heaps of coal that were to be burnt to produce coal tar or coal breaks. The whole area was covered in ash and fumes from the burning coal. Donkeys transported coal from the mines to men wearing makeshift masks who stoked the fires for the coal tar. There were six mines, referred to as 'wells', which were identified by numbers.

We were billeted in the mud huts and the next day twenty-nine of us were sent further up the mountain to look for iron ore, which we would have to carry back. The remaining twenty people from our group were ordered to work in the coalmines.

There were mines in different parts of the mountains, from which workers had to go to a central canteen for food, or arrange for one or two people to collect food for them. One day it was my turn to go and collect food; I arrived to find it was not ready. While waiting I heard the sobbing outside. I stepped out of the canteen to find five or six teenage youths crying. I never thought there would be young people here in the mountains.

I walked up and asked, 'What's the matter? Why are you all so upset'? They blinked away their tears and one who looked most confident replied, 'Six of our friends

---

3   *In order to show the superiority of communism over capitalism, Mao started the Great Leap Forward (1958-1961) movement, aiming at surpassing the the UK's economy in 15 years and the US's economy in 20, through rapid industrialisation. Every ordinary citizen was encourage to participate in iron and and steel refining work, often by donating the metalware they owned at home to produce iron and steel in the communes with the most rudimentary facilities.*

have just died from gas poisoning in the mine. We were all from the same village.' The students began weeping uncontrollably.

'Where have you come from?' I asked.

'From Khotan', answered the teenager sadly.

'Khotan!' I said in surprise. 'But that's so far away! Why are you here?'

'Our parents sold all of their possessions and arranged for us to go to the university in Ürümchi. Originally there were fifty of us recruited by the government agency. Six months ago we ended up here and have worked without pay ever since.' The others affirmed his story.

I was saddened and shocked by their story, particularly as they were only about 16 or 17 years old. These young, handsome and intelligent boys had been duped by the system and their lives ruined forever. 'Are your parents aware of your situation?' I enquired.

'No, how could they be? We don't even know where we are in these mountains, or where we could post letters to tell them of our situation. When we first arrived, we didn't even understand the language since the government agency workers are all Chinese, so we couldn't communicate at all. We can understand them a little now but we don't know where they took our other classmates or what will happen to the bodies of our six friends who died today.' They looked at me in the desperate hope that I could help.

I was upset by their story and I wanted to help them, but I was powerless. I promised that I would do everything in my power to find the address of this place that we were in, and urged them to keep trying to find a way to contact their families. I comforted them as best as I could before leaving. When I returned a few days later, with the address, they had disappeared. No one knew of their whereabouts. To this day, I have wondered what happened to them.

After I had been searching for iron ore for a month, I was transferred to the smelting kiln work unit. We built five or six ovens. This was done by digging a hole in the ground about three metres deep and two-metres square. We collected flat pebbles from the riverbed to make a chimney style parapet to release smoke. To complete the kiln we required mud. I was given the task of bringing water from the river running through the coalmine. The Chinese manager gave me a donkey that had wooden panniers strapped across its back. He explained that all I needed to do was to fill the panniers with water using the bucket that had been left on the riverbank. I was instructed to follow the donkey as it knew where to go, and once the panniers were full the donkey would start back without being told. I requested a torch but he said he didn't have one. 'Don't worry! The donkey will guide you to the exact place where you are going'.

My classmates laughed, 'What ever you do don't get separated from your tour guide and make sure you hold onto his tail tightly!'

I set off, holding the donkey's tail. As we entered the mine, the donkey broke into a brisk trot forcing me to jog down the unlit tunnels. The donkey sped into a gallop, making it harder for me to keep up, but I didn't dare let go of its tail since I would certainly get lost in the pitch-black tunnels. Suddenly I banged my forehead on an overhanging rock and my eyes glazed over as I slumped to the floor holding my head. The pain was excruciating and there was a rapidly rising lump the size of an egg. Recovering from the initial shock, I realised that the donkey had gone and was nowhere to be seen. In a dazed state, I felt my surroundings and deduced that I was in one of the tunnels rather than a cavern.

I decided to return to the entrance of the mine, but was embarrassed at not completing my task and losing the donkey. I trailed my hands along the sides of the passageways as I went, but was constantly hitting my head against the roof and overhanging walls. In the distance, I heard the sound of bells and trotting hooves; it sounded like a train of donkeys. I knew the animals would be carrying coal from deep inside the mine. I trembled at the thought of being squashed or trampled by the cantering animals in such a confined space. It sounded as if there were at least forty or fifty of them. As the sound grew louder, a twinkling light brought a rush of fear. Not knowing what to do, I began shouting, 'Help! There's someone here, I'm here!' A man, carrying the lamp, shouted back, 'there's a side passage to hide in, get in there quickly! Quick run!' The donkeys were approaching fast. I felt along the tunnel walls as quickly as I could to find the hole. I squeezed into it with a sigh of relief. The donkeys clattered past, used to this routine and knowing that they could rest from their burdens when they reached the mine entrance. As the last one went by, I emerged from my bolthole. I couldn't stop coughing from the dust in the air that they had kicked up.

The donkey-herder carrying the oil lamp approached me and asked whether I had come here to get water. I cringed away from the tall and solidly built, donkey-herder, who looked terrifyingly demonic in the flickering light of the tunnel, but summoned up the courage to respond, 'Yes,' I told him, 'but I've lost my donkey and I can't find my way in the dark.'

He said, 'Your donkey is waiting for you by the river, once you fill the panniers with water it will bring you back again this way. Make sure you don't return before these donkeys have returned to the coal mine, otherwise there will be no room to pass each other.' He passed me his oil lamp before leaving.

I slowly worked my way deeper into the mine, towards the coalface, holding the lamp with one hand and rubbing my tender forehead with the other. After some distance I came upon a wide-open space with lamps fixed to timber supports. They reminded me of streetlights at about two metres high. I was intrigued by what I saw and looked around. There was a narrow gauge railway here in the mine and approximately ten wagons passed by as I was looking. Streams of clean water flowed along both sides of the cave walls fed by a reservoir at the far end. The donkey was standing patiently by one of the streams, waiting for me to fill the panniers.

From the end of my tunnel, I could see that the road forked after about fifty metres, with each fork leading into two coalface tunnels. As I waited, the second group of now-empty wagons rattled past back down to the coalface. I told myself that the most intense activities were actually happening right there. As advised, I waited until the other donkeys returned, before filling my donkey's panniers with water. Then, I followed the donkey back out of the mine.

The cadres, who were in charge at the university, and the head of the Student's Union, visited us daily to report on our progress and encouraged us to work harder to complete our tasks.

Having worked in twenty-four hour shifts, we completed the kilns faster than expected. We sat in front of the kiln breaking the ore into smaller pieces with hammers, which we piled up in layers in the centre of the kiln, surrounded by coal. After we ignited the coals, the kiln would be heated continuously for seven days, before being left to cool down. Then, we would sift out the melted ore from the ash. After two months of this backbreaking work, it became clear that it was a total failure, as we ended up with nothing. What a waste of labour, time, and resources. The cadres in charge didn't know what to say or do, and frantically scurried around with long faces. We were angry by the amount of time and hard work that had been involved in such a fruitless project.

One day I went to the toilet along with Rukiye, Nesihe and a few other girls in a gorge on the other side of the mountain. My eyes caught a sparkling object in the earth, which I dug up and wiped with my hand, I picked a small sharp stone to scratch the object and with a jolt, realised what might have found. I leapt up, shouting, 'Hey girls look! Quick, over here, I think I've found iron ore!' Everyone rushed over to look, and agreed that it looked like iron ore. The supervisor was called to examine the rock. He came over with a few other people. After scrutinising the object they all concluded that it was indeed iron ore. A sample was taken to be sent to Ürümchi for further examination.

The following day a truck arrived to collect the ore that we had found. Once the truck was loaded the ore was covered by a velvety material and was taken to the city. A day later, the chancellor of our university arrived with a group of officials. We were hurriedly summoned to a meeting where we were presented with a certificate of excellence and praised for achieving the number one place above all other universities in finding high quality iron ore deposit. We were all relieved that we could finally be freed from the mind-numbing hard labour of the past year, and we returned to the university just before the new year.

We were allowed two days to resettle, before we were called to a meeting and informed of the outcomes of the 'Thought Reform Movement'. We learned that those who were branded as 'rightist' or 'nationalist' had been imprisoned. Many of the staff, and the doctors such as Tursun Qasimov, Abduréhim and Zeynal, were among those who had been arrested and jailed while another group of doctors and students had been placed under the university supervision rule. There were no Chinese involved in the 'Thought Reform Movement', as it was directed only at the ethnic minority people living in the area.

The meeting distressed me, since I could not understand why people who had been encouraged to speak freely were now being imprisoned. What crimes had they committed? They had highlighted issues that needed to be addressed so what harm had they caused? Why destroy a person by sending them to prison and ruining their future? These questions ran through my mind again and again, but I had no answers.

I went for a walk around the university campus with Melike and told her of my distress and confusion about these questions. Melike agreed, 'I have been thinking about the same. There has to be some kind of conspiracy, don't you think?'

What she had said made me think long and hard. How could a people be downtrodden and their identity vanished? It seemed that the real motive of this so-called 'Thought Reform Movement' was to silence knowledgeable experts and skilled practitioners. We talked for hours until dusk.

Years of Hunger

University started soon after New Year's Day of 1959. We were supposed to have studied foundation courses during the first semester, however as we had been engaed in the Thought Reform Movement, and doing hard labour, we had missed the Chinese language course. Now the pressure was on to catch up, since the Chinese professors delivered their lectures without considering whether or not we understood them. We complained, but the management ignored us.

During our second year, all the ethnic minority students were divided among the Chinese students classes, so we had to attend the same lectures without extra support. We found it difficult to follow the lessons due to our limited of Chinese. Although we asked the teachers to speak slowly, the Chinese students insisted that they were taught at normal speaking speed. The Chinese students outnumbered us, so our voice didn't count for anything and teaching continued as normal for the Chinese.

During this time ethnic minority students were separated and placed in Chinese dominated dormitories. This was a method of placing the ethnic students under the Chinese Civilian reporting Regime. This brought into conflict different cultural practices of communication, religion, personal hygiene, and eating practices; these differences were all detrimental to our studies.

We were criticised for every little thing at the Wednesday evening group meetings, for taking too long with personal hygiene, or brushing our long hair. It was even suggested that we cut our hair like the Chinese girls. Pressure was brought to bear on the Uyghur girls who had long beautiful hair. Management issued an edict that all ethnic girls with long hair must cut it like the Chinese girls' did. The edict also required us to use a bucket for washing our faces, and a mug for cleaning our teeth. We queried this; why should we have to use buckets and mugs for washing, if we have running water? The only people who followed the edict were those who were pro-Chinese.

The nationwide famine of 1959-1960 saw the introduction of ration vouchers for the purchase of household items including food and cloth. No one was allowed to purchase anything without the allocated vouchers. It was difficult to find a mouthful of food in local stores around the city. At times people queued for hours, just to obtain a kilo of stale cornflour biscuits, or a kilo of insect infested sweets.

These would sell for fifty to sixty yuan per kilo, but there would be days when they weren't available. All that could be found in the local shops were iron tools. Many people poisoned themselves trying to ward off starvation by foraging for wild foods. Hospitals were also full of people dying of starvation there were ten to twenty deaths in one hospital per day. These were the hardest times ever experienced in the history of East Turkistan, and will never be forgotten.

At our university, we also had very little food. Students stopped studying for a week to forage for alfalfa grass, more usually horse feed, and edible tree bark, to supplement the food stocks in the student's canteen. Bread made of corn flour, water and ground up grass would be made for the ethnic minorities. The bread was so unpalatable and chewy that it was difficult to swallow without gagging from the taste. During this time the Chinese and the ethnic minority canteens were merged, although while we were served this horse food, the Chinese students enjoyed food like fish, tofu, and pork.

During this period, an anti-religious movement was instigated, in which it was claimed that God does not exist. Government propaganda said that religion is a superstition, people shouldn't have any religious views, neither should they be separated by superstitious ethnic beliefs. Rather, we should all live as one nation, we should live and eat and think as one. As an opposition to progress, religion should be crushed.

Young people led this movement and held 'In the Fight against Religions' meetings, during which believers were condemned. Students who were members of the communist party or the pioneer youth group were ordered to combine the Muslim and Chinese canteens in which all university students must eat. There were three in my group: Patime, myself, and Babay, who was Kazakh and a member of the youth pioneer corps. Although he was a Muslim he had to set an example by eating Chinese food. The first day he ate Chinese food he sat next to me in one of our group discussions, I slid away from him,

'Don't sit next to me; I don't want to smell the pork you've eaten.'

He looked away from me and stared at the floor, 'You aren't the only person who's disgusted by what I've eaten. I am disgusted with myself. I only just managed to make it to my dormitory before I threw up and I still feel sick now.'

He looked deeply upset and all I could say to him was, 'Babay, your face shows that your faith can't accept what you have thrown at it.'

I next saw him a week later and I was shocked to see the state he was in; he looked fragile and emaciated. I asked if he was ill.

He told me, 'Söyüngül, I can't continue with this; my body won't take the change of diet. You can see the reaction all over me, even though I haven't eaten for five days. I wish I could only eat from our canteen now'. We secretly brought food for him everyday from our canteen until the cooking conditions became so bad that we stopped eating on campus.

After three days, Turahun, the head chef, reported concerns that ethnic students were boycotting the canteen. He questioned why we were not receiving the same food allowances as the Chinese, and said that he was extremely concerned about the possibility of deaths among the students. To resolve his complaint, he was told that in future, all students would be treated the same. The same day he was given permission to make tandoori samosas for the students.

When the samosas were ready, Turahun went to the dormitories and shouted, 'Ladies and gentlemen, I have freshly baked samosas ready for you in the canteen, come quickly!' People yelled in delight, and rushed to the canteen, where they chanted, 'Long live Chef Turahun!' The samosas looked and smelt fantastic; the boys took ten to twenty and scoffed them like hungry wolves. The samosas had been filled with alfalfa grass, so some people removed the alfalfa and ate only the pastry.

While we were eating, Mr Tang, the university chancellor, who had never visited the canteen before, arrived and smirked at us, asking, 'How are the samosas?'

As he walked around the canteen, he noticed that the alfalfa filling remained uneaten by many people. His voice roared across the canteen, 'Why have you remove the filling and not eaten it?'

With one voice we all replied, 'Try a samosa and you'll find out.'

The chancellor spoke, 'Don't forget in the olden days your ancestors cried out for a piece of bread. Food is not to be wasted.'

Ablikim picked up a samosa from a tray on the table and took it over to the principle and said, 'Try it. The alfalfa is rotten, pigs wouldn't eat it.' Students near Ablikim agreed, 'We're human beings, not animals, and even the animals know not to eat rotten grass.'

At this point Ablikim spoke, 'So when word got around that we were having samosas today, you decided to visit us for the first time. Why don't we have the same ration allowance as the Chinese students?'

Chancellor Tang looked uncomfortable at the unexpected confrontation with the students. He responded, 'The allowances are the same.'

But voices from the back of the canteen queried, 'If that's, so why don't we get cooking oil, vegetables or meat?'

The chancellor was momentarily flummoxed, but relaxed and spoke with contempt, 'This has nothing to do with me, you must speak to the Canteen Management Team.'

'Why doesn't the Head Office manager monitor this? Surely it's his responsibility to ensure that we are all treated equally, which hasn't happened here.' The students' questions came thick and fast.

Afterwards, I left the canteen with Melike, Shemsijamal and Turnisa. We were lighthearted and laughed as we hopped from one step to another on our way back to the dormitories.

Secretary Deng walked past, stopped and winked at us, 'Hey girls, you look very attractive in your beautiful dresses. How lucky you are!'

'Ew, What's the matter with him today? Look, he's ogling us like a starving wolf.' Shemsijamal grinned.

Deng didn't understand us, but joined in the laughter and said in Chinese, 'You all look so beautiful in your lovely clothes. You are all very lucky, given that in the past you would not have been able to afford to even buy underwear, never mind a dress.'

Our laughter was abruptly replaced with anger. I retorted, 'Have you ever seen any ethnic girls without underwear? If so, tell me where and when?'

Before he could gather his thoughts Samshijamal snapped, 'You listen to me, old man. Now I know why you've been so friendly to us; you wanted to find an opportunity to sting us with your poisonous tongue.'

The boys who'd been walking behind us overheard the exchange and were furious, 'We Muslims always ensure that our girls are always dressed in pantaloons made from the finest silk, satin and the most beautiful fabrics available regardless of whether or not we have food. Have you ever seen any of our girls without long pantaloons? You, as the secretary of this university, how could you make such an insulting statement against the us, the native people?' Mr Deng was stunned and said, 'Ok, ok!' and walked quickly away.

Since there was no edible food in our canteen, students increasingly turned to the Chinese canteen out of desperation. Then the University Management Team informed all students that they must eat in the Chinese canteen and ordered the head of each year to register those who did so. Ahmet Toxti, our year leader, started the registration process by talking to each student individually. Some agreed to the ruling, others didn't. The disagreement escalated with the food rules taken as symbolising the identity and beliefs of people. To me, eating in the Chinese canteen was equivalent to losing my own ethnic identity as I felt I was being denied the freedom to follow and practice my faith. As a Muslim, I would not be forced into eating pork or any other *haram*[4] food. I would rather die from starvation.

During a meeting about the canteen arrangements, I voiced my opinions –

'I disagree with this. We are all Muslims with our own ethnic identity and faith. If we don't stand up for our own rights what will be the consequences for us in the future. My friends please think about what has been proposed. I will never agree to this proposal now or in the future, even if I was the only one to disagree. If I am told that it is not possible to have a canteen for one person, I will request my individual ration quote and I will try to find a way to survive. I think that if we accept these changes we

---

4   *Arabic word meaning 'forbidden (by Islamic law)', the opposite of halal.*

will be held responsible for the travails of future generations. And so I say to you that I will not accept these changes regardless of what happens to me.'

A dead silence settled over the room, it was to be broken by Melike who stood up and said, 'I stand with Söyüngül.' One by one, everyone else voiced their agreement. Then Ahmet Toxti, our supervisor, said, 'I agree with you too.' He wrote his name at the bottom of the registration list. 'Being the first group of students to reject the proposal, I am now going to inform your colleagues of your decision. Those who have reluctantly agreed to the changes may now change their minds and join us.' He hurried out of the room.

Mr Ahmet came back one hour later confirming that all the students including those who were eating in the Chinese canteen agree with us.

'What about Babay?' I asked eagerly. 'He agreed as well. I came to tell you the good news that now we are all united.' We were delighted with the success of our united front against unfair demands. If only we had realised the problems that were to come.

In the past it was difficult for friends to visit us, as the Chinese would tell them to leave or to speak in Chinese so that our meeting could be reported to the administrators. This was one of the many issues that led to our criticism at meetings, which increased the tension between both groups. Another contentious area was personal hygiene. We had to ask ask the Chinese students to use the washroom for personal hygiene and washing of clothes, since they would not use the purpose-built bathroom blocks to wash their clothes or themselves, but would instead use buckets of water in the dormitories for washing, then leave the buckets of dirty water in the rooms. In the end, we had to throw the water and the buckets away ourselves, to force the Chinese students to use the bathrooms.

The students from my year voted against combined study, responding with a large poster signed by everyone and pasted on the entrance wall to the campus. The message of the poster was delivered to the university head office. In response, a numbers of managers went to see the poster. They were outraged by it, and called all student Communist Party members and the Youth Pioneers to an urgent meeting. The head of the Student's Management Team deemed the poster racist and counter-revolutionary and demanded that whoever was responsible for creating the poster was found.

To his surprise the students riposted that the poster was neither racist nor counter-revolutionary and that the only reason they wanted to study separately from the Chinese students was because they found the language barrier hugely detrimental to their studies. Since the manager had not received the response he expected, he called for group meetings made up of one or two ethnic students to every fifteen Chinese, so that he could try to flush out the designers of the poster. It didn't work.

So the following day, Chancellor Tang called a meeting where he as asked us to reconsider the situation and give up our demands. He repeatedly asserted that it was wrong for us not to study with the Chinese, and accused us of being confused by and following misleading ideals espoused by local nationalists and counter-revolutionaries.

Kazakh students led by Nusret agreed with the chancellor but couldn't provide convincing evidence on the benefits of study with the Chinese. Nothing came of the meeting, so ultimately we all stopped attending classes in protest. To resolve the protest, the university requested the assistance of the Provincial Educational Department, the Public Security Bureau and the head of the Communist Party Bureau. We were also watched and subjected to random searches in our rooms, by officials hoping to catch secret meetings or letters. Nevertheless, we remained united and the university officials were unable to find the perpetrators of the strike. In the end, the university decided that the semester should finish earlier than normal.

I left for home with a sigh of relief, only to find that there had been changes while I was away. The government had imposed a commune system on everybody. This meant that you were no longer allowed to own anything. People's livestock, cooking utensils and a number of personal belongings were removed by force. The only things that people were allowed to keep were one spoon, a plate and a bowl and everyone had to eat in a communal canteen. At the same time, communal nurseries were established, which all toddlers had to attend. In order to set up the nurseries, bedding, carpets and rugs were requisitioned from family homes.

In our village it was decided that a dairy factory would be developed at personal cost to the village; cream separators, buckets and milk jars were taken from my home and my mother's sewing machine and table were removed. I looked around and was saddened by the emptiness and the pain my mother must have felt at the loss of her most precious possessions. To be able to eat in the commune kitchen, everyone was issued with vouchers for two meals a day, a breakfast of steamed bread, and a dinner of soup. The portions were too small to fill us up. I worried for my parents; they shared their food with us children because they believed we were hungry. I asked my father why people were facing such poverty and hardship.

My father, the commune accountant at that time, smiled and said, 'The water is polluted at its source, the same problem is everywhere at the moment. And to reach the food targets demanded by central government, we had to supply nearly all of the harvest as well as the crops we held in reserve. We've also had to supply an awful lot of livestock. As a result, we no longer have enough livestock or agricultural produce to feed ourselves or build reserves for next year. Added to which, the harvest has been poor...so we don't know how we're going to cope, I just pray that we won't die of starvation. There's no extra milk or food for the babies, so they are suffering too. I am very concerned.'

He looked around cautiously before continuing: 'This so-called commune system is designed to suck blood from everyone. The Chinese Communist Government is shamelessly robbing us of our resources; it's taking all our food to feed others, so those who've worked hard in the fields and on the farms are dying of hunger. It makes me so angry.' My father grimaced. He was a private, calm person, so his show of frustration was very unusual.

My father studied in a Russian school and trained as an accountant in college. He was a highly qualified accountant, fluent in Russian, Arabic and Chinese, and also trained other accountants in the region. I learned a lot from him during our heated discussions. My mother would join in too, after she'd put my siblings to bed. She would slump into her chair and ask 'What are you two talking about now?'

I laughed, 'We are praising the commune system.'

My mother snapped, 'What? Is there anything good to praise? To hell with it! Everything has been taken away from us, look at us we have become naked and poor. First we lost our house, in the Socialist Transformation Movement,[5] and then we were stripped of all our possessions. Their imposed system means that the Chinese can legally rob us!'

My father calmly interrupted my mother's tirade, 'What can we do? We are helpless. We are not the only victims in this situation; the whole East Turkistan nation is suffering. We will get past this eventually. Don't let it get you down, we have to be strong and patient.'

My mother seemed convinced by my father and relaxed, 'You are right, May God keep our nation safe! As long as we survive, anything is possible.' Like most mothers in the world, my mother was caring, kind, cheerful, and hard working with the good sense of humour. She had raised a large family and was also the community tailor, helping with the family income.

---

5   *A socio-politico-economic movement in the newly established People's Republic of China from 1953 to 1956, aiming at implementing rudimentary socialism in society.*

January 1961

In the first spring after the introduction of food rationing, food deprivation became critical. There was no bread, nothing. Deaths from starvation were common. Some people resorted to eating animal feed, wild plants and seeds. Deaths by poisoning were common. Whole communities were devastated. That year, most children in the commune nursery died. Only two survived. They died the following spring from malnutrition.

Famine in East Turkistan continued through 1960 and 1961. Even the rich agricultural regions of Ghulja and Chöchek couldn't meet the food rationing needs because the government requisitioned the food for the rest of China, and left them with no seeds for new crops. No one in East Turkistan knew of such famine in our history.

These were the early years of the 'liberation' by the Chinese Communist Party.

After ten days at home, I returned to university. Those students who had remained during the vacation had continued their campaign of separate classes from the Chinese students. The university leadership threatened to expel and have arrested anyone who didn't comply with the mixed classes regime. Matters came to a head a few days before the start of the new semester. Our tutor, Mr Abdushükür, was informed by senior management that all students must participate in mixed classes from the 22nd of February or face the consequences. We wanted to finish our education and did not want to be imprisoned. We had no choice but to give in.

The Chinese students were overjoyed that that we now had to study with them. Some of our more frightened students confessed to senior management and informed on us in the hope of avoiding punishment. The division between the Chinese and non-Chinese students widened.

Melike returned to university from Ghulja. According to her, radio and newspaper reports had suggested that food production from Ghulja was enough to feed the entire population of East Turkistan for the next twelve years. I asked, 'If that's so, why are so many people starving, in the cities and the country, everywhere?' Melike was frustrated and said, 'Every day, everything in our country from raw materials and gold, to food is being taken into China. They are deliberately ravaging our country and causing the deaths of thousands of people.'

Nothing like this had ever happened in our country. Every day, we asked 'What is happening to us?' We grew more and more frustrated with the government misinformation. Leaders who dared to defend our interests and our voices were either executed, or interned in prison and labour camps. Those who actively supported the regime were given important roles within the government. They were puppets who were only concerned with personal gain.

We were so angry. Although we were only medical students, we worked as practicing doctors in the hospitals, where we witnessed the deaths of young and old first-hand. It hurt so much that we could do nothing to save them. Daily, the numbers of dead rose. I felt sick and exhausted. We all did.

June 1961

It was a beautiful evening bathed in a mellow moon, with the leaves of the trees rustling in a gentle breeze. I walked into the garden and sat on a bench opposite the dormitory. With the breeze stroking my face and hair, I drifted, at peace with the world. Two of my peers, Ablikim and Abliz, saw me on their way back from the revision class and interrupted my serenity to talk. Shortly afterwards we were joined by Melike.

As we chatted, Ablikim started complaining about the Chinese and Melike joined in. She mentioned that she had a Uyghur patient from the oil-rich region Qaramay, who had told her about ethnic conflict and grievances against the Chinese authorities in that area. Once again, we were talking about the problems that beset our country. I had been thinking about things for a long time and had some ideas on remedies for our people. But I hadn't told anyone until now. I spoke out –

'My friends, the only way out for us is to establish an Independent East Turkistan. Without this, we will always be slaves to the Chinese system and we and we will always suffer as we are now.'

'Yes, I agree. I don't believe there is any other choice', Melike spoke quietly and glanced around to check that no one was listening. She leaned in and said 'It could have been so different if we had been the victors in the 'Three Districts Revolution'. We would be living in our own country, ruled by our own people, and not having the discrimination of these Chinese people. And we would be taught in our mother tongue, not Chinese.'

As she spoke, I remembered the conversation I had with my father, where he explained the failure of the revolution. I told them what my father had said, 'When the Ethnic Minorities Army reached Manas Bridge, the Kuomintang[6] nationalists and

6   Kuomintang was the ruling party and government of the Republic of China (1912-1949) before losing the civil war to the communists. Because the name of the party means 'People's Party', their adherents are usually referred to as 'nationalists', which has a different meaning from how the word is usually interpreted in English.

their ethnic conspirators fled East Turkistan. Afterwards, people in Ürümchi waited to welcome the Ethnic Liberation Army. Instead, the fully armed Chinese Red Army arrived wearing masks and protected by tanks. People shouted in confusion, 'What's happening? Where's our army? These are Chinese.' They were told that the Red Army had arrived.

My father had said, 'after all the sacrifices made by our army to drive out the nationalist Kuomintang, we expected freedom. Instead, we were taken over by the Red Army. We had swapped one Chinese regime for another worse one, the communists. We waited for our liberation for four years, but our army was kept at Manas Bridge.' I had asked my father why the army had never left Manas Bridge? He had explained that the senior army commanders were Russian, so when they received orders from the Russian authorities to maintain their position at Manas until the Chinese Red Army arrived, that is what they did.

'But why did the Russians change their minds in supporting our fight for independence? Why were they interested in us? Why did they get involved in the first place?'

'There are many conspiracy theories and a lot of undisclosed information in politics. Remember this, regimes only benefit those that control them. These people don't care about anyone else. Only you can solve your own problems. If you feel that you must, then stand alone, don't wait for help from somebody else or you could wait forever. In other words, don't expect another country to liberate us. People have to fight for their own liberation.'

When I told my friends of this conversation, they were transfixed and as I finished, they looked at me as though I should continue. All was quiet for a while, then Abliz broke the silence, 'The reason why the Three Districts Revolution failed was that we were naïve and believed in the Russians. We gave them the power to control the army and our destiny. If the senior commanders had been our own people we would have gained our independence.'

'What a way to lose everything that we fought so hard for! We had a golden opportunity to gain our independence and we lost it.' Melike shook her head.

'It's just awful! It'll be very difficult to get that opportunity again, not least because our present occupier is bigger and more powerful than the last one. It'll be a bloodbath if we try fighting them for independence,' said Ablikim.

Abliz nodded, 'No one has any passion for liberty. The socialist and communist propaganda has seen to that. We live in poverty and confusion. People have no will to fight for their rights. They just want a peaceful life; they are sleepwalking through their lives. So we need to wake them up, but that will be hard in the current political climate, because people are so frightened of saying anything against socialism.'

I snorted, 'We'll achieve everything we want once we attain communist ideals, they'll give us ever lasting happiness.'

Melike spoke, 'We'll disappear as a nation one day if we don't take action now. We need to wake the people so that they can claim their rights. They must be told the truth behind these ideologies.'

The more we talked, the more ideas we had and the more enthusiastic we became. We grew confident that we could make these changes.

'The government is fooling people about the benefits of socialism and communism. They are very generous to those who support the regime, supporters were given the title of 'Senior Officials and extra benefits. Ordinary cadres were given puppet positions in the regional government and were happy enough with the extra benefits for them and their families. Meanwhile, working-class people and peasants have been deceived by the promise that communism would bring everlasting happiness. This is not going to happen. Instead, the Chinese government has taken control of East Turkistan. Of its people, its land, and its resources.

'Our resources are disappearing. We must make people aware of the propaganda they are being fed. We must reach people, but we need more people and resources to do that. Then we must go to every region, city, and village to tell people of these lies. If we do that, we can begin to make a future for our country', I said.

Abliz was silent for a while before saying, 'It's a bit too early for us to start anything yet, we'd better wait for the right time.'

Ablikim was infuriated by this and spoke up, 'Wait for the right time to come? When do you think that'll be? Will we ever even see it? The Chinese are arriving at the rate of a thousand a day like a river bursting its banks. If this continues, we'll be a minority in our own country. Do we wait until we are one in a thousand before we do anything?'

I interrupted him, 'Don't you think there are other people out there who are thinking the same as us? We're young students with hardly any experience of life. I believe we should find others share our idea, but who have more knowledge and experience of dealing with such problems. It's possible that there are already people secretly working against the communist regime. If I could find them, I would join them today.'

Before I had even finished speaking, Melike spoke up, 'So would I.' Ablikim and Abliz also agreed that they would join if they could. All four of us felt a bond of comradeship as we shared our innermost thoughts for our country and its people. We agreed to begin an intensive search for underground organisations or people who could help us, during our summer vacations, and to share anything we found out.

28 August 1961

The same day that I arrived back at university, after the summer vacation, a group of my friends ran up to me shouting, 'Great news! We're now allowed to have separate dormitories and classes away from the Chinese.'

I couldn't believe my ears. Everyone was so happy and hugging each other. I ran to the dormitory and found that all the beds were filled by my ethnic minority friends. I couldn't understand it after what had happened. We'd had to fight so hard and put up with such awful circumstances, after we were told that the separatism we wanted was impossible. What had happened to change things? We wanted to know. So we asked our student rep, Ahmet Toxti. He told us that our strike at the university had been reported as one of the 'bad elements' that had blighted Xinjiang. Chairman Mao had heard of our disruptive strike and asked Seypidin Eziz, the Governor of Xinjiang, about it.

Seypidin had explained the cause of the incident and the demands of the ethnic minority students. He had told Mao that the students had first petitioned the university, then had protested, and finally had gone on strike, but had been forced to accept the decision of the university board. Seypidin had also told Mao that the Xinjiang Ministry of Education and the Xinjiang Public Security Bureau had been involved in suppressing the students' revolt.

Mao had not been pleased. 'This is not a good sign. Student movements could course further unrest. This will have a detrimental impact on our socialist society, and if news of this unrest spreads abroad, then we will lose face with the international community. We cannot afford to be criticised for our internal policies by western countries at this time.'

'So Mao ordered a change of policy in favour of our students' demand.' Ahmet Toxti laughed.

I couldn't believe what I was hearing. 'Mr Ahmet, you are joking, aren't you?' Deep down, I felt this was just another ploy to keep us sweet and quiet. I had my doubts. 'I'm still not sure about this. Only one year of the students went on strike after all. So how was it possible for Chairman Mao to be involved in such a small matter?'

Melike overheard us and commented, 'Yes, it is true. Ahmet Toxti was given the news personally from the chancellor of the university.'

So, from the start of a new term, we studied in separate classes and had the lessons designed for us. Extra teachers were employed to give us additional lectures so that we could catch up on the work that we had missed. We were very happy and enjoyed our classes, and so we made rapid progress.

November 1961
In Search of Comrades

One day, Melike and I were walking around the hospital after lessons.

Abliz and Ablikim came by. They bombarded us with questions about whether we had found anyone who could help us. It sounded like there was an emergency. Melike did not respond directly. Instead, she asked them if they had just come from a secret meeting or had met someone with the same goals as us and also had the experience.

They looked at each other and laughed. 'Truthfully,' said Abliz, 'we have spent last two months looking for anyone who could advise us and lead us. Every Saturday after classes, we visited universities, colleges, and factories, including places where we have friends, hoping to identify any experienced person in the independence movements. We couldn't find anyone … and so we think that there is very little hope of success in our quest.'

Ablikim interrupted, 'And the people we had hoped to find were like ghosts. Most of them didn't know very much about Xinjiang's past and weren't bothered about its future. When we told them what we knew, they were shocked. They have begun to understand what is really happening, right here, right now. And they have started to worry about the future. Many are now calling for open war with the Chinese.

They listened to us and engaged with us. We would talk all night. But I'm sorry to say that our own people just don't know what's happening.' Ablikim took out his handkerchief to wipe the sweat off his face and continued, 'what can we expect from them when they don't even understand what's happening around them?' He looked dejected.

'Melike and I have also been looking for underground leaders. We looked in the city, and we talked to all kinds of people from teachers, cadres, and civil servants to factory workers. When we spoke to them, we emphasized how unfair the treatment of our people was, and how all of our daily lives are getting worse. In the end, I bluntly told them that without independence, we would never be free of this subjugation.'

People would gasp with their hands over their mouths, and quietly caution me, 'Sister, aren't you frightened of speaking so openly? Who do you think can help us to achieve independence? You'd do better to abandon your ideas and just try to live a peaceful life.'

'Tell me who will bring us independence, if we do not help ourselves?' I demanded of them. 'If we don't protect ourselves, no one else will care whether we live or die! At the moment, the Chinese government is taking away our homes and possessions. In the future, women and children might be taken, if we don't do anything, and this degradation will continue until we have nothing, no homes and no future.'

Some people walked away, while others would say, '"leave us alone. You're too young to advise us. Go back to your university and finish your studies." So, we also were not able to find the people we'd hoped for.'

While I was talking, Nurnisa Rozi came and called Melike away. The three of us continued talking, and I told them what I had been thinking about, 'I have tried to imagine what the characteristics of a leader were, like being strong in mind, courageous, passionate, resilient, and calm but decisive. Since we haven't been able to find such as person why can't we set up our own organisation? I believe that people who are heads of organisations are ordinary people just like us. What do you think? I would willingly accept the responsibilities for any position I was offered.' I looked at them calmly as I awaited their reply.

Ablikim said nervously, 'No! How can we possibly do this on our own with no experience?' Abliz backed him up, 'This is not a simple matter, and not one that students can do.'

I tried to convince them, 'Yes, you are right. It is a complicated and difficult task, but I believe it can be done. It is not as if we're going to declare war or start carrying guns. Our frontline is words. We've already agreed that the first course of action is to visit universities and colleges, to talk to anyone who would support our cause. Once we've recruited people, we can better inform the public through posters and word of mouth. By doing this, we can reach as many people as possible. Then, with public support, things will become easier. During this initial period, it is still possible that we may find the experienced person we want. But at the same time, we must not forget the danger we put ourselves in if things go wrong. We could be imprisoned or even executed for this. But you are born to die! So isn't it better to die in the cause of justice and freedom than as a slave to communism or by surrendering to your enemies?'

Abliz said, 'I agree with you.' We walked back to the dormitory in silence, deep in our own thoughts, before we said good night.

December 1961

We were given four days off for the New Year, so I decided to go home to see my family. After lunch, I packed my bag, said goodbye to my friends, and headed to the milk factory that collected milk from Nanshan, in the hope of getting a lift home. At the front desk in the Nanshan office sat a Chinese man. I asked him, 'Is the milk van going to Nanshan today?'

'Yes,' he replied, 'it might be leaving in an hour's time.'

'Can I get a lift?'

'Why are you going to Nanshan?' he asked.

'My family lives there, my father's name is Salih Weliyet', I said.

'Oh, I know him. He is a good man. You can wait here for the driver, as he may not be leaving for an hour or two,' He said with a smile.

I thanked him and went outside, as the office was crowded with people because of the cold winter weather. To kill some time, I walked to the railway station, which was close by, since I had never been there before and went to the far end of the platform. I stood, looking at the railway lines and the trains with fascination, when I heard the sound of a train whistle. I looked in the direction of the sound and saw the approaching train in the distance. This was the first time I had seen a moving train. It looked like giant ugly monster and made the most unpleasant terrifying noise. The train shook the earth beneath me as it slowly neared the platform.

When the train finally chugged to a halt, I was unable to see the end of it. All the carriages were crammed full of people. A few minutes later, I saw people shoving past one another as they squeezed out of the carriage doors to disembark. They were Chinese immigrants arriving from the Mainland China. They were like ants coming out of their nest; they were all dressed the same way in black except for a different coloured balloon tied onto their hats. Most were accompanied by two or three children but some had five of six children. Mothers carried babies in slings on their chest and back and held onto children with either hand.

They all looked the same to me, tired and filthy; they must have come from areas of extreme deprivation and poverty. When I arrived, the station had been empty, now it was a heaving mass of people who were being directed to coaches by uniformed officials.

In less than an hour they had all disappeared, leaving the station once more in silence. I was shocked by what I had seen, yet impressed by the speed and smooth management of the exercise. Surely, this was the state organized migration service.

I told myself, 'Not many people were aware of this, most of us are oblivious to these daily changes.' I was deep in thought when I heard the sound of a train coming from the opposite direction, from the West Mountains. When it passed slowly by the platform, I noticed it was a cargo train transporting petrol or gas and was longer than the previous train. It had about eighteen to twenty wagons. A third train arrived not long afterwards, heading for Mainland China, only this time it was loaded with horses, cattle, and sheep, and timber, coal and manure.

I was so preoccupied with watching the train and thinking about the effects it would have on our people and future that I completely forgot about the lift home. When I realised, I rushed to the office, only to find the milk van had left. I was bitterly disappointed, but had no alternative other than to return to my dormitory. Everyone was surprised when I entered the room and asked me what had happened. I told them what I had seen. We didn't sleep until after midnight since we talked about the forced removal of our nation's wealth and the future disasters that would occur as a result.

31 December 1961

After breakfast, I returned to the railway station with some of my friends. There was an old Uyghur man sweeping the platform who glanced at us a few times, then asked us, 'My children, have you come to meet someone?'

'No, Uncle. We don't have any family living in Mainland China. We're just visiting the station to find out how many trains are arriving and departing for Mainland China from here. We've never seen so many Chinese in all our lives!'

'I am a cleaner here.' said the old man. 'People arrive by train all night long. I wonder where they are taken. They all disappear like water soaking into the sand. There are always buses ready to collect them. I hope they don't swallow us alive one day.' He sounded distressed as he left us.

We spent all day at the station, counting how many trains arrived from Mainland China in twenty-four hours, how many carriages there were to each train, and approximately how many people were squeezed into each carriage. We were shocked by what we found.

'Oh my God, in another thirty or forty years time, we will become the minorities in Xinjiang and our land will be occupied and controlled by the Chinese. What can we do! What's going to happen to our future generations if things continue like this?'

'There is nothing we can do. This isn't our problem.'

'If this isn't our problem, whose problem is it, then?'

'Who do you think can resolve these problems for us, if everyone thinks this is not their problem.'

'If we don't do anything now, then it will be more and more difficult in the future, when their population exceeds ours!' My friends and I were all frustrated. We continued the debate all the way back to the university. Soon, our findings from the visiting the train station spread throughout the university by word of mouth and were much discussed by the students.

February 1962

We started our winter holidays on the first day of February 1962. Melike came to stay with me at my home in Nanshan.

Abliz came to see me a day before we were due to leave. 'I need to talk to you.' he said. So I asked him to come with me to my dormitory. Melike was alone in the room waiting for me when we arrived. Abliz said with a smile: 'Oh good, Melike is here'. He continued, 'As you are all aware, we did all we could in searching for comrades to lead us, but were unsuccessful. So I think we should set up our own organisation. Let's start our activities as best we can, while continuing to look for a leader. If we can find anyone, we can always join them and work together as a team. I feel we are wasting too much time and energy on this one task, so I believe we should start of on our own.'

I jumped up and said with excitement, 'let's get started! Even if I have to sacrifice my life I will have no regret.'

Melike hugged me smiling and said, 'We will continue this fight until our last breath.'

'We will not give in unless we die.' Abliz looked into our eyes with joy and happiness as he put his arms around our shoulders saying, 'Now we are like brothers and sisters. We will remain this way until the end of time.' Tears trickled from Abliz's eyes as he spoke.

We talked enthusiastically about our tasks, the future plans and the difficulties we might face in the future. Abliz left just after midnight. Melike and I carried on discussing things, our spirits had been lifted and we felt as if we had started a new journey. Our hearts were filled with hope and happiness. I felt stronger with the thought of being able to carry out such a huge task on my shoulders; above all we will be leading a meaningful life. A newfound feeling of power and strength erupted inside me when I dreamed that one day we would achieve freedom for our people.

5 February 1962
The founding of the East Turkistan People's Party

It is Chinese New Year today. Ablikim, Abliz, Melike and I held a secret meeting in our dormitory at ten o'clock that morning. We laid out a chess set on the table, so that it would look like we were playing chess if someone walked in.

We discussed the founding of the East Turkistan People's Party and its aims: to free East Turkistan from the Chinese authoritarian regime and its repression, and to establish an independent East Turkistan Republic. We also planned our future activities:

Founding aims of the East Turkistan People's Party

1. To visit all the different universities and colleges to secretly propagate our proposals in order to gain support. To visit all the factories and enterprises to recruit reliable members and to educate people about the current political climate. To call on citizens to resist the repression of the Chinese Communist Regime and to fight for an Independent East Turkistan Republic;

2. To study the history of East Turkistan and find a way to obtain sources like history books from which we can produce booklets summarising the history of our origins;

3. To set up an underground network to educate and recruit more people to the cause;

We decided that we would name the party, design the party flag, and draft the party goals and its future agenda once the party was formalized, and we agreed to meet again that evening to formalise the party's policies.

To celebrate the Chinese New Year the students union organised a dance evening. Almost all of the students attended the party; the music was great and the students danced all night. Around midnight, we sneaked out to gather in my dormitory. My room was the most convenient place for us to meet at the time, since all the other students in the dormitory had gone home.

We locked the door before starting the discussion of the formal establishment of our party, The East Turkistan People's Party; Ablikim read out the party oath which he had prepared:

'I swear that I will fight for the independence of East Turkistan and never give up until the day I die. I will not surrender to the enemy under any circumstances. I will never betray my comrades under torture. I will fight to free my country from the enemy until my last breath.'

We all swore the oath separately, declared our formal membership of the party, and a founding member in its establishment. We congratulated one another, and then burned the oath. After Ablikim and Abliz left my room, Melike and I returned to the dance party. The party was in full swing and continued until five in the morning.

I went to bed but tossed and turned before deciding to go home to Nanshan to collect a book that had some chapters on East Turkistan history. It was the text we had used in history lessons back in the Tatar School. Ablikim and Abliz decided to study the book then look for more information about our history during the vacation.

Melike came with me to my home in Nanshan. We returned to the university at the end of our vacation to find out that Abliz, and Ablikim hadn't found any new material. So they only used the information from the book I gave them for our campaign.

When we set up the organisation, we decided that the four of us would remain as core members on the board with all other recruits just being members. Although we campaigned in and around the universities, we didn't achieve much, not least because all four of us were young inexperienced students. We realised that we needed to discuss things further in order to find appropriate methods that would further develop our organisation.

After some discussion, we decided to expand the board, as we desperately needed someone who was intelligent, calm, well respected by the people and had experience in society, and also had a broader knowledge of the history of East Turkistan and the world. We all agreed to approach Ahmet Toxti, the student representative of our year. He was thirty-three years old, and had previously worked as an associate dean of academic affairs in the School of Science and Technology. He had extensive knowledge of the Three Districts Revolution, and was a well-respected and trustworthy person.

Another person we considered was Ghopur, a deep thinker, calm, confident, quiet, and knowledgeable. He had the right attitude and personality for this sort of task. It was agreed that Abliz and Ablikim would approach him while Melike and I were to speak to Ahmet Toxti.

Melike and I invited Ahmet to study with us in the department of orthopaedics. Ahmet Toxti had recently returned from Korla after visiting his wife, who was a teacher at the Korla Science and Technical School. We started our conversation by asking about his wife and the general situation in Korla. He told us about the changes taking place in the region and the unfair policies of the regime, which is causing so many grievances among the ethnic population. We all expressed our frustrations at the situation.

Eventually, I said, 'Brother Ahmet, are we going to remain passive forever without doing anything? Why not set up an opposing organisation and do something about it?'

He was taken a back by my statement as he stared at me before glancing at Melike saying, 'What can the three of us do? We don't have the ability or knowledge to do anything. It is better that we concentrate on our own studies, finish our degrees and leave the university quietly.'

We told Abliz and Ablikim of Ahmet Toxti 's reaction to my request. They decided to talk to him again in the hope that he had thought about what had been proposed. The next day after the evening revision we saw Abliz and Ablikim leaving together with Ahmet Toxti. The following morning while I was waiting to go into lessons, I received a little note saying, 'Good news, now we are six.' Later that day we arranged to have a meeting in the physics laboratory after dinner to formalize the joining of the two new members.

After dinner, I went straight to the physics laboratory, went in and locked the door behind me, where I started preparing the necessary documents for the meeting. Soon afterwards there was a knock at the door. I opened it to see Ghopur staring at me in surprise; he hesitated to enter. I realised that Ghopur was cautious so I said to him, 'Come on in, let's do our homework together.'

'What homework?' he asked as he slowly entered.

'I'm revising the lessons we had today.' I calmly replied. We chatted until all the others had assembled.

Abliz told Ahmet Toxti and Ghopur that I was also a member of the organising committee. Ghopur explained to everyone that when he had first seen me in the room, he thought he might have come to the wrong place. While Ghopur was speaking, Melike arrived, Abliz told them that she was also a member. We all continued chatting for a few minutes before we got down to the serious business of the meeting. We first explained to them about the set-up of the party including the activities that we had been involved in so far, and then we asked them for their personal opinions before accepting them as members of the party.

Since that first meeting, we have regularly met to discuss the party agenda, the party name, its charter, and the history of East Turkistan. Naming the party has led to many meetings, discussions and debates. Abliz suggested the name of 'East Turkistan Islamic Party', but the majority of us did not approve the name since having Islam in the title would brand the party as being pan-Islamist, just like the name East Turkistan was being accused of being pan-Turkist. Melike told us a story about the 'Rahmanov group' of Ghulja –

Rahman was her aunty's brother-in-law, a good looking and an intelligent young man. During the land reform, religious leaders were arrested and many were executed. This was followed by an anti-pan-Turkist campaign during which many young men were arrested, accused of being members of the Pro-turkists Rahmanov group, and executed. Rahman avoided capture by hiding in his sister's home in a remote village. His brother-in-law hid him in a cave where the vegetables were stored, and made a kennel for the dog, which was placed in front of the cave entrance. He stayed there for over a month. The government arranged for a secret agent to watch his sister's family. One day, the agent observed the brother-in-law buying cigarettes. The agent knew that no one in the family smoked, so he arranged for more agents to follow put all of the family under surveillance. As a result, Rahman was found. He was taken away and shot.

Melike continued, 'Many innocent people who had nothing to do with the so-called Rahmanov Pro-Turkists were also implicated during this campaign and were brutally murdered. This resulted in negative publicity towards pan-Turkism, in the misunderstanding that Xinjiang was to be absorbed into Turkey. There were similar negative feelings about Islamic groups.'

Melike's story silenced us. Someone suggested the name: 'East Turkistan Uyghur Party'. None of us approved of this name because this would easily mislead people into believing it is a Uyghur Nationalist party, which could damage the unity of the many Turkic peoples who have been coexisting in the area for generations. It was considered that the title should represent the all the Turkic nationals in the region. Since the term 'Turkistan' represents both Turkic people and the religion of Islam, we all eventually agreed on the name: 'East Turkistan People's Party'.

We talked about the precautions necessary to avoid exposure and what would happen if we were caught, we had to prepare ourselves for the worst. We were aiming to raise people's awareness about the current situation, and our right to seek independence. We wanted people to wake up from the nightmarish injustices and start fighting for their own rights. Even if the party was exposed one day and all of us were arrested, we wanted it to cause a big impact on the general public so that more people would stand up to the regime and its leaders.

We also discussed the party flag. None of us had ever seen an East Turkistan flag because they had been banned since the Chinese occupation, but we had heard from elders in the community that it was a blue coloured background with a moon and stars in the middle. I was given the task to design and make the flag.

We had a lot of meetings about the party agenda. In the end, Ahmet Toxti was given the task of drafting the manifesto. After much discussion, he drafted the party's manifesto in three parts. The first part exposed the current situation of the country under the Chinese Communist Regime. The second part outlined brief history of East Turkistan, and the third part highlighted the importance of gaining independence and called on people to unite and fight against the imposed communist regime.

As we now had goals and a plan, we decided to research the history of East Turkistan. The information we obtained would be used to produce a booklet containing our own history of our country, which challenged the official histories of the Chinese government, in which they claimed that Xinjiang had been part of China for centuries. We wanted to let the public know that this was not true. We decided to seek historical evidence to destroy their false claims. Melike, Abliz, and I were given the task of researching and finding the relevant materials. I was appointed to take care of all documents, correspondence, and money for the party.

As the 1 May International Workers' Day holidays approached, we agreed to use the holiday to produce and distribute leaflets containing information about the situation in East Turkistan and to call on the public to join our cause for an independent East Turkistan. In order to produce a large amount of leaflets, we needed a printer. However, printers were only available in the main public offices. We had tried to find a way around this but had had no luck. We had fifteen-yuan membership money in our group account, so we decided to purchase a mimeograph and paper.

The next day Melike and I skipped lessons to look for a mimeograph. We visited almost every shop in the city and found a few shops which sold these machines. However, they were only sold to customers who had an approval letter from their workplace. After going from shop to shop we returned to the university empty-handed in the evening. As a result we had to write the leaflets by hand using one box of black ink and duplicating paper.

Although we had identified the people and places for our leaflets and made a note of what we should say and the number of leaflets we needed. However, we realised it would be impossible to produce the leaflets in time for the May Day holiday, so we decided to defer the leaflets until the following year so that we would have more time to plan them and ensure that we did not get ourselves into trouble with the authorities.

The board decided to recruit new members after the International Workers' Day celebrations. I recommended Sajide and was given the task of bringing her on board. Sajide and I had shared the same dormitory from when we had started university, and had become quite close friends. I was initially very cautious when I began talking to her about things. However, with time I became confident that we shared similar aims and approaches so I began to speak more openly about my thoughts.

I had planned to formally accept her as a member, but in our meeting, the board appointed Abliz to carry out the formalization process. Meanwhile, I was asked to influence Nurnisa into becoming a member, while Ghopur and Ablikim were to recruit Halide and Abley. I opposed Ablikim's recruitment's of Abley, since I was aware that they had had disagreements in the past, but I was overruled. Abliz suggested that we should also start trying to recruit university staff especially cadres, and that we should reach out to people outside university. However, Ahmet Toxti didn't agree; he thought that we should move slowly so as not to attract the authorities.

Abliz tried very hard to convince everyone, 'We are not going to do this by ourselves. For instance, the writer Elkem Ahtem is receiving treatment in our hospital at the moment. Wahit, who we know shares our ideals, could visit Ehtem to discuss things and ask him for advice. As a writer he must be very open-minded and knowledgeable, with an in-depth understanding of the current circumstances and some good ideas about future possibilities. I believe he is a patriotic person, and so I want to make some arrangements; please leave this with me.'

'I wonder what kind of person President Iminov is', said Ablikim suddenly, looking at each of us as if searching for the answer. 'I'm thinking that if it's possible, perhaps we should arrange to meet him one day.'

Ahmet Toxti abruptly stood up and shouted, 'What are you thinking? You cannot rush into this! You want to know what kind of man Iminov is? He is the one who authorized the Ghulja massacre. People went to the government building to petition the government, women, children, and elderly, and there were many bystanders too. Suddenly, the army opened fire, killing almost everyone. Do you know how many innocent people died? Countless! No one knows the figures, even now. The blood ran like a river in the street, but the soldiers dragged all the bodies inside the government courtyard before quickly cleaning up the street, so quickly, it seemed like nothing had ever happened. People who witnessed the bloodshed that day have been scared ever since.

Ablikim was very embarrassed and said, 'Down with Iminov! I didn't know that he's such a brutal man.'

'All the misery and suffering of this nation were committed by those ruthless traitors.' Ahmet Toxti was still shaking with rage as he finished speaking. Feelings ran high as we continued debating until late into the night.

Three days later Abliz told us the shocking news about Wahit's visit to Elkem Ahtem. Wahit went to see him, introduced himself and asked Ahtem how he was. Then Wahit moved onto the focus his visit; the welfare of the people under the communist rule. To Wahit's surprise, Mr Ahtem held completely different views about the Chinese Communist rulers. When Wahit raised his concerns over the miserable circumstances of many people and the disastrous future prospects, Elkem lost his temper.

He shouted, 'People in Xinjiang cannot live without the Chinese; Xinjiang will become an easy prey to American imperial power, if Xinjiang separates from China. Don't waste your time and energy on this, be happy with what you have and go with the flow, otherwise I will report you to the university authorities.' Wahit left the room quickly, before Elkem had finished lecturing him.

News of this exchange between Wahit and the writer spread among the students very quickly. Many students were angry and called the writer a traitor, a bootlicker, and a Chinese lackey. The university board organized a meeting for all the Turkic students, during which the conversation between Wahit and Mr Ahtem was discussed. The board criticized the students' attitude towards Mr Ahtem and warned them of the consequences if they didn't stop. We were quite used to these meetings as they occurred frequently even for very minor matters, since there were always students ready to report the most menial things to the board.

During this period, we were disappointed to hear that Abley who had initially agreed to join us had now declined, two days before his enrolment. Ablikim received a warning at our next meeting and was temporarily suspended from recruiting.

The board were concerned that Abley might turn in our organisation, so we decided that he should be watched. I was appointed to keep a close eye on Abley because I was in the same study group. However, I trusted him completely, knowing that we shared the same ideals. As I had had many discussions with Abley in the past, I was confident that he was a conscientious person who truly cared for his nation and its people. I told the other board members that we shouldn't worry about him, and indeed, their worries were eventually put to rest.

One day at the beginning of June, I was alone in my dormitory and quickly took the opportunity to tidy up; I moved two pots of flowers from the windowsill to the table and placed two party flags in each pot. The colourful flowers and the flags added a special beauty to the room, where later, we held a quick ceremony in accepting Turnisa as a formal member.

In the middle of July Sajide became a member. Soon after the recruitment of Turnisa and Sajide, all the minority students and staff were called to attend a meeting at which there were a large number of student representatives from Xinjiang University, The Petrochemical Institute, the First August Agricultural Institute, and The Science Academy.

Mr Enwer Jakolin, an officer from the Provincial Public Security Bureau made the following speech,

'Kazakh students from Xinjiang University, The Coal Mining Institute, the Agricultural Institute, and The Science Academy, and some other colleges and institutes have been involved in setting up an anti-government organisation. A number of cadres have also been involved with this illegal organisation. Action has already been taken – a number of arrests have already been made.'

He read out the names and charges of more than fifty people who had been arrested. Among them, I knew Orunbay, Elmiqan, Örkünbek, and Atmishbek. Orunbay was in his second year at our university. Elmiqan was a student in the Department of Physical Sciences. Örkünbek had done his degree in the Soviet Union and was now working in the Science Academy, while Atmishbek was a student at the Agricultural University. According to Mr Enwer Jakolin, they planned to unite the three regions of Ghulja, Chöchek, and Altay to establish a Kazakh independent state, which was to be united with the Soviet Union. In the end, Mr Enwer Jakolin declared their crimes as, 'traitors for conspiring to divide the motherland, for spying and engaging in counter-revolutionary activity, and for being rebellious nationalists.'

The hall was silent. People sat frozen to their seats, motionless with fear. Once the report had been concluded, the other students returned to their own universities. The remainder of us were divided into groups and were instructed to carry out a case study of the party principles. The university stopped normal teaching. Instead, we were ordered to undertake political study in groups, and talk about the need for the current changes of communist rule. This lasted a week.

It was a big blow to have so many young students arrested. More arrests followed: Kobe from the Xinjiang University, Keken from the Coal Mining Institute, and Qali from The First August Agricultural institute. We held a secret group meeting to discuss the failure of the Kazakh student's movement. We all condemned the Kazakh student's plan to divide East Turkistan, because we believed that the native Turkic peoples should unite, rather than divide, to fight the Chinese occupation of our lands.

We also discussed the shortcomings of our own organisation. First and foremost, we didn't have a strong charismatic leader and we were inexperienced. Furthermore, we didn't have any financial support. If we wanted to recruit members, we could easily recruit about eighty per cent of the students within our year, plus at least fifty per cent of students from other years. However, simply increasing our membership would not solve our problems. What we desperately needed was a dynamic leader with strong financial backing. At this point the board decided that we should temporarily suspend further recruiting to concentrate on underground publicity to seek out a strong existing organisation.

During this period, we heard that Abliz's relative Mahire, who was working in the Technical College, was emigrating to the Soviet Union. This prompted us to consider how to make contact with influential people in the Soviet Union. It was decided to write a letter to Mr Ziya Semedi, a prominent Uyghur separatist who had been imprisoned and had then fled to Soviet Kazakhstan. Abliz went to see Mahire and asked her to deliver the letter, to which she happily agreed. Later Ahmet Toxti, Melike and I went to a study room in the Orthopaedics Department to write the letter, which read –

'We are the committee members of the "East Turkistan Youths" and we are seeking to liberate our country from Chinese communist control. We have recently set up an organisation to implement non-violent anti-Chinese communist activities. We are now seeking an experienced leader, with strong financial backing, and as such we are desperately in need of your support. Even though you live a long way off, we would still appreciate your advice. We hope that you would consent to be our backstage director, and maybe at a later date, provide us with funds and weapons should it be necessary.

We learned later that the letter had been successfully delivered to Mr Ziya Semedi. We waited anxiously for a reply, but never heard anything.

We always suspected that there must have been an organisation behind the May 1962 Ghulja Massacre. We hoped that we might find the people responsible for organizing the protest, since we might be able to work with them.

During the summer vacation, Ahmet Toxti, Ablikim, Abliz, Ghopur and Melike went to Ghulja for holiday; they all planned to use the opportunity to look for other similar organisations. I hoped that they would come back with some good news. My heart sank upon hearing that they had been unsuccessful. I was bitterly disappointed.

Later In 1962, the Chöchek border incident took place. Over forty thousand people crossed the Soviet border in a rush to the safety of the Soviet Union. They left all their belongings and properties behind. From the Chöchek city all the way to Dorbojun Village almost everyone disappeared within days. Soon after the Ghulja Border Incident occurred. Once again, thousands fled to the Soviet Union this time by crossing the Ghulja Soviet border. These events brought more misery and uncertainty to the people of East Turkistan. However, they also initiated a new wave of anti-Chinese movements and anti-Communist regime movements among students in schools and universities. The Chinese authorities could never be under-estimated; they immediately clamped down on things getting out of hand.

One day during this period there was a note on Feizulla's desk when he came back to the class after the break. The note was directed at Tursun and said, 'When we demanded that we study separately from the Chinese students, you opposed it. Yet after we obtaining this right, you shamelessly joined us in the Turkic classes. The people of Chöchek fled, why not join them instead of sitting here?' Tursun was furious. He crumpled the note in his palm and questioned nearly everyone. Even if anyone knew who had written the note they would not have told him. We shook our heads, shrugged our shoulders, and pretended to know nothing about it.

Tursun was related to Enwer Jakolin's wife Patime. We knew that he always reported any minor infringement that occurred among the students to Enwer Jakolin. And for him, because Enwer Jakolin was his patron, he was very unpopular among his fellow students. Enwer Jakolin was a patient in our hospital at the time, so Tursun took the note to him and read it out. Enwer Jakolin declared it to have been written by a counter-revolutionary who must be found and exposed immediately, and insisted that a detective from the Public Security Bureau be instructed to investigate it. The investigator was named Ömerjan. He was a fair skinned, a tall slim built man with deep-set eyes and bushy eyebrows. He looked odd when he smiled because he had a gold front tooth.

The staff in the Security department of the university assisted him with his investigation. All the students were interviewed separately. Some interviews lasted for hours. In the end they found the person who wrote the note. It turned out to be Ruqiye Ilaji. She was interrogated for days and nights in the university detention centre. They believed that there was an organisation behind her note. Ruqiye fell ill. She had recovered from tuberculosis in the past, but during her incarceration and interrogation, she relapsed and her condition became very serious. In the end, the university informed her family. Her brother came and took her back to Ghulja. Years later, I learned that Ruqiye never recovered and died in 1966. Her young life ended in such tragedy. I pray for her to rest in peace in paradise.

They focused their investigation on our year when they didn't get any information from Ruqiye, because they always suspected that there must be an underground student organisation. We were very vigilant during the investigation. The investigating team spent most of their time with students from our year, and frequently called individual students for questioning. We managed to obtain information about who was called for interrogation and what was said.

The pro-government student activists Nurnisa, Pida, Hebip, Kerime, Nurnisa Rozi and Nurnisa Yüsup were all very busy. They spent most of their time in the investigation team's office reporting details of the students' activities.

After Sajide became a member, she told us that she had heard from a friend who worked in the Science Academy, that among the secretly kept documents there was an East Turkistan history book. We wanted to read the book and, if possible, make a copy of it. So Sajide was given the task of getting hold of the book. Soon afterwards she brought us the book. Melike, Turnisa, Helime and I started to hand copy it on the top-floor balcony of the accommodation block in our campus. We chose the top-floor balcony because it was the quietest and most out of the way place; hardly anyone visited.

It took us two sleepless weeks to finish copying the whole book so that we could return the book. We were so happy that at last we had some material for our East Turkistan History programme. We were really pleased with our achievement.

November 1962

Rumour spread among the students that Shemsijamal was pregnant. At the beginning of the year, the university had announced that students were not allowed to get married during their academic studies. Should anyone become pregnant, both parties would be expelled from the university. A number of students had already been expelled for this reason.

Melike, Shemsijamal, Abliz, Ablikim and I had become good friends since starting at the university, and later, our group was joined by Helime and Turnisa. We were so close it was like being a part of a large family. Any time we faced difficulties, we were there for one another, and we shared almost everything. We were horrified when we heard the rumour, so I asked Shemsijamal frankly about her condition. My question embarrassed her. She stared at the floor and replied softly, 'Yes I am pregnant.'

At that moment she looked so vulnerable and helpless. I felt my heart missed a beat. I exclaimed, 'Oh my God! What is going to happen now, do you know? If you're thrown out of the university, what we are going to do?' Then I realised that she didn't need any more pressure from anyone. I calmed myself and comforted her instead. I told her we would all be there for her, for anything, and we would do our best to help.

Shemsijamal hugged me tightly and cried uncontrollably. The thought of Shemsijamal, and her boyfriend Sétiwaldi, being expelled from the university was really upsetting me. I didn't want to lose my friend.

Shemsijamal's boyfriend Sétiwaldi managed to find an influential contact, Mr Yüsup, who was the director of the Machine Repair Factory, and was originally from Jaghastay, where Sétiwaldi came from. He was also a very close friend of Sétiwaldi's older brother. Mr Yüsup was able to persuade the university to give the two of them permission to get married, and he also helped with the registration of their marriage. For some strange reason, the Public Security Bureau was in charge of all the arrangements of their wedding, which was arranged to take place within a week. Mahmut's wife Meriyem made the wedding dress at their family's sewing factory. Abliz, Ablikim, and I helped with all the other bits and pieces.

The wedding took place in November, with the girl's party held in the house of our classmate Xalide Seydi, whose husband Abdukerim was a lecturer at Xinjiang University. We had enjoyed ourselves so much, and voiced our deep appreciation to Xalide and their parents for providing us with such a perfect evening. The wedding took place in a hall at the Public Security Bureau Building. Ablikim was best man, and I was the bridesmaid. Almost all our classmates attended the wedding, but half of the guests were Public Security officers.

Tables were set in the middle of the hall covered with white tablecloths, on which different types of delicious food and drinks were laid out. We were all impatient to sample the dishes. Music was played throughout the night, with guests enjoying ballroom dancing and dances of different minority groups. However, there was a dark cloud hanging over the hall, as it felt that we were being closely watched under microscopes by all the security officers. The wedding party lasted until midnight after which we accompanied groom and bride to Brother Yüsup's house. The Yüsup family loaned their house to the newly married couple for few days. When I emerged with Melike and Abliz after settling them in, all the other people had left.

It was snowing heavily, but with no transport available, we walked back to our campus, which took about two hours. I had been thinking about the reason for the involvement of the Public Security Bureau at their wedding, when suddenly Abliz said, 'Its strange that the Public Security Bureau was directly involved in taking full responsibility for this wedding.' He looked at us with a question in his eyes.

'They are looking for us, using Sétiwaldi as a torch', I said.

'You're right; they want to use Sétiwaldi as bait in order to catch us.'

Abliz looked at us with concern and said, 'I'm worried. They may be suspicious about us and possibly be setting a trap for us. We must take every precaution possible in this dangerous situation.

'I have been thinking the same; do you think they have sensed something about us?' Melike asked in a troubled voice.

After some thought, I said, 'No! They don't have any clues yet. They did this because Shemsijamal is pregnant, and the bureau did them a big favour in helping them to avoid being expelled from the university, in order to obtain their future loyalty.' Sétiwaldi must be very grateful and he won't hesitate to do anything for them from this day onwards. He will endeavour to satisfy their requests. Both Shemsijamal and Sétiwaldi will forget our friendship. They will not retain any loyalty to us whatsoever. This is a bad omen for us.'

Everyone trudged on in silence through the deep snowdrifts. The only sound was our shoes crunching into the snow. I broke the silence once more saying: 'I don't believe the security personnel know anything about us at the moment. If they had known they wouldn't have wasted all their energy and money in splashing out on such a big wedding, simply to keep the couple at university. Instead they would have detained us all immediately.'

'If the six of us keep our mouth closed, nobody will know anything.' said Melike.

'That is the problem', started Abliz, but I interrupted him –

'When you got drunk with Sétiwaldi, did you ever reveal anything about the party?'

'No, never!'

He continued after some thought, 'We have to be really cautious; let's pretend to be just like normal classmates in front of others. We'd better not raise anyone's suspicions. Sétiwaldi and Shemsijamal don't know anything about us so they can't provide any information. If we can go on to graduate without arousing suspicion, we'll be able to achieve our goals outside the university.' We carried on talking without realizing we had reached the campus.

12 December 1962

Melike's family decided to move to the Soviet Union, taking Melike with them. It was a sad day for all of us to lose such a good friend. I was devastated. Having been close companions since starting at the University, we had spent most of our free time together sharing our lives and ideas. She and I agreed about many different things. We organized a leaving party for her on her last night and talked until dawn.

We discussed our organisation and its future development before I said to her, 'My dear friend, you are leaving us and going far away, but the good thing is that you will be with your family and not alone. The bad thing is it may take you a while to settle in your new environment. Once you've settled in, please contact Mr Ziya Semedi and tell him about our organisation. Listen carefully to any advice and ideas that he has, it would be a great achievement if you could get him to help us. If that happens, you can work over there, while we continue over here. Things will run more smoothly if we can co-operate with each other by working as a team. You know the situation here. As the university rules tighten, things are getting harder day-by-day. Our entire society is coming under increasingly strict control. We don't know what's going to happen in the future. When I write to you about our organisation, I will use 'flower' as a symbol, remember that 'flower in the jar' represents our organisation.'

Melike was very keen to coorporate; she said that she would do her very best to help us in every way possible. Abliz, Melike and I had a long discussion about the organisation. With dawn was breaking; it was time for Melike to leave. Helime, Turnisa, Abliz and I accompanied her to the airport. It was with heavy hearts we said goodbyes to our dearest friend. With tears in my eyes, I gazed at the plane until it disappeared into the blue sky.

Back on campus, we found out that Nusret had spread rumours of our disappearance causing unrest in the student's union. Her followers were looking for us everywhere. I decided to skip the afternoon classes to sleep instead.

I was about to have a nap after lunch when Ablikim rushed in. He looked very upset and asked, 'Did you get back alright?', then sat on an empty bed.

I asked, 'What's happened? Are you Ok?' Other girls in the room also asked similar questions, but he just said, 'I'm ok' before leaving the room in a hurry.

I was worried and wondered what could possibly have happened. Abliz arrived, looking very anxious, but pretending to be normal. He sat for a while, hinting to me to come outside and then left. I waited for a short time, and then went to see him in his dormitory. Sétiwaldi was lying on his bed staring up at the ceiling and Ablikim and Abliz were sitting next to his bed. They all looked distressed.

'Hey, what's happened to you all, you look like gamblers who've lost everything in the game', I said jokingly.

'Sétiwaldi has been questioned by officers from the Public Security Bureau. He was interrogated and forced to provide information about our activities. They have specifically asked about Ablikim, Ahmet Toxti, you and me. He was warned not to mention anything to us about today's questioning', Abliz replied.

I didn't say anything for a moment, but I was very surprised because Sétiwaldi has had no knowledge about our activities, and in a way I was glad he didn't know. So many questions went through my mind, 'So what made the Public Security Bureau start to investigate us? They must have had some ideas about us; but how?'

I was worried because I knew that we were in a dangerous situation. Sétiwaldi suffers from heart disease; he said he almost had a heart attack during their interrogation. He said he was very nervous and didn't know what to say. Sétiwaldi didn't have any knowledge about the organisation, however he always worried about the consequences of the activities we had carried out when we petitioned the University to be separated from the Chinese students for lessons.

I wanted to calm Sétiwaldi down and said, 'Don't you worry. They are free to investigate anything, because we have nothing to hide. Although we initially encountered some problems after we petitioned to study separately, they eventually accepted our request, because it was reasonable. With everything now in the past, why do they want to investigate again? So what did they say when they asked you to expose us? What did they want to know exactly?'

Abliz and Ablikim looked at Sétiwaldi, waiting for his response. He thought for a minute, then said, 'They asked me to tell them about your daily routine, like what do you do? Who are you in contact with? What is your personality like? All those types of questions.'

I wondered why their investigation had focused on the four of us? This question kept bothering me.

From that day Sétiwaldi was questioned daily by the Public Security Bureau in their office. At the same time, other officers from the Public Security Bureau paid daily visits to the university to assist with the interviews of the students. The increased coming and going of police cars heightened tension among members of our group. I remained positive in the thought that no one in the party would betray us because of our determination and resilience, and because of the promise we made on joining the party. No one would break his or her word, I reassured myself. I truly trusted all the members. I thought perhaps Sétiwaldi might have said something about us during the questioning triggering their suspicions.

The investigations began not long before the end of term. Sétiwaldi went home with Shemsijamal to Jaghastay for the winter vacation. Turnisa and I spend the vacation in Nanshan with my family. Sétiwaldi returned to the university where we learned that Shemsijamal had had a baby boy, and they had named him Dilshad. Shemsijamal rejoined the university one month later, leaving the baby with the mother-in-law.

At the start of the semester, we were all allocated different work places and hospitals for practical tuition. Abliz, Sétiwaldi, Meriyem and Mahmut were placed in the No.2 Hospital; Ablikim was sent to the Military Hospital, Ghopur, Turnisa, Ahmet Toxti, and I were at the University Hospital. With the increased workload we had little free time. But the officers in the Public Security Bureau were busier than us because of an increase in their ongoing investigations. The students who were active in the Communist Party were the busiest of all, because they spent most of their spare time informing on other students or watching the events taking place in the investigation office.

One day Abliz came to see me, saying, 'Dear Söyün, I think that there is a traitor in our own group. You must be very vigilant. At this point we still don't know why they've suddenly started investigating us. It could be that someone in the party has provided some clues or details. So we can't trust anyone. All I know is that they are watching us very closely and we must cease all activities at this time. If we are exposed, I want you to burn all the party documents because we can't afford to let them fall into their hands.'

I said, 'Ok, I will. However, the question is, who has betrayed us?' It stuck in my mind. I was staring, frozen in horror at the thought.

Abliz agreed, 'We both have to be very careful when meeting or talking to each other.'

'May God protect us!' I replied. We said goodbye with heavy hearts.

After Abliz left, I had second thoughts about Abliz's request, as destroying all the party documents is like destroying the whole organisation. I didn't feel it was right to destroy everything! So I decided to move all the documents to a safe place for the moment and only to destroy them should the situation worsen. I still hoped and prayed that the authorities didn't have any evidence against us. I couldn't imagine anyone in the group betraying us.

One day I had a very strange dream that I planted a huge amount of bamboo in the desert. Suddenly Ömerjan, the man with the gold tooth from the Public Security Bureau appeared on the other side of the bamboo patch, he put a bamboo pole in his mouth and then blew towards the top of the first bamboo I had planted. Suddenly it burst into flames, from the root up, and disappeared in a matter of seconds. Ömerjan smirked. I was so distraught by what he had done that I woke immediately.

Although it was only a dream, it left me feeling unsettled. I tried to convince myself that no one in the party had betrayed us by telling myself, maybe they're just suspicious and I shouldn't worry. I don't think they know anything about our activities.' However, the next minute I would start worry again, 'You can't really trust anyone, as sometimes a disaster can be caused by the closest friends or family. Perhaps one of them has betrayed us, if so what shall we do now? What is going to happen to us?' these thoughts tumbled over and over in my mind.

'I must prepare myself for the worst', I said to myself as I got up from my bed and took out all the letters, journals, books, and other material. Once I had gathered them all, I burned them. Among these documents were a number of journals called 'The Truth of East Turkistan' which were published during the Three Districts Revolution, and which contained all kinds of information and sources from people who had been involved.

With the situation getting tenser every day, Ablikim reacted oddly and was very nervous. He would come to see me and would wish me well before he left for the hospital. He would always return to see me, no matter how late it was. Even when he finished from the late shift, he still came straight to see me.

He always said, 'Just popped in to see you, to make sure that you are fine.'

Sometimes he would knock on the door even if we were already asleep to say, 'As long as you are safe and well. I am happy.' Then he would leave.

I found his behaviour was very strange, however, I thought that he must just be scared, because he is a nervous and hotheaded person. Some days he called me into the corridor and said, ' Söyüngül, it seems as if they will arrest us soon, would you come to visit me in prison if you were free?'

'Ablikim, why are you so worried? Have you heard any bad news?' I asked him.

'No, I haven't, but look at the present situation and the atmosphere; you can feel and taste it. They are looking at us, and are carrying out an intensive investigation into our activities. If they continue, they will find out about our organisation eventually. It would have been so much better if they didn't pay attention to us, but now we are in their line of sight. They will destroy us one day; no matter how much I try, I still can't see any hope.'

I became even more worried after hearing what he said.

Nevertheless, I told Ablikim, 'Let's wait and see what happens, we have to hold ourselves together and stay calm. They have no evidence against us unless someone has betrayed us. It is all up to us. If we don't admit anything, anything at all, they can't make up anything against us. Even if they accuse us of any crime, without any evidence they have no chance of a conviction.'

He listened to me quietly as I tried to calm him down. 'Don't worry too much, if all five of us keep our mouths shut, they won't get anywhere', I added.

Sometimes, Ablikim called Helime and Turnisa to his side and said 'If they come to arrest me, I am going to walk like this towards them.' He showed them how he would walk, head held high like the heroes in the movies, as he strode backwards and forwards in the room.

'If they torture me, I will remain resolute and dignified, no matter how painful it is or what they do. I wouldn't reveal anything to the interrogator.'

He would act out the scene of a man shackled and chained, as he described the conditions of the cell in which he would be held, and say, 'I would gaze at the stars in the sky through a little narrow window at night, reciting the international poem for freedom.'

He would then passionately recite the poem. The two girls would be moved by his performance, which had brought tears to their eyes. Then, he would ask the girls, 'Would you come to visit me if I was imprisoned?'

The girls regarded him with sympathy, 'Of course we will come to see you, no matter how difficult it may be. Nothing can stop us from visiting you.'

I would laugh, 'Don't be silly, you're mad.'

Ablikim would continue, 'if you come to see me, just bring me cigarettes, nothing else.'

'Ablikim, why are you so worried? Why would they arrest you? After all, nothing has ever happened.' I looked into his eyes while he was speaking. He was acting as if some thing real would happen.

'They can accuse me of organizing the student strike and arrest me for it.' He replied. Ablikim continued playing different dramas like this almost every day. I started getting worried that by behaving like this, he would expose himself and reveal everything.

Soon after Melike left us, we received a letter from our classmate Riza, who was living in Soviet Union. He wrote, 'I am very pleased to hear that you are all well, and I am excited to hear about your future plans, as I feel I am working with you towards the same goal. We are starting our new life, but it is similar because we want to embrace all things anew, like you along with our other friends in the country. Although we are far away from each other, our hearts will always be as one. Let's continue our close friendship with you in the motherland and with me seeking a new future in a foreign land.'

I understood what he meant: he would also like to set up an organisation like ours and support us from abroad. I was extremely happy. I felt as if there was extra input being added to our organisation at last. The letter was read out at one of our secret board meetings. Ablikim and Abliz were overjoyed.

Abliz said, 'Riza is a courageous and righteous person who shares same ideology and approaches as us.'

I remember when we worked on the railway in Seyapul, Riza had once said, 'Work slowly girl, do you know once the railways completed and the trains start running from Mainland China? It will bring disaster to Xinjiang.' He was right, that was exactly what is happening now.

Ahmet Toxti said, 'Officers from the Provincial Public Security Department are in and out of the university all the time, they are carrying out a very intensive investigation. So we have to be very careful; don't reply to Riza or Melike under any circumstances because of the current political situation. Also if possible, we need to let them know that they shouldn't write to us as this will cause trouble for us all if our mail is checked.'

Ablikim nodded, 'When I was at last dance party organised by the university, I met the director of the Central Postal Control Office. He told me that the students in this university were writing letters too openly, that university staff have been stamping them off to their destination up until now, however, that if some of those letters landed in the wrong hands, it could cause serious consequences. He asked me to pass this information on to the students, that they have to be careful about what they write.'

Abliz added, 'Oh yes, I learned today that the letter we wrote to Mr Ziya Semedi was delivered. The strange thing is that we didn't receive any reply from him until now.'

30 March 1963

Days passed in wretchedness and uncertainty. One day I was studying in the Orthopaedic Department, when Ahmet Toxti came to see me. He dropped a scrunched up piece of paper on the desk in front of me saying, 'Please read this letter starting at the second paragraph', then hurried off.

The letter was written by his wife Mariyem, and said,

Ahmet, do you know how much I have missed you having spent so many years apart and waiting for your return. We have not lived together since we were married but I have never complained because I wanted you to finish your education without disturbing you. With your graduation approaching, I had started counting the days to our reunion.

However, I have just heard that officers from the Public Security Bureau are investigating you; they have interviewed a number of your close friends in Ghulja, and they have been to Jaghastay as well, talking to your close friends over there. What is happening? I cannot understand it! I fell ill after I heard this terrible news. Why don't you think about me, what else do I have apart from you? What can I do now? I am in a state of shock from what I have heard.'

Having read the part of the letter which Ahmet had asked me to read, I folded it up feeling terrible. While I had been sitting here thinking that they don't know anything about us, they had, in fact, been carrying out investigations in our hometowns. They wouldn't have wasted their time focusing on us specifically if they didn't have any clues about our activities. Clearly they have evidence against us.

Ahmet Toxti returned later and asked me in a low voice, 'Did you read it?'

'Yes, I did. It sounds like they already have some evidence against us because they have been incessantly checking on us. Has someone in the committee turned us in?'

'I have been wondering the same. This is not the right place to talk, let's go back to the dormitory.' He spoke quietly.

We continued our conversation as we walked back to the dormitory.

Ahmet said, 'I think the five of us should not contact one another for the time being. You need to stay away from Abliz, Ablikim and Ghopur. You are a young lady; it is going to hit your family hard if you are arrested. Your family has endured financial hardships in order for you to attend university. I can't imagine what the consequences would be, given that this government is shameless and ruthless. You have read the letter and you can see the awful things that are going to happen. We must prepare ourselves for the worst possible scenario.

Tell Ablikim that he should move to the Military Hospital where he is working as a practicing doctor, ask Abliz not to come to see you anymore and don't visit them either. If you really must speak to them try to find a safe place where you will not be noticed. There are eyes and ears everywhere; the situation is becoming more and more dangerous. If the worst should happen, it is going to be difficult for you being a girl.'

I told Ablikim of the developments that same day; he moved to the Military Hospital immediately. Although I tried to tell myself that nothing would happen, unpleasant thoughts kept bothering me. I repeatedly told myself, 'Why should I worry? I haven't committed any crimes. We don't have guns or go on the street to incite fighting, or kill anyone. We simply asked for our own independence. That is not a crime. It is every human being's right to ask for their freedom.'

However, the question kept returning again and again about who it was that had betrayed us. This troubled me. I couldn't find the answer no matter how hard I tried even though I considered all the possibilities.

Sétiwaldi, Ablikim and Abliz all came from Jaghastay. They had all been friends since primary school. Both Ablikim and Abliz had suggested in the past that Sétiwaldi was a trustworthy person, and as such, was a suitable candidate for membership of our organisation. I considered it possible that one of them had told Sétiwaldi about our organisation, and he had revealed it to the Public Security Bureau during one of their interviews. This was the only possibility I could think of.

In the beginning Ablikim visited me regularly even after he moved out from the student campus. However, he suddenly stopped seeing me. I heard from other students that he had been seen in the university. Ablikim was going out with a girl from Chöchek. I knew the girl; as she was a well-known pro-active student who regularly reported any students' activities to the university board. Later, I heard that they had ended their relationship, but I also heard that Ablikim continued to visit her from time to time. This news bothered me a lot.

'What was going on? Why is he seeing this girl again, knowing what she's like? Is it because he made a mistake? Maybe he is trying to cover some thing up.' I had all kinds of horrible thoughts constantly running through my mind.

10 April 1963

I was writing up a patient's medical history in the Inpatients department when the phone suddenly rang. I was alone in the room. I ignored the phone and continued with my work. The phone continued ringing, until a nurse rushed in and picked it up.

'Ok, alright, I will.' She put the phone down and said depressingly, 'My God, I don't know what happened this time but they are asking all the minority staff to gather in the university board meeting room.'

Doctors, nurses and other staff members all left for the meeting, returning after a short time. As she was putting on her white coat, the Uyghur nurse who had answered the phone, said, 'Do you know what this is all about? We were told that all the ethnic students and staff would stop their normal studies and work programmes to attend political study meetings as from Monday. They mentioned about 'organisations' and such. I don't know how many poor people are going to be in trouble this time. They're terrorizing everyone, which is creating pain and worry for so many people. Oh, and please don't tell anyone what I've told you.' She left the room.

When I heard the news, I froze in my chair and my heart fluttered; it was a disturbing feeling. 'If someone hadn't revealed our organisation it wouldn't have been mentioned at the meeting. Has someone really betray us? Who? Was there any other organisation apart from ours? The name of members went through my mind one by one, but I just couldn't believe any of them could or would betray us. Who can I trust and talk to, if anyone, about what I have been told? What could be done if we are exposed? Is it possible to disappear and go into hiding?

There is nothing we can do, except face the consequences.' I was so unsettled that I wanted to run out of the office to confide in someone, but who could I talk to? It wouldn't be possible to do anything if we were being denounced. I felt so alone, like a stranger in a foreign land. Then I started to calm myself down, as always by saying comforting words to myself.

'It is going to be alright, but why am I thinking of so many problems? Perhaps it is just a different type of political study programme, and nothing to do with us. Also it's impossible that our organisation is being exposed, each of the members are trustworthy, resilient, honourable and loyal individuals. No one would do something evil like this. I shouldn't worry myself too much without knowing the truth.' With all this to think about, I hadn't realised that lunchtime had come and gone. I rushed to the canteen to find no one there. I went straight to the dormitory; no one was there either. I went back to the hospital for my evening shift. I found it difficult to focus on my work as my mind was still in turmoil. No matter how much I tried to console myself, deep down in my heart I knew that dark and horrifying days lay ahead.

Once again, I was the last in the canteen for breakfast, so I didn't see anyone before I went to work in the hospital. When I returned to the dormitory after lunch, I found Shemsijamal and Turnisa talking. They both looked very unhappy and worried.

As I walked in Shemsijamal said, 'Söyüngül, I received a phone call from Sétiwaldi, he said he just wanted to inform me about a new political study programme starting at the university.'

I told them that I already knew about it and outlined what I knew. After the break, we saw all the students that were on work placement elsewhere returning on the university buses. Everyone looked worried. I heard some students say, 'We may lose some of our best friends.'

There is no laughter or jokes on the lips of the students now. Instead, there is only a look of fear on their faces, with people talking in low tones.

Our classmates gathered in the dormitory, looking very apprehensive, as if the world was about to end and we must say goodbye to one another. They looked at each another with love in their eyes, yet all were deeply troubled and only spoke quietly to relieve the tension.

Ablikim sauntered into the room, looking like he didn't have a care in the world and loudly joking. His behaviour didn't seem normal, as he looked casually in my direction, as if he didn't know me. He didn't even speak to his best friends, Abliz and Sétiwaldi, as he carried on joking with some proactive Kazakh students, before he turned and left.

I wondered if he was simply trying to divert attention away from us by acting in such a way. 'Perhaps he is doing the right thing', I said to myself, not suspecting him at all. As dusk approached, everyone left the room except Abliz and Sétiwaldi. They both looked so miserable and said, 'After we heard the news, we went to the shower room so we could talk quietly and wash, and when finished we hugged each other before saying our farewells.

Sétiwaldi sadly said, 'I don't think we will be safe this time, especially not Abliz!'

I noticed Abliz was gazing at us girls with his gentle compassion on his face, but I could see the sadness in his eyes.

13 April 1963

Today, all us ethnic minority students and staff were summoned to a political meeting in the conference hall of the administration department.

Mr Baodun, the head of the University, gave the opening speech about the anti-Chairman Mao, anti-party activities, and revisionism among the students.

He said, 'The most outrageous thing is that some students have shown no respect to our great leader Chairman Mao. For instance, some students cut the picture of the Chairman Mao and Khrushchev in half and kept the Khrushchev's photo as a wall poster while discarding the half that was Chairman Mao. Some students have turned Chairman Mao's poster around to face the wall, then hit it and cry 'I hope hell strikes you down!'

He gave many different examples of the incidents that had occurred. While he was speaking, he kept looking in our direction. It was as if he was saying, 'Yes, I am talking about you!'

To make matters worse, we were all sitting together. Although this was accidental, it draw the attention of other people in the hall. Mr Baodun talked all morning without a break.

14 April 1963

We formally started the political study programme today, with the students of our year divided into two groups. Ablikim, Abley, Shemsijamal, Turnisa, Ghopur, Helime and others were in the first group and I was in the second group with Abliz, Ahmet Toxti, Sétiwaldi and some other students. The leadership of the political study project was formed from three different organisations. Mr Turdi, Mr Yüsup, and Mr Ömerjan were from the Public Security Bureau; Mr Gozjang, Mr Ghopur Réhim, and Mr A. Réhim were from the Student Union; and some other cadres from the hospital. These leaders were invited to be in charge of our year, making it clear that we were the only targets for this political study programmeme.

The police cars kept scouring the campus, like hunters waiting for their prey. During the meeting, students were asked to give their understandings about the political study project, and their thoughts before and after the study. After some students finished their report, the organizers turned their attention to us.

One of them asked me, 'Söyüngül, why don't you tell us your opinion?'

'I need time to think before I can say anything', I replied.

They moved on to ask my friends, 'Abliz, tell us what you think.'

'How about you, Ahmet Toxti, what do you think?'

Abliz answered. 'Ok, let me tell you what I think.' He talked about 'the Three Unities'.[7] When he finished Ahmet Toxti carried on from Abliz. This lasted until three in the afternoon. No one has spoken about party policies as clearly and comprehensively as those two, and their discussions became more interesting when they asked each person one after another.

Security at the university was tightened during this period. No one was allowed in or out without special permission. The proactive students were frequently called to the meetings. I could sense that something terrible was waiting to happen, but I tried not to think about it.

Every time we heard the wail of a police siren as they entered the campus, Sétiwaldi became very nervous and unsettled. He would murmur, 'They're coming to arrest us now.' The pro-active students watched us closely, as if they knew something.

Turnisa's attitude had suddenly changed towards me from the day we started the

---

7   *Mao's dictum, referring to the unity of political action within the insurgent forces, spiritual unity between the insurgents and the people, and unity of political action targeting the enemy's cohesion.*

political programme. She stopped talking to me, and whenever I tried to speak to her, she either ignored me or responded coldly. She became so disturbed that she would no longer eat or sleep. She had never before treated me this way, since we had become friends. We had never kept secrets from each other, and had always been there for each other. This made me very sad and lonely. I felt I was gradually losing everything close to my heart.

Unlike many previous political meetings, where people had been dragged out to the front, violently intimidated, and forced to confess their crimes, this campaign was conducted relatively peacefully. There was sadness in the eyes of my classmates, I could tell from the way they looked at me. I sensed that they felt loss towards me, and sympathy for me. During the break, some of them came to me and said 'We will never forget you!' When I returned from the break, some of my classmates asked me to sit with them. This comforted me greatly, as I felt I was being deserted by my best friends.

16 April 1963

On the second day of the meeting, Abliz was asked to tell the officials what he had learnt during the political study, and whether there were any changes about his ideas and political views. He lectured them for one hour on the subject of 'the Three Unities.'

A special meeting was held for pro-activist students. Before the meeting, students who had a good working relationship with us were asked to speak to us privately. During the break, Meriyem's husband Mahmut, looking uncomfortable, called me into the corridor.

He cautiously said, 'Söyüngül, I was asked by the leaders to speak to you because we have always maintained a good relationship, so please don't take this the wrong way or be angry with me. They have asked me to tell you that you should confess what you have been doing because in today's meeting we were told that there is 'an anti-government organisation'.

I was shocked and saddened to hear this.

'Is it true, Söyüngül? Please don't be cross with me. To be honest with you, my friend, I am totally devastated. I don't want to lose you or any other classmates. What is going on?' He asked with tears in his eyes.

'No, there isn't any such organisation. It is all in their minds. To be honest with you, there is nothing to confess. I thank you for your concerns and kind words.' I smiled.

During the meeting officials repeatedly stated, 'We are offering you this last chance to redeem yourselves and get out of a difficult situation before it is too late. Otherwise, you will regret your actions for the rest of your life. Do not lie or try to mislead us, we are aware of everything. We are being generous in giving you the opportunity to admit your mistakes in order to correct yourselves. This would enable you to continue with your studies without interference.' They glanced in our direction while they spoke. We acted normally, laughing and joking as if unaware of anything.

After lunch I went to the dormitory, only to find Turnisa pale and trembling. She saw me and called, 'Söyüngül, quick, come quickly!'

I thought she wasn't feeling well, so I asked 'What's the matter? Are you feeling sick?'

She whispered in my ear, 'Our organisation has been exposed, I have been interrogated for the past three days. I denied knowing anything about such an organisation, however, today when I repeated the same story to them, they said, "If you don't know, then let us tell you what we know." They told me in detail of how and when and through whom I had become a member. I didn't know what to say. They also asked me about Ablikim, Abliz, and Ahmet Toxti. I told them that I didn't know anything about their activities. Finally, they warned me not to tell you anything, otherwise I would be held responsible. What shall we do now? Söyün, my dear, I don't know what to do? I am so scared!' She burst into tears.

'It's ok! If they have already found out about the organisation, there is nothing we can do. I don't think anything serious will happen to you if you show the right attitude towards them. Please remain calm and composed.' This was the only comfort I could offer.

I sensed something serious was about to happen and jumped up from my seat to retrieve my diary as it contained a story I had written in 1959 titled 'Dream'. I passed it to Turnisa saying. 'Please take this, hide it inside your jacket and throw it in the toilet behind the university grocery shop.' She took it and left the room.

I started to tidy my things; I gave Ahmetjan Qasim's picture to Shemsijamal. 'Please accept this in remembrance of our time together. Ahmetjan Qasim had been the former president of East Turkistan. He died along with ten other high-ranking officials of the East Turkistan Republic in a mysterious plane crash after boarding the plane in Almaty to attend the First Chinese People's Political Consultative Conference in Beijing.

When my roommates realised that I was sorting out my belongings and preparing myself for the worst they tried to ease my tension by saying, 'Come on Söyün, don't make us feel sad, don't be negative, nothing bad is going to happen to you. We will pray for you! This awful news has also left us shaken but we still have high hopes that nothing bad will happen to you' I hugged them one after another, and thanked them for their compassion. They all had tears in their eyes then. I was moved by the thoughts and love which they had shown for me.

After the break, we returned to the conference. I sat next to Meriyem, keeping a seat next to me for Abliz. The conference started when Ömerjan came in and took the seat facing me. I noticed that he was closely observing Abliz and me. I wrote a quick note for Abliz on a piece of paper, saying, 'Abliz, the flower in the pot was broken by the wind.' I passed it over to him.

He wrote back, 'Was it just the flower that was broken or the roots as well?'

I wrote back, 'When the pot and flower was broken, the roots were destroyed with it.'

He returned with 'What is this all about? Tell me what has happened?'

So I wrote another note explaining what I had heard from Turnisa. He wrote back, 'Do you know who damaged the roots?'

I answered, 'I have no idea.'

We were exchanging the notes as quickly as we could while were being watched, but I had prepared myself to chew and swallow each note as it came in case anyone approached me for them. Luckily nothing happened.

Ömerjan opened his conclusion to the political study programme by saying, 'We have completed our three-day political study programme successfully, which has had an impact on the thoughts and attitudes of the students. By doing so, we have been able to resolve many questions, which we had failed to address in the past. To be frank, a secret anti-government organisation has been exposed. The political study programme we organized was to give those people who were running the organisation an opportunity to confess and reform. These students still stubbornly believe that we don't know anything.

But I can tell them that we are aware of everything. We have spoken to them separately as we consider them to be young and impressionable, and we have shown them understanding and compassion. However, they have not appreciated our offers of help and forbearance. A number of students were not questioned; perhaps this should be carried out today. The government has special exonerating policies towards young people, but in your case this hasn't been appreciated. You should also remember that we have very tough policies in place for our enemies.' He carried on with a long speech about policies, principles and punishments, during which he kept glancing at Abliz and myself. We gave him our full attention and friendly smiles.

Ömerjan came to the dormitory after dinner requesting that I report to his office at seven o'clock.

I sent Shemsijamal to ask Abliz to come and see me, then I asked Meriyem, Helime, and others to kindly leave the room. They didn't mind, instead they said that they would stand guard near the door. Abliz arrived with Shemsijamal.

I asked Shemsijamal to act as a lookout, then spoke rapidly to Abliz, 'I have been summoned to the security office later. What shall I do?'

Abliz replied, 'Let me speak to the other comrades first.' He hurried off and returned just as quickly, saying 'I have spoken to the other board members about your problem. If the authorities already knew about our group, there is nothing we can do to keep it secret anymore. Now we have to try to show the desirable attitude in order to save ourselves from persecution. Our priority now is to conform to the rules of society; if we can even save one of us, we have to try. Maybe we will have the opportunity to carry on our work in the future. We will have to make many sacrifices, but may God grant our people the freedom and independence they desire one day!'

He looked sad as he continued, 'Söyüngül, It is hard to believe that our organisation is being exposed before we have managed to do anything.' He shook his head. I saw tears in his eyes.

I tried to comfort him by saying, 'Abliz, this is only our first step, nothing will be in vain. We will still have the chance to carry on the fight for our dreams in the future, with God's will. The next generation will carry on in our footsteps. They might achieve the goals that we haven't been able to. It will not be a failure if we are arrested, on the contrary, it will be good publicity for the independence movement of East Turkistan. Abliz looked at me with sympathy and said gently, 'Goodbye. I pray to God that you'll be safe and well. I leave you in his care.'

I stood staring at nothing, lost in a world of endless thoughts until I was distracted by Shemsijamal saying that Ömerjan was coming. He followed her in and said, 'Let's go, they are waiting for you.'

I followed him to the office where there were seven people waiting to question me. Those present were Mr Deng, the party secretary; Mr Tang, the university chancellor Mr Tang; the head of the University Security Department; the Chinese head of the Public Security Bureau; a Chinese official whose face was familiar but I didn't know his name; Ghopur Rahim, the head of the Students Union; and another Chinese official whom I had never met. I sat down on the chair that I was directed to. The head of the Public Security Bureau was the first to open the conversation. 'You are Söyüngül, is that correct?' He grinned with little humour.

'Yes, I am Söyüngül.' I tried to make myself comfortable and to relax as I sat straight on the chair and responded to the question with a smile.

'Ok, tell us about your experience over the past three days. What did you learn from the study programme?'

I told them about the 'Three Unities', as the other students had done.

He said, 'Is that all you have learned? Aren't there any changes in your ideas and thoughts? We know all about you and have waited a long time for you to come forward to confess your crimes. Open your eyes wide now and look around you. It is impossible for you to fool us any longer. You should understand the leeway the party has allowed you. All of your members have woken up and have accepted the right path. Who can you trust now? You'd better consider your future by confessing your crimes right now!'

'What do you want me to confess?' I responded.

'So you still don't know what to confess? Expose your organisation, don't act like a fool,' he barked, 'Your people have already exposed it to us. You can't continue to cover it up any longer. All of your members have confessed every thing.'

'If they have already told you everything, then there is no need for me to say anything.' I replied.

'Do you think you did a good job?' he snapped.

'No, I wouldn't say that I did a good job, but I don't think I did anything bad either.' I said.

'What are you talking about? Are you trying to mock us?'

'From your point of view, it wasn't a good thing, but from our point of view, we haven't done anything bad. We didn't use weapons to kill anyone or organize people to rebel. We were only hoping to appeal for independence.'

'What did you say? You come here to bargain with us for independence? Remember, Xinjiang is an inseparable part of China.' Ömerjan shouted. 'What did she say? What did she say?' the Chinese officials asked urgently.

'Xinjiang is Chinese territory, do you have any evidence for claiming independence?' the head of the detective department asked me.

'Yes, I have. History itself is the evidence.' I replied.

'What history is that?'

'The history of East Turkistan' I said.

'Those histories were written by reactionaries like you. Xinjiang has been a part of China's territory since ancient times, and it will always remain a part of China. No other power can ever separate Xinjiang. Stubborn reactionaries like you cannot achieve anything. The party is not alarmed of any such powers as those people only digging a hole for themselves.' The man was almost screaming at me with rage. Everyone in the room was furious.

The Chinese official whom I never met asked me, 'Do you have any backing? Who are they?'

'We have none!' I said firmly.

He shouted, 'Your comrades have already exposed them! We are checking your attitude and lies.'

'I have no knowledge about any backing, maybe the person who exposed them knew better.' I responded.

'Are you certain that you really don't know? Everything has been revealed to us. You'd better carefully rethink your answer. We have been very patient with you but don't forget the party's heavy-handed policy towards its enemies. We have been very tolerant with all of you because you are students, especially with you as you are a young woman. If you hadn't been students, you would have been arrested and locked away in prison by now. You should understand that we don't use such a forbearing policy with everyone. Time is running out, because we have many other matters to deal with. We ask you to think again and give us a full and detailed account of your wrongdoings. Try to cooperate with us in order to be pardoned by the Party.'

Ömerjan interrupted him before he finished what he was saying. 'You will hand over all your documents regarding this organisation to me by tomorrow morning. Furthermore, you are not allowed to hold any meetings as from today.'

All of them stood up and got ready to leave. As I walked out of the door, they all followed me. There wasn't anyone in the dormitory when I arrived back because they were still at evening revision. I sat alone in the room thinking through everything I had said and been told. The thing that bothered me the most was the request that I hand in all the organisation's materials and document to them. As long as I was alive, I told myself, I would never hand over any of our documents. I had to find a way to safeguard all the documents. It was my responsibility to do so. "What shall I do?' I asked myself - should I go home to sort things out? No! I cannot. I am being watched; also someone would definitely follow me. If someone walks in while I am dealing with these documents it would ruin us all.

Can I leave after everyone has gone to sleep? No, I can't. There are no buses after 10 o'clock, in addition, it would raise more suspicions if they found out that I wasn't in the dormitory. What shall I do? I'm stuck. My head started to spin, faster and faster. By then all the students had retuned to the campus from classes.

Shemsijamal came to me and said in an undertone, 'We were told that it was Ablikim who betrayed us.'

Abliz followed her in and asked me, 'What happened? What did they ask you?' I told him everything.

Abliz wanted to know, 'Who exposed us? From what they were saying they knew everything. They believe that we have backers. I don't know if it was Ahmet Toxti who betrayed us.

I said to Abliz, 'Whatever happened is in the past. Now we have to face whatever comes our way. Don't be sad, we couldn't have continued to hide this forever.' Abliz stared into space while I spoke, 'I told them that we didn't do anything hurtful, that we didn't use weapons to kill anyone or organize people to rebel.'

Abliz said thickly, 'Are they going to do something serious to us for what we have done? The worst might be we will be kept under the University Surveillance regime. They may even pardon us if we show the right attitude.' At that point, he smiled at me.

'Honestly, I am upset that we didn't achieve anything. I wouldn't have any regrets whatsoever, if we had been able to achieve something before ending up like this. I feel deeply sorry for our failures and the position we are now in.'

After some thought, Abliz spoke, 'we didn't have as many chances as we had obstacles in every direction, leaving us with plans and ideas unfulfilled. It is possible that we may achieve our goals in the future, God willing.' He smiled at me and said, 'don't worry too much now, go to bed and have a good sleep. We have little choice but to face whatever comes our way. Good night and sweet dreams.' He left the room, then popped his head back round the door, 'Hope to see you safe and well tomorrow.' He left the room, still smiling.

18 April 1963

Everything carried on as normal, so after breakfast I put on my white coat and picking up some of my books I headed off to the hospital. As I was walking down the stairs, Kamil strode up behind me and barely breaking stride as he passed me, handed me a letter and said 'Be careful!'

I held the note tightly in my hand and went to the toilet to read it. It said, 'Söyüngül, we never thought you were on this path. After we learned about what you have been doing, our respect for you increased. Your noble character will remain in our hearts with the highest respect forever, and whatever happens, we will never forget you!'

It was a very beautiful hand-written note, and every word touched me. I finished reading the letter with tears in my eyes. This simple letter gave me so much comfort and strength, it made me feel like my well-wishers were my backbone. Whatever happened, I didn't want the note to fall into the wrong hands or cause any kind of trouble for them, so I tore the letter up before throwing it away.

As I walked on outside Zubeyde was looking for me. She told me that Ömerjan was waiting for me outside our dormitory. I became very nervous, 'what should I do now? He must be here for all the party material. I won't give him those documents under any circumstances! I have to find a way to stall him.'

With all these thoughts churning round my head, I returned the dormitory. Ömerjan was standing outside my room. When he saw me, he walked towards me, 'You must hand over the documents to me right now,'

'The papers you want are not in my room. They are at my house in the city', I said.

Ömerjan turned around and looked at me saying, 'You have a house in the city?'

'I mean in my grandparent's house. I keep them in a cloth case there.' I tried to explain.

He said, 'Ok, let's go there to get them.'

'Oh God, what shall I do now?' I thought.

A number of thoughts crossed my mind as we walked on. When we reached the bus stop, Ömerjan asked me,

'Where do your grandparents live?'

'Down past the Xinhua Bookshop[8] near the Russian Club.' I told him.

A police jeep sped past us heading to the university, but it turned around and drove back in our direction.

Ömerjan said, 'This is our jeep, We'll go by jeep.' He raised his hand to stop the vehicle.

I prayed, 'Please don't stop!' The jeep didn't stop and Ömerjan looked embarrassed. He said, 'The driver is new, he didn't recognize me. Let's catch the bus.'

I was trying to figure out what to do next to prevent him from getting the documents. In the end, there was only one possible solution. In the basement of the house where the papers were stored was a cellar, three metres deep by one and half

8   *A state-run chain of bookshops in China*

metres wide, for the storage of food and ice to keep the food cool in summer. When Ömerjan comes with me to the basement, I will push him into the cellar and burn all the materials before he can get out. I will then face the consequences, whatever they may be. I felt more relaxed after I had decided on my course of action. While I was still preoccupied, we arrived at the Xinhua Bookshop.

As soon as we got off the bus, Ömerjan asked, 'Which is your house?' I pointed at it.

He said, 'Ok, you go and get the documents and I will wait for you here.' This took me by surprise. 'Is he serious or is he just playing with me? If he doesn't follow me to the gate, I can lock the door from the inside and burn everything before he can force entry.' I walked fast towards the gate, but as I approached it I saw a large padlock on it. I was relieved and turned around to find Ömerjan smiling smugly at me.

'So no one is at home, where do you think they've gone?' he asked.

I lied, 'My grandma's sister is going to the Soviet Union, maybe she went to say her farewells.'

'Check with the neighbour to see if the key has been left with them, and ask them if they know their whereabouts.'

I ran to my neighbour's house, my aunty Zeynus; she was doing embroidery on the sewing machine, but stopped, came over to me and kissed me, inviting me in for a cup of tea. I thanked her and told her that I was in a hurry.

'I came to see my grandma, but she is not at home. Do you know where she is?'

Aunty Zeynus replied, 'She went to attend a meeting in the commune; and should be back within the next five or ten minutes. You are welcome to wait here for her if you wish.'

I thanked her and rushed out. I told Ömerjan, 'My grandma has gone to see her sister; the neighbour said that she'll be back in the evening.'

Ömerjan looked at his watch and said, 'It is ten o'clock now maybe your grandfather will be home for lunch. I think we can just wait for him here.'

I improvised and told Ömerjan that my grandfather always took his lunch to work with him, he doesn't come home for lunch, and that he normally finished work around five or six o'clock.

Finally, Ömerjan capitulated and said, 'Ok, its best if we come back around five o'clock tonight.'

We returned to the university. I rushed to my dormitory, changed my coat, took some money for the bus ticket and the house keys, and then headed out to the hospital.

'I have to go back to the house during my lunch break and burn all the documents, otherwise I won't get another chance. I fear this man knowing where the house is, because he might go by himself and take everything away I have hidden. I must act quickly.'

I was fighting time. When I arrived at the hospital, it was twenty past eleven, and as I was changing my uniform my supervising doctor arrived to instruct me, 'There is a new patient allocated to your care, you have to diagnose the patient independently, carrying out all the relevant checks, including urine samples and blood. Making sure you've taken a detailed notes of the patient's medical history, and decide on the course of treatment needed. I will assess how well you have performed and you will be marked accordingly.'

My head began to spin, 'Oh God, I can't take any more pressure. How can I deal with a patient in my present state of mind?' I took the necessary equipment required for the medical checks and went to see the patient. She was a young Chinese lady, whose temperature was very high. I asked her to tell me about her illness. As she was very weak she spoke slowly and very softly, which made it very hard for me to concentrate. I was constantly watching the clock; it was now twenty to twelve and I could no longer take anything in.

I had to ask her to repeat what she had said, so she once again outlined her problems with a struggle. I still could not comprehend what she was saying. Then looking at me she said, 'Doctor, I am very ill. Please help me!'

At that moment I felt guilty, it must have been the feeling of guilt that made me pull myself together and focus on making my diagnoses. She was suffering from a kidney infection. I explained this to the patient saying, 'You need to rest. I will instruct the nurse to administer some medicine, just stop worrying and you will soon start feeling better. I wrote out the prescriptions and gave them to the nurse with instructions to take urine and blood samples for testing. It was now ten to twelve. I walked through the outpatient department towards Paediatrics where I took off my white coat and hid it under the staircase before quickly leaving the building.

Fortunately, as I rushed out of the main gate there was a bus waiting at the bus stop, so I ran and was able to catch it. On the bus was a man who looked like one of the Chinese men who had questioned me the previous day. I was terrified, so I looked down and sat on one of the front seats quickly so that he wouldn't recognize me. I was so jittery, waiting for the bus to leave, but it didn't. Time passed so slowly, unlike my rapidly beating heart, which jumped every time there was movement. What worried me most was that at any moment, I would be recognized and dragged off the bus. Every time someone passed by, I felt as if they were going to arrest me.

The bus moved off at last and when it stopped at the Bei Min bus stop, the man I recognized left the bus. I looked at him again, more carefully, and realised that he wasn't the same man I had seen last night. I took a deep breath and sat up straight. There is an expression in the Uyghur language - 'When you fear something badly you have double vision, and you see one thing as two'. The bus stopped at the Bei Min bus stop for about fifteen minutes. I was getting so impatient that I felt like getting off the bus and pushing it myself. The more I wanted the bus to move, the longer waiting became. Time was passing very slowly, I felt like screaming to the driver to get a move on.

Then, I was distracted by a police jeep. It was the same one I'd seen earlier in the day at the university and was heading towards the city.

'Oh my God, they might be on their way to my grandparent's home; perhaps they want to check if my grandfather has come home from work for lunch. What shall I do now? Shall I return to the hospital? It will only make things worse for myself, if I walk into the house while it is being searched. No! I have to go on. I must take a chance no matter what happens, I have to try to do something about those documents. Maybe the police jeep went somewhere else. I shouldn't frighten myself with all these negative thoughts.'

By this time I was already at the Xinhua Bookshop stop. I rushed off the bus, and ran to the house, which had the police jeep parked outside. 'Oh God, they are here!' I looked in the jeep, but no one was inside. 'They must be in the house, what shall I do? I thought. 'I have no choice, I'm here now, I'd better go inside'

I pushed the gate open and dashed in. My grandmother was sitting in the middle of the courtyard performing wudu in preparation for afternoon prayers. I couldn't believe my eyes; I stopped and stared at her.

She looked up, saw me and spoke easily, 'Come in my child, come in!' She came over and gave me a warm hug.

I asked her, 'Did anyone visit the house grandma?' I was scanning everywhere while I waited for her reply.

'No, my dear. Are you expecting someone?' She asked.

I sighed with relief, quickly locked the gate with a padlock , and told her not to open the door to anyone. I then explained, 'I came here to take something from storage room. I don't want anyone to see me.' I opened the storage door and hurried in.

'I need some coal from there.' said my grandmother as she followed me carrying a bucket in her hand. While she was filling the bucket with coal I started collecting the documents as fast as I could. I put the Xinjiang history book, duplicate papers for the leaflets, the picture of the East Turkistan flag aside, but hid one of the flags inside my jacket, as I wanted to keep it as a memento. The rest of the documents, including the party manifesto, sworn in declarations, the draft of the brief history of East Turkistan, the history of Xinjiang, handwritten by Melike, Turnisa, and myself, I put together and carried them to the room where the stove was burning.

I threw them into the fire. I stood watching until they were all burnt to ashes. I felt sad that all our hard work had gone up in smoke in a matter of minutes. We had so many dreams and great plans. Now, the feeling of looking forward to achieving our ultimate goal seemed increasingly impossible. But I felt relieved that at least I had managed to destroy the evidence, which would otherwise have brought more complications for a lot of people. There were poems written by Ablikim, and a collection of poems by the famous poet Abdul Aziz Mehsum, which he wrote while in prison. I didn't want to destroy them, so I put them in a bottle, dug a hole in the courtyard and buried them.

My grandmother was still bringing coal to the living room and not paying much attention to what I was doing. When I told her that I was leaving, she insisted I stay a little longer to have some lunch with her.

I explained that I had to go back to the hospital quickly. 'I will return here again around five o'clock with some other people; please don't let them know that I have already been here. Greet me as if it is the first time we had met today. Say that I heard you came this morning, but I was in your aunty's house. Remember this alright, it's very important. They are investigating me but I don't want you to worry too much, just do as I have asked.' She looked a little confused. I kissed her goodbye and left the house quickly.

The jeep was still there but there was still no one in it. I ran all the way to the bus stop, people in the streets stared at me as I sped past, because it's unusual in our culture to see girls of my age running around in the street. Waiting at the bus stop I felt unsettled, so I said to the lady standing in front of me, 'Excuse me, could you save my place while I dash into the shop to buy something I have forgotten?' I went to the shop and stood in the doorway looking through the window for the bus to arrive.

The shopkeeper approached me, asking, 'do you want to buy some *osma*?[9] He brought some over for me to look at when I visited my grandmother, I always bought some *osma* from him for my friends, so he knew me.

I replied, 'Not today thank you I'll buy some later.' Before I have finished speaking I saw the bus arriving so I rushed out to catch it.

---

9   *A type of eye cosmetics.*

Fortunately, the bus was non-stop to the Big Bridge. I saw police drive past near the Friendship Hotel, going in the direction of the university.

The bus didn't stop at the university, so I disembarked at the hospital. There wasn't anyone around so I quickly entered the hospital from the rear door of the Paediatrics department, and took my coat from under the stairs. I put it on and carrying my books, I left for the university. On the way I bumped into Nusret.

She exclaimed when she saw me, 'Where have you been? We have been looking for you everywhere; everyone is looking for you in the university.'

'Really, is it that serious? I didn't go anywhere; I was in the laboratory doing some tests. Who needs me so urgently? Why were you so worried about me?' I asked her easily.

'Oh, we didn't think of looking in the laboratory. Even the officials went out to look for you.'

'What a shame I didn't know anything about that; I was so preoccupied by what I was doing that I only came out when I felt hungry. What's the problem? Let me go to the dormitory to have something to eat first.' I hurried off to the dormitory.

Shemsijamal was in the room, and as soon as I walked in, she said, 'Oh Suⵏyün, where have you been? They have been in a frenzy looking for you. I was worried that something bad had happened to you.'

When I told her what I had done, she jumped off her bed and hugged me tightly. 'Oh my God, how did you manage that? Were you not scared? It's like you are a female hero in the film. My dear friend, I'm so worried about you! What am I going to do if they take you away? My heart aches so much every time I think about it.' Tears streaked her cheeks as she spoke.

I heard footsteps in the corridor coming towards our room. We stopped talking and Shemsijamal wiped away her tears, I sat at the table with the food she brought me for lunch, and picked up a spoon. I was really hungry. After knocking on the door, Nusret walked in and spoke,

'They said you can have your lunch when you come back. They have asked you to meet them with the house key. You will find them waiting for you at the gate. Don't forget!'

I was laughing inside as I looked at Shemsijamal from the corner of my eye. I winked at her as I was leaving.

A black police van was waiting at the gate, and there were six Chinese inside. The van drove off as soon as I got in, and sped to the house. We sat in silence, the driver didn't even ask me for my address when he stopped outside the house gate. We all got out of the jeep and walked to the gate. At the same time, Ömerjan arrived with a group of people. We entered the house without looking left or right.

I didn't want my grandmother to be frightened by the sight of all these people. So I tried my very best to look relaxed, greeting her with a smile, but her face turned pale when she saw me with so many serious looking officials. She said, 'How are you, my darling? I'm sorry I wasn't in this morning when you came to see me.' She repeated everything I had taught her earlier on, but her voice was shaking with fear. She added, 'What are you doing my child?' and broke into tears. My heart ached, but I couldn't say anything to comfort her. I went straight to the small room.

The officials marched into the room, where I showed them the box,which I had prepared earlier. It contained cloth for making the flags, the books, and the duplicating paper.

'Is that all?' shouted Ömerjan, 'Where are the other documents? Where are the flags, the membership documents, and other papers for your organisation?'

'I burnt everything two months ago. This is all I have. This book was my primary school history book, this is carbon paper I bought from the shop, and this is one of our flags', I replied calmly.

One of the Chinese officials said, 'We were told that there were two flags, where is the other one?' He ordered officials to search the house. They looked everywhere, opening boxes, turning the house upside down. Nowhere was left untouched except the cellar in the middle of the house. They looked at the yard a few times where I had buried the bottles with the poems in. My heart jumped each time when they looked at it. Ablikim's poem was not a big problem, but the poems written by Abdul Aziz Mehsum, which were smuggled out of the prison where he is serving his time was a problem. I didn't look in that direction even once, as I was afraid to draw their attention to it.

The search continued for over an hour. As they failed to find anything, they decided to leave. I asked them to help me carry the box because it was very heavy.

They opened the box and went through each item carefully, before putting in a bag. In the end, they closed the bag and we all left the house. More than ten of us squeezed into the black minivan, the rest of the officials said good-bye at the door. I guessed that they must be from the local council. The minivan stopped in front of the Public Security Bureau. All of them got out of the van carrying the bag into the police station, as if they had found something very important. I was the only one left behind until they returned to drive me back to the university.

I was dropped off near the university, and as I was walking towards the gate I met Zeynure. She was a student in our university who married Murat, a mathematics lecturer from Xinjiang University, two weeks ago. Murat's family were citizens of the Soviet Union. The government had issued orders that all Soviet Union citizens must leave the country. So they were in the process of moving back home. Zeynure had been expelled from the university after being accused of marrying illegally. She told me that she was going to the university to sort out university documents. We discussed quite a lot of things while we walked.

I gave her Melike's address and asked her to pass on a message about our situation, and that she shouldn't write to us. As we don't know what will happen to us, I told Zeynure, 'It doesn't look good, and I don't think I will be able to say a proper farewell to you before you leave the country. We've been sharing the same desk since middle school and we're like sisters you know that. I wish we could hold hands and say good-bye to you properly, exchange forget-me-not gifts, but I don't think that will be possible.' We unhappily took our leave of each other, with the feeling that we would never see each other again, which turned out to be true.

I didn't go to the evening revision session, instead staying in the dormitory. Jin Hua, a Chinese girl from Shanghai came to see me asking, ' Where were you today? Mr Ahmet passed out during the lesson and was revived by the doctors who gave him an injection. He was then assisted by two doctors back to his accommodation. He is really poorly and I feel sorry for him.'

As I listened to Jin Hua, I wondered if the present situation was affecting him. We also thought that Mr Ahmet had been the person who sold us out! Now it seems not likely to be him. So who could it have been?

19 April 1963

The doctor under whom I was training told me that I was to be transferred to the General ward. The following morning when I was collecting all my books and was ready to go to the new department, Mr Ahmet hastened into the room. I was shocked to see how much weight he had lost, and his face was pale with sunken eyes. When he saw me with all my books, he asked in surprise, 'Where are you going?'

'They have moved me to the General patient's ward', I said.

'Maybe they want to separate us,' He said.

I left the room but before reaching the stairs, Mr Ahmet called, 'wait a minute, can I write a letter to Mariyem and leave it with you? If I am arrested you can post it to her for me. I believe that they may not arrest you because you are a young woman.'

'Ok, you can give it to me. If I'm still here, I will post it for you as necessary.'

'Just wait for me here, I'll be back shortly.' He dashed off to his office.

I was left waiting for him in the middle of the corridor. A Chinese doctor who was passing asked, 'Why are you standing here?' She told me to follow her to her office.

I believe that all the staff may have been informed by the university board about my activities, because everyone started to keep a close eye on me. Maybe we are already under University Surveillance. I was unable to get Mr Ahmet's letter before being sent on my way.

I was documenting a patient's medical history when a member of staff entered the room to tell me that someone wanted to see me outside. It was a cadre from the administration office who informed me that the chancellor was waiting to see me. I removed my white coat and went to his office. This was the second time I had visited his office since starting at the university.

The office was spacious, clean and bright. Modern tables and soft comfortable chairs stood on a red carpet. Chancellor Tang, Party Secretary Deng, Head of the Educational Affairs, a female interpreter, and two Chinese whom I had never seen before were present. I sat on the chair indicated. They welcomed me politely before party secretary Ding opened the conversation,

'All the students in the university are like my own children. I therefore decided to speak to you as a father and as the head of the university. Being a vulnerable young woman, you must also consider your parents along with your future. I heard that there are young siblings in your family, so you should also think about their welfare and happiness.

'As you have disgraced yourself, you must endeavour to change your ideology. You don't understand about life yet. You will live to regret so much if you don't listen to our words. We are making a special effort and taking the time to try to save you from sinking too far into the mud. You should return to your commonsense and your family background, unlike Abliz who comes from a rich and evil aristocratic landowning family background. We know how our enemies go against us; however, we also know how to fight them. They will all be destroyed in the end.'

My heart sank with the thought of poor Abliz being arrested and taken away. Secretary Deng continued, 'There was a girl named Oljanhan in the anti-government organisation that was organised by the Kazakh students, which was exposed last year. You know her. Later, she saw the truth, and after realised her mistake, she co-operated with us, by exposing the details of the organisation and its members. We pardoned her because of her assistance. Today she is carrying on with her studies at the university.

You will even be rewarded with incentives should you expose your organisation. Tell us who your sponsors are. Where are they?' He looked at me questioningly, expecting me to give him answers.

'We don't have any backers', I replied.

They became angry. Chancellor Tang shouted, 'Students wouldn't be able to set up such an organisation without any outside support. You'll not be able to hide this information from us for much longer, all will be revealed soon. No matter how devious and clever you people think you are, you will all fall into our traps, it's just a matter of time. You'd better think about your future, following the capitalist ideals will be your downfall, but if you follow the socialism dream your future is guaranteed.' He went on to praise the future of socialism, and eventually stopped to ask me, 'what have you learned from our conversation? Now is the time to reveal who the people are behind the organisation. That is your best option.'

'I repeat to you all that we don't have any other sponsors, whosoever. I am not personally concerned about capitalism or socialism, people will choose what is best for them.' I replied.

They looked at each other, then secretary Ding turned to me and said, 'Good, you can leave now.'

20 April 1963

In the morning I didn't feel up to very much or very interested in anything, as I left for the hospital. I didn't want to see patients or to review my books. New patients had been admitted for whom I am responsible. But I had still not completed their medical histories or organized the necessary tests for them. I was unable to focus on my duties, so I spent my time chatting with the patients instead.

Suddenly, I heard people in the corridor calling my name. I stayed where I was and tried to ignore them, but the shouting increased as more people rushed about and called me, 'Söyüngül, Söyüngül! She isn't here, where has she gone?'

I went out to ask, 'What is the problem? I am here, what's the matter with you all?' A Uyghur man standing near Ömerjan saw me and shouted out as he pointed at me, 'Look, she's here.'

Ömerjan looked at me and then informed people through his radio that I had been found. 'We came to look for you,' he said.

'Why? What's the matter?' I asked as I walked towards him. We have spoken to your tutors and they have allowed you a day off in order for you to write a detailed report of your activities within the organisation. Now go back to your dormitory and write your report.'

I didn't say a word and started taking off my coat. He watched me before saying, 'that white coat suits you, we've looked at all the other student doctors, but that white coat suits you the most. You shouldn't waste your time and energy involving yourself in unworthy matters, which will ruin your future. Just try to concentrate on becoming a good doctor.'

I returned my coat to the department before leaving for my room. No one was in there so it was very peaceful. I sat down to think about what to write. I was unable to think of anything no matter how hard I tried, my mind was totally blank. I felt drained from all this searching. In the end I decided to go and tell them that I had nothing to say or report. Otherwise they would question me later on what I had been doing all day, since I hadn't written one word.

I went down to the university administration department's Public Security Office. Ömerjan was in the office talking to a man. When he saw me, he asked the man to come back later. The man immediately left. Ömerjan then looked at me and asked, 'So why are you here? Is there anything you want to tell me?'

'I don't have anything to say or anything to write. I came here to tell you that I cannot write anything today.'

'So you have nothing to write?' He asked.

'No' I replied.

'So setting up an organisation is nothing? Recruiting members is nothing? Don't you think that there's plenty of information you could put down on paper?' He asked angrily.

'What is there to write? Is it a crime to be asking for independence? East Turkistan has always been an independent state. So we have now become criminals because we are asking for the return of our independence?'

Ömerjan paused for a while and then spoke, his voice rising, 'What are you talking about? When did Xinjiang become independent? Xinjiang has always been the territory of China. Who told you that Xinjiang was an independent country? Where did you get all these ideas from?'

'This has not all been made up. History speaks for itself. I gave you that book for a reason; don't you know or understand that? I wanted you to see the truth of the historical evidence. We have not committed any crimes in asking for our rightful independence. So there is nothing to confess or write about', I said.

'So, if you are demanding independence, why do you have to set up an organisation to carry out anti-Party activities?' Asked Ömerjan.

'It is well-known that anyone who speaks out openly is accused of being rightist, racist or anti-government, is tortured, thrown into prison and in some cases murdered by the regime. Well aware of the consequences had we spoken out, we realised that the only way to obtain independence was to mobilise people with the aid of an organisation.'

Ömerjan became so angry that his face turned puce and his eyes almost popped out of his head. 'Did you come here to lecture me with your reactionary propaganda? You should think before you speak, don't you understand what will happen to you if you carry on with this attitude?'

'Yes I have considered the consequences of my actions, and I am I am aware of all the possible results. If it is my time to die, then I cannot change that no matter where I am.' I riposted.

'You are treating the present situation too lightly. You forget you are a young woman who has not experienced any hardships in life. Unretractable attitudes will be your undoing in the years to come.' Ömerjan cautioned.

I sensed that he was being sincere. 'No, I disagree. I will never have regrets! Not having killed or caused misery to others, I have done nothing wrong. My soul, heart and mind are free of pain, I was only trying to help my people obtain their freedom.'

He replied, 'In ten or twenty years time you will regret every word and action you have taken.'

I retorted, 'You are working for the Chinese authorities, helping them to catch your own people and assisting them in destroying your own nation. You are a true patriot of the system in their eyes because you carry out their orders. However, once you have fulfilled their requirements you will be surplus to theirs. Chinese authorities never catch Uyghur people using their own men or women. They have always used people like you to do their dirty work.'

'What are you talking about? Are you here to propagate your ideas or to show me how defiant you are before your death?' he bellowed.

'No, not having done anything wrong I have no regrets or fear of dying for my beliefs.' I asked him, 'Are you Uyghur?'

'Yes, I am, what does that have anything to do with you?' he replied.

'How could you turn your own people in to the Chinese? Don't you have a guilty conscience, and heartache from shame?'

Deep down I knew that I would be arrested so I thought it would be better for me to say everything that was on my mind. Maybe one day he will recall this conversation. Ömerjan looked shocked by my outburst. I was overjoyed by being able to express myself so frankly to him. To me it was a sweet revenge in that I told him of his origins and responsibility to our nation state. Repeating myself once more I said, 'I have nothing to confess or write about.' before I turned and walked out of his office.

Arriving back at the dormitory I spent my time cleaning and tiding up. I was about to sit down at my desk when I heard footsteps in the corridor and a sharp knock on the door, the door opened and Ömerjan entered the room. I thought he had come because of what I had said earlier but to my surprise, he spoke to me in a mild manner.

'You are not the only one given a task today, we have asked other members of the organisation, and some other students we are suspicious of, to write a report, which they are all doing now. As a vulnerable young woman, you have no idea what you are facing. I warn you once again that you will find it very hard. The party's dictatorial regime is not something you can joke about or take lightly. You don't want your young life wasted in prison and as such I feel sorry for you.'

I remained silent. 'We sympathise with you but please change your direction. Try to find a way out by completing your report and do it properly.'

'Ok, I will.' That was all I had to say.

I was just thinking about Sajide when she rushed in coming to hug me tightly, 'Söyün, I will stand by you no matter what happens. Let's face the situation together.' She burst into tears. Sajide was a very kind-hearted person whose uniqueness was incomparable. I always felt happy when thinking about her being my friend. It was such a blessing. Not long afterwards Abliz arrived to tell me about his experience with the investigation team, and gave me suggestions on how to deal with them.

I said nothing as he continued, 'Yesterday, I saw you from my window when you left the campus with the security team, did they accompany to your home of your grandparents?'

I explained everything that had happened the previous day. I then showed him the flag and observed, 'I am going to keep it. If we survive and meet again one day we will continue to fight for justice and freedom. If God is willing we may be able to raise and wave this flag.' I smiled at him.

'Of course we will. May God bless us with health and strength, to live and see that day. If we can't live to see that day, I hope and pray that our children will take our place', he said.

'Yesterday you told me that you burned everything two months ago. Why did you lie to me?' Abliz asked.

'Abliz, to be honest with you I did not trust you. We still don't know who exposed us; we're still in the dark about that. At this moment I can't trust anyone', I replied.

'Come on, do you think I would do something as disgraceful as that?' He sounded disappointed.

'There are times that people don't even trust themselves', I replied.

21 April 1963

Mr Turdi of the Public Security Bureau came to my dormitory last night to say, 'You're not allowed to go outside the university without permission as of today. If you need to go out you must obtain special permission.'

'I am on duty at the hospital tomorrow, am I not allowed to go to the hospital either?' I enquired.

'No, you can go to the hospital and the canteens but no other places outside the university grounds. These is the orders of the university leadership; these rules are not something you can joke about!' He snarled.

After he left Shemsijamal said, 'I feel so sad for you. What shall we do now?' She wept.

I was feeling upset myself but I tried to comfort her, so I said, 'Don't get upset; we just have to overcome whatever is thrown our way.'

The following day at the hospital, my first duty was to check my patients and then update their records. This seemed unnecessary to me; my thoughts were elsewhere. Instead of doing my work, I gazed out of the window at the beauty of the sun high in a blue sky with birds flying in and out of the trees. I couldn't get enough of these sights, since I felt everything would become dark and dismal from now on.

Shemsijamal suddenly appeared, gasping. 'How are you? Thank God you're here. I saw a small car parked in front of your door, my heart almost popped out, so I ran all the way from the corridor to check you're safe.' She sat with me for a while, then left. Turnisa was also on-duty today but she kept her distance. When we bumped into each other, she ignored me completely. She had been one of my best friends up until now.

22 April 1963

I returned to the dormitory for lunch find that Shemsijamal was alone in the room. I asked her where the others had gone. She replied sadly, 'I heard that Nurnisa Rozi, Nurnisa Yüsup and other student activists were called to attend a meeting organized by the university administration department. I asked Turnisa about it, but she didn't want to tell me anything. I think something may happen today and I feel very uneasy. I didn't sleep very well last night.' Her eyes filled with tears again.

'Shemsi, please don't upset yourself any more, we will always be able to overcome difficulties as long as we are alive', I comforted her.

After our organisation was exposed, I didn't go to the canteen anymore, because my roommates decided to bring food to our room and eat together. Since doing that, I noticed that the room had become very untidy and dirty because no one was in the mood to clean up. This made me feel very uncomfortable, so I decided to clean the place up. I started with the dishes and ended by scrubbing the wooden floor to a shine. I went to the communal bathroom to collect hot water to wash myself, then sprayed the room with perfume. It was now a warm welcoming place.

I saw Nurnisa Rozi standing on the balcony opposite our dormitory when I came for lunch. As I had finished all my chores I was surprised to see that she was still there. I was suspicious of her actions. I decided to go to the hospital, picked up my white coat and left the room.

In the connection corridor, Nurnisa Rozi dashed in front of me asking, 'Where are you going?'

'I am going to attend my tutorial', I replied.

'I have been told to tell you not to attend any lectures as you have more important things to complete', Nurnisa said.

I returned to the dormitory as Shemsijamal and Turnisa were about to have an afternoon nap. I told them, 'I think they are coming to arrest us today.' Turnisa quickly lay down, as I started packing all my things, and closely watched my every move. As soon as I finished packing, Ghopur Réhim, Nusret, Gozjang, Heyip, Ömerjan, Nurnisa Rozi, and two Chinese students and some Chinese officials entered the room.

Ghopur Réhim looked at me and said, 'You are placed under a surveillance regime as of now. We are giving you your last chance to provide information about your criminal activities. One more thing; I am informing you that Nurnisa Rozi, Nurnisa Yüsup and these two Chinese girls are appointed to monitor your activities and your whereabouts to the University Security Bureau. They will accompany you wherever you go and you are not allowed to go to the canteen, so they will bring food for you.'

He continued, 'Secondly, we are going to search you and your belongings because you failed to hand in all your documents to us. This is an order from the Public Security Bureau and you have no right to oppose it. Now you will be taken to the Chinese students' room.'

'That is fine', I said.

Nurnisa Rozi and two other Chinese girls escorted me to the Chinese students' room. Upon entering, they locked the window and pulled the curtain across.

'Draw the curtain and open the window!' I requested, as I walked across to do it myself.

All three of them rushed towards me, yelling, 'You can't have the window open!' and started to close it again.

'I haven't been imprisoned yet so don't treat me like a prisoner.' I opened the window to sit looking outside as I had always enjoyed the light of day from when I was a child.

The Chinese students' dormitory was like a pigsty; messy, dirty, smelly and unpleasant. It was already difficult for me to cope with the present situation without having the windows closed and curtains drawn. The two Chinese girls remained next to me as Nurnisa ran out of the room and returned with Nusret.

As she came in, Nusret shouted at me, 'You don't have any right to question any orders given to you from now on, come away from the window and close it now! 'She walked up and tried to drag me away.

'Leave me alone, get away Nusret, don't treat me like a prisoner! You have no right in ordering me to do anything!' I said firmly. I didn't move and continued to look outside. Nusret left helplessly.

The head of the Investigation Unit came in not long after Nusret had left. 'Where are the party programmes and other materials?' he demanded.

'I don't have them. I burned them all two month ago', I replied while sitting on the windowsill.

'You are lying; you didn't destroy them two months ago. Where were you at lunchtime on the 18th of April?

'I was in the laboratory of the Department of Internal Diseases. I replied without blinking my eyes. I tried my best to look relaxed.

'You are lying! You are the smartest and the most cunning one of them all, we know you are trying to deceive us. Tell us the truth!' He barked.

I remained relaxed, saying, 'It's true; I burned all the materials two months ago. I was in the laboratory on the 18th of April. You can check if you don't believe me', he shouted at me for a while and then left.

At around seven o'clock Ghopur Réhim came to see me to tell me that they had completed their search but failed to find anything.

'Stay here for now; we are trying to arrange special accommodation for you. We will let you know once it has been finalised', he said. He left to return not long afterwards to tell me that it had been arranged for me to stay temporarily in Nurnisa Yüsup's accommodation. He took me to her room.

All the students in our year and in Sajide's year were called to a meeting organized by the university administration department, which lasted until eleven o'clock that evening. Nurnisa Yüsup brought me a bowl of noodle soup. I didn't feel like eating anything, so I didn't touch the food. She asked me why I wasn't eating, I told her I had no appetite but I would like some tea. She said all right and left to get some.

Hörnisa came to see me after the meeting, she said, 'Oh Söyün, why have you not thought about your future, the future of those around you, and the impact on your parents and siblings if something happens to you? Didn't you realise what would happen if things went wrong?'

I knew she was sincere and kind-hearted. Not wanting to show my misery, I said with a smile, 'Hörnisa, I don't mind sacrificing my happiness for that of my people. I don't mind sacrificing my freedom for the freedom of my people. I have no regrets! Instead, I feel blessed in that I never have to consider myself as being ill-fated, my only regret is that I may never become a doctor. The change from university to imprisonment in my mind would be one of learning the hardships of life as people struggle to adjust to a regime of evil – and I will see good and bad in that. If I don't die, this will all become a thing of the past.

'If God wills it, I will live through these times. I have always wanted to help people, now unfortunately, I will probably not have the opportunity to fulfil my desire, but maybe if I am arrested, it may well encourage others to take up the fight for independence. I believe, by the grace of God, my parents will forgive me. Also they have other children.'

'Oh Söyün, your words are so inspiring! I now understand the ideals that are driving your body and soul. I admire your courage in the belief that you will overcome the difficulties to come as if they had never happened. Don't forget, I am truly your friend', she said.

'No, I will never forget you! You will always be my friend', I replied.

'What did they say in the meeting?' I asked.

'They said that all of you were placed under surveillance from today, because you set up a reactionary organisation against the party and socialism, and they said the usual stuff as well, you know, the things repeated in every meeting. They announced that the leaders of the reactionary organisation were Ahmet Toxti, Söyüngül, Abliz Sewridin, Sajide.'

'Didn't they mention Ablikim?' I asked.

'No, his name wasn't mentioned at all', Hörnisa said, giving me a meaningful look.

Knowing Ablikim's fearful, anxious characteristics, I thought that not to have been implicated was lucky for him. If he wasn't implicated at least he would be able to carry on with his studies, otherwise he might have gone insane. However, part of me cannot help but ask, 'Why was he excluded?' As he was one of the four core members of the organisation, I still didn't wish him any harm. On the contrary, I was pleased that he was safe. I asked myself why I trusted Ablikim so much? It had never crossed my mind that he might be the one who had betrayed us.

The girls brought hot water for the tea even though it had been a lot of trouble to find some, because it was so late at night. One of the students had a small electric hob, so they were able to boil some water in her room to bring it for me. Although I sipped my tea, I didn't feel like drinking.

Nurnisa Yüsup was annoyed when she saw I wasn't drinking the tea, and said, 'You made us run looking for hot water to almost every dormitory in the corridors, is that all you're going to drink?'

'Don't be upset, I will finish the tea in a moment', I replied.

No sooner had we retired to bed, Ghopur Réhim, Gozjang, Ömerjan, Nusret and few other cadres entered the dormitory saying, 'We have arranged a new room for you downstairs, you must go there now.'

We carried our bedding to the room downstairs on the ground floor in the female section opposite the ladies' toilet. In the room, was a table with four chairs, a double bed and a single bed. The window was covered with newspapers, making it darker than the room we had left. I settled into the single bed as it was already one o'clock. The others sat around with no sign of retiring.

So I asked, 'What's the problem? Why are you not going to bed?' 'We will. You just go to sleep.' Said Nurnisa Rozi as she placed one chair at either end of the bed. Nurnisa

Rozi said to Nurnisa Yüsup, ' Pang Zi and I will be on-duty tonight; you and Jing Ziying watch her during the day. The two of them came and sat on the chairs. I couldn't help myself but to laugh out loud.

'Why are you laughing? Has something funny happened?' All the girls demanded.

'I am laughing at your stupidity. It is not enough for two of you to watch me, so why don't all four of you watch me all the time?'

Nurnisa Rozi became upset saying, 'This is none of your business as we are carrying out the orders of our leaders.

'As you are interfering with my personal life, why can't I be involved in your affairs?' I said. 'Turn the light off please!' I requested as I turned my head the other way.

'We were told not to turn the lights off so cover your face with something', stated Nurnisa Rozi.

This was difficult as I normally can't sleep with the lights on. I turned away from the light and tried to fall asleep.

After a while, Gozjang walked in, and asked, 'Is she sleeping?'

'Yes, she is', replied the girls.'

'Watch her carefully, don't fall asleep otherwise things may go wrong. You can sleep tomorrow during the day. We have installed a telephone in room number seven, if anything happens you can call us on this number.' He told them to write it down. He also gave them a Chinese man's name and number. Finally he told them that he would be on duty in the administration department. He repeatedly urged them to be vigilant and careful before he left.

They sounded nervous, as if enemies were waiting to launch a sudden attack at any minute. The two girls spent the whole night watching me intently.

23 April 1963

In the morning, I got up, washed my face, combed my hair and made myself more presentable. After I finished tidying myself up, I walked to the window to tear off the newspapers and open it.

'You always have a problem with windows, don't you? Why do you have to do this? The covering of the windows with newspapers was done at the request of our leaders', Nurnisa Rozi said in frustration, as she endeavoured to close the window.

'No, you can't close the window. Why don't you go and tell the officials what I have done!' I said.

Nurnisa stormed out of the room. I thought she had gone to report the incident, however, I was no longer stopped from opening the windows.

After breakfast, I was questioned for a long time by an officer, named Eli Yüsup, from the Public Security Bureau. In the afternoon, the questioning was repeated by the party leaders from the university, then by the senior detective. The amount of people involved in the investigation was remarkable. I found it difficult to understand how nervous all these people, from senior detectives in the country to the cardres at the university, had become with regard to such a minor matter caused by four students. Security guards were placed at every corner in the university as police cars continually came and went from the campus.

A week passed, with me being questioned by various officials three or four times daily. In addition, I was forced to write a report about my role within the organisation and confess that I was a part of an anti-government movement. Despite spending hours with a pen in my hand, I couldn't find anything to confess. In the end I wrote, 'It is not a crime to demand a nation's independence. On the contrary it is our duty and right. I also wrote quotes from articles praising Chairman Mao, and Lenin, and Stalin about their heroic actions during their struggles in the fight for independence. I always concluded with the statement that our movement was justifiable, and we were innocent of any wrongdoing.

29 April 1963

Today, the campus sounded very noisy with people rushing around and looking very nervous. Police vans came and went at least six or seven times during the morning. I saw party secretary Mr Deng with Chancellor Mr Tang, Ghopur Réhim, and Ömerjan Mr Turdi, and a number of unfamiliar faces in a group of twenty to thirty people, who were trailing from one building to another with uneasy expressions on their faces. It felt as if a heavy cloud was hanging over my head, particularly as I wasn't questioned that morning.

I stood by the window looking outside, but every time someone passed, they closed the window. I would immediately reopen after that person had walked on. This happened a lot, but it didn't bother me. I was examining everyone's body language, facial expressions and their movements. One thing was certain that there had been some sort of new developments today.

Nusret and Heyip were also exceptionally busy running back and forth as if they were the ones running the whole operation. They had always played an active role in reporting even the most minor student incidents to the school management department. They considered themselves to be very useful and were excited at having the opportunity to play a major role against our movement. For many student activists, this was the golden opportunity for them to show how strong their loyalties were to the Communist Party, which in the future would serve them well in obtaining a desirable position within the status quo.

I was worn out and decided to have my usual nap after lunch. I was almost asleep when I heard the all too familiar sounds of police sirens. I jumped out of bed to look outside where I saw two police vans approaching the campus. I instinctively said, 'They are coming for us.'

'Here we go again, stop your incessant fabrication', Nurnisa Rozi sounded exasperated. I didn't pay the slightest attention to what she had said, as I was looking at the police vans to see where they would stop. I turned to Nurnisa saying, 'Let's go to the toilet.'

'Which one would you like to go to, the one in the corridor or the one outside?' she asked me. I made my way to the door without answering the question.

Entering the corridor, it looked strangely chilling to me. I saw some school cadres hurrying past. Instantly, it dawned upon me that this might be my last free moments. I saw Nurnisa Yüsup coming towards us. Suddenly, she stopped and screamed, 'You're not allowed to go outside! You must use the toilet in the corridor!' She didn't sound like a student, rather she gave the impression that she was a prison officer. Her voice was cold as she bawled her chilling orders. She was out of breath and her skin looked darker than usual. In my eyes, she looked evil. I turned around and made my way back to the stairs in order to go to the second-floor toilets.

While I was walking up the stairs, I looked out of the window again noticing the two police vans parked in front of our campus building. There were students popping their heads out of their windows, looking with interest at what was happening. Some of them looked up and saw me. I could see shock on their faces. I made myself believe that this might be the last time I would walk these stairs. I started running up to the second floor. Nurnisa couldn't catch up with me because she was heavy and always slow. She looked much older and more mature than her age.

She shouted, 'Söyüngül, stop!' Before she had reached the top of the stairs, I had already come out from the toilets and was making my way back.

I looked outside from the corridor window in a panic, to see that one of the vans had gone. This left me thinking that they may have already taken my friends away, and now it was my turn. Returning to the room, I frantically started packing my things in a bag. I emptied the pockets of my white medical coat and gave it to Nurnisa Rozi. She accepted it without saying a word. I had twelve yuan and a voucher for two-metres of cloth which I gave to Nurnisa Yüsup, and asked her to pass them to my family through my friend Helime. I also pleaded with them to treat my family with respect and to comfort them if they ever came to the campus.

Both Nunisa Yüsup and Nurnisa Rozi said, 'You don't have to worry about that, we will do our best.'

After packing my bag, I proceeded to roll up my bedding. At which point Nurnisa Yüsup said, 'Don't pack everything as we need to check what you will be allowed to take with you.' She opened the door and turned around to look at me, saying, 'They are already here.'

I heard the sound of many footsteps tramping down the corridor. There were roughly fifty to sixty people coming in my direction. They filed into the room and within seconds it was crowded with people. Those unable to enter the room remained in the corridor. People were staring at me with icy looks on their faces. I could see and feel the hostility in their eyes, as if they were trying to break me. In the group, were my long-term classmates Nusret and Heyipe, who were staring at me with more aggression and hostility than the interrogators from the Public Security Bureau. They looked as if they would kill me on the spot. I was not at all surprised, since they had always taken an active part in supporting the regime. They were hungry for power and this was a vital opportunity for them to show their devotion to the party. Having prepared myself mentally that arrest was inevitable, I no longer felt nervous or fearful at all, in fact, I was now strangely calm.

Holding my head up high and standing upright, I felt taller and stronger than those around me. The head of the university's Security Department read out the arrest warrant issued by the Public Security Bureau. In summary, it said that the arrest warrant was issued due to the suspect's refusal to confess and correct her criminal activities. Therefore, the case was handed to the Public Security Bureau which deals with such cases.

'Do you understand this fully? Asked Mr Turdi, 'If not we can interpret it into Uyghur.'

'Yes, I do understand.' I replied firmly.

'Good. Sign this for me then', Mr Turdi commanded and coldly passed me a piece of paper.

I put it on the table and signed my name in Arabic, Chinese, and then in Russian, before handing it back.

He looked at the document and queried, 'Why did you do this?'

'I want to make sure that everything is clear', I replied with a smile.

'If that is the case, pick up your belongings and come with us', Mr Turdi shouted at me.

I hadn't even packed my bedding, and someone had taken my things and left the room in a hurry. I suddenly remembered my favourite black jacket and asked Nurnisa, 'Where is my black jacket, I need to take it with me.'

'It is in your old dormitory. Everyone is in a meeting right now so no one is in the room', he replied.

'I have to take my jacket with me, please go and get it for me', I insisted. All four girls who had been watching me for days went immediately, returning with my jacket very quickly.

I put my jacket on, and slowly buttoned it up before checking myself from head to toe. I then slowly left the room. Everyone followed me. The student activists who had been assigned to monitor the four of us under the 'school surveillance regime' were standing outside. With every step I took, I paced past motionless guards lining the walls on either side of the corridor, the stairs, and the road in front of the school club, blocking the school gate. Students stood on both side of the roadway looking at me with raw emotions in their faces. I could see their sympathetic looks, and the tears in their eyes. Some even managed to say kind words as I passed by. I was deeply moved by their support, and returned their looks with a warm smile as I said goodbye.

As I arrived at the police van, Anwar Jakolin's car pulled up. He got out and asked Mr Turdi, 'Have you finished?'

'Yes, she is the last one', Mr Turdi replied.

They stood for a while talking. I took the chance to look around the campus and at the students for the last time before Mr Turdi turned and shouted out, 'Go back to the meeting hall right now, every one of you. Enwer Jakolin is here to inform you of the latest developments.'

He came over to the van, opened the door and ordered me to get in. Once I was inside, he got in to sit next to me. Nurnisa Yüsup was trying to indoctrinate me with the theories of Marxism and Leninism while she stood next to the van window. Then, Mr Turdi closed the window.

The van was moving now, and leaving my beloved university behind. As I stared out of the reinforced window with a metal grill over it, Mr Turdi suddenly asked, 'How are you feeling now?'

'I feel as if I am moving from one institute to another', I replied.

'What kind of institute is that then?' He asked.

'The institute of life', I replied.

He looked at me for a second before saying, 'Oh, life's institute! In a way you are right. You're a very interesting young woman. Do you have a boyfriend?'

'No', I replied.

Mr Turdi's expression had now changed, he was no longer relaxed, but looked as angry as he had been all along.

He said, 'If you had lived your life like other pretty young girls, finding a nice boyfriend, studying hard to complete your medical education to become a successful doctor then you wouldn't have ended up in this situation. What a pity. You had so much going for you, but you have ruined it all, think about it.' Suddenly, he turned shouting at the driver not to drive so fast. The driver was an old Chinese man who looked like he had been born and brought up in East Turkistan. He kept looking at me in the mirror. I returned his gaze and smiled. He looked puzzled but sympathetic. I felt as if he was trying to say, 'You don't know what you are about to face, so why are you smiling?'

The prisoner in the next cell knocked on the wall where I was leaning. Suddenly this brought me back from my daydreaming. I responded by knocking on the wall.

After some time of knocking, he shouted, 'Who are you? Are you Mahmut Sidiq?'

I shout back, 'No, I am not.' Everything went silent.

30 April
Life in prison

I was woken up by noises in the corridor. It was the inmates delivering water to prisoners for washing. After that, a bowl of wild green leaf soup and a piece of mouldy steamed cornflour bread was served for breakfast. The soup tasted bitter and smelled horrible. It was off. I didn't feel like trying the bread, as it was clearly rotten. As I was very hungry, I told myself that I must not fall ill so I started to force myself to eat. In my case, I had some sweets which had been given to me by Helime. I bit a small piece of the sweet then had a bite of the steamed bread. I also managed to finish the soup sip by sip.

The prison cell was very cold. I was wearing my thick jacket, but I was still freezing. I swept the floor and then sat down leaning against the wall. The man in the next cell knocked on the wall again and shouted, 'Who are you?'

I didn't know whether I should tell him; I thought for a while and then replied.

He was startled, 'Are you Söyüngül'?

I was shocked, so I asked, 'Do you know me?'

'If you are the daughter of Salih Abliz, then I know you.'

'Yes I am Salih Abliz's daughter, Söyüngül.' I said.

'How did you end up here?' He asked.

'I was accused of setting up an illegal organisation in the Medical University.'

'Who are you?' I asked.'

I am Mewken.' He said.

'Oh, you are Uncle Mewken! What happened to you?'

'I didn't commit any crime; I was arrested on suspicion of having links with the Soviet Union.'

Uncle Mewken used to live in the capital Ürümchi. He was ethnic Kazakh who used to teach in the primary school. Later he was transferred to the City Education Department. I held a newspaper in front of me pretending to read out loud while I spoke with him.

'I am in cell No.5. You are in No.3, the one next door to you is No.1, and there are two people in that one, a Chinese and a Uyghur. We can't trust them, as we don't know who they are, so be careful when talking to them! In cell No.7 is Tashmuhemmed who was secretary of the Soviet Citizen Union. I have forgotten the name of the person in cell No.9. In No. 2 is a Tatar girl called Sefide, who worked as an interpreter in the Soviet Embassy in Ghulja. In No.4 is a Kirghiz man, Sultan, he was the president of the Soviet Citizen Union, while in No. 6 is a Kazakh called Zeynula , the former vice president of the Soviet Citizen Union. In No.8 there are eight people, brought here for various crimes. Mehmut Sidiq is in corridor 4.' He also mentioned about my head teacher Mehmut Abliz.

The prison guard came and opened the door as I was talking, so I switched to read the newspaper aloud. He shouted, 'What are you doing?'

I said calmly, 'I am reading a newspaper.'

'Stop reading out loud!' he ordered.

'Ok, I will. But I am very bored and frustrated. It helps me to relax when I read like this.' I said.

'You know you are not on holiday. This is a prison, remember!' he shouted at me for a while then left.

Uncle Mewken knocked on the wall again, 'do you want to sleep?' he asked.

'No, I am just sitting', I said.

'Don't sit all the time, try to do some exercise regularly. Another important thing is you must eat whatever food they give you. I know it is disgusting but you must finish it all otherwise you will fall ill. It is hard if you fall ill here.'

Lunch was delivered, a bowl of hot water with a tiny piece of cornflour steamed bread. It tasted and looked horrible, and made me vomit. I didn't eat. I never ate lunch all the time I was in prison, from that day on. After lunch I walked in the cell back and forth until two o'clock. Hearing a knock on the wall, I knocked back.

Uncle Mewken said, 'There is a major interrogation taking place today, Enwer Jakolin is here. No one is allowed to work. They have taken two male students who arrived here on the same day as you, and they are also questioning your female friend at the moment. You may be next, so don't be afraid! Don't admit anything! If you do, they will hold it against you. Don't give any information about any other members of your organisation. They will interrogate you using various methods. They may even threaten to kill you, but stay strong and be brave. You will be alright. I am praying for you!'

I stood up, to get ready for questioning. I changed clothes and tidied my hair. I paced backwards and forwards in the cell to prepare myself mentally for the attitudes and questions of my interrogators. The words of my teacher from the next cell were encouraging, offering me strength and wisdom at a time when I needed it most. The door of the cell opened with a loud screech. Two armed prison guards entered the cell, pointing their machine guns at me, and shouted, 'Come!'

I walked in front of the two guards. There weren't any other people outside today, apart from the armed guards who were standing on the walls, along both sides of the road and either side of the prison gate. I saw two guards standing outside one of the offices near the prison gate. The door was open, so I went straight into that office. My two escorts left. Scanning the room, I saw an empty soft chair on the right, near a sofa filled by Enwer Jakolin's corpulent figure. He was leaning backwards, squinting at the door, with his hands behind his head. His small beady eyes were barely open in his ugly fat face.

Ali Yüsup, the secretary was sitting in the left hand corner of the room, next to the window and a cabinet. In front of the secretary, was Abliz Niyaz, who was the main interrogator and sat at the desk. On the lefthand side of the desk was a rickety stool made from rough wood. I thought it must be for the prisoner to sit on, so I walked straight over and sat down. All of them had been staring avidly at me from the minute I had walked in. They were examining my every move.

Enwer Jakolin was the first to question me,

'What is your name?'

'What is you ethnicity?'

'Where are you from?'

'Do you have parents?'

'Who are your relatives? Are you related to Zekiy Weliyef?'

I answered all his basic questions truthfully, except for the last one,

'How did you end up here?'

When I replied, 'I don't know', he became so angry that his eyes almost popped out of his head. He said –

'You *don't* know? So we brought you here even though you are innocent. We have made a mistake then. So let's say that we're wrong. Tell me why did you set up a reactionary organisation? What activities did you carry out in the organisation? Who are the members within the organisation?'

'We dreamed of independence. Every human being has the right to fight for their country's independence. Lenin, Karl Marx, even Chairman Mao supported independence movements in the world. Is it a crime to have a desire for independence?'

'What are you talking about? What kind of independence are you asking for? Xinjiang is an inseparable part of China. You are a separatist, your action is to destroy its ethnic unity. You are counter-revolutionaries and nationalist saboteurs. Watch your mouth; don't you know where you are now? This is a prison, what do you think you can achieve by going against us. Do you still believe that all your comrades are continuing to resist us, like you? All of them have pleaded guilty to their crimes and apologized for their wrongdoings, now they are waiting for the party to handle their cases with leniency? However, you are still resisting our assistance instead of accepting your crimes. You are the enemy of the people and you are walking towards death', he was enraged.

'Only time will tell who the people's enemies are', I said.

Enwer Jakolin snorted.

'Look at you, so brave you are! Ok, you have the right to choose your own destiny. We thought you were a young immature student who had committed a crime by mistake, so we wanted to help and re-educate you.' He looked at Abliz and shouted, 'Remove her from here now.' I stood up immediately before he finished speaking, walked out of the room and went straight to my cell, escorted by the guards who locked me in the cell.

4 May 1963
Qurban Eid in prison

Today is the Qurban festival. I was dreaming when I was awoken by the loud noise of the water buckets being brought to prisoners for washing. I opened my eyes to find myself still in prison. I have made myself familiar with the prisoners who have delivered the food and water to my cell over the last four or five days.

They shouted through the door hatch, 'It is the Qurban Eid festival today, Happy Eid! Unfortunately, you are spending your Eid here in prison, but there is good news, you are having carrot Pilau Rice for lunch today', said the man, handing the water over to me. I thanked him.

After I washed my face and exchanged well-wishes for Eid with my teacher through the wall. He said, 'All of your comrades send you their Eid blessings.' I thanked him and also asked him to send my kind wishes to them. He continued, 'We have also sent our well wishes to Mehmut Sidiq and we have also included you in our message.'

I am starting to get use to life here. Every day I rise early and complete my daily routine before breakfast. After breakfast, I start exercising by walking from one end of the cell to the other, which is seven steps each way. I do this nonstop for two hours. I imagine that I am walking from the Medical University to the North Gate, which is about three thousand steps. In the afternoon, I imagine that I am going from the North Gate to Victory Road, which is about the same distance. Visualizing all the scenes along the road such as, the shops, buildings, trees, streets, and the people, helps. While I do this, I almost forget where I am and my sense of the passing of time. It makes me so tired that I have to sit down and rest. I finish my morning exercises before we are taken to the toilet between ten and twelve.

As I wait for my turn to go, I stand next to the door, peeping through a little hole, trying to see and hear the people passing along the corridor. At other times I write in my diary or write letters to my friends. I would tear the letters out after I finished and by then it would be lunchtime. After lunch, I would try to take a nap, however an overwhelming feeling of sadness would overtake me, as if I had just returned from a graveyard after burying a loved one. Looking around the cell, it felt like a grave to me, and one I found it hard to sleep in during the day. The radio was played through the loudspeakers today, as it was the Qurban Eid festival; it relayed many beautiful songs on this special Eid programme. The sound of the songs echoed throughout the corridors and the courtyards of the prison.

Normally, this was the happiest time of the year for me but I couldn't stop thinking of the times I used to spend with family and friends. I enjoyed spending such times with my friends, particularly when visiting everyone's house in turn. When I was little, I didn't sleep all night long, as I would constantly check the clock, waiting for daylight and Eid to arrive. I used to spread my new clothes on the bed and go to touch them every few minutes. I would frequently wipe my new shoes with a cloth, even though they were shining. I was so excited that I didn't know where the best place to display them.

We used to wake my parents early, not caring how tired they became preparing the perfect Eid for us. We would go to their room, wake them up from their deep sleep, and shout while jumping around, 'Eid is here! Eid is here!'

When my father left for the mosque, we always followed him into the street. I loved to watch people stopping every ten steps to call *tekbir*,[10] one group after another. The constant stream of people entering the mosque reminded me of an endless piece of string. The sounds of the *tekbir* were so beautiful and uplifting; it always made me feel happy and blessed to be a Muslim. After prayers, men would first go to the graveyard to pray for their loved ones, before returning home to distribute Eid money to the children. After this, they would start visiting families, friends, neighbours, colleagues and acquaintances in turn, regardless of whether people are rich or poor. This would last for three days.

It was also traditional for families that could afford it to buy a sacrificial sheep for Eid, tradition that had started by the prophet Abraham. Families would offer some meat to the poorer families and cook the rest for relatives and visitors. Eid is the most exciting and happy time for children, especially the purchase of new clothes. All of these scenes played out in front of my eyes in sequence, just like a film.

Today, I'm spending my Eid in prison. I can't imagine how sad my parents and siblings must feel inside. The thought of them being sad because of me was unbearable. I always tried my best to drive my despondency away by telling myself, 'Dictators can never break us by terrorising us or caging us in prison. We will always live above them, empowered by our greatest dreams. We have friends everywhere; even in prison we are not alone. I must stand up straight and proud with my comrades, in happiness, regardless of where I am. These uplifting ideas sustained me.

---

10   *An Arabic word meaning 'to say "God is Great! (Allahu Akbar)'.*

9 May 1963

I haven't been questioned since the 30th of April. I am alone in a dark cell and haven't seen the outside for the past ten days. I made a paper calendar and hung it on the wall cabinet. Everyday, as soon as I wake up, I flip a page over. No matter how much I tried to make time pass faster, it feels like I have spent months incarcerated here. However, when I looked at the calendar only ten days have passed. When I was at the University, months flew past without you noticing, I constantly checked and re-checked the dates on the calendar, but time didn't pass any faster. I tried to keep myself busy. I started to watch people who were working outside by standing on top of my bedding, which I piled as high as I could. People outside also noticed me and we exchange greetings by sign language. They passed messages to me while pretending to talk to each other.

The prisoners outside were busy constructing a new building. My teacher also took the opportunity to chat to me when the guards went to patrol the other corridors. I would stand in the sun when it shone through the window but the sunshine usually only lasted about five minutes.

Other times, I would sit on the bed and review movies that I've seen in my mind. I would visualize myself sitting in the theatre to watch them. On other occasions, I sang songs nonstop while pacing in the cell. The guards would shout at me not to sing, but I ignored them. I drew a picture of a beautiful girl on the wall. It lifted my spirits, when I looked at the wall to see her smiling back at me. Gradually she became my close companion. She seemed so warm to me. I would talk to her about my boredom and thoughts. One day, when I returned from the toilet the drawing has gone. It had been wiped away by the guards. They warned me not to draw anything on the wall again.

I was taken for questioning around two o'clock. Eli Yüsup and Abliz Niyaz were in the questioning room. Eli Yüsup began questioning me as soon as I sat down.

'Have you thought about your problems?'

'What kind of problems should I think about?' I asked.

'I mean your problems, how can you ask me what problems?' he said with irritation.

Abliz Niyaz glared and shot a question at me, 'Do you know who Enwer Jakolin is?'

'Yes, I know him.'

'Did you meet him before you were imprisoned?'

'Yes.'

'Where did you meet him?'

'I used to see him often in the University.'

'What was he doing in the University?'

'Enwer Jakolin was admitted to the hospital and stayed for a while when he suffered some health problems. He also sometimes attended university functions with his wife, and he presented three or four reports at university meetings.'

'Who interviewed you on the 30th of April?'

'Enwer Jakolin.'

'Why were you so rude to him when you knew who he was? He is a high-ranking official. Senior personnel would not dare to look him in the eye or antagonize him. He is a busy person who would not normally come here question someone but in your case he felt it necessary because you are a young female student with little worldly knowledge. He felt that you should be given the opportunity to be re-educated. However, instead of showing your appreciation of his forbearance, you were extremely rude. What was your intention? Why are you resisting our approaches so strongly? Who is influencing you?' Niyaz shouted as he thumped the table with his fist. Do you understand how much tolerance you were given? But you show no awareness of this.'

The two of them took it in turn to shout at me. When one stopped, the other took over. They continued their interrogation.

'Who is your leader?'

'We don't have a leader', I replied.

'I mean the one who directs your organisation and acts as your mentor. Who are your sponsors? Where are they now?'

'We never had such a leader', I said.

'I am asking you to tell the truth! Your comrades have already exposed them. You can't protect them any longer.'

'I am telling the truth. We don't have any leaders. If my comrades told you differently then perhaps they have a different leader who I don't know', I said.

'Don't treat us like fools! You're saying that you have your own leader and they have theirs? You are all very close friends, so how is it possible that you could keep such secrets from one another? You know everything. Do not continue to try to mislead us! Answer my question! Abliz Niyaz slapped me and screamed in my face.

I said, 'No matter what you do to me I can only tell you the truth.'

'Ok. I will give you time to think about what we have said. To lessen your crime you'd better give us a written statement.'

'I keep telling you that there isn't anyone else involved. I can't make something up from nothing. I can't promise you that I will be able to write a statement. If other people can give you answers to your questions, let them be the ones to expose the people you are looking for', I said firmly.

Suddenly, they changed the subject. 'What was the content of the letter that you wrote to Ziya Semedi?' they enquired.

I was shocked. I had been promised that the letter would be kept absolutely secret. 'Who had told them?' I thought, 'No, I can't admit anything.'

'No such thing ever happened', I said.

'What kind of person are you? You wrote the letter and sent it to him and now you're telling us that this never happened. Who you trying to fool? You won't resolve any of your problems by being so stubborn. It is just not possible to remain lenient with you any longer.' They shouted.

'You can say what you like, but I don't have any knowledge of such a letter', I said.

'If you don't have any knowledge then let me tell you', said Abliz Niyaz, 'You are still trying to cover everything up but your comrades have already informed us about this. Do you believe that they would also hide everything, like you try to do? Although you've burned all the documents, Ahmet Toxti rewrote many of them for us. You cannot beat us with your arrogant manner! Let me tell you the contents of the letter you wrote to your godfather Ziya Semedi, and listen to me carefully! 'Please support our movement and assist us with weapons. Isn't that what you wrote?' said Abliz Niyaz.

'No, I don't remember', I said calmly.

'Oh, you don't remember! Listen to this. If they agreed to provide you with weapons, what was your plans for transporting them here?'

'I don't know what you're talking about. I have never heard about this', I said.

'You never heard about this?' Abliz Niyaz's voice had turned cold.

'You are one of three people who wrote the letter to Ziya Semedi. Don't you remember that Ehmet Toxti, Melike, and you wrote the letter? Why are you saying that you have never heard of it? Do you not consider your future at all? We can only help you so much. You will have to bear the outcome alone, because we are unable to share your suffering despite our efforts to help. You have rejected our assistance and, as such, you will suffer a great deal from your continued stubbornness. As a young woman we are considering your wellbeing. You are more fragile than a man, that is why we are treating you so differently. You all have life ahead of you, don't ruin it. If you aren't thinking about your future, you are taking the matter too lightly.

'While you are refusing to say anything, other people are revealing everything. We are only checking whether you are willing to cooperate with us, in order to benefit from the party's lenient policy. We are here to help you, do you understand? Let me tell you this. In one of the meetings, you discussed how to transport the weapons into this country should Ziya Semedi agree to supplying them. Ahmet Toxti said he would go to the border and collect the weapons because he had been to the Soviet Union in 1950 and 1951, was familiar with the routes, and as such, it would only take him one or two days to make the round trip. Isn't that right? Do you remember now?'

I was struggling to believe that someone whom we had trusted the most could have reveal such detailed information to them. Who has told them? This question replayed time and again in my mind.

'So, do you recall what was said now? You have no choice but to admit it, now that the evidence has been laid in front of you.'

'No, I don't remember anything about what you are saying. Maybe I wasn't at that meeting', I replied calmly.

'What are you saying? There was never a meeting without your presence. We know that.'

'I can't recall anything at all', I said while thinking of my promise not to admit to anything under any circumstances.

'Do you really believe you can escape from the responsibilities by denying everything? We know you are more intelligent than most people and have an extraordinary memory. You may have made up your mind to stick to what you believe, we have wasted enough time and tired of talking to you', they yelled in unison.

'What are you expecting from me? I am not guilty of any wrongdoing. Wanting independence is not a crime. What surprises me is how you have exaggerated a minor student activity into such a big thing', I replied.

They glanced at each other and asked, 'Do you still believe that what you have been involved in is such a small student activity? Since the investigation of your organisation began, a programme of political study has been introduced into all the work places throughout the province. And while the investigation is ongoing, you sit here and think that what you have been involved in is only a little student game. You still fail to recognise the seriousness of your crime.' They repeated these accusations for about an hour before I was returned to my cell.

After I was locked back in, I heard my teacher, on the other side of the wall, 'Don't be afraid, they can't do anything to you.'

18 May 1963

Two prison guards came to the cell, ordered me to collect all my belongings, and wait in the corridor to exchange cells with Sefiye from cell No.2. This cell was brighter than the one I had left because the window got more sunlight. I think the reason for the change was that they might have realised that I've been communicating with Uncle Mewken. As I have mentioned, I've also found a way to communicate with people working outside. We exchange greetings, they keep me informed about the people who visit the prison, and they send me their best wishes. Someone informed the prison manager about this, so I was immediately taken for questioning.

I discovered that some of the prisoners were kept in dark cells for days, for a breach of the rules. My new cell window faces the rear yard. No one works on this side, so it is very quiet. Prisoners were taken out in turns, once a week, to air their bedding and to wash themselves once a month. I was able to watch the prisoners through the window when they were outside. My neighbour in the next cell, Sultan, was always very quiet. I never heard any footsteps or other sounds. Some days, I heard Sultan calling God in agony, which made my heart ache. I heard later that he died in prison.

I became very ill on the second day after I moved into this cell. My hands, feet and face all became swollen. I lost my appetite and became very weak. On the third day when the guard came to take me to the toilet, I told him I was very ill and desperately needed to be seen by a doctor. About an hour later a tall slim Chinese doctor came, escorted by two prison guards. One guard stood by the door and the other one stood next to me.

The doctor asked questions about my illness and then examined me. He told me there was a problem with my liver, and he prescribed me a glucose drip and three different medicines. He explained that I would need to take the medication for three days. He also said that he would write a request to the prison management for a special meal to be provided everyday until I was well. 'I will ask them to give you white bread instead of corn bread for dinner.' He then told me that he would visit me the next day.

The two prison guards escorted him out, giving me the impression that he was also a prisoner. I was given a drip everyday for fifteen days, by the doctor. The first four days I stayed in bed, only going to the toilet. As I walked past, the prisoners from each cell would call my name saying, 'Salam Söyüngül! Salam girl.'

Sometimes when the guards were not close to me I would respond. However, this time they said, 'Salam Söyüngül, are you feeling better? May God protect you and give you good health!'

These words comforted me greatly. The encouragement of the prisoners in cell No.9 always gave me great comfort. Although I had never seen their faces, we developed a special bond, and they became my close friends. Some prisoners who worked in the front courtyard would come to my window and ask how I was doing. They would pass on get-well messages on behalf of all the comrades. The kindness, care and support expressed by everyone gave me the drive to recover.

22 May 1963

On the twenty-fourth day after I had been arrested, my family were granted permission to contact me, after repeatedly pleading with the authorities. I was walking back and forth in my cell when one of the guards, Qaynil opened the metal slot and passed me a letter with ten yuan. I read the letter immediately. It said that my mother, my sister Zekiye and aunty Mehfuse had all come to prison to visit me. I wrote a quick note back to them, saying that I was fine and not to worry.

Also I had received the 10 yuan that they had sent. I passed the note back to Qaynil. After Qaynil left, I read the letter again and again. Memories of how hard my mother had worked in order to raise all ten of us racing back to me. There was the housework, and the tailoring that she did day and night, sharing the financial burden with my father. They had faced so many hard times. Sometimes they hadn't even had enough food for themselves, but they never stopped supporting me in my education. They always said that they didn't have anything for their children to inherit, other than a good standard of education.

I could only imagine how my mother would have sobbed in front of the prison gates when gazing upon the high prison walls and beyond. My father's words echoed in my ears, 'My girl, you are finishing university soon. Once you have graduated, there will be less pressure financially.'

I also remembered how my younger sisters and brothers would sit on my lap and have the same conversations so sweetly each time when I visited them, 'Sister, when are you finishing your studies?'

I held the money tightly in my hand. I was deeply upset by the thought of how hard it must have been for them to spare this 10 yuan for me.

25 May 1963

I was taken for questioning around 10 o'clock. On my way past the prisoners working in the courtyard, I greeted them. Abliz Niyaz was in the room and as soon as I walked in he said. 'Your mother came earlier and brought you these things. You need to write a note confirming that you have received them.'

I wrote the note, signed it, handed it to Abliz and said, 'All my clothes are still at the university. I haven't been able to change for a month now. Can you please arrange for someone to bring them here?' I gave him my keys for the chest of drawers. Abliz went out to make a phone call to the university and returned shortly after to tell me that someone would bring me my clothes that afternoon. I was questioned for two hours then escorted back to my cell. At about 2 pm, I heard people talking outside my cell. I always found ways to watch what was happening outside my window, although I found it hard to identify people because they all had long beards, and were frail and slim. Long hair and moustaches can change a man's looks completely.

Listening to people talking loudly and clearly, 'Among the different flowers there are red flowers, roses, lilies, peonies and Söyün flowers.[11] I jumped up and started listening more carefully. One of them repeated, 'Among the different flowers there are red flowers, roses, lilies, peonies and Söyüngül.' At that moment I said to myself, 'Oh God, that must be Abliz.' I was so excited and didn't know what to do. I remained frozen in the middle of my cell.

In the past when we had student parties at the university, my friends always requested that I sing the song Sermen Küyi. So I started to sing that song, hoping to catch his attention, then he would know which cell I was in. I then tried to climb onto the window frame, however because the metal frame had been removed there was nothing for me to hold onto and hoist myself up. I waited for an opportunity when the guards had walked away from my window to try to look through the widow. I was stopped when suddenly my cell door was opened with a bang.

A guard entered shouting, 'Come with me!' I was escorted to the office in which I had filled the forms when I first arrived. A cadre from the university's Security Department had brought my belongings as I had requested. I chose the clothes and books I needed, before tying the rest of my things together and carrying them all to the prison storage area. The storage room was full with suitcases and boxes. I noticed Sajide,

---

11   *The second part of the author's name, gül, means 'flower' in Uyghur.*

Abliz and Ahmet Toxti's belongings were scattered all over the floor. As I walked back to my cell, I was informed that all my course books had been confiscated. Although I knew there was no chance in hell I could ever go back to university, I felt deeply sad realizing once again that my university life had ended forever.

28 May 1963

It has been a month since I saw the light of day. I feel more settled now than when I first arrived. I bought a bucket in the prison using some of the money my parents had sent me. I had become familiar with the people who delivered water in the morning. They agreed to leave me any leftover water after completing their distribution duties. I became friendly with one of the men who delivered our food and on one day as he was handing over my food tray I saw dumplings on one side. Just like the ones my mum used to make. They smelled so delicious that my tummy rumbled in anticipation.

I asked him, 'Are the dumplings made in the prison?'

'Yes. You eat normal prisoner's meals but there are wealthy people here that eat top quality meals which cost fifty yuan a month. Their food is specially made according to their requirements, and includes fresh milk, fruit, and special drinks. They are Soviets from the Soviet Union. You and I are different from them. Oh no, the guard is here. Got to go.' He quickly closed food slot.

This surprised me, that there is a class system even in prison. The ordinary people only earned an average of 30 to 40 yuan a month, high ranking cadres and top doctors earned fifty to 60 yuan a month, which was enough to feed their families in that time. That was an interesting comparison with what Soviet prisoners were paying for their food. Ninety per cent of prisoners were of Chinese origin. Prison governors, guards, chefs, and staff were all Chinese. Only those who involved in questioning the prisoners were of ethnic minority origin.

It rained so heavily one day that the water leaked through the ceiling of my cell all over the floor. Only a tiny area near the door was left dry. I placed my bedding in that area and sat there all night. The next day I noticed that the wall where the water had run down had become whiter. I thought that if I washed all of the walls they might also become whiter, so I saved a little water every day to wash the walls. It took me a week to complete this task, but it brightened up my cell. I washed the wooden floor and fittings twice a day, and the floor became so clean that I was able to dry my white cloth on it.

One day upon returning from the toilet, I saw that the prison governors and other officials were inspecting my cell. They were looking at the walls and talking amongst themselves. The governor looked at me and asked, 'What did you do to make the walls so white?' I replied that I had washed them, but he didn't seem to believe me. He touched the walls and said nothing.

A Chinese man who was standing next to him said, 'Do you know she's a doctor, they like to be clean.'

The prison governor said, 'I have been working in this prison so many years and I have never met a prisoner who has kept their cell so clean. I can't believe my eyes. Who would have thought that by washing the walls it would brighten the room so much. We have had many female doctors who were prisoners in the past, but their cells were so filthy and smelly that you didn't want to step in. Many people don't clean their cells once a week let alone once a day. Look at the floor; you can see the footprints we are leaving behind.' He was right. Every time I returned to the cell after leaving it, I immediately knew how many people had been in my cell by counting the footprints on the floor.

After lunch I was sitting on my bed, deep in thought when I heard Sajide singing,
My darling.
Where have you been wondering? Oh my darling.
You are my treasure my beautiful darling,
I am still yearning for you to come back to me, my sweet heart.
I am still longing for you day and night, my darling.

I jumped up from the bed and tried to climb up to the window. The window had recently been painted over, yet I managed to see the people outside through a tiny gap that had been left between the window frame and the bricks. I started singing the lyrics in tune with her. The guards who were watching Sajide shouted at her to stop singing, then one approached my window and shouted at me to stop.

Someone from the No. 4 corridor had also joined in the singing as well. The guard escorted Sajide away. I was able to see that she was wearing a long green coat and boots. She looked undernourished and pale. It saddened me to see her fragile appearance. The man who joined in our singing sounded very much like my teacher Mehmut Ewzi, enough that I believed it was him. I later learned that he had died in prison. I was devastated when I heard the news.

10 June 1963

I was taken for questioning today. As soon as I walked in the room Eli Yüsup asked, 'How are you finding prison life? Is it hard? What are your feelings?'

'There is a saying you can get used to life in Hell after three days. I am getting used to it', I replied smiling.

'If that is the case, have you thought more seriously about your mistakes?' Eli Yüsup enquired.

'I have not committed any crimes or made any mistakes, therefore there is nothing for me to think about. I have always believed that our demands for independence could be justified. I would like to ask you a question if you don't mind. Has Xinjiang always been a part of the China? If so the past and all the history books written about Xinjiang are incorrect.'

Eli Yüsup looked a little angry but he answered my question after some thought, 'Xinjiang was an independent country in the past, what was written in history books was correct. However the founder of the socialist ideal, the great leader Lenin, said that it is best to set up a socialist system by uniting small states into larger nations. What is wrong with combining this country with China? You won't get anywhere or gain any benefits from being involved with big issues such as this. You must have realised this after you received your belongings from the university.'

'I knew what my future would be from the day I stepped out of the university gates', I said.

'Right! Well having predicted your future, it is not easy to fulfil that kind of life. We are concerned about you. As a young girl and your life will be wasted. Let me tell you something, do you know why Ablikim was not arrested? Just like you, he was one of the founding members of your organisation, in fact, his crime is more serious than yours. His class background is that of a rich farmer's son. But he was not arrested. Why do you think that was, Söyüngül?' he asked.

'I have no idea. Can you tell me why?' I asked.

'It was Ablikim who came forward exposing everything to us. The party decided not to punish him because of the information he provided. As a result, he was not punished by the university authorities. Didn't you know that?'

What he said hit me hard. I had had doubts about Ablikim many times, but my trust had always overridden any concerns. The integrity he had showed and his views about the revolution were demonstrable in his actions and words. He was so angry with

Abley when he chose not to join the organisation. He threatened that he would kill Abley if Abley revealed the details of the organisation. All these scenes played in my mind like snap shots from a movie.

So he was the one who revealed everything! We had been best friends for so long. How could his conscience bear such a burden? I had now lost any respect and feelings of friendship that I had for him. 'You have not heard this before, have you?' asked Eli Yüsup.

'No, I haven't', I said truthfully.

'It's very painful to be betrayed by your best friend. Don't you think?' he said looking into my eyes, 'I have been working in this prison for many years, and I have questioned numerous prisoners but I have never interviewed anyone for setting up an organisation like you did. You are among the first group of young people who have been imprisoned here for political reasons and for setting up an illegal organisation, particularly young women like you and Sajide. You are different from others because most people deny their responsibility, it is normal to hear, "I didn't do it, so and so is the one who did it." However, when I questioned Abliz, he clearly stated that he was responsible for everything. And you are also saying that you are the one who had set up the group. Interesting! Very interesting.'

5 July 1963

Having been surrounded all my life by people, I found it increasingly difficult to cope with solitude. One day, a noisy fly flew into my cell. I sat on the floor scrutinising its movements. Normally I hated flies, and would always be quick to swat them, but this time I didn't want to kill it. Instead I enjoyed its company hoping it would stay longer. After it had flown around for a while it found its way out and flew away. Even the fly didn't want to be trapped in this cell, I thought.

It had been sixty-eight days since I was arrested and incarcerated in this tiny dark cell. It was not just the loneliness and boredom driving me crazy; but the sound of men in other cells crying day and night was unbearable. Some cried out from the pain of torture, others screamed for fresh air and freedom. Sometimes I heard, 'Oh, naan bread, where can I find you?' I knew the man was suffering from starvation.

The constant sounds of people pleading for help tormented me. I often forgot my own problems and I felt so desperately sad at not being able to help anyone. Sometimes, I heard arguments and fights breaking out in cells. One day I heard a loud argument followed by the shouting of the prison guards, followed by a heart-stopping scream. I looked through a crack in the door, trying to figure out what had happened. As I couldn't see anything, I went to the window and shouted to cell No. 4 asking them what happened.

A man replied, 'There was a fight in the cell. The guards have chained up the prisoner's feet.' They must have been tortured a great deal. The screaming coming from the cells made me feel ill and depressed. That same day, I also heard people shouting words of comfort like, 'Dear friend, be strong! Everything will be ok! One day all of this will be in our past!'

The singing of moving folk songs continued every evening. I always looked forward to these singing sessions. All the prisoners from different cells would sing like a choir, and if an individual began to sing other prisoners would join in. Every word of the lyrics expressed the suffering of mankind, and touched everyone's heart. They were so uplifting. The guards would react in the same way every night. It was their busiest moment as they ran up and down the corridors banging the doors and commanding the prisoners to stop singing.

This demand was ignored by everyone despite the threats of torture. The guards sometimes enlisted the assistance of other cadres to gain control of the situation. The singing would eventually stop, but only in the prisoners own time. It was the prisoners' only pleasure and a way of expressing pain to ease their suffering. On a few occasions I heard the moving sounds of someone reciting the Quran, which was spiritually uplifting.

I saw Sajide and Abliz twice through the window. On one of the days I jumped up to the window seal, and by holding onto the metal bars, I was able to look outside. I saw Abliz with four other prisoners in the courtyard. Then I heard him calling me, 'Söyün?'

I replied, 'Yes.'

As I looked at him through the gap of the window, he asked, 'How are you? How is your health? I heard you were sick, are you feeling better now? Are you alone in your cell?'

After answering all of his questions, he said, 'I think they will be charging us very soon and sending us away to different prisons. I may not see you again. Has your family visited you? And do you need any help?' I told him that my family had visited me, I was fine and he did not need to worry about me.

He continued, 'I felt terrible on hearing that you were ill, I hope you get better soon, look after yourself. Also I have heard your attitude towards the governors and officials is not good, please don't be difficult and try to cooperate with them so that you will receive a lighter sentence. I know it is very difficult and I do worry about you two girls a lot. Sajide is alright, she is in the first room in the third corridor, also Ahmet's brother is alright. Do you have anything to tell me?'

'Yes' I said. 'Thank you for everything, I wish you well. May God protect you wherever you go!'

He replied, 'I leave you in God's hands and wish you well.'

I said, 'I wish we could meet again in happier times.' He then replied, 'May God bless us with a long life and live to see happier days.'

The other prisoners who were with him added, 'We wish you well, wherever you go, may God protect you always.' I couldn't restrain my tears as I wished that things would change.

One day as I was looking through the gap in the window frame, I saw some prisoners from other cells airing their bedding outside. They were all middle-aged men, scruffy, and non-shaven with hair that had not been cut for a long time. They looked emaciated and frail. It was hard to recognize anyone in such a poor condition. One of the men came and sat not far from my window and started singing. His voice sounded very familiar to me, as if he was my teacher at school, Mr Ahmet. He was well known at school because of his beautiful voice.

But due to his appearance I couldn't decide if he was Mr Ahmet or not. Then one of the prisoners called, 'Hey Ahmet-jan come over here, let's clean out this ditch. If we're lucky we might be praised in the Reform through Labour Newspaper for behaving extraordinarily well!'

After they cleaned out the ditch, the prisoner returned to sit in the same place and started singing the song Biwapa (The Unfaithful). It was our favourite song and the girls learned to sing this song from him at school. He also used to sing Ghulja style songs for us. It was Mr Ahmet! The way he looked shocked me. I would never have recognized him without hearing his singing. I felt sad at how time and hardship had changed him. This was the only time I saw Mr Ahmet during my time in prison. I never saw my teacher Mr Mahmut Abliz, although he did regularly send his salaams and asked about my well-being.

8 July 1963

The morning when I returned from the toilet, one of the Chinese prisoners who was responsible for taking prisoners outside for fresh air, was waiting for me. He ordered,

'Collect all your belongings together.'

My heart jumped and I felt sick. I asked, 'Where are you taking me?'

He said with a smile, 'You are to be taken back to your university.'

'You are lying', I said.

He continued with a smile, 'You will be working with us as a doctor in this prison.'

I am kind of used to his joking by now, because every time he saw me he would say, 'Your mother is here to visit you.'

I always replied, 'You are joking.'

He always took the opportunity when the guards were not around to open the food slot and chat with me. He passed me information about other prisoners who were in the cell-block. He told me that I would not be here for too long. Once a decision was made on my case, I would be transferred elsewhere. Being a kind-hearted man, he also kept me informed about Sajide.

He said, 'Your friend cries all the time, some time she sobs aloud. But you sing all the time. You two are very interesting.'

'You are kidding me, please tell me the truth', I begged.

'Well, we are taking you to your friend's cell', he said.

I was so happy but I doubted him as usual so I kept asking him, 'Are you sure? Is it true?'

'Yes, get your things ready now. Let's go', he replied.

I started packing my things as fast as I could. I was over the moon at the thought of meeting my dearest friend Sajide after being alone in this dark cell for so long. I kept thinking about how Sajide would react when she saw me. 'Oh God, I don't mind being kept in prison as long as I am with Sajide' I thought. I almost ran to her cell. The door was open but there was no sight of her. She had been taken to the toilet. I returned to my cell to collect rest of my belongings.

There were three sets of bedding laid out on the floor in the new cell. It looked as if the bedding was never tidied up. Also, the cell was dark and filthy with buckets, bowls, brooms, and clothing, lying around everywhere. I recognized Sajide's bedding from her blanket. I waited anxiously by the door. Other prison staff were also standing around waiting to see how both of us would react the reunion. I heard footsteps in the corridor, but not wanting people to see me, I moved from the door to inside the cell.

Two Chinese women walked in carrying buckets, they were taken aback and stared at me coldly. I then heard the familiar steps of Sajide. She walked into the cell with her head down, looking very sad. She was wearing her green long coat, black boots and wool headscarf. She didn't even notice me because I was standing in shadow next to the wall. I stood quietly with a smile on my face. I wanted to hug her, but I controlled myself because people were watching from the doorway.

Sajide walked in a few more steps before suddenly seeing me. Her big round eyes widened. 'Oh Söyün', she sighed, and threw herself into my arms, weeping uncontrollably.

I told Sajide to stop crying, because people were waiting to see our reactions. 'Don't let them see your tears.' I said. But she couldn't control her emotions. The tears poured from her eyes like rain. It was heart-wrenching to see her so upset. I said, 'Sajide, my dearest friend. Please stop crying. I have missed you so much since we were parted. Now I am here, we are going to share everything.' People standing near the door closed and locked it as they left.

Sajide looked frail. She had lost so much weight she was like a skeleton. My heart ached for her. 'What's happened to you my friend? Are you ill and hungry? Hasn't anyone from your family visited you?'

'I have been suffering from dysentery for the past three or four days, I can't tell you how much I want something oily. My elder sister brought me some sweets and snacks. I don't know if my mother knows I have been arrested. Oh my poor mother, she waited so many years to see my elder brother Hekim come out of prison. Before he has even finished his sentence, I have ended up here. I feel so miserable when I think about my poor mother. I can't imagine how much pain she must be going through every day.'

The tears began to flow again. I said, 'Saji, please don't cry so much, you are going to make your condition worse. When we started the organisation, we prepared ourselves for all kinds of difficulties and hardships. We promised to sacrifice our lives for the freedom of our country and happiness of our people. We also promised to stay strong in the hands of our enemies. Do you remember? Unfortunately, the hard days arrived sooner than we expected. This is only the beginning of the difficulties that we will face, there are more dangerous days to come. We cannot run away and there is no going back. We have to remain strong.

We need to have extraordinary will power, to maintain high spirits and good health. We didn't consider our own benefits or those of our parents and families when we started this journey, and we can't think differently now. We are no longer the old Söyüngül and Sajide, we have became different people. We are the representatives of our dreams and the voices of freedom. So we must act as role models, we must reach out to hold a special place in the hearts of our people. Don't cry from now on, tears are signs of weakness. Our parents love us and they wish us to be strong and healthy. They will understand and support our dreams.'

'Oh my dear friend, what would I have done without you? What you are saying is absolutely right. I've missed you so much!' Her beautiful eyes filled with tears again while she was talking.

I tried my best to lift Sajide's spirits because she was so downcast. I took out some fried white bread, which I had bought from the prison trolley the day before, and some cream which my family had brought. We had tea together and spoke nonstop.

I said, 'Saji, we are not going to be bored from now on. It is so hard being alone; you don't know how much I have missed people. At least you have these two Chinese in your room.'

'Oh, you don't know how racist and suspicious they are; they have been watching my every move, reporting me to the prison guards constantly. I have been searched and questioned many times. I didn't feel free even in this cell.

'Söyün, on the day I was brought here, as the guard locked the door with a bang, my mother appeared in front of my eyes as if she was crying for me on the other side of the door. I couldn't help myself from crying aloud for about an hour. These two were taken outside for fresh air at the time and Abliz was in the cell opposite. He tried to comfort me with kind words. I didn't cry for about a month after that. I find it so difficult to stop thinking about my mother.

'She is such an unlucky woman, never having had happiness in her life. My father went abroad on business and died, leaving her with all the young children at the age of 27 to bring up. It was a life of hardship. My brother Hekim spent two years in prison, and Ablihey fled to the Soviet Union. I was her only hope, now look at where I am.' The tears filled her eyes again. It took me some time before I could stop her from sobbing.

It was all very emotional. 'Do you know it was Ablikim who exposed us?' Sajide said.

'Yes, I learned that during my questioning. I knew someone among us had sold us out because the interrogators had such detailed knowledge about the organisation. It is hard to believe it would turn out to be Ablikim. It just goes to show that you can't really judge a person from their words and actions. I believe that Sétiwaldi provided the clues while Ablikim provided the details in order to save himself. I am disappointed and sad that we were sold out by the one person whom we thought to be our most loyal and best friend.'

'Words fail to express how much anger I feel towards him, he is the lowest of the low.' Sajide said tightly. We spent all night chatting and gazing at the moon through the cell window, it was like old times, and reminded us of the times we spent at the university on moonlit nights. I recited a poem written by a famous Tatar poet Abdulla Tuqay when he was in prison:

> *The stars brightened the sky as the darkness spread.*
> *My Lord lightens my heart amidst the clouds and darkness of my fate.*

I recited all of the verses. Sajide joined in and we recited it again together many times.

LIFE IN SOLITARY PRISON
AND LABOUR CAMPS

9 July

We chatted away until sunrise the next day, without sleeping a wink. The prison governor opened the cell door at ten o'clock, ordering us to pack all our belongings and place them in the corridor. We looked at each other anxiously, eager to find out where we would be taken. On the way to and from the toilet we exchanged farewells with the other prisoners. After collecting our cases from storage room, we were told to go outside and stand by the gate. Prison staff helped carry our belongings and put them in a black jeep that was waiting outside. They also said their farewells before leaving us. Eli Yüsup took me to his office while Abliz Niyaz called Sajide to his office. As I sat down he started to read the decision on my case:

'You are the first young woman to have been brought to our attention for setting up a political organisation. We hereby present our verdict based on careful consideration of your case. Considering that you are a young woman and a student without any social experience, and your family members, as we have checked, seem to be well-respected members of the community, we have therefore decided to sentence you to three years of Reform Through Labour. You are very lucky to have received such a light sentence, given the seriousness of your crime. You could have easily been sentenced to over fifteen years.'

'How could you even say that I should have received fifteen years sentence just because I was involved in such a trivial matter? I don't deserve such a long prison sentence. Everyday, every month and every year is a precious part of a person's life. What damage have we caused for our life to be ruined for so long? I find it difficult to take in.' I protested.

Eli Yüsup was visibly upset at my words and shouted, 'Do you understand how much time and effort was put into defending you so that you could get just three years? Your crime is no less serious than Abliz's. The only difference is that he comes from a different social class. You really should be grateful to us and stop taking things for granted! Everything is politics these days so put aside your grand ideals and focus on how to serve these three years without fuss. It will not be easy for you.' After a short and tense pause, he continued, 'You are now going to the Mechanical Repair Factory. Malashof works there and I understand he is related to your family. The director of the factory Yüsup knows both of you. They will take good care of you. There is a hospital, which the Public Security Bureau is in charge of. They might be able to arrange work there for you as well. Be very careful in what you say and do. It's a shame that three years of your life is to be wasted and I feel very sorry for you. But this is all we can do.'

I thanked him after he finished with his admonition. As I came out of the office, I met Sajide at the gate. I quickly asked Sajide how many years she had received. At the same time I made a gesture to impart to the prisoners working in the courtyard that I had received three years, while Sajide did the same to indicate two years, in the hope that this news would reach Abliz.

Eli Yüsup escorted us in the jeep to the factory where we signed the documents confirming our sentences. He then left us standing in the courtyard where twenty to thirty people sat waiting. I thought that they might have served their sentences and were now ready to leave. Since the time of our arrival, people emerged from different places to look at us.

A Kazakh official in army uniform came out of the office and asked politely, 'Where have you come from, girls?'

'We have just arrived from the Public Security Prison', Sajide replied.

'You are prisoners then.' There was a harsh tone in his voice.

Sajide whispered to me, 'A minute ago he sounded so polite and now he sounds so rude.'

'Ignore such attitudes. They have no respect for anyone here', I said coldly.

A pregnant Chinese woman came and told us to follow her to the clinic, where we had a medical check-up. After that we were taken to the inner courtyard. We passed through three gates and workshops before arriving at our destination. One of the Chinese women shouted loudly, 'Mahinur, Mahinur!' Then a young woman came out of a building on the right hand side of the courtyard. She was slim with thick dark eyebrows and her hair was tied in a ponytail. Her skin was very dark from long hours of labour in the sun. She was wearing three quarter length trousers with a Chinese style high collared blue blouse and velvet slippers. She greeted us then led us to a two storey building on the left. She guided us to a room where there was bedding on the wooden floor next to the window for two people. At that moment four men entered the room, searched us and our belongings and left. We started chatting to Mahinur to find out more about the place when the team leader Mr Malashof walked in.

'What a surprise, Söyüngül! The girl that we couldn't get to come to the party even if we'd offered you a lift in a limousine! Now look at you, coming here on foot!' He looked at Sajide and asked, 'How many years have been given?' 'Two years', she replied. He then looked at me and asked the same question. 'Three years!' he smacked the palm of his hand on his forehead then shook his head, 'Your parents have almost gone insane because of what you've done. Have you ever thought about your parents, Söyüngül? Your father has become very ill. The pain is too much for them to cope with.' His lecturing continued for a while before he finally left.

I heard a bell ringing calling people for lunch. A young woman walked in to the room wearing a floral long dress, a blue jumper, a black *shalwar* and a white scarf. She had fair skin, a round face, grey eyes and light-colour hair. She came across as a very warm and down-to-earth village girl. I couldn't help but also notice her gold tooth every time she smiled, and thought it looked oddly amusing.

Mahinur introduced us another girl, Zohre, a butcher's daughter from Qumul, who had been sentenced to two years of Reform Through Labour. Mahinur then told us a little about herself. She used to be a singer and a dancer in the National Dancing and Singing Ensemble and now she is here serving a three-year sentence. We chatted while having lunch until the bell rang for work. Initially we were given half a day off, but the team leader changed his mind and called us to work. Sajide and I worked in the courtyard in front of the blacksmith. The news soon spread that we had been transferred from the Public Security Prison. Many people gathered in front of the windows and in doorways of the workshop to look at us. There were many rumours about us circulating around, and our arrival became big news within the labour camp. The Mechanical Repair Factory had many different types of work units with at least two hundred people allocated to each work area. We felt embarrassed and intimidated by the large number of people staring at us from all directions. We did not know how to react.

It was a scorching day and our workload was extremely heavy. After work we quickly washed ourselves before placing a piece of clean cloth on the floor and sitting around it to eat our dinner.

'I heard that you were spies. They told me that a spy is an ugly and very bad person, but neither of you are anything like that. You are both too pretty and too stunning to be spies,' said Zohre with a blushing smile.

We both burst out laughing at her words. We had not laughed so hard for a long time.

'We were students, Zohre, not spies. We've been accused of setting up an anti-government organisation', I explained. She looked confused and did not understand much.

'Now tell us, Zohre, why are you here?' enquired Sajide.

Zohre told us her story. She used to be part of a group of young thieves who travelled to various cities to steal money from people. 'We worked as a team and divided everything we stole evenly amongst us. We used to make between one to three thousand yuan a day. However, stolen money never had much value, as it was normal to spend our illicit gains within the same day. After some time people started to recognise our faces it was impossible to stay in one place for long, so we were constantly on the move.

I will never forget the last time I stole money. It was in Tuli city. An old Kazakh man came in the shopping centre and I was there looking for an opportunity to steal. I hid myself quite well behind him, checked the inside of his bag and managed to find his money. It was wrapped in a handkerchief and place on the side of the bag. When he was at the counter and realised the money was missing, he shouted, "My money is gone! It was in a handkerchief in my bag!" He checked his bag inside out, again and again, shouting and sobbing, "Oh my God, the money has gone. What am I going to do now? I saved that money for my son's wedding over so many years and he is getting married next week. What should I do now?" The old man's tears were rolling down his cheeks, into his beard and onto the floor. People surrounded him immediately showing him their sympathy and offering words of comfort, but he was crying inconsolably with a look of someone who had suddenly lost everything in life. It was the look on his face that affected me the most. I was so ashamed of myself and did not know what to do. If I gave him the money back the police would certainly arrest me, if I didn't I would feel guilty for the rest of my life.

I wandered around the department store for almost half a day. My friends kept pressuring me to leave, which I did in the end. We counted the money. It was three thousand yuan. And that evening we checked into a hotel. The police then came and arrested all of us at the hotel that evening. We were locked in a room, after midnight we broke the window and jumped down into the courtyard before climbing over a wall to escape. When I jumped off the wall, I landed on a wooden board with nails sticking up, one of which went through my foot. My friends helped me pull my foot off the nail, but it bled so badly that my shoe was full of blood. We decided to flee to Mainland China and went straight to the train station. The blood from my foot left a trail all the way, which the police followed to the station where we were arrested again. That is how I ended up here. I was already on their arrest list before this anyway. In April I was sentenced to two years.'

All three of us listen to her story intensely forgetting to eat our food. I then asked Zohre if she had to hand over the money to the police. 'No, when we reached the train station we only had enough money left to pay for the tickets. We had stolen a lot more money but we had spent it all', answered Zohre calmly. Silence fell as we were wondering about the old man's fate.

'We were cursed by him. I will never forget him', added Zohre. Then she went quiet.

After we finished dinner, Sajide asked Mahinur, 'I heard you were a singer and dancer for The National Ensemble. What's your story, then?' I had been looking at Mahinur with curiosity, as I was also impatient to know. She hesitated for a moment before speaking –

'I was a singer and dancer in The Song and Dance Ensemble for the Ethnic Groups in Beijing. I have travelled to many countries to perform with the group and was becoming very popular. In 1961, as you know, the nationwide famine hit Beijing and we were all affected by the shortage of food. There was a singer in our Ensemble called Guli, who had connections in the Pakistani embassy. She used to visit the embassy frequently and return with lots of food, drinks and many other things. We didn't suffer from hunger all the time thanks to her. In 1962, Guli introduced me to a friend of hers at the embassy, and we started to get invited to the parties there. Of course we knew that we'd get into trouble if the authorities found out, so we were very careful to cover our tracks. We would hide inside Embassy cars every time we went in or out. We enjoyed the lavish banquets and dancing parties, sometimes we even stayed in the embassy overnight.

'In April 1962, Guli left Beijing for Ghulja without telling me. Later I found out that she had left Ghulja to go to the Soviet Union during the Ghulja Border Incident. She married a Tatar man and settled in Tataristan. After she left I continued to visit the embassy alone. I naïve and thought no one knew about it, until one day one of my Chinese colleagues told me that she'd heard from someone that I'd be arrested soon, and that my photos taken at the embassy had been leaked. "They are investigating your involvement and I think they will most likely arrest you within days", she said.

'I was terrified by her words and packed and left Beijing by train as quickly as I could. When the train pulled into Ürümchi station, I was so relieved that everything had gone smoothly. I felt safe and made plans for my next move: I should go to Ghulja and find a way into the Soviet Union. I got off the train with my luggage when a very handsome young man came straight to me and said, 'How are you, Mahinur? How was the journey? I hope you are not tired after such a long trip.' I was taken aback, since I had never met him before. I asked him, "Who are you? How do you know me? How did you know I was arriving today?"

"'I have known of you for a very a long time. I've seen you on stage many times and have become your biggest fan. I think I've even fallen in love with you. I know you were living in Beijing, and I've always hoped I could meet you one day. I called your theatre a few days ago and one of your colleagues answered the phone, when I asked for you she said that you had left Beijing. Ever since I have been coming to the railway station to await arrival of the train from Beijing in the hopes of catching you coming off the train. I am so glad to have found you today." He looked so excited and joyous. It did not surprise me that a man should express their admiration and interest in me, but at that moment I was flattered and happy to hear such words from this handsome young man in particular. Anyway, he helped me with my luggage and asked me to be his guest. I walked with him to his car and we drove to a luxury hotel in the city. We had dinner together before he left me in the hotel, promising that he will be back tomorrow. The next morning I wanted to go out for a walk but a member of the hotel staff told me not to leave the hotel, as someone had planned the day for me. I guessed it was him and waited, but he didn't show up. In the evening I received a message from him saying that he was very sorry for breaking his promise due to some emergencies at work. Then he asked me to meet him at 10am the next day.

'The next morning, I made an extra special effort doing my hair and makeup as if I was going on stage. I put on my long earrings with matching beads and my best clothes, along with my favourite high-heel shoes, and waited for him. He finally came by around noon and was very apologetic about being late. He said, "I am so sorry! I must make up for everything. I'm going to take you somewhere better than this place." I could see all his love and affection by the way he looked at me and was over the moon, as I had liked him from the moment I had set my eyes on him at the train station.

'After quite a long drive we arrived at a large manor house on an estate. "Where are we?" I asked anxiously. "This is the place I talked about,' he said calmly. I was very disappointed as I was expecting to go somewhere spectacular but this place looked cold, chilling and unpleasant. He got out of the car saying that he was going to ask where to park the car. Then another man arrived from nowhere, got into the car and started to drive off. I was in a state of shock. I asked nervously, "What's happening? Where are you taking me?" The car was now entering a remote courtyard where it stopped suddenly and the man asked me to get out.

'My tight skirt hitched up to my hips as I got out of the car. I looked around and saw a large group of young men standing not far from the car, looking at me mockingly. I was confused and in shock. "Who are these people? Where am I now? Why would they be welcoming me?" My mind was flooded with questions. I heard the men speaking about me as they looked in my direction. "Wow, a singer has arrived! A famous singer is here!" Some men whistled as others made distasteful jokes and laughed. I was confused; I didn't know how to react in such an awkward situation. Only later was I to find out that these men were workers from the Mechanical Repair Factory, which was a part of the prison, and I had been brought to a Labour Camp. Two men came over to take my luggage from the car and told me to follow them. It finally dawned on me that I had been fooled, and how naïve I had been to trust an attractive stranger. I was taken to an office where an official told me that I was under arrest and I had been sentenced to three years' hard labour. I almost fainted as he read out my sentence and I cried uncontrollably. It felt as if my world had ended. The next day I gathered up all my valuables: my clothes, my jewellery, my makeup, my duvet covers… I put them all inside the suitcase to be locked away. Since that day I haven't lived. I am only surviving…' tears rolled down her cheeks as she continued, 'When I saw you two, I felt I was once again among friends and family.'

I tried to comfort her, 'Mahinur, in this life there are good days during the bad times and bad days during good times. One's life does not end just because something tragic has happened. We live each day as it arrives, and each day becomes a part of our existence. We cannot give in easily. We have to be strong, resilient and fight every day for a better life. When we've overcome all the hardships, good things will come our way. Don't feel so down; you are not alone. From now on all of us are friends, we all belong to this large family. We will support one another and get through this together.'

'It's true, Mahinur, don't feel so down. We all have to pull together to win this battle. We must support one another like best friends', said Sajide, completely supporting my optimism.

Mahinur, moved by our words, said with tears in her eyes, 'Oh my dear friends, I am so lucky that God has sent you here to me.' Zohre, who had been silence since Mahinur started her story, looked at us with teary eyes and said, 'You two are so kind, I am so, so glad to have met you. Let's be friends from now on.'

We continued in conversation late into the night. After Zohre and Mahinur went to bed, Sajide and I went outside to chat under the moonlight.

13 July 1963
Abliz and Zunun's arrest

We started work early in the morning, the heat was unbearable and I quickly got sunburnt, and my skin itched as I sweated. I felt uncomfortable standing in one place as the sun became hotter and hotter. But we had to carry on. I went to get some water from the hut in the middle of the workshops. I had just filled the cup and was about to take a sip when I was interrupted by a tall and broad-shouldered man in his twenties, who walked in from one of the work units behind the shed.

'Söyüngül, how are you? How is your health? Do you need any help?' he asked me as if he knew me well.

I looked at him for a while, trying to figure out if I had met him before, but I failed to retrieve any memory of him. Ready to simply walk away after responding to his greetings, I was stopped by him.

'Söyüngül, please wait', he said, 'I've come to talk to you. My name is Tursun, I used to be a driver in the city bus company. I was sentenced to ten years for selling ten bus wheels illegally. I was in the Public Security Prison before being brought here two weeks ago. I shared the same cell with Abliz Sewirdin. I saw you once when you were taken out for a break. Abliz used to speak about you a lot...'

My suspicion dissipated, and I stopped to talk with him like he was an old friend. He then explained that Abliz had been informed of my situation. Suddenly, six men walked by before he could finish his words. I was startled and ready to leave when, unexpectedly, they greeted me caringly.

'Sister, how is life? How are you getting on? Please let us know if you are in need of any help. We will do our best to help you. Also, the comrades from the work unit told us to send you their regards.' Surprised and puzzled, I didn't know how to respond. As I stood in bewilderment, Mr Hadi, our work unit oversees suddenly walked in yelling, 'Hey, you! What are you doing?' The friendly strangers fled promptly as Mr Hadi approached.

'Slacking off again, are we?' said Mr Hadi with a threatening stare, 'From now on you will not be allowed to get water yourself. We will bring it to you!'

He escorted me back to work. I was overwhelmed by the sense of being under constant surveillance. There were times, however, when people still managed to distract Mr Hadi's attention in order to contact both of us regularly. Sometimes we would find things like soup, towels, gloves, tooth paste and food vouchers among our belongings.

This didn't provide any comfort, as we were always worried that we'd get into trouble because of these 'wrongdoings'.

We were having dinner when we heard the team leader Malashof shouting outside, 'Welcome, doctors, welcome! Everybody, we now have the most experienced doctors from the Medical University among us!' He shouted as if he was selling goods at the bazar. Sajide and I jumped up, rushed to the door, and saw Malashof walking in our direction.

'We have the most experienced doctors from the Medical University! The most experienced doctors from the Medical University!' he shouted, again and again, as if it was some sort of chant. I was surprised to see Zunun and Zeynidin holding their belongings and standing outside the building. 'What are you both doing here? What's happened?' I went up to them and asked. Malshof interrupted me and said sarcastically, 'They missed you so much that they have followed you here.' Shaking his head in disappointment, he continued, 'They wouldn't have ended up here if they had concentrated on their studies only.' The two were then taken to the male side of the accommodation block.

14 July 1963

I was washing my face in the courtyard when brother Seley came over and said, 'I understand the two young men that came yesterday know you girls. Zunun and Abliz were so upset that they didn't sleep at all last night. I don't know how to comfort them. I feel very sorry for you all, you are too good to be here', he had tears in his eyes, 'Could you please come and say something to them, may be you can offer them some sort of emotional support?'

Sajide and I quickly went to the Male dormitory. The building was almost empty as most of the men had been taken to Xigobi over the last month to repair the river banks. Only two old men were left behind because of their poor health. Zunun and Abliz were sitting on the raised wooden sleeping area in a sorrowful state, staring into the void. Abliz's eyes were red, and when we asked them how they were, tears fell from Abliz's eyes. Zunun tried not to show his tears but we could clearly see his eyes glazed over.

'Hey, what has happened to you two?', I asked, 'You look like the zombies. Have you given up on yourselves this easily? Listen up, you are the most precious sons of our nation, don't lose your spirits, pull yourselves together! Everyone feels very depressed at the beginning, but you will get used to it slowly. We've never done anything wrong or bad to anyone and should not have any regrets. Our conscience is clear. You are still young. You have a whole life ahead of you. We will face all sorts of hardships in this life and our battles have just started. Every one of us needs extraordinary strength and power within ourselves in order to win. Don't allow the bad things to kill your spirit. Find ways to laugh and enjoy life, no matter how hard it is right now!"

They both cheered up a little after listening to what I had said, and seemed to agree with me. I then asked them what had happened for them to be arrested. Abliz Seydi said, 'I drew a picture on the blackboard. It was a skinny cow stretching its neck out to eat flowers in the field. I named the cow Chairman Mao and the field Xinjiang. For three months I was persecuted during the University Denunciation Meetings. They built a strong case against me with lots of exaggerations and lots of lies, then I was given a two-year sentence. The university launched a "Clean-up Campaign" after you were arrested and a number of students from your year were expelled, and our chancellor, Mr Baodun, was replaced by Governor Seypidin's wife Ayim Ezize. Zunun interrupted and said, 'I cut the picture of Chairman Mao and Khrushchev into two and I kept Khrushchev's photo as a wall poster and threw Mao's away. Like Abliz, I was also targeted during the Denunciation Meetings for three months. They also made a strong case against me, and was given a three-year sentence.' Sajide and I sat in silence, our hearts aching for them. I thought of the Chinese saying, 'To scare the monkeys by killing the chickens' – Abliz and Zunun had become the scapegoats of the Clean-up Campaign; they had received harsh punishments only to serve as a warning to the rest of the students. We sat chatting for a long time, during which Abliz expressed his concerns over his mother's health. We comforted him as best we could before going to work.

17 July 1963

Bad day - the sunburn blisters on my legs became infected. Working constantly under the scorching sun among the dust and dirt only made things worse. I asked Mr Hadi to take me to see the doctor. He agreed after seeing the condition of my legs, and he asked Sajide to come with us.

Just before we reached the gate, Tursun, who shared the cell with Abliz and another young man, approached us. Tursun came close to Mr Hadi and greeted him warmly, 'Brother Hadi, how are you? How is your health?' Tursun kept him distracted as another man came close to Sajide and started talking to her, as they both walked two paces behind us. Tursun suddenly dropped a letter in front of Sajide and signalled with his hands that she should pick it up quickly while he was still talking to Mr Hadi. Sajide quickly picked up the letter with an expression of shock on her face. I walked ahead with Mr Hadi pretending not to have seen anything. We saw inmates gathering in front of the windows of the workshop pointing at Sajide and me. 'It's just those girls', I heard their manager shouting: "Come on, back to work. What are you waiting for? Come on!' We walked on as fast as we could to get to the hospital quickly. The doctor prescribed a different cream. I quickly rubbed it on my burnt legs and felt its soothing effect.

Sajide and I found a quiet place to read the letter after lunch. The letter was addressed to me. It was about how to get in touch with Abliz Sewirdin. It suggested that I should write to Tursun's mother's address. Then the letters would be forwarded to Abliz at the Security Prison with secret arrangements. It also mentioned that Abliz was informed of our present location. We decided to write Abliz a letter. After we finished, I placed the letter in my case and locked it before leaving for work. As soon as I arrived back, the team leader Malashof called me to his office. Sajide, Zunun, and Abliz looked at me with questions in their eyes. I stood worried, wondering why I had been suddenly summoned to the office. Upon my arrival I found two men sitting there. I took the seat that was offered to me.

Malashof's started the interrogation before long, 'What is the content of the letter which Tursun gave you? Where is it now?'

'I'm sorry I don't know what letter you are referring to. I haven't seen any letter', I said calmly. 'Don't try to lie to me. When you went to the hospital with Hadi, Tursun and Erkin met you on the way. Tursun dropped a letter on the ground in front of Sajide while you were talking to Hadi. She picked up the letter and gave it to you. Didn't she? Don't deny a thing, I'm not a child', said he, bursting with anger.

"I don't know what you are talking about', I replied firmly, 'Sajide never mentioned anything about a letter to me. I didn't see anything.' No matter how hard he insisted, I repeated the same answer firmly, again and again. In the end he gave up and said, 'You can go now, but I am sure Sajide will tell me.' 'It is impossible, as no such event occurred', I said before leaving his office. Malashof followed closely behind me as I left the office.

Sajide dropped the tools and walked towards us looking confused and worried, as she moved her eyes backwards and forwards from Malashof and myself inquisitively. I made a 'hush' sign with my finger on my lips, telling her not to say anything. Both Abliz and Zunun saw me do this and Abliz quickly approached Malashof and pointed at things to do with work asking questions to distract him, Zunun asked Mr Hadi to go and get some water. I took the opportunity to pull Sajide quickly outside the gate and said, 'Someone has reported the letter to them. Tell them that after you picked up the letter you were so frightened of getting into trouble that you destroyed it without reading it. Tell them that you didn't even tell me about the letter.' I then quickly thanked Abliz and Zunun and returned to work.

As expected, Mr Malashof came over to Sajide and asked her to follow him. They went off to the office. Sajide returned before long with Mr Malashof and two other men. 'Come with us!', Mr Malashof ordered impatiently, 'We are now going to search your room as neither of you are telling the truth.' He then called Mr Hadi to join them. My heart started beating faster with fear. We were going to be in big trouble if they find that letter, as this would implicate a lot of people, especially those who are working in the Security Prison providing secret connections. I had to try and find a way to hide the letter from them. 'Oh, God, please help me!' I prayed silently, desperately in need of consolation. Sajide kept looking at me, her eyes filled with terror. 'What can we do now?' she asked, and I wished I had known the answer.

We reached the dormitory. I opened my suitcase for it to be searched. Mr Hadi started picking up each item of clothing, one piece at a time, groping and feeling to see if there is anything hidden inside it. Mr Malashof and the other two men stood watching nearby. As Hadi removed my underwear from the case, Malashof left the room, perhaps out of embarrassment. Mr Hadi moved on to search the duvet, he removed the cover and, having found nothing, he tossed them aside. 'Have you finished with these?' I asked, pointing at the duvet. 'Yes!' he replied with anger. I picked the duvet off the floor, draped it over my suitcase and started putting it back into its cover. With one hand under the quilt pulling the cover on, I took the opportunity to put my hand quickly into the side pocket of the suitcase where the letter was. I then removed it and quickly placed it inside the quilt cover before folding it up neatly, and placed it amongst the other items, which had already been searched. Sajide was sitting on the edge of the wooden platform at this time looking extremely nervous. I winked at her discreetly. She understood the signal and sat back on the platform looking relieved. They continued to search all our belongings including every corner of the dormitory for over three hours. As the bell rang for the end of the working period they announced that search had been completed and left the room.

The dormitory was in a mess with our belongings scattered everywhere. We quickly tidied up before we went to the toilets. Sajide stood outside while I went in to tear the letter into small pieces and threw them into the toilet. A group of young men had entered the courtyard upon our return from the toilets. Some of them engaged the doorman in conversation, while two other men walked cross the yard to us and asked about the search and if they had got hold of the letter. They told me that they needed to tell Tursun, who was due to be interrogated as well. I reassured them and they immediately left with relief.

20 July 1963

When I returned from work, I saw a man sitting on the woodpile where brother Seley used to sit. He stood up and greeted me, and I returned his greeting.

'I saw you in Public Security Prison, You are Söyüngül, aren't you?'

'Yes, I am', I replied.

'I am Ibray. We were in the same corridor, I was in cell No.8', He said with a smile.

Ibray was between twenty-five and thirty years old, a tall, handsome looking man with big, affectionate brown eyes, thick dark eyebrows and brown wavy hair, which accentuated his pale complexion, which I imagined was the result of him spending a long time in the dark cell. His looks reminded me of my father when he was younger. I remembered his writings while he was in the cell No.3, which made me chuckle.

'Oh, so you are the drunk who turned up at the Public Security Prison and asked them to lock you up!'

'Yes, you become your own worst enemy when faced with disasters. I initially bought a ticket to go home the following day, so my friends invited me that evening to a farewell party, and I drank too much.'

I laughed as I visualised his drunken state, walking unsteadily in front of the Public Security prison, shouting for them to arrest him.

'How did you manage to find the prison in that state?' I asked.

'Don't mention it, I don't think I could have found that place if I was sober, I always wondered how I ended up there. I don't know why my friends left me alone in the street knowing that I was so drunk.' I thought of the Kazakh saying: You die of whatever you're scared of.

He continued, 'I try not to think about things too much. I was really drunk. Apparently I stumbled upon the prison and started banging on the gates, stupidly calling for the guards to come and arrest me. Two of the guards dragged me back to the streets and told me to leave, however I returned to the gates again, shouting and banging on the door. I must have done that at least three times. I even told them to arrest me in Chinese. I had come to Ürümchi with forged documents. My thanks be to God that at that moment of stupidity I didn't reveal any other sensitive information. I am still grateful for that – well, at least I am pleased with myself for that. The following morning, I woke up in a prison cell, at first I thought I was dreaming and shook my head and looked around, and realised that I was indeed in a prison cell. At that point I was utterly shocked. I banged on the door shouting to be let out. A guard opened the food slot and shouted, "What's the matter with you? What are you shouting for?" I asked, "Why did you bring me in here?" He said, "Be quiet! This is a prison, and you will soon find out the reason when you are questioned."

Later I learned that I had told them that I had come to Ürümchi with a forged letter of introduction. Having checked the document, they confirmed it to be forgery. I had one thousand yuan with me, which they confiscated before sentencing me to fifteen months in prison. I was interrogated many times and asked why I had come to Ürümchi using a forged letter of introduction and, on top of that, with so much money. They insisted that I was here for secret arrangements, even considering that I had told them constantly that I was just a simple carpenter who had borrowed money from friends and family to come Ürümchi to buy materials for my carpentry business. Finally I was given a three-year prison sentence and was brought to here today." Sajide arrived at this moment, and Ibray introduced himself and it turned out that they both came from the same area of Chöchek. We sat talking until dinner.

After dinner I went to collect some water. On my way back, I saw an old man performing *wudu*[12] sitting on the woodpile. He was short and slim, and his clothes suggested that he was a native of Kashgar. He stood up to greet me before introducing himself, 'I have just arrived today. They had given me a two-year sentence of which I have served one already in the Security Prison. I am grateful to God that I am now able to see the blue sky in an open space.' I asked him where he is from and why he had received two years. He replied, 'I am from Kashgar and so is my entire family. My daughter married a man from Chöchek, and settled there with their two children. My daughter wrote to me asking me to visit them. I'd missed her so much so I went on the trip. But before I could even arrive at Chöchek, the border incident happened and as you know, many people tried to flee to the Soviet Union. I was arrested by the border police who accused me of trying to escape to the Soviet Union! I insisted that I was on my way to see my daughter and didn't know anything about what was happening. But they refused to believe my story. I was sentenced to two years of Reform Through Labour...'

'Did your daughter flee to the Soviet Union then?' I asked.

'Yes, the whole city became a ghost town. They had left two days before I arrived.

---

12   *Muslim ritual washing before prayer or worship.*

I missed them', he said with eyes filled with melancholy.

'Do you have any other children?' I enquired.

'No, she is my one and only child. Her mother has passed away, so I am alone now', he said sadly.

I suddenly felt as though I knew him. His voice sounded eerily familiar to me. So I asked him, 'Which cell were you in when you were at the Security prison?'

'I was in the first cell of the last block on the right hand side after you had walked through the prison gate. I shared the cell with a Chinese man. He was Chinese, yes, but when I recited the Quran he always said, "I like your voice. Don't worry and continue your prayers." During our time together he even taught me some Chinese.'

It was him! The beautiful voice reciting the Quran when I was in cell No.3! It was such a joy to see the face that was behind such a magnificent voice.

28 July 1963

We were moved from the current building into a small room at the rear of the watershed. It was a cozy room with a cooking stove and fire in the corner. Half of the room had an earth-sleeping platform. Also there was a small desk and a small window from which we could see the courtyard. We liked the room very much as it had a homely feeling. Sunday was the only day that the prisoners were allowed visits from their families, which of course took place in the presence of the prison authorities.

Abliz's older sister Patime visited him today, after which he came to see me straight away. 'Your family sends their love to you', he told me, 'They have applied for permission to visit you many times, but it has always been turned down. They have been informed that you are still under investigation because they have not been able to find members of the organisation you set up and who it's key figures are.'

Two days after moving out of the main building, all the men who had gone to rebuild the riverbanks returned. There were hundreds of them. Sajide and I were now sent to work in the fifth courtyard, where a guard was placed next to the gate to stop anyone from speaking to us. However, prisoners still found ways to come and say hello to us. What amazed us the most was that, among the prisoners accused of attempting to go to Shanghai, there were Chinese youths who would regularly visit and try to help us. Sajide and I found this rather odd and we couldn't understand why they showed so much interest.

4 August 1963
Banished to Xigobi

I was woken up by a sudden noise outside. The girls were still fast asleep. I got up quietly to wash my face before going outside. The sun had already risen quite high and was shining bright, signalling a hot day. Men had gathered in front of the canteen, waiting for breakfast. Some of them were laughing and cracking jokes as others stood watching and laughing. I also noticed that others were busy the every day routine of washing their faces or clothes.

Having observed this early morning ritual with its buzz of activities, I returned to wake the girls for breakfast. Abliz walked in soon after, carrying a *nan* in one hand and a plate of grapes in the other as we were eating.

'My sister Patime visited me today and brought me some *nan* and grapes, I'd like you to share them with me. Take these', he said with a joyful smile on his face. We accepted them gratefully.

'Has she seen my family lately?' I asked.

'Yes, she spoke to your mother. Unfortunately the poor old lady still has not been granted permission to visit you. My sister was not able to say much because the guards were standing near us', he replied. We enjoyed the *nan* and the grapes. This was the first time I had fresh homemade bread since I was arrested.

Abliz came back again before we finished our tea. Normally, men were not allowed to enter our room without permission from the team leaders. Abliz visited us frequently, obviously ignoring this rule.

He looked upset, sat down on the edge of the platform in pensive silence. We were all staring at him, wondering what had happened. Before we asked, he told us why. Mr Hadi had told him that all the girls were soon to be moved to Xigobi, and a truck would come at ten o'clock to collect us. Abliz had been designated to announce the bad news to us and to help us with packing.

This was indeed very bad news. A heavy silence lingered among us until it was broken by the sobbing of Mahinur. The grief on the girls' faces upset Abliz. 'I will be back before you leave', he said, got up and left the room in a hurry. Zohre started crying with Mahinur as Sajide sat silently staring at me.

We heard two knocks on the door, and Mr Hadi walked in with two other men to confirm the fateful transfer. 'The Head Office has decided to send you all to Xigobi Labour Reform Farm. Get all your things together quickly. You will be collected at ten o'clock.' Mahinur and Zohre's faces were awash with tears.

'Guess this is true then. Come on, let's pack.' I stood up and started packing my belongings while hurrying Sajide to do the same. Some men came to the room to help Mahinur and Zohre. We were ready in ten minutes.

We left the room with our belongings and headed towards the first courtyard. Mahinur and Zohre couldn't stop weeping, no matter how hard friends tried to comfort them words of encouragement and support. The truck arrived on time, our friends helped load our bags and bedding onto it. Mahinur and Zohre were still sobbing as they said their goodbyes to everyone. I thought I had to say something to cheer them up.

'Girls, what are you crying for? At least they are not taking us to Mainland China. Xigobi is a part of our motherland. Let's go and see what it looks like. I am certain the people living there are no different than us. It is just like going to another university. Come on now, let's get in. We haven't been on a trip in a long time; let's treat it as a tour and enjoy it. Didn't they say that everything is like a game, except death?' I said jokingly.

'Söyüngül, you are absolutely right. You're a great friend', they said and finally stopped sobbing. We set off.

On the way, everyone on board sat in silence, looking at the scenery as we drove passed the city. When the truck turned in the direction of Wujiachu, one of the men broke the silence.

'Where were you arrested?' he asked.

'At the Medical University', said Sajide.

'Do you happen to know a Kazakh student who was also arrested there?' he pursued his question.

'Do you know where he was taken? Is he in Xigobi now?' Sajide and I asked him simultaneously.

'He was in Xigobi indeed but he didn't work for a year as he pretended to be insane. He ran away in early spring but obviously didn't know where to go and got rearrested and jailed in Liudawan Prison. We were supposed to collect him today and to take him back to Xigobi, but we then received orders to collect you instead. I believe we will deal with him tomorrow…'

'Who are you, actually?' Sajide interrupted as if suddenly reminded to correct a mistake.

'I am Barat, the team leader of the male prisoners in Xigobi', answered the man with a smile.

He then pointed at two Chinese men sitting on the opposite side. 'Those two

escaped from Xigobi, but they were stopped in Zhejiang.[13] We are now taking them
back.' There were two other guards on the vehicle, who kept staring at us throughout
the journey without speaking a word. After travelling over many bumpy old tracks, we
finally arrived in one of the bases of the Chinese Construction Corps[14] at Wujiachu,
where the local residents were mainly Chinese migrants from Mainland China. The
truck stopped and we were ordered to get down on the road. A number of Chinese men
came dressed in grey came and spayed us from top to bottom with some chemicals. They
then also sprayed the truck. Seeing our puzzled faces, Barat explained, 'There is a severe
disease out in the desert; this fumigation is to stop the spread of the disease among you
and others in this area.'

We got back on and continued our journey without further delay. The truck drove
along bumpy winding roads, gradually leaving all greenery behind as we drove deeper
into the desert. At about 1 pm we arrived at Xigobi. We stopped in front of the head
office of the Construction Corps. The men who had travelled with us unloaded our
belongings before leaving with the rest of the male prisoners.

It was extremely hot. This place was so quiet that the only thing you could hear was
the buzzing of the flies. The atmosphere was mercilessly depressing. We were dehydrated
and our parched throats were desperate for water. The four of us looked at one another
in deep shock.

'What a sad place!' said Sajide with a deep sigh.

'It is strange. There is no one around. Where have they all gone? Looks like no one
is going to be overseeing us', Zohre said and sat down on her suitcase.

Mahinur took her water flask out from her bag. She pointed at the running water
from a well in front of a kitchen and said, 'Shall we go and get some water, I am really,
really thirsty.'

We were just about to go to the well when we saw a short slim Chinese woman in
a blue blouse coming in our direction. She had short hair with small beady eyes and a
flat nose. She looked filthy and ugly. She ordered us in Chinese to pick up our suitcases
and follow her.

'Oh, now she is giving us commands. Look at what state she's in', said Zohre coldly
in Uyghur.

13   *A coastal province in southeastern China.*
14   *Xinjiang Shengchan Jianshe Bingtuan, or Xinjiang Production and Construction Corps (XPCC), is
an economic and paramilitary government organisation in Xinjiang. Many see the XPCC as colonies, because it
has administrative authority over several medium-sized cities as well as settlements and farms in Xinjiang. It also
has its own administrative structure, fulfilling governmental functions such as healthcare and education for areas
under its jurisdiction.*

We picked up our suitcases and followed her on a narrow path. We walked past two single-roomed brick buildings and the ruins of some derelict buildings to stop in front of a one-metre high hummock of earth. I wondered if our new home would be one of those brick-built rooms as I wasn't able to see any other sort of buildings around us. She then approached one of the hummocks where there were stairs going down to a door at the bottom. It reminded me of the vegetable storage cellar at home. She pushed the door open. 'Where is she taking us', I asked myself as I followed her, 'Maybe it's a cave house?' As I stepped through the door, a swarm of flies stormed out right in my face. I was lucky to stop them from entering my mouth and nostrils by covering my face with my hands. Inspecting my surroundings, I saw the rough wooden table with at least twenty dirty dishes of what looked like leftover food on them, now turned into an ignoble feast for the flies, which were startled by the opening door and flew away like bees from a hive.

The room was approximately ten metres long with a long wooden platform on one side. The floor was covered with straw. I noticed half-naked women sleeping on the platform and the floor. The room was dark, damp and stuffy, and reeked of sweaty bodies and rotten food. The unbearable odour made me nauseous. The women who were sleeping woke up one after another as we entered. One of them raised her head and shouted angrily, 'Where have you come from? Don't you see we are sleeping?' The others raised their heads, looked at us in sleep-heavy silence before turning aside to catch up with sleep. One of the girls raised her head and asked in a friendly manner, 'Where have you come from? When did you arrive?' She then pointed at the free space in the room, saying, 'You can put your belongings here and over there, too.' Sajide and I had no choice but to put our bedding on the bare floor, as there was no space left on the straw. Mahinur and Zohre spotted a Chinese acquaintance from Qumul, who kindly made some space for them next to her bed.

We went outside after putting all of our things in the allocated space. We sat leaning against a delapidated wall near our dormitory. The Chinese woman who were giving us orders earlier returned, bringing us from the canteen four steamed sorghum buns the size of a baby's fist. We asked her if we could go and get some water to drink. She insisted on bringing the water for us herself. She went down to the room and returned with two filthy cups, we refused to use the cups and asked her to fill Mahinur's flask. We also begged her to fill bucket so that we could wash ourselves. She agreed and took Mahinur and Zohre with her. Soon they returned with the water. We drank and washed, and I felt so much better having washing my hands and face with the fresh cold water.

Then it was silence again. The four of us sat leaning against the wall like strangers lost in a foreign land.

Suddenly, a very pretty teenage Uyghur girl came out from the dormitory next to ours, smiled and went back in. Then another dark-haired and dark-eyed Uyghur girl of similar age walked past and did the same. Then a third girl with light brown hair and fair skin did repeated the kind gesture, followed by a tall, dark-skinned chubby lady who came out from one of the brick rooms and shouted, 'Ma Shuying!' Ma Shuying was the name of the bossy Chinese women who had collected us at our arrival. She said to Ma Shuying, 'It's time for work. Wake all the girls up right now.' She went back into the room pretending not to have seen us. Ma Shuying stood outside the dormitories and blew a whistle. The women came out from the rooms one by one and dragged their feet down the hill behind the accommodation units and disappeared from sight. The three Uyghur girls who had come out of the dormitory earlier appeared once more in front of us. They were followed by a tall and good-looking woman in her forties who looked straight at us with her head held up high as she walked to the team leader's dormitory. She knocked on the door and asked, 'Team Leader, are these new arrivals working today or not?' 'No, they start tomorrow!' was the answer that came from behind the door.

'What a loyal follower of the system and a running dog of the authorities!' mumbled Sajide, visibly offended by how she referred to us.

Zohre looked at her and said, 'I know her. She is Altunxan. She used to work in the Qumul Singing and Dancing Troupe with very famous singers like Aynisa. They travelled to cities like Shanghai and performed for Chiang Kai-shek.[15]

Mahinur interrupted Zohre and said, 'Oh, so she worked with celebrity singers such as Munewwer and Aynisa who now live in Beijing?' And I became curious myself and asked what she was doing here.

Zohre continued, 'There was a man called Séyit who was a hero of the people, perhaps you have heard of him. He was accused of setting up an anti-government organisation in Qumul. Many people in Qumul were arrested under the suspicion of being members of the 'Séyit Organisation'. I heard that Altunhan was also arrested because she was in a relationship with Séyit…'

'So was Altunhan a part of that organisation?' I asked.

'No, the authorities believed that she had a lot of information about Séyit and the organisation, that is what I heard back then. I was surprised to see her here.'

'Isn't she married?' Mahinur asked.

---

15   *Chiang Kai-shek (October 31, 1887 – April 5, 1975) was the President of the Republic of China before the communist takeover and the establishment of the People's Republic of China.*

'She was married, and she has sons old enough to get married. Her husband divorced her after the affair went public. Her sons are living with their father after disowning her.'

'Did the organisation have a lot of members? And how many people were arrested?' asked Sajide.

'I think it attracted a large number of people because afterwards, countless people were arrested. I also heard that Séyit was locked in a metal cage with his hands and feet chained to the roof and the floor when he was transported to Ürümchi', Zohre explained.

At this moment, we heard a voice calling from behind us. We turned around saw a woman waving at us. 'Come on now, get down here, all of you', she shouted impatiently. We followed her order. She led us to one of the brick rooms that served as an office. There was a table with two chairs in the middle of the room and light sieved through from a small window on the wall. All four of us stood in a line near the wall facing her. She introduced herself, 'I am the team leader of the female workers of this farm. My name is Gülnisa. I am responsible for everything. If you have any queries or problems, come and speak to me.' Then she opened a drawer and took out some forms and started to fill them in with our information. When it was my turn, she looked at me and asked, 'Are you Russian?' I answered, 'No, Team Leader, I am not. I am a Tatar.' 'You are lying. You look like a Russian to me. I know what Russians look like so stop lying to me', she said, full of confidence.

All four of us burst out laughing. Sajide said, 'Team Leader, she is a Tatar, honestly.' Gülnisa gave her a threatening stare and continued with the bureaucracy. After completing all the documents, she said, 'We've never had such highly educated women like yourselves since this place was built. It is also the first time any Tatar has been sent here. I want you to be model prisoners for the others to look up to. Prisoners in Xigobi are convicted criminals. They are thieves, burglars, prostitutes, hooligans, gamblers, drug addicts and drug dealers. We have to use corrective methods appropriate and relevant to their behavior, otherwise we cannot control them. You will start to understand this when you have lived among them for a while. If you have any valuables, don't keep them in the dormitory, they will be safer if kept in the storage room. If you want, you can go and get the things you don't need right now and we can place them in the storage.'

We sorted out the items we did not need and took them to the storage. By the time we had finished and returned to the dormitory the other women were returning from the fields. As we started to settle down in the dormitory, Altunxan arrived and asked us to go to dinner. We went outside and found that the floor had been cleaned, and a large blanket had been spread out across it; a long duvet had been placed along the edges for us to sit on. A colourful tablecloth was placed in the middle of the blanket with the food laid out on the top of it. There were steamed sorghum buns and some vegetable soup next to bowls of different sizes filled with hot water. They had put dried horse manure on metal plates and placed them on the four corners outside the sitting area, and had lit them to create a smell and smoke to repel the flies and mosquitoes, making the area more comfortable and pleasant for the consumption of food.

As usual, we started with a cup of tea and took the opportunity to introduce ourselves. We soon learned that that there were four Uyghur women in this Labour camp. Altunxan and a lady named Tilaxan, both from Qumul; there was a young teenage girl called Xasiyet, who looked about sixteen years old. Xasiyet started to tell us about her past timidly.

'When I was fifteen years old, I went to town with my neighbour for shopping. While we were there my neighbour said that she needed to see someone and asked me to accompany her. We went to a house and I was asked to remain outside while she went in. She came out afterwards with a young man who was a truck driver and asked me to join them for a ride in the truck. I agreed and we drove off. We stopped outside a bakery where my neighbour got out to buy some *nan*. We waited in the truck for quite a while but she didn't return. The driver asked me to stay in while he went to look for her. After a while he returned, but my neighbour was nowhere to be seen. I started crying as I was very frightened at being left alone with a strange man. He promised to take me. I was naïve and believed that he meant it. After a while, I realised that we where no longer in the town, but in a deserted area. I started crying hysterically and shouted and screamed for him to stop and let me out. He ignored my pleas as we left my beloved hometown Kucha behind.

We travelled long and hard over a few days during which I was raped again and again. When we finally arrived in Ürümchi, we stopped at a restaurant to eat, he finished his food quickly and left the restaurant. I was too frightened to leave, so I sat there till it was closing time. The owner asked me to leave and I tried to explain what had happened. He said, "He won't come back to get you. That kind of men are all the same. They get what they want then abandon you." He closed the restaurant and left, leaving me crying outside. It was getting dark and cold as a middle-aged man with a long mustache walked pass me. he stopped to turn around to look at me. After a while he approached me and asked why I was crying. I told him what happened to me and he asked me to go with him. He took me to a hotel where he got me a room and stayed with me before leaving the next morning. I was left on the street without a penny. I had tried to find work to survive but there wasn't anything available. In the end I had no choice but to start doing things against my will in order to survive. To be honest, I feel I am better off staying here, at least I am in peace…'

As the conversation turn into a dead silence, we all felt deeply sorry for her ill fate and cursed the men who had destroyed such a beautiful young girl.

I broke the silence and asked, 'Do people get beaten up here?'

Altunxan paused for a moment and said with a sad look in her eyes, 'The government's policy is written beautifully on paper, but the reality is not so beautiful. From team leaders to the most ordinary cadres, they all beat prisoners and no one is allowed to say anything against them. They use wooden sticks and thick ropes to beat the prisoners until they collapse unconscious. If you are unwell they won't allow you to stay behind in the dormitory and rest. If you refuse to work, they tie your hands and feet with rope and drag you into the fields, leaving you on the ground regardless of whether it is burning hot or freezing cold…'

'Really? Have any women actually received such treatment?' I asked, shocked but unsure if I should even be shocked.

'I haven't seen any women falling ill since I arrived here, but I have witnessed men being beaten and dragged to the fields.'

Zeynep joined in and said, 'We have seen it too, we were called to a big meeting recently where we were threatened that if we did not obey the rules, we would be beaten. Also if we try to escape we would be shot. They said, "We have one solution for those of you who try to escape: it is a bullet to the heart that will finish you immediately." We later heard of a man who did try to escape, when he was told to stop, he didn't, they shot him there and then.'

All the girls spoke one after another about the brutality of the camp and what they had witnessed. They spoke of a small dark cellar three or four metres deep underground in the camp where anyone who broke the rules would be locked up after being tortured. It was also reported during the meeting that a man who had escaped was attacked and eaten by wild dogs. So there is no way out as no one can escape to safety.

The mosquitoes continued stinging us, but we didn't want to end the conversation. The team leader suddenly appeared on the narrow road, shouting, 'Why are you still sitting there and not studying? Go back inside now! Altunxan, I want you to be a group leader for the new comers and, Söyüngül you will be in charge of political studies. Get on with it now!' She then went and told two Chinese girls to move to the dormitory next door so that Altunxan and Zeynep could be with us in our dormitory. We started our political studies lesson as we were told, but soon changed to our previous conversation.

I was looking forward to a relaxing sleep on the clean bed sheets in the new dormitory, even though the floor was hard. But as soon as I dozed off, I was suddenly woken up by an unbearable itch. I opened my eyes and saw Sajide sitting up. 'Söyün, look at this!' she screamed with disgust. I took a look and saw her white sheets covered in blood spots with fleas jumping everywhere, I then looked at my body and was horrified to see it dotted with red spots. We picked up our sheets and shook off the fleas as best as we could before going outside to sleep.

As we spread our sheets, Ma Shuying, who was on-duty that night, came and told us sternly that no one was allowed to sleep outside. We told her about the fleas, but she insisted that we should back inside the room. We ignored her. It was fresh and pleasant outside in the beautiful moonshine. In frustration, Ma Shuying told Altunxan angrily that we had refused her orders, and that she should do something. We hid our heads under the covers and heard Altunxan saying, 'Those girls just came from the university and don't understand the rules here very well yet. Just keep an eye on them and make sure they don't run away. I will deal with them tomorrow.' Relieved and pleased, we let out a muffled chuckle. The joy didn't last long, however, for the mosquitoes started attacking us just as we were falling asleep, and they were large and many. They always said that the mosquitos in Xigobi could carry steamed dumplings, and to our dismay, that was not an exaggeration – they were biting me through the blanket. It was so bad we had no choice but to return to the room and didn't fall asleep until after sunrise.

I was once again woken up by loud footsteps as people came in and out of the room. 'What should we do?' I heard them saying, 'They are going to kill him!' I woke up. Disoriented and weary, I couldn't figure out where I was for a few seconds. 'What's happening?' I asked, concerned, 'Why are you all running in and out?' Zeynep rushed into the room and said in distress, 'They are beating a young man very badly in the tomato field.' Then she ran out again.

Listening carefully I heard the heart-wrenching pleas of the man, 'Oh God, help me!' His cries for mercy chilled my blood. I got out of bed, walked outside and looked towards the field, which was not far from our room. I saw a man hanging from a tree by his wrists. Two Chinese men were beating him ruthlessly with thick wooden sticks. After a while the man stopped screaming, but the beating continued. I couldn't bear the sight of such an atrocity, so I turned around and returned to the room. I heard the Chinese girls cursing with rage, 'Beasts! How can they beat someone to death over one tomato? Evil, heartless, inhuman murderers!' I could not hold back my feelings and was anxious to know what was happening, so I went back outside. I noticed that they had already taken him down from the tree and laid his motionless body on the floor. Just before we went to work they dragged him by his arms and took him to one of the men's rooms.

I felt sick. Not just because I had barely slept last night, but also because I had to wake up to such a bloody scene in the morning. Before I could recover from the shock, we were ordered to go out to pull out the rampant weeds in the turnip fields. Each of us was allocated three large areas of a field and mine was at the far end. I always enjoyed how my mind would drift far away and think about all sorts of things during work, so that time could past quickly. After finishing my tasks, I looked around to see what the others were doing. I saw Mahinur, Zohre, and Sajide sitting closely talking. I walked up to them to listen to their conversation with curiosity. As soon as they saw me, they welcomed me to sit down next to them, telling me that they were planning something 'important'.

'Sounds good, what is it?' I said as I sat down.

They looked at one another and had on their faces a smile of enthusiasm with a hint of secretiveness.

'Hey, what's happened to you all? You all look you are excited. I hope this is going to be something good.'

'Well, we are making big plans. Do you want to know more?'

'But of course', I said impatiently.

'We are planning to escape from here', Sajide replied solemnly.

'Well, thank God I arrived on time then! I wouldn't have the opportunity to say goodbye to you all otherwise!' I said jokingly.

'Oh come on! As if we'd escape without you!'

'Even if you did, I'd risk my life to run after you. So don't ever try to get rid of me!' I laughed.

'Great! So if you all agree, I will cover all costs for us all, you don't need to worry about that', said Zohre with a shy smile - she was holding her chin with her thumb and fingers and looked almost embarrassed as she made this promise.

'Where can we go, though?' I turned serious, 'You know there are communists everywhere. If they catch us, we will be handed back to prison again, and then God knows what will happen. I don't think there's any safe place for us. Perhaps we are better off giving up such silly ideas…'

Sajide, who was sitting with her hands on her knees, moved closer to me and said, 'Söyün, what happened this morning is torturing me. I'm still burning with anger. I want to go to the Public Security Bureau to report what had happened. "Oh, we have the best systems in place compared to all others around the world" they always say, don't they? And how about "We educate and reform people's thoughts and don't resort to any sort of physical violence." Pah! Their "best system" just killed someone for stealing a tomato grown by his own hands, and you saw that! I'd rather die than stay in this "best system"!'

Zohre stood up with a determined look on her face, 'Sajide, why should we go to the Public Security Bureau? We can escape to Mainland China and stay there for a few years until our prison sentence has expired. They cannot arrest us after that, can they?'

Mahinur agreed with her, but we had doubts. I said, 'How could we survive in Mainland China without *hukou*[16] or a job? We will only ruin our lives further there. No, we can't go there.'

'We must escape from here to Ürümchi, and then we can go our separate ways. No matter what happens, Söyün and I would try to find a way to report the officials here who are mistreating people against party policy. Party policy does not condone such acts, and I'm pretty sure what these people are doing is illegal', said Sajide.

'Don't be so naïve. The reason these officials dare beat and kill is that they have the blessing from higher authorities, we will not achieve anything by reporting them to the Public Security Bureau because they are all there together against us', I objected. However, Sajide still insisted that something should be done with an ideological justification, 'I am sure there is no such policy which allows anyone to be murdered for stealing a tomato. This is fascist behaviour in a socialist system, and it's our duty to report it.'

In the end I said, 'Look, I don't want to be separated from you all, my life will be hell if you all run away and I am left behind. I know people should experience all different kinds of situations during their life. So let's try to escape and, if we succeed, then we will go straight to the Public Security Bureau and hear what they have to say. They may even be surprised and say, "We thought we got rid of you so why have you come back?"' We all laughed. The four of us carried on discussing our plans to escape,

---

16   *In China, the hukou, or family registration system dictates that citizens with a rural registration must obtain residence permits if they wish to live in the city.*

and decided as a first step to save some food everyday for the journey ahead and to pick which valuables to bring with us. We were all very excited with the thought of escaping.

As soon as we had finished our work, the weather changed, and dark clouds covered the sky bringing a sudden downpour of rain punctured by lightning and swayed by strong gusts of wind. We ran to our room before we were soaked. Two girls from each dormitory went to get dinner while the rest of us started putting ash and earth on the mounds of earth that covered our rooms to prevent the rain from soaking through. We also blocked the surrounding areas to stop the water running down the steps into the rooms. We worked as fast as we could, but the rain fell so heavily we could not finish the job. We abandoned what we were doing and ran into our rooms. After we finished dinner we had political studies. Finally, having completed the things that needed to be done for the day, we were able to lie down and rest. But water started to run in at the corner of the room where we were lying. 'My dear Sajide', I said jokingly, 'looks like Xigobi is welcoming us its own special way.' We quickly got up and rolled up our bedding just in time to stop it getting wet, and found a tiny space on the raised wooden platform where all the other girls were sleeping. With no room to lie down, we resigned to sitting there all night. The rain did not stop for four days, and the room was flooded. We had to use buckets to bail it out.

On the fourth day, Altunxan came to inform us that the river had burst its banks and, despite the hard work for the past four days, the male inmates had not managed to stop the flooding. 'They need more assistance, so we will leave at three in the morning, you must get yourself ready tonight', she said before leaving.

When we were left alone again, Zohre said, 'The best opportunity to escape is tomorrow after we finish work. We should try to stay behind and make a run for it if we can." We packed our suitcases and put the *nan* in a separate bag. We got up at midnight, ate some food in a hurry, and started our journey in darkness. A Chinese team leader plus four armed soldiers on horsebacks escorted us as we walked along the riverbanks passing through the edge of the fields. The road was extremely muddy and slippery. We had to walk barefoot as we didn't have the right shoes for these situations. In some places, the mud even went up to our knees; in others, where the wheat had been freshly cut, the sharp stems made our feet bleed. At the same time the soldiers kept rushing us, shouting impatiently as if they were herding kattle. We arrived in the work area just after eight o'clock.

The whole area was surrounded by armed soldiers. Hundreds of people were working in the river with water up to their waist. When we arrived, they stopped working to look in our direction, only to be told off harshly by the guards, some of whom took the opportunity to whip the workers every time they stopped to look. Then, out of nowhere, we were surrounded by policemen, shouting and pointing in the direction we should go, as if there was an imminent catastrophe. Our felt our feet cut badly by various sharp objects hidden in the mud, and didn't have time to stop and check our wounds.

We were taken into a wooded area to collect wood that had been cut back to the river. Sajide and I walked carefully up the hill towards the piles of cut wood. Men who were cutting down bushes raised their heads to look at us as we passed by. Suddenly I noticed a very familiar face and stood frozen for a second.

'Oh my God…' I murmured in disbelief.

'It is Zeynalov', said Sajide quietly.

He recognized us immediately. 'Söyün! Sajide! What are you doing in this hellhole? You don't deserve to be here!' he said with tears overflowing in his eyes. People around him also showed us their sympathy as much as we felt the same way for them. Then a white-haired, long-bearded old man who had been working next to Zeynalov said with a trembling voice, 'Oh my girls, may God give you strength! You are far too young have to suffer like this!' He then burst into tears.

The guards started shouting at us, urging us to work faster and the men warned us to be careful or we might get beaten. They then stopped speaking and carried on cutting the bushes as fast as they could. We picked up the wood and carried it to the side of the river. We worked all day without rest. At about four o'clock, we started our journey back.

Mahinur, Zohre, Sajide, and I walked on slowly at the rear of the group, hoping to find an opportunity to escape, but it never came, as two armed soldiers walked behind us throughout the journey. After hours of walking we arrived at a reservoir. It was at least one kilometre round which was surrounded by clumps of bamboo. There were wild ducks and swans swimming around. The water was clear and transparent, you could see fish swimming at the bottom while above flew beautiful multi-coloured birds. Every time a flock of birds arrived, another would fly away.

As we sat by the water wearily the mosquitoes came to irritate us, they were many of them and yet we were thankful for being a part of the beautiful natural surroundings and able to forget the harsh reality of life at this moment in time. All of this was constantly broken by the ruthless cracking of the guards' whips and their vehement shouting, 'Get up and start walking! Now!'

On reaching our dormitory we washed and ate before our political studies class. As we were ready to go to bed, Sajide and Zorhe said, 'We must leave tonight after everyone has fallen asleep. We must also check the Chinese women who is on duty is asleep before we quietly make our escape.'

I was in deep sleep when Sajide suddenly woke me up and whispered, 'Zohre has gone outside to check if the woman is asleep. If she is we need to leave right now.' Zohre returned just before Sajide could finish her words. She walked in carefully but mistakenly squeezed Altunxan's foot and said, 'Hey, Ma Shuying is sleeping. Quick!'

Altunxan jumped up quickly from her bed and said suspiciously, 'Sorry? What's happened?'

Realising that she had made a mistake, Zohre replied nervously, 'Oh, um, I wanted to go to the toilet but I am scared.'

'Ma Shuying is outside. You should have asked her to company you and not me!' said Altunxan, obviously unimpressed.

Then she walked outside with Zohre and shouted at Ma Shuying, 'Hey, wake up! You are supposed to be watching, not sleeping! If something happens you will be the first to be held responsible!' The three of us couldn't stop ourselves from laughing. After Zohre came back with Altunxan she lay down next to Sajide and said, 'I thought I touched Söyüngül's feet!' and started laughing uncontrollably. Despite the failed attempt at escape, the four of us laughed so much that it took us a while before we could go back to sleep.

11 August 1963
Sajide beaten up by Wang

We worked in the vegetable field all this morning. Then, in the afternoon, we were moved to the wheat field behind the horse shed. Our task was to separate the wheat grains from the hay. We were given some wooden tools like garden forks. I had never threshed wheat before and didn't have a clue about what to do. So I started mixing the straw with the fork from the top to the bottom. One of the Chinese supervisors rushed towards me, swearing, pointing at my nose, and acting as if he was going to hit me. 'You stupid bitch! What the hell are you doing? Who told you to mix the straw with the grain?!' I was embarrassed, ashamed and above all, angry - I had never been treated by anyone in this a way in my life.

Sajide, who was next to me, could no longer bear to see his behaviour and stepped in, 'What's your problem? We've never seen wheat threshing done in our lives, and it is *your* job to teach us what do to first. If we don't follow your instructions *then* you can come and tell us off!'

The Chinese girls who were working with us looked shocked, perhaps by Sajide's courage, and perhaps fearing the consequences of such courage. They begged her to stop confronting the supervisor, who was fuming at her words.

'You should be glad that I haven't hit you already!' said the supervisor with a threatening stare.

Intrepid, Sajide continued her speech, 'The Party's policy clearly states that "the purpose of our job is to reform through education and labour, and no one should be subject to physical abuse." I'm sure you know the Party's policy very well, so tell me which party policy justifies your actions at the moment? Furthermore...'

Before Sajide could finish her words, he stepped up and gave her a slap so loud and hard that she staggered backwards and nearly lost her balance, if I hadn't rushed over to grab her. I was so sad and hurt that I wished it had been me who had been beaten. Tears tumbled from my eyes. I held her tight and stroked her beautiful cheek, which was angrily red with the imprint of five fingers.

Sajide didn't utter a word. After a few moments, she stood up and walked away towards the head office in defiant silence. The Chinese girls came to my side and said, 'Söyün, come back and get on with your work. No one dares to question his authority as he always beats people with a big stick until they cannot move. You are lucky he didn't treat you the same way because you are university students. All of these people in charge are the same, the head of the farm unit instructs them to beat anyone who disobeys their orders. What could we possibly do?' I listened to their warning and went back to work, anxiously awaiting Sajide's return. Then after an hour, she came back, looking terribly upset and depressed.

'What happened? Did you speak to anyone?' I asked.

'The water is polluted from its source. They are corrupt to the core. I am too naïve', she replied coldly.

The cadres kept checking on us to see if anybody was eating the wheat grains. Later the male inmates joined us after retuning from the threshing fields. They told us that a week ago one man died of eating too much grain. The truth is that all of us were constantly tired from the workload and from not having enough to eat. Many men who could not cope with huger stole grain to eat without cooking it. The man in question therefore developed indigestion problems. When the cadres found out the cause of his condition they refused to take him to the hospital and his condition worsened. He passed away as a result. A meeting was then organised for all the prisoners in the farmyard, where the deceased was criticised for being greedy, and everyone was warned against stealing food, the punishment for which, as we were told, would be severe.

One hour before we finished work a truck appeared in the distance throwing up thick clouds of dust, which mercilessly reminded me of the meaning of the name Xigobi, 'The Western Desert', where the whole area was a flat and barren wilderness under the majestic stature of the Heavenly Mountains in the distance. The head office of the Labour Reform Farm was built of mud bricks and painted white. On the courtyard there stood a horse shed, a small canteen at the front, and a larger one for the party cadres close to the office block with a well in the middle of the yard providing water for everyone, including the livestock and irrigation for the vegetable fields. It was the only source of water in the area. The accommodation for male inmates was located inside the adjacent courtyard with only one gate for both entry and exit. Inside there were approximately twenty rooms in a circle. Xigobi, with its harsh environmental conditions, was one of the most miserable places on God's earth to live in.

A truck drove in our direction, which caught the attention of the prisoners' soulless eyes. As it came closer I noticed that it was fully loaded with people. It drove past us to stop in front of our dormitory, discharging a number of women.

We were taken back to the dormitory earlier than usual. The women who had arrived earlier were talking loudly amongst themselves as they stood outside the dormitories holding onto their belongings and looking around confused. They stopped talking to stare at us as we walked passed them to our dormitory, and then their chitchat resumed. From their body language it was clear that they were talking about us. The team leader entered our dormitory ordering Altunxan, Sajide and I to remain while the rest of the girls were moved next door. She told the three of us to be in charge of settling in the new comers and of the political studies. After our roommates moved out, Sajide, Altunxan and I rearranged the room. We placed the wooden boards on both sides of the room, leaving walking space in the middle, we replaced old straw with new straw, which we spread over the wood. The new girls finished their dinner as we finished preparing the room for them. The team leader then brought them to the room, told us that there was no political study that evening and left.

We started introducing ourselves when I noticed that some of the women didn't have any belongings. 'Where are your bedding and clothes?' we asked, 'Didn't you bring anything with you?'

'We were arrested in the street and we didn't have anything with us.'

'Didn't your family bring your things to you?' we were curious.

'They don't know where we are, and even if they did they wouldn't be able to bring anything for us. We are not from Ürümchi. We are from the southern part of Xinjiang.'

Suddenly one of the women lying at the far end of the room started swearing, using the most foul words possible. She was a large and an angry looking woman in her fifties. We were all in a state of shock, wondering who she was cursing at and why. Then a girl in her twenties sitting opposite us cursed back and started pointing at her. I found it difficult to listen to such disgusting language and to see such rude gestures. Feeling uncomfortable, I left the room as quickly as I could and sat against the wall opposite the dormitory. Sajide followed me and sat next to me and said, 'Söyün, how are we going to get through the months and years to come with people like these? What part of society have they come from?' Before she could finish speaking we heard loud screams coming from the dormitory, we went back inside to see what was happening.

They had started fighting, the dust in the air spread by the flying straw made the room look even darker. The guards who were patrolling the area heard the screaming and ran into the dormitory, the team leader also rushed in as the guards handcuffed the two of them and dragged them outside. The young women's eyes were red and swollen and barely open. Her hair was all over the place and her dress was torn. The older women's face and clothes were covered in blood from a deep wound on the top of her head. Her clothes were so badly damaged that her breasts were exposed. They continued shouting insults at each other regardless. We left the room for a while for the dust to settle and things to calm down, and upon our return, we could hardly recognise our room. Our bed sheets had been trampled on and where covered in footprints. There was broken crockery everywhere. It took us quite a while to clean up the mess and tidy up our sleeping area. The team leader entered the room to denounce the women's behaviour. Once again repeating the same rules and regulations, she warned everyone not to start fights, and informed us all of various methods of punishment for the perpetrators. In the end she said, 'Those two women will spend the night in the dungeon where they can fight all night long until they've had enough.'

As it was time to rest and go to bed, we gave some of our blankets and quilts to those who didn't have anything, three to four of the girls had to share the same bedding.

The fleas were a pain as usual and would not let me sleep in peace. I didn't rest fully until after midnight, only to be waken soon after by loud screaming and swearing.

'Oh what now!' I grumbled.

'I don't understand these people. Haven't they had enough fighting?' Sajide said angrily.

I shouted, 'Hey girls, go outside and fight if you have to. Leave the others in peace, will you?'

A woman in her forties stood up, she was medium height with eyes that kept moving spontaneously. She shouted back at me furiously, 'Shut up bitch! Go back to bed and mind you own fucking business!' I was stunned by her rudeness and sat on my bed as my head started spinning. Holding the collar of my pajamas tightly, I mumbled, 'Oh God, what on earth is going on?'

'Now, if you don't stay quiet, I will make you confess more!' she wouldn't leave me alone.

A girl lying opposite me said, 'Stay quiet and don't worry. She's a mad woman don't let her bother you.'

The mad woman then walked furiously passed everyone to jump on top of the girl who had spoken to me and started beating her. The woman next to her stood up to drag the mad women off the girl and started beating her, and other women joined. Altunxan went to push all the women out of the way and helped the mad woman up from the floor. Although she was bruised and bleeding, she didn't want to stop fighting and was about to run towards the other women when the team leader rushed in shouting, 'What the hell is going on?' The mad woman wiped the blood all over her face saying, 'These women ganged up against me and beat me up', as she pretended to sob.

One of the women who had not been involved in the fight spoke out, 'Team Leader, please allow me to explain to you exactly what has happened. We were all sleeping when Nuriye and Tajisa disturbed us by starting a fight.' She explained things from start to finish in great detail. The team leader called the six girls who were involved in the fight to her office for further investigation, from which they didn't return until breakfast time. As we finished eating, the two women who had been locked in the underground cellar came back. They were now holding hands and smiling as they walked towards us. I found this strange, having witnessed their aggressive fight of the night before. It seemed that they had put everything behind them, as they stood smiling like they had just returned from the theatre after watching the most amazing play.

'What a joke!' said Sajide, 'They don't seem to take anything seriously.'

'I know. Just look at them. They are behaving like heroes returning victoriously from a war', I concurred.

I felt more tired today than usual. After work I freshened myself up before changing my clothes for dinner. The others had already laid the food out and poured celery soup soup into everyone's bowl. I collected my bowl along with a portion of steam bread and was ready to leave when I heard Ayshe Mahmut complaining angrily while picking up her bowl. 'Everyone here is discriminating against me. I have been given less soup than everyone else!' she whined. I glanced at her bowl and saw it was indeed not as full as the rest of us. She carried her soup and walked towards the dormitory when she suddenly collapsed on the floor just before the doorstep. I noticed that she was shaking uncontrollably with white saliva coming from her mouth. Her hands and legs were clinching together as she rolled over the floor. It frightened all the women and they kept their distance from her. I ran over to her to hold her hands tightly, pressing them hard against the floor. Ayshe was a tall and chubby woman. As I struggled to hold her, she managed to loosen one of her hands and hit me hard. I fell over onto my back. Sajide hurried over to help, as the other women stood their ground saying one after another in horror, 'Don't touch her, she will infect you with the disease that she has!' The two of us held her as tight as we could, I pressed her upper lip hard with my finger, and minutes later she started breathing normally again as her body relaxed. She opened her eyes and started moving weakly, we helped her stand up, and she walked away slowly to the room alone. Sajide and I were exhausted as if we had just come out of a wrestling competition. It was the first time I had caught someone having a seizure.

Before we went to bed, Zohre came over to ask quietly, 'Shall we go tonight if there is an opportunity?'

'No, Zohre, we are not going. Even if we go to Beijing to make a complaint it will not make any difference. They are all the same. The policies are only fair on paper but not in reality. If you want to go, then go ahead. We are not going to have this conversation again', Sajide said firmly.

'I will only go if you are going. Otherwise I wouldn't dare. I would be scared to run alone…' said Zohre, her voice full of disappointment and frustration.

It seemed that we'd made the right choice. Two days later the team leader asked to see me in her office after dinner. Unable to guess any reason for this, I was nervous the whole time during dinner, and hurried to her office immediately after eating.

'Why did you want to see me?' I asked her directly as I sat down.

'There are a number of issues that have come to my attention which I want to talk to you about', she said in an ominously flat tone, while I sat looking at her with questions in my eyes.

'I have heard that you made plans to run away', she continued, 'Is this true?'

'Team Leader, where would we have run away to?' I said calmly, trying my best not to show any signs of being under immense stress, 'party members are everywhere and there is no place for us to hide or run to. No, I never considered anything of the sort.'

'Ha! You are lying again. People have informed me of your plans', she said threateningly.

'No, no, Team Leader! Please don't believe these rumours as they are not true. Why are you convinced that I'm lying but not those who spread rumours? How is it possible to escape from here? Where would we go? We don't have any money, we are not thieves so will never steal money. We are good girls who don't swear or fight with people, as you have witnessed. We are here for reeducation and will never try to bring trouble to you!' I said confidently.

She sat quietly for a few terrifying seconds before saying, 'I didn't believe what I had heard anyway, and that's why I decided to speak to you alone. Don't ever think about such stupid ideas of escape or follow other peoples idiotic ideas.' She paused for a bit and changed the topic, 'Have there been any major changes since you arrived here?'

Not knowing exactly what she meant, I replied without directly answering her question, 'To tell you the truth, I find it very difficult to accept some things in this camp. Human beings should always be treated with respect, and it is with kind words that one can truly reeducate people. Don't you think so? People are being beaten so often here and it's affecting me deeply. In our course books we learned that only in fascist capitalist countries can people be treated unfairly, unequally, and their human rights are often violated as they are abused physically. However, in a communist society like ours all human beings are meant to be equal. I regret to say that I feel that sometimes, this place looks similar to a fascist regime. And I wonder why that is…'

The team leader looked at me, half surprised. 'What you are saying is absolutely correct. However, having just come from the university, you don't understand the reality of life. The reality of life is that you can't control these criminals if you don't handle them with a heavy hand. I hope you will begin to understand it slowly', she paused for a while before letting me go, saying, 'Don't think too much about these things. Just concentrate on working hard.'

I went back to the dormitory and explained to Sajide what had happened.

'Unbelievable', she commented, 'Only Mahinur and Zohre knew of our plans, perhaps one of them informed her? I can't believe this!'

'I don't think they would do that', I said in defence of my friends, 'Maybe it was Altunxan? You know Zohre woke her up that night by mistake, may be she suspected something and told the team leader.'

And we both made a decision that in the future we would trust no one and be very careful in what we say or do.

Mahinur's Trick

A week after the new prisoners arrived, our dormitories were reorganised, with some of the Uyghur women and Chinese women now split between the two dormitories. Sajide and I were allocated to Dormitory 2. Sajide was appointed as work supervisor along with Altuxhan, who was appointed assistant supervisor. My duty was to be the supervisor for political studies class that took place every evening, where I would read article from newspapers and journals to the group. I was happy for Sajide, because she was not a physically strong person, and her emotional state had deteriorated since arriving at Xigobi. I was under the impression that by managing other people's work at which she was very good, she would be able to lift her spirits and have hope for the future. The majority of women were pleased with the decision of Sajide being their work supervisor. However, some disagreed: Mahinur and Zohre, who we had considered to be friends, didn't look happy at all.

After the evening study session, I was leaving the room to return reading materials to the team leader, when Sadet, Helchem, and Mahinur came in. Sadet and Helchem asked Sajide to go outside for a few minutes. When I returned to the room Sajide was already in bed and I was about to get into bed myself when Asiye entered the room, shouting, 'Sadet and Helchem had run away!'

I was shocked and looked at Sajide, who looked at me, concerned and wary, 'They were standing outside the door earlier on. How is it possible for them to run away?!' She got up and went outside. Then Mahinur walked in with a group of women behind her as soon as Sajide left the room and shouted, 'It was Sajide! Sajide told them to run away!' I looked at her in disbelief: I suspected that Mahinur, in a fit of jealousy, set up the whole scenario in order to have Sajide replaced by herself.

The two girls were brought back within less than five minutes. I later heard that they were taken to the team leader's office. About fifteen minutes later they entered the room smiling, and got into their beds saying, 'Sajide told us to run away.' It felt like someone had poured boiling water over my head. I turned looked at Sajide who was in a state of shock with her mouth half open. She sat up in bed and asked angrily, 'What are you talking about? Why would I want you to run away? In what way would

I have benefited from it? You should take responsibility for your own actions. Don't make false accusations against me!' The team leader walked in before Sajide had finished reproaching the girls and asked her to come to the office. The situation angered me as I found it difficult to understand how people could make up lies so blatantly and shamelessly to benefit themselves while hurting others.

Sajide returned one hour later coming to sat next to me with tears rolling down her cheeks, 'I can't believe this… They have blamed me for their own failures and for something that I have not played a part in! I can't believe this!'

'Did they mention anything to you about escaping?' I asked.

'Oh! So *you* also have doubts about me now!' she stared at me furiously.

'No, no, Sajide, please don't get upset with me!' I hugged her tightly, 'how would I ever suspect you? It's Mahinur that's behind all this. She wanted your position so she is doing this in order to discredit you.' It hurt me to say these words about a friend, and it hurt me more to realise that perhaps this 'friend' is no longer one. 'Listen to me, my dear sister', I continued in tears, 'don't take it too seriously, because for us there is more evil than good in this place. We have to remain strong and not let these people destroy us!'

We didn't sleep that night, tossing and turning anxiously in bed. Mahinur woke everyone at sunrise and proactively organised everything. She visited the team leader a few times before giving instructions. She called us out of our rooms telling us to go to our work place. Mahinur returned to the dormitory soon after we started working, and almost immediately, one of the Chinese officials named Luo Ganshi summoned Sajide to the head office. Sajide returned to the dormitory only at lunchtime, looking angry and distressed. She had been interrogated about instigating people to break the prison rules. She went to bed early with an empty stomach, complaining of a persistent headache. She was restless that night, mumbling in her sleep condemning the Communist Party and it's officials.

I watched over her all night, as I was worried that she might get into more trouble if someone reported the contents of her sleep talking. Her temperature rose after midnight and she was red as if on fire. At sunrise I rushed out to find doctor Li, who was also a prisoner but now living in a small room behind the team leader's accommodation. I spoke to him about Sajide's situation. He accompanied me to the dormitory and examined her. Sajide's temperature was now 40.5 degrees. The doctor immediately went to the team leader's room to explain how ill she was and that he needed to prescribe some medicine for her.

Upon my return from work, Sajide was still lying in bed with a high temperature. I went to see the doctor again who followed me to the room and gave Sajide an injection. She was unable to eat but did drink a little water.

As expected, Mahinur was appointed as work supervisor on that day by the head office. She didn't try to hide her happiness and laughed joyfully all day. She made herself look superior to all others as she bossed everyone around often ordering me to do things for her. It still puzzled me why she went to such lengths to make Sajide suffer so much. The Mahinur we knew was dead and had transformed into this a soulless and petty creature without any sense of morality, having sold her conscience to satisfy her greed for power.

A Chinese girl and myself were ordered to water the vegetables. We worked non-stop from midnight to midday: we had to carry a lamp in one hand while walking along the water channels to open and close the sluice gates to ensure that the field was not overwatered and, at the same time, guarantee that the vegetables had all the water they required.

I came back to the dormitory after our shift, exhausted and famished. Sajide was lying in bed in a miserable state. She had no strength to get out of bed; I helped her sit up and drink some water before pulling her up slowly to take her to the toilet. She remained in that state for fifteen days with a persistent high temperature. I was worried that she might lose her life. Mahinur and Zohre, on the other hand, never enquired about her condition. I wasn't too bothered by Zohre, thinking that after all, she had lost her way at a young age was still very naïve. It was Mahinur that I could not be more angry and disappointed with. She had betrayed our friendship and torn my heart into pieces by treating Sajide with such cruelty. I visited the doctor everyday to discuss Sajide's condition, begging him to do his best to save my friend and make her better.

'I am doing everything I can. But unfortunately, despite the various antibiotics I have used, she is not responding positively to them. Her temperature persists. I think her problem is psychological, caused by the harshness of prison life. I worry that she may develop serious mental issues. You two are like my own daughters, we have the same background in medical studies, and we share the same views. I am trying my best to save her.' I don't know if I should feel consoled or more worried by the doctor's words.

One day, I visited the doctor after work as usual to ask about Sajide. He smiled at me, saying, 'I have good news for you. She is a lot better today. Her temperature has returned to normal. I assure you that she will recover very soon. I have spoken to the team leaders with regards to her vulnerability and warned them that, unless she's treated with great care, she could develop mental issues.' I was overjoyed and thanked him sincerely on behalf of Sajide. I walked into the dormitory and saw Sajide sitting on her bed leaning against her pillow. She looked frail but happy. When she saw me, she called to me with a smile that had been absent from her for so long, 'Oh, Söyün! I am feeling better but I still have no strength.' She took me into her arms.

'Don't worry, my dear friend, you will recover your strength soon! Look at you, you are much better today', I said with happy tears in my eyes.

It is September now. It was becoming colder day by day, and the temperature would drop sharply at night. I put on a heavy coat to try to stay warm but still shivered all night long, as my feet were constantly soaked in cold water at work. On top of that, the hunger was unbearable. Since arriving here at Xigobi I had never had a full meal with the same monotonous three meals given to us every day: a small steamed sorghum bread and a little bowl of watery celery soup. I suffered constant stomachaches from hunger while being forced to work long hours in severe weather conditions. My physical strength was waning as the days went by.

One night, my Chinese workmate in the sunflower field, Luo Shufang, came to me and said, 'Söyün, I am terribly hungry. You know there is a sweet melon field not far from here. I'm going to go and pick some melons. I can't bear this hunger any longer.' She was ready to go and left the lamp next to me. I was frightened by her decision and said, 'Shufang, don't! If they find out they will hang and beat us. Please don't take the risk.' She replied with timid confidence, 'I will be fine. There is no one in the melon field at night. I have been watching the guards. They usually go into the guards' room to sleep after a while. There is no one to catch me. If I see someone I will pretend I'm going to toilet. Don't worry. I've thought this through. I will hide the melon under my arm inside my jacket. No one will notice it.' I was unable to retain her.

About ten minutes later she came back with a huge smile on her face. She sat down and dropped two melons on the ground. My heart was beating so fast with joy and fear that it almost jumped out of my chest: the thought of someone watching us terrified me, and I quickly checked our surroundings attentively to make sure no one was around.

'Don't be afraid, Söyün. Come on, let's sit down and have one now', said Luo Shufang, unbothered by any potential danger. She hit the melon on the floor and it cracked open. We left the lamp on the edge of the stream that irrigated the sunflower field, sat down and ate the melon. I finished my share as fast as I could while telling Luo Shufang to hurry up. We hid the second melon among the sunflowers in the field before resuming our work. At dawn we returned to eat the second melon quickly under the pressure of being caught. I had never taken such a risk before and, although I was satisfied by the sweet and juicy melon, I felt awful. After that incident I promised myself never to do such a thing ever again.

When I returned from work to the dormitory I found Sajide looking much better and in a happier mood. When I asked her if she needed anything, she replied, 'I feel very hungry today, can you make me something to eat?' Her request pleasantly surprised me, had she forgotten where we were? How could I make her anything to eat when I didn't have access to anything? Without any immediate solution, I left to see the doctor and told him how hungry Sajide was, and asked if he could write a note requesting special food for her from the kitchen. He agreed. I took the note to the team leader who signed it before I went to the kitchen. The chef took the note before giving me 500 grams of flour and one courgette and asked me to sign on the doctor's note. Returning to Sajide with the flour and the courgette, I explained that there was no oil or meat and I didn't know how to make the flour and courgette into a nice meal. 'You can make me some *leghmen*',[17] said Sajide with a smile, 'have a look in my suitcase. There is a red bottle with some lamb fat in it. You can use the fat to fry the vegetables.' I took the bottle out of her case, only to notice that the lamb fat had turned red in colour, but she didn't seem to mind.

I made the dough and cut up the courgette. Before frying it, I tried my luck in getting some more vegetables from the vegetable field enclosed by bamboo trees, which supplied vegetables to the cadres. An old man worked there as a security guard, who we called 'Ren Daye'.[18] I went and stood among the bamboo calling Ren Daye. After a while he saw me and came over. I told him about Sajide's illness and asked if he could give me some vegetables. He checked to make sure that there was no one watching before quickly passing me one tomato and a green pepper. I quickly returned to make a simple fire stove outside the dormitory to fry the vegetables. I then used the dough and pulled it into noodles. When I finished and presented the rare treat to Sajide, she was overjoyed. The noodles did taste delicious, and, after finishing most of it with her newly gained appetite, Sajide happily proclaimed that she had never had such good *leghmen* in her life.

---

17   *A common Central Asian dish consisting of hand-pulled noodles, vegetables and meat.*
18   *Chinese for 'Grandpa Ren'.*

18 September 1963

It was a bright sunny day, but the atmosphere of working on the farm was making us depressed. We had been working since early morning without a break. I carried on my shoulder two big baskets of horse manure hung on a pole to fields located two kilometres away from the stables. My shoulders ached constantly from the pressure of the weight. I had to stop to rest at least three to four times on the way there. The cadres refused to let us take a big break, so we had to take any opportunity we could find to catch our breath. I was a short distance away from the field, but I couldn't bear the pain on my shoulder any longer. I looked around and, convinced that no one was watching, I put the baskets down on the ground cautiously. Other girls behind me saw that I had stopped and did the same. Suddenly we heard screaming from the field. My heart skipped a few beats, as we looked horrified at each other. We picked up the poles and baskets quickly and rushed towards the fields. I put down the baskets and looked in the direction from where the screaming was coming.

On the edge of a ditch next to the sunflower fields I saw Wang Jishu sitting on top of a woman whose trousers were pulled down to her knees, exposing her bottom. She was hitting the woman's bare bottom with a thick wooden stick as she screamed in agony. I was shocked by what I was seeing and turned my eyes to avoid seeing her suffer. I felt I had to do something to help her. I threw the pole to the ground and ran in their direction. To Chinese girls, Zhan Yulan and Wang Shuhua quickly grabbed my arms and said, 'No, Söyün, don't! You still don't know anything about the rules of this place. If you help her you will be beaten and they will make allegations against you. Remember, to them you are no more than a political criminal. If you go there and try to stop it, Wang Jishu will shoot you or beat you until you are crippled for life. You will then be accused of acting against the Communist Party, a counter–revolutionary conspirator, and of organising criminals to attack officials and all of those serious crimes. It is better for you not to get involved in any of it.' They pleaded with a sincere look in their eyes.

I was touched by the way they expressed their care for me and thanked them for their honest advice. The other girls around me were crying helplessly. I recognised the woman beaten by Wang from her clothes and sound of her voice. It was Aygül, a chubby woman of medium height in her forties from Kashgar. This surprised me, as she was not someone who would normally get into trouble. Wang, on the other hand, was an ugly, severe and ruthless woman who specialised in brutality and had a cold gaze that instilled fear in people, which had won her a senior position of power within the farm. She was a typical racist who despised people of other ethnic backgrounds and would often beat up ethnic minority girls merely for talking to each other. When she was around we wouldn't dare even to look at one another. We all hated her from a bottom of our hearts, and wished that she would die soon and go to hell.

After she was satisfied by her beastly act, Wang threw the stick on the ground, stood up, and looked in our direction. 'What are you standing there for? Work faster!' She yelled. At her order, all of us quickly picked up our shoulder poles and emptied the baskets before running back towards the stables. We worked as fast as we could for fear of being beaten, forgetting about the pain and hunger.

Aygül was lying in bed sobbing when I returned from work. I sat next to her, stroking her hand gently and asking her if she needed help. Weeping uncontrollably, she pulled up the blanket and showed me her back, 'Söyün, look what she has done to me!' Her body was covered in black and purple bruises inflicted by the beating, and her legs were angrily swollen. The open wounds on parts of her body were oozing blood. My heart ached and I couldn't hold back my tears. I offered to go and see the doctor for help but she refused.

'No, I don't want to see any Chinese person! I hate them all!' she said with tears falling down her face.

Under Wang's brutal supervision, we managed to finish five days' work in three days. Many girls were beaten by her, including Atiqe, who was beaten for tipping the manure too far away from the vegetable plants.

20 September 1963
A visit from my mother and Sajide's brother

Team leader Gülnisa ordered me, Sajide, and a few other girls to thresh corn, while she took the rest of the team to work in the vegetable fields. As we passed the men's dormitory on our way to the cornfield, a man approached us.

'Have you got a Söyüngül and a Sajide among you?' he asked. We introduced ourselves.

He continued, 'Very good. I met with your families in Sanji. They were on their way here to visit you. They asked me for a lift, but I couldn't offer it. They should be arriving later today.'

'Oh Söyün!' Sajide screamed with joy and hugged me, her face brimming with excitement. After the brief celebratory moment, I asked the man who he was, and learnt that he was working as a driver for that farm.

'But why didn't you give them a lift? How will they manage such a long journey on foot?' Sajide asked in a sad tone.

'My apologies. I didn't know they were your family at the time. Otherwise I would have found a way to bring them here', he said with deep regret.

As we walked on a chicken stopped in front of us and laid an egg. Sajide picked up the egg and giggled, 'Söyün, it really is our lucky day today. We received good news from that man, and now the chicken has laid the egg for us. Her words cheered up all the girls.

As we passed by the male canteen, we saw a man boiling water with a black stained pot. We were just talking about giving the egg to him when Sajide suddenly stopped. She looked at me and said, "Oh my God, it is Khali from Chöchek! Don't you remember? He was arrested with Kamal Bek at the Agricultural Institute?" I had heard that he was here but have never met him; it was difficult now to imagine him as a University student from how he looks now. He was terribly thin with the black prison uniform looking too big for him. He stood up slowly to greet us. His voice trembled as he spoke: "I had heard that you were both here and wished that it was just a rumour. You don't deserve to be in this place! I have been ill since the day I arrived here, my father is coming to collect me very soon to take me for medical treatment. I hope I will be leaving this place." We noticed the cadres in the distance coming in our direction, so we quickly passed the egg onto Khali and left in a hurry.

My mind had become occupied completely with the thoughts of my father and mother along with my siblings. The longing to see them over rode my thoughts. Every now and then I gazed out into the distance hoping to see them appear. The desire for freedom, which was burning inside me, kept making me sigh constantly. The day was now passing by slower than usual, and as such I couldn't wait to get back to the dormitory. As soon as we finished work, I rushed back hoping to see that they had arrived, but found no sign of them. Having finished dinner there was still no news of them. The girls in the dormitory took it in turns to go to the well pretending to drink while checking to see if our family had arrived. In the end, we went the hill behind the yard to stand on the top to look and wait for their arrival. Team leader Gulnisa spotted us and shouted: "What are you doing there? Go back to your room for evening studies." Reluctantly we did as we were told.

About half an hour later, Hasiyet went outside to have a look returning quickly saying: "Good news, they are here. There are five or six people who have arrived on a donkey cart. I have seen a woman with a little girl, plus some old men with a young man standing in front of the office."

I wanted to run outside to throw myself into my mum's arms, but I knew that I must remain calm and wait for permission from the team leader before I could see them. Some of the girl's had tears in their eyes as they said, "We are so happy for you both, because you will get to see your family. Our families live far away, and being poor will never be able to visit us." I comforted them by saying: "Don't lose hope; we will all finish our sentences in two or three year's time. It will pass quickly. If we stay strong, we will all go home one day to be reunited with our families." At that moment the team leader walked in calling Sajide and I. "Your mother and Sajide's brother is here. You may go and see them. However, I am warning you not to tell them anything about the prison camp!"

We agreed and then ran to the office.

My mother and sister ran over to me and hugged me tightly. The team leader took us to a room next to her office where I introduced my mother to Sajide who in return introduced her brother Hekim to me: "This is Söyüngül, Hekim" Said Sajide smiling. "It is good to meet you at last as I am sure everyone must know the two of you by now. You have both become very famous as you are paying very heavy price for the patriotism you shown for our nation. You are not the only ones who are suffering from your actions, all of our families are affected by the current changes. You have no idea how much all this is impacting on our lives." We stayed quite just listening. There were no words that could express our deep feelings of guilt and sadness for the troubles we have brought to our loved ones.

My mother then broke the silence: "You are here now and there is nothing anyone can do about it. I want you both to remain strong, to speak out less and finish your sentence quietly." My mother and Sajide's brother both gave us a lot of advice on how to cope with the present situation. We sat quietly listening. My younger sister Gheyshe sat on my lap with her arms around my shoulder, stroking my neck gently with her little fingers, kissing me now and then saying: "We miss you very much." I caressed her beautiful curly hair while holding her tightly in my arms, I replied: "I miss you too."

We talked about my father, also my brothers and sisters at which point the team leader walked in saying: "It is time for you to return to your room."

Our families remained overnight in the office room. How I longed that night to be able to sleep close to my mother and sister. They left the next morning after saying their farewells. It was heart breaking to see them leave so reluctantly with tears in their eyes.

15 October 1963

As soon as we returned from work, we were told to move all our belongings to the mud brick buildings next to the canteen, which was opposite the cadres' quarters. We quickly did as we were told. Our new accommodation was a large room that held fifteen people. Sajide and I placed our bedding in the two corners of the room opposite the door, the rest of the girls settled on the straw along the two sidewalls of the room. We were very happy with our new room as it was on ground level, and we no longer had to put up with a dark, damp cave, suffering constantly from leaking rainwater which soaked our bedding and clothes. We hoped that it would be free from fleas, but to our dismay, the situation with fleas and mosquitoes was no different, and they tortured me all night as usual.

Mahinur, having become the group supervisor, would always blow the whistle, symbol of her power, inside the room, which annoyed everyone. There were times when we jumped out of bed from deep sleep, with the sudden, hellishly loud whistling. We cursed her for almost giving us a heart attack. Despite all our complaints, Mahinur never changed this evil habit of hers and seemed to take great pleasure from it.

Today, after we got up, Ayshe went to get the broom from the old dormitory, from which she returned quickly, shouting, 'Girls! You can't believe how lucky we are! The roof of the dormitory has collapsed, if we hadn't moved out last night we would have been trapped in the rubble and crushed to death.' We all looked at each other in shock upon hearing the news and thanked God for keeping us safe.

20 October 1963

It was Sunday, our day off. We got up later than usual. After breakfast, the team leader distributed duvets and blankets for those who didn't have any. There was a sigh of relief from some of the girls to have received such a treat, while others were shouting and fighting as usual. We were now used to such fights, which would happen a few times daily. We had learned not to pay any attention to it.

I had decided to stitch the duvet cover on my duvet. I spread a blanket in the courtyard and started sewing. Sajide came and sat next to me. We could hear Ayshe singing beautifully in the distance as she walked towards us.

> *Who wouldn't experience the loss of a mother?*
> *Who wouldn't experience the loss of a father?*
> *Who wouldn't feel like a wonderer in another's land?*

When she approached us, I looked up at her with a smile as Sajide shouted out, 'Well done Ayshe! Long live Ayshe! God bless your voice!' That cheered us up.

Ayshe was a fair skinned girl of medium height, with a face covered in pockmarks. She was a bit of a tomboy, and could sometimes assume the characters of a hooligan, but she was never a bully and was never interested in any type of gossip. People called her Pockmark Ayshe, which she didn't mind at all. She had the most extraordinary singing voice. She could sing songs from both Ghulja and Kashgar[19] better than some of the professional singers I had heard in the country. When she sang, people could hear her resonating voice from miles away. She was our nightingale in the barren lands that had become our abode, deprived of beautiful flowers that would usually accompany a nightingale in a garden – an image often evoked by our greatest poets and song-makers.

Ayshe came over to us, shaking her head and saying, 'Oh, our beautiful doctors, what are you doing in this nightmare of a place? I feel sorry for you both.'

'We are all in the same boat Ayshe, look at how many of us are in this living hell. We are all the same here, doctors or not', I replied earnestly.

Ayshe came and sat down next to us and stayed silent for a while before saying, 'In 1959 a girl called Patigül from your university was brought here, too. She was from Chöchek. She was such a beautiful and kind-hearted girl. Perhaps you know of her?'

Patigül! That name rang a bell, and the event of 1959 came back vividly to my memory.

On one winter's day we were all called for a meeting in the main conference hall, and students from the Technical Institute were also present. All members of staff from the university from the doctors to the cleaners attended the meeting. The atmosphere was cold and depressing. Everyone had a look of horror on their faces. The meeting had started with officials giving a speech in a strident tone, condemning the anti-party, anti-government activists and rightists. During the speech, I noticed that there were people

---

19   *Uyghur folk songs vary greatly in style from region to region. The Ghulja style and the Kashgar style are so distinct from each other that singers used to one either style often find it challenging to master the other.*

looking out of the windows. Realising that something was going on, I also turned around to look out of curiosity. I saw armed police getting out of jeeps and rushing towards the conference hall entrance where they stopped.

It terrified me and I pulled the arm of the girl sitting next to me, saying, 'Did you see that? The armed police have surrounded the hall. It looks like something terrible is about to happen. I wonder how many people will be taken away this time.' Before long, four policemen entered to stand by the door. The official who was delivering the speech stopped and started announcing the names of the students who were going to be arrested.

The first name he read out was Imam, a student from the Technical Institute, his crime was 'being reactionary and a rightest'. Imam walked to the front, and two policemen pulled his hands together and locked them in handcuffs. After that they hit his head hard with the butt of their guns before escorting him out of the building.

Imam was a tall, slim, dark-skinned handsome young man who had just turned 18. I remember he had big deep dark eyes like those of a deep thinker. We had previously seen him being dragged out during many denunciation meetings, and this was to be the last time we would ever see him.

Following him, a lot of students and cadres were called onto the stage where they were handcuffed and taken away. The last person to be called was Patigül, who was branded a thief. Apparently she had worn her best friend's blouse to a party without her permission. The so-called best friend then reported her for stealing the blouse. Patigül was not in the meeting hall that day when her name was called out, but her roommates informed the officials that she was in the dormitory. Two cadres and two policemen went to the dormitory and arrested her.

Everyone arrested that day was herded at gunpoint into an army truck before being driven away. I was shocked that Patigül had been arrested for such a pathetic 'crime'. What kind of friend was that? How could she report such a thing? I was upset for many days as I struggled to understand how someone could ruin a friend's life of another over a piece of clothing.

'Yes, I knew Patigül very well', Sajide started speaking, bringing my wandering mind back to the present, 'She is from Chöchek, and has a twin sister named Zohre. Their mother died when they were young and their father never married again and brought them up alone. Zohre worked as a machinist in Chöchek, unlike Patigül, who was accepted by our university as a medical student. So unfair that she was arrested for something so trivial.'

'Exactly. I remember her, too. She was such a nice person, she died one year after arriving here, suffering from constant headaches. We had a small funeral for her. One of the women here washed her, and wrapped her body in a *kaftan* before saying the prayers and burying her. Her grave is not far from here. If we ever pass by it I will show you. The poor girl has been left alone in the desert...' Ayshe said, her voice full of sympathy and sorrow.

We all sat quietly for a while before I broke the silence and asked, 'You mentioned that she was buried after being wrapped in a *kaftan*, has anyone ever been buried without following the Islamic procedure?'

'A lot of shocking things have happened since I came here', Ayshe answered with a sigh, 'In 1959, more than six hundred prisoners arrived here from a place called Eighty Walls. In those days life was extremely hard. Our three meals a day was a small bowl of watery vegetable broth, far less than what we are receiving now, and there were hardly any vegetables in that soup. We lived with hunger pains day after day. People would eat anything that was edible. The men started eating any small animals that they could find, even rats. In winter we were ordered to dig a canal on the other side of the graveyard to bring water to the reservoir. Every time we walked past Patigül's grave we would leave little pieces of wood or stones on its top as symbols of remembrance. The workload was unbearable. People died from hunger gradually. Each day one or two people would die while working or on their way to or from work. At first the people that died were buried with some dignity: their bodies were washed and wrapped in *kaftan*s before being buried. When the number of deaths increased to five or six every day, sadly no one had the energy to wash and bury the dead, so most of the corpses were left on the ground to be eaten by birds and other wild animals. Eighty people survived out of the original six hundred that had arrived here. The majority of those died were all well educated young men and women who'd been accused of being rightist and reactionary. It makes my blood boil every time I think about this tragedy... Those who did survive were too weak to continue digging the canal, so the project was abandoned.'

26 October 1963

Having worked extremely hard under constant pressure, we finally completed the vegetable harvest for the year. The weather was getting colder by the day. After work the team leader distributed winter clothes to everyone. We were given Chinese revolutionary style black cotton winter jumpers along with winter trousers and cotton shoes. We tried them on eagerly to see how we would look. I didn't like my outfit at all as it looked dull and ugly. Some girls were in tears because they were being forced to wear something that they didn't want to, while others just laughed. Many of the clothes were too big so we had to spend hours altering them.

After dinner Sajide and I went to the well for some fresh water. We filled the bucket and were about to leave when four men came to us in a hurry. They stopped in front of us smiling.

'I am Keken from Xinjiang Petrochemical Institute', one of them introduced himself couteously, 'And this is Koben from Xinjiang University. There are two other students brought here, Kali from the Agricultural University and Kamalbeg from your university. Kamal went nuts when he was brought to this place, and somehow he managed to run away later. Unfortunately he was captured and brought back again. These two are our fellow prisoners and they have come with us to meet you. I was shocked when I first heard that you were here and felt extremely sad for you both. We returned from digging the canal last night and have been waiting near the well, hoping you would come for water at some point.'

Their arrival gave me some comfort. We chatted for a while about life in the labour camp. They told us of their terrible experiences of torture while digging the canal. Keken then said, 'We have worked like slaves for long hours with constant hunger. I am so sorry to see that girls like yourselves are suffering in this place, too.'

They were terribly thin. It was heart breaking to see such handsome young men now turned into skeletons, enslaved by monstrous human beings. Yet at the same time, it was consoling to see that them in good spirits despite the circumstances. They made us laugh with their sense of humour. Before leaving they asked us try to find a way to keep in touch and advised us strongly not to trust anyone.

28 October 1963

Our winter work started today. We stood in two lines with all our tools, ready to head off to the reservoir. Most of the girls were cheerful, joking and laughing, trying to keep their mind off the task ahead. Gülnisa, the team leader, had arranged for us to work in pairs. As it was quite a distance from the field to the reservoir where we have to move an insurmountable mountain of earth. We worked non-stop in pairs carrying a basket of earth hung backward and forward, between the reservoir and fields. After a while we felt worn out, and the stomach pains resulting from hunger made it worse. At the end of the day I could hardly walk back to the dormitory. The skin on my shoulders starting to peel off and the bare flesh rubbed against my clothes. It was nothing but torture.

Mahinur blew the whistle as usual. I jumped out of my bed, having had little sleep. It took a while to realise and gather my senses. Mahinur certainly enjoyed this game of power: instead of showing some love and respect to her fellow prisoners, she abused them whenever she had the chance. Her actions antagonised everyone. She had become an unhappy and bitter person to us all.

I put on my work clothes and bent over to grab my shoes. To my astonishment, one of them was filled with sunflower seeds. I wondered where all these seeds had come from. May be a rat?

'What's happened? What are you staring at?' Sajide asked curiously.

'I don't know. It seems that a rat has filled my shoe with sunflower seeds!'

Tajnisa, who had been sleeping opposite me, spoke out cheerfully, 'Alright, if you don't like the seeds, give them to me. I'm hungry.'

'Oh don't be ridiculous', I said, 'How can you eat something from a rat's mouth? They carry diseases!'

'We will be fine', Ayshe and Tajnisa said simultaneously. They took the seeds and washed them up before starting to eat them. From that day on, I would check my shoes every morning as soon as I woke up, and, to my amazement, my shoes would always be full with different things: sometimes with wheat seed, sometimes with corn, and sometimes with sunflower seeds. The girls were very pleased with the friendly rat providing them with these treats. They thanked God for this providence and didn't give it much thought. I, on the other hand, was curious and determined to meet the friendly rat, so I stayed up one night and, to my disgust, I saw it: it was as big as my hand.

The harsh winter had finally arrived with heavy snow and strong winds. At night, the temperature would drop to -30 °C. The working conditions became extremely difficult as the wind blew snow into our faces; also walking on the icy ground carrying heavy baskets of earth was extremely hazardous. No matter how we tried to stay on our feet we couldn't avoid slipping and falling to the ground frequently. As we continued to build a wall encircling the reservoir, the walls were already quite high and it was becoming harder and more and more dangerous to reach the top. Every day it would take us at least an hour to break the ice with the hammer to reach the earth that lay beneath the snow and ice. After which we filled the baskets before carrying them to the reservoir. Once the earth had tipped on top of the wall we had to stand and compress the earth with a long tamping pole by hand, which was exhausting.

Later it was Sewirnisa's and my turn to compress the earth; we had to walk from one end of the wall to the other pressing using the tamping pole all day without a break. By the end of the day my arms and legs started aching as I lost the strength in my body.

Xigobi is an extremely cold place in winter. If you don't have the correct clothing you can easily freeze to death or catch pneumonia. The leather gloves my mother brought when she visited me protected my hands and helped to keep them warm. When we were outside we were completely wrapped up with only our eyes left uncovered, as we had to protect our skin from frostbite. Thick ice would always build up on our facemasks, eyebrows, and eyelashes. And you could see condensation from our mouths as we breathed. It was difficult to recognise one or another: we were all dressed the same with our faces were completely covered. Sometimes the temperature was so low that even the facemask couldn't stop the frostbite on our faces and we had to put on cream to repair the damaged skin. Some girls couldn't go to work because of their skin conditions.

Our accommodation was narrow and dark, and it looked more unpleasant in winter compared to the summer. The small window was always covered with thick snow and ice. The room was always cold, as the heating provided by the small wall stove was insufficient to heat the whole room. Everyday as soon as we got back from work we would hang all our clothes and wet shoes around the stove to dry them. The odour coming from the shoes filled the room, and made me want to vomit. Sometimes when we couldn't cope with the smell any more, we would open the windows to allow fresh air in even though it was freezing cold. As there was no shower facility; some of the girls didn't wash themselves at all during winter.

28 December 1963

Due to the biting cold, we were only able to work for few hours in the morning. New year was approaching, and we were lucky to be given a week off. Two days before New Year's Eve, we cleaned out the dormitories and the kitchen before we went to collect some thorny shrubs with which to make some brooms. We also gathered some wood for the fire. I was about to bundle the wood up when Ayshe came to my side and said, 'Söyüngül, come, I will show you Patigül's grave.' I agreed and went with her.

We arrived at an area where all the dead prisoners were buried. She pointed at the far end of a row and said, 'Look, that is Patigül's grave.' I dropped the firewood in my hands as I looked at the grave. My whole body started to shiver. I was deeply moved by the poor souls who had been left in this God forsaken place. I felt the pain and misery that they must have been through before death finally came. I couldn't move. Tears fell from my eyes and soaked my cheeks. I remained standing and staring at the graves for a long time.

I suddenly remembered to pray for them. I recited all the *suras* that I knew in Arabic and then asked God to forgive all their sins and grant them paradise. I cried loudly inside me, 'Oh my unfortunate friends! I wonder whose dearest loved ones you are, whose dearest parents and most precious children you are. You are victims of this cruel system. I can't imagine the suffering you must have all been through before you the dark soil of this treacherous barren land claimed your bodies. We don't know what kind of fate we are to face in the future or what our final days will be like. Only God knows our fate.'

Suddenly Sajide appeared in front of me and interrupted my thoughts, 'Söyün, What's happened?' She looked very confused. I pointed at the graves, 'These are prisoners' graves. Look, that one is Patigül's.' Sajide walked to the grave and kneeled down while we stood quietly. The team leader spotted us and shouted from a distance, 'Hey, what's going on with you lot? Hurry up and finish your job! We are going back.' We quickly collected the firewood and made our way back to the dormitory.

25 June 1964
Threshing season

The days are extremely hot, with the temperature exceeding 40 degrees. People had died from heat exhaustion and our working hours had been changed to four till ten in the morning, and four till ten in the evening. During the work break it was difficult to get any rest as the heat in the room was so suffocating. The flies and fleas made our lives a living hell. If winter was bad, then summer was infinitely worse. Since the end of winter we had been working in the vegetable fields. We were also ordered to build earth walls around the wheat fields. Each person was ordered to construct a 200-metre long, 1-metre high and 1.5-metre wide section each day. We were not allowed to leave the work area until we had finished our allocated tasks.

Having finally finished the task for that day we moved to the threshing fields located fifteen kilometres away. We had settled into a new unfinished building without doors or windows. A mobilisation meeting was held during which each person was ordered to complete two *mu*[20] *of threshing in one day. The threshed area must be clear of all wheat without one seed being left on the ground. Anyone that can manage more than two mu* would be rewarded with extra food for that day. Anyone who failed finish the required workload will not receive any food. We were also informed of the various types of punishment for those who did not obey the rules and orders and did not work hard enough to complete their given tasks.

After the meeting Ayshe came over to me and said, 'Söyün, this area was once the centre of Xigobi. There were thousands of prisoners who used to work here. Among them was a famous writer called Ziya Semedi.'

'Oh really, did you ever get to meet him?'

'I only saw him in the fields. I heard after that he was accused of being a rightist and nationalist. During the famine lots of people died here, as the water from the mountains dried up and stopped the fields from being irrigated. Eventually this place was abandoned and we moved to where we are based now.'

After dinner we went to bed early, as there was no electricity. Lying in her bed, Emine said, 'Hey girls, do you know I have never slept in such a spacious room since my arrest. It is such a nice, cool and fresh feeling, I wish we could spend the entire summer here!'

'What I am pleased about the most is that there are no flies here, thank God!' Zeynep added.

'And the fleas, there are no fleas!' Sajide rejoiced, 'We will definitely enjoy our sleep tonight free from flies and fleas. I don't think you could find more flees or flies anywhere in the world than in Xigobi. This is a treat!'

Helchem then interrupted, 'Have you all forgotten the famous mosquitoes? There aren't mosquitoes either!'

'I know I should be grateful and happy for all of this, but I'm petrified of wolfs', Tilaxan sounded concerned, 'What if they come and eat us. We are in the middle of this wildness sleeping in a room open to any creatures ready to attack us.'

'Oh come on Tilaxan, why are you spoiling the peace we have been longing for? Sleep tight, God will protect us', said Helchem impatiently.

Everyone laughed, I prayed quietly before falling asleep.

---

20   *Chinese unit of measurement; 1 mu = 666.7 m², or 7,716 ft².*

26 June 1964

The sound of the whistle woke us up from our sweet slumbers. It was only two o'clock in the morning as we rushed to get ready in pitch darkness. By half past two we were all lined up, ready to go to work. On reaching the fields, the first rays of the rising sun gradually lit up the earth. Each of us went to our designated work areas in the wheat fields to start threshing as quickly as we could. Team leader Gülnisa came over to me at about seven o'clock, saying, 'I want you to be in charge of supplying hot water to all the women until we have completed threshing here. I have chosen you because you are fast and reliable. I know this is a difficult task but I believe you will manage it well.' I wasn't happy with the new job, it was much harder to carry hot water from a long distance in the heat than threshing, but I could not refuse.

It took me an hour and half to carry the hot water on a shoulder pole from the hot water room to the fields, this was the first time I had used a shoulder pole to carry water, I found extremely difficult to balance. I had to walk fast otherwise I would have been told off by the team leader for being too slow. But when I walked fast, the hot water splashed and blistered my skin. No matter how careful I tried to be it was simply impossible to stop the splashing. My feet were red with blisters from the splashes. The burning sun made the task even harder, and the steam rising from the water buckets around me increased the temperature further. I was soaked in sweat, which I could see evaporating off my clothes in the heat. As soon as the girls saw me coming they started shouting, 'Walk faster! Come quickly! We are thirsty.' When I reached them they cheered happily, 'Long live Söyüngül!' But the water containers were only half full and wasn't enough to quench everyone's thirst, so I had to run back to the hot water room again. I was thirsty but didn't get any chance to have a drink of water. The second time when I returned I was completely fed up. I went to the dormitory to collect three flasks, which I filled with cold water before hanging them around my neck. This time I managed to walk faster than before and less water was spilt.

I finished one flask of water on the way. The sweat from my body was dripping like raindrops onto the ground with every step I took. Slowly I started to get the hang of things and was now finding it easier to balance the pole as I walked. But the heat was getting worse as time went by. We had our breakfast in the field, and were given one extra potato each. We stopped at ten returning to our dormitory. I went straight to the tap, washed my face and feet and cooled myself down with a wet towel before going to the dormitory.

'Oh my God', Méhriban complained, 'It was as if the sun had moved from the sky on to earth. I would have been cooked like kebab if I had stayed any longer in that field.'

'My darling, it would have been so nice if you had been cooked, at least we could have the opportunity to eat some delicious meat. We have not had any meat for so long that we would have appreciated you so much', Emine said jokingly, and we all laughed.

We returned to work at around three o'clock. I delivered water to the girls at least ten times before we finished for the day. The girls were all exhausted, having worked the fourteen-hour shift. The hardship of having to thresh two *mu* a day under the scorching sun was beyond description, and, fearing punishment, everyone had one target in mind: to complete the job within the time given. The wheat we had threshed was thick and of good quality. It was hard to understand with such an abundance of wheat and vegetables why we were always kept half starved. Where was all this food going?

I went to the dormitory with Sajide after we finished washing ourselves. Everyone was already asleep. When I lay down in my bed that night the pain in my legs and shoulders finally kicked in.

We worked intensively for one whole month to complete the threshing as planned before being transported back to the Xigobi head quarters.

3 August 1964

After returning from the threshing fields we were given a two-day break. We were then divided into two groups, one to work in the vegetable fields and the other at the site of the combine harvester. The workload, as usual, was inhumanly heavy.

Sewirnisa and I were told to work as a pair to collect the grain falling through the sieves of the combine harvester. My job was to seal the bags as soon as they were full and carry them to the lorries. Each bag weighed over 50 kilos. The speed at which the grain travelled through the sieves was incredibly fast, so there was no time to pause in order to take a breath. As soon as I ran back from the truck, another bag would already have been filled, and I had to get it sealed as fast as I could and stumbled to carry it to the truck again. The dust from the machine was everywhere and our faces became unrecognisable with a paste of sweat and husk particles mixed together.

'I really wish I was never born!' said Sewirnisa, looking at me and holding the open bag, 'I'm going to pass out. Every time I struggle to reach the truck and throw the bag in I feel as if I am fighting for my last breath!' She was trying very hard to hold back her tears as she spoke. The mixture of dust and sweat made Sewirnisa's face look as if it had been painted with grey mud.

'Söyün, if someone sees the state we're in, they will run away in fear thinking they've come across two ghosts. 50 kilos of grain! 50 kilos! Who could do this? I don't think I have any strength left to carry on.' She then carried the bag with great difficulty, after throwing the bag into the truck, she collapsed and fell to the ground. I stopped immediately what I was doing and ran in panic to her side and, after noticing that one of her legs was bleeding, I called for help and she was taken to the clinic. I wanted to accompany her but I had to carry on with my own work. We stopped for our lunch not long after the incident.

I quickly washed myself before sitting down. Turaxan, who was sitting opposite me, shouted with rage, 'Where is my bread? Who ate my bread?!' She stared angrily at Tilaxan and Zeynep who were sitting next to her and started swearing at them. Both of them told her that they had not even seen her bread. She didn't believe them, and a fight broke out – the usual result of life in prison. I went over trying to pull them apart, but it took a good while to calm them down.

When we finally all sat down again, Sajide said, 'Turaxan, I saw you eating your bread while you were chatting. No one took your bread but yourself. Maybe you didn't realise you'd eaten it? I was watching you all the time when you were talking.'

Turaxan thought for a while before replying in protest, 'But I don't remember eating anything! I'm sorry!'

Silence resumed, until Turaxan spoke again, bitterly, 'The bread is so small that I don't feel like I have eaten anything. Listen, my stomach is still empty and rumbling with hunger. Why don't they give us more food if they ask us to work like donkeys?' She left the room with angry tears in her eyes. No one knew what to say to this, but the incident did come to the attention of the supervisors very quickly: about fifteen minutes later, Turaxan was called to the office.

We were forced to work day and night for twenty days in order to complete the workload in the threshing fields. All the grains were transported to Ürümchi, from where it was dispatched to Mainland China by trains.

24 August 1964
Dispersing the East Turkistan National Army

Yang Zi and I were ordered to wash and dry ten bags of grains each day, each bag weighing 50 kilos. We started the job at dawn near the well. We washed the grains before spreading them onto the ground to let them dry under the sun, and then we had to pick out the small stones among them. We then refilled the bags with the grains ready for transportation on a wheeled cart back to the warehouse. Before finishing for the day, we had to collect the next ten bags of the grains for the following day.

As dusk fell, I was pulling the cart towards the well when I saw a truck loaded arriving with armed Chinese police. My heart immediately started beat faster. I noticed the worried look on Yang Zi's face.

'Why have armed police come here?' she asked me.

'I don't know, something isn't right. It is very strange.'

Half an hour later, the soldiers of the National Army carried all their belongings and got on to the truck. They took off their caps and waved us goodbye as they drove off. It was clear now: The National Army had been replaced by a Chinese one. Later I found out that the National Army had been dispersed into the villages and communes.

The people of East Turkistan had lost their own military. I sank into immense sadness. We were surrendering the control over our land and its people until there is none left. In simple terms, the loss of our own army is a symbol of complete surrender of our rights to another nation. It was devastating for me to realise this.

Team leader Gülnisa's husband was also removed from his position in the Ethnic Minorities Army and placed in the labour camp as an ordinary labourer earning 30 yuan a month. The once proud army personnel became worthless citizens. All our hope for a bright future was woefully collapsing and there was nothing that we could do to turn the tide around.

27 September 1964
Ismail's tragic fate

Our team leader ordered me, along with eight other women, to work with the male prisoners in the sweet potato fields, helping to load the horse carts with the potatoes. The rest of the women were taken to the vegetable fields. We were picked up by a horse cart whose driver was called Ismail, a very handsome young man. He pulled out two sweet melons hidden under a coat and gave them to us, which made the girls very happy. As we were wondering what to do with the melons, Ismail took out a knife and said, 'Hey girls, patience. Give me the melons and let me cut them for you.' The girls passed the melons to him and he started to cut them. The girls would grab a slice as soon as he cut one, and some of them enjoyed the rare treat so much that they even ate the hard skin. When he gave last piece to me, I refused politely. Before he could even say a word, another girl quickly grabbed it and ate it up within a second. He looked shocked but didn't say a word. Putting the knife back in his pocket, he said, 'Söyüngül, you still manage to keep your politeness and grace despite your terrible hunger and the miserable conditions of this place. You seem to have adapted well in such a harsh environment. I truly admire you and have no doubt that you will survive in any place.' I thanked him with a smile.

Upon our arrival, we saw men digging up sweet potatoes, which they had piled up on the side. The discarded green leaves were scattered everywhere and added to the beauty of the autumn scene of harvest. The horse cart stopped next to the field, where a huge amount of sweet potatoes had been piled up like a small hill.

As we were getting off the cart, Ayshe Mahmut shouted, 'Hey, Söyün, look!' I looked in the direction that Ayshe was pointing at and saw some men eating sweet potatoes in a hurry. Ismail saw us looking at the men and said, 'Poor guys. They can't cope with hunger, the food they given to them is no way enough to keep a grown man going, so they always look for any opportunity to eat whatever is edible in order to ease the pain of hunger. Please don't mind them.'

Suddenly Heytem Qalaq, who was working not far from us, started singing loudly, 'Check your front and back, ho! Hide everything, quickly, ho! Work hard, very hard, ho!' The men got the warning and quickly buried the leftovers and went back to digging. I could see in the distance that six officials were coming in our direction.

As they arrived, we started loading the potatoes more quickly. Ismail had transported five carts of potatoes up to this point. As we were loading the sixth cart, Ismail asked me a question unexpectedly. '

'Do you know the meaning of the Three *Talaq*s?'[21]

I raised my head and stopped loading for a while before answering such an awkward question, 'I remember when I was little I used to hear my elders talk about this subject. As far as I can remember, its not a nice word to be used, and it is also sinful when listening to it. Even the thought of such a word is sinful. And it brings bad luck to the

---

21   *'Divorce' in Arabic. According to Islamic law, a man can legally divorce his wife after uttering the word 'talaq' three times.*

place where it is said. They used to say that that if the word was uttered by someone in a room, the walls would tremble. I don't know the exact meaning of the word, though, but I do know it is sinful to say it.'

'Oh, really?' said Ismail. He went quiet and thought for a while then continued, 'I lost my parents when I was little and was brought up by my elder brother. I never had the opportunity to learn anything about Islam, our religion. I joined the military and attended the military college. When I finished my studies, I was employed by the Shanshihangzi Council, a district in Ürümchi. I don't meant to sound arrogant, but overall I did quite well compared to many people, and I also had quite a lot of female admires.'

I noticed again his tall figure and handsome face as he continued, 'My destiny had already been written by God as I married a beautiful girl who came from a good and conservative family. We had a very happy family life for the first few years. And then… I don't think I need to explain to you what changed in our country. I was forced to work longer hours each day. I was extremely unhappy with what I had been forced into, which gradually affected my mental stability. I suffered from nightmares because of the pressures of work and the changes that I had to implement under the new regime. The stress finally took a toll on my marriage. My wife never understood my problems or how I felt and was ready to argue any time, despite me explaining to her again and again how hard my work was. One day I had experienced an extremely difficult and unfair situation at work, I returned home depressed. My wife started complaining as soon as I entered the house. I tried to explain to her how mentally exhausted and weary I was, asking her to give me space and peace for five minutes. She flipped and started screaming and shouting at me, telling me how unhappy she was as my wife. So I also said, "You know what, I am so fed up with you." And she shouted back, "Ok then, divorce me if you are so fed up with me!" To avoid having any further arguments I tried to leave the house in order to calm down and give her the chance to calm down too. But she grabbed my arm and pulled me back and screamed, "Come on, man up and divorce me!" She really provoked me and I lost my mind. I remembered the words I had heard earlier in my life and said automatically, "I give you the Three *Talaq*s." And I left slamming the door. But believe me, I only wanted to warn her and didn't really understand the seriousness or the consequences of the words. Then she looked shocked, stopped shouting and turned away from me immediately.

'I went out for a while and upon my return she had already packed her things ready to leave. I asked her where she was going but she left the house without saying a word. I naïvely thought she would return once she had calmed down. I waited for two days before I went to her parent's house to collect her. Her mother opened the door. I explained that I had come to collect Ayshe to take her home, but she interrupted me angrily and said, "Ayshe is no longer your wife, you have given her the *talaqs*. You are no longer her husband and have no rights over her any more. You can now leave." I was completely devastated. I returned home feeling lost. Later she made a complaint about me to my managers at work and revealed to them something I shouldn't have said about work. My work unit then exaggerated the problem and turned it into a big case against me and that is how I received a two-year sentence and ended up here. The three *talaqs* cost me my marriage and my career, and look where I am now...' He sighed deeply.

'Did your wife get the divorce paper from you? Was it ever confirmed in writing?' Ayshe Mahmut asked after a long moment of silence.

'She came asking me to sign the divorce papers the week after I was sentenced, and I have never heard from her since. So I don't know what has happened. All I know is that anger can destroy a person completely.'

After lunch we waited for Ismail to collect us from in front of the canteen. As his horse cart approached us, the horse was suddenly disturbed by something, and started dashing towards us. At the same time, a Chinese cadre's son about four years old appeared on the road out of nowhere. Everyone was terrified that the horse might hit the boy. Ismail quickly pulled the reins to make the horse's head to one side, making the horse change direction and run away from him. The horse reared up and as a result Ismail lost his balance and fell under the wheel of the cart. Everyone watching the scene screamed in shock; some men ran in front of the horse and managed to grab the reins and stop it. Ismail was lying on the floor covered in dust. I was terrified, and felt as if my heart was going to jump of my chest. People started to gather at the scene, surroumding Ismail who was lying unconscious on the ground. He was taken to the dormitory. Two days later he was taken to the City Hospital for treatment and brought back. We later learned that his lower spine was broken and he was paralysed, and there was no treatment the doctors could give him. The prison had contacted his brother to take him home but his brother refused saying that his family could never manage to take care of him. As a result he was kept at the camp where one person was appointed to take care of him.

4 October
The male prisoners moved out from the camp

The rays of the rising sun were gradually brightening the earth. The weather was turning cold day by day. The cracking of the crows brought life to the silent atmosphere of the labour camp. As I stood washing my face I heard the sounds of vehicles in the distance. I looked in the direction of the sound and saw lorries approaching fast, leaving a plume of dust behind them. I wondered why they had come so early in the morning. As I stood watching, they passed by the barn and headed towards the men's dormitories. There were five empty lorries in total. I went back into the dormitory to tell the girls what I had seen, and they were all curious to know what was going on. Méhriban volunteered to go and bring breakfast from the canteen so that she could try to find out what was happening on the way.

Later we could see that the men had suddenly come out, and the atmosphere looked tense. We all ran to Méhriban as soon as she came back. She placed the bucket she was carrying on the ground she said, 'They are moving the male prisoners to Shabahu Labour Camp, close to the Sanji city. They are leaving after last breakfast here right now.'

'What about us? Do you know if we are moving somewhere too?' Ayshe asked with excitement.

'I haven't heard anything so far. I was only told that most of the male prisoners, including some of the horse cart drivers and a number of cadres are leaving today.' Méhriban replied.

Our morale dropped. Some of the girls even cried at the thought of it, which also affected me. In this open prison camp in the middle of the wildness, the only happiness we had was to be among the people around us. It was them that made this place alive and the loss of any inmate would make a big difference.

As we finished our breakfast the lorries had been filled with prisoners ready to leave. Each vehicle had five armed soldiers and four armed officials encircling the prisoners, who sat motionlessly on the floor of the truck. We stood in the courtyard watching the trucks disappear into the distance.

20 December 1964
The wild boar chase

It was one of those extreme cold winter days with thick snow covering this bleak open prison camp. The wind was strikingly sharp as the cold penetrated deep inside our bones. There was no other sign of life apart from us, the female prisoners, who were forced to work non-stop under such harsh weather conditions. We were repeating the same work we had undertaken during the last winter: building a wall to encircle the reservoir.

Suddenly Turaxan shouted in excitement, 'I can see someone coming in the distance! He must be a post man or someone's relative.' We all looked in the same direction and saw a man coming, and everyone tried to guess who he was and what was he coming for. The team leader saw us talking between ourselves and yelled, 'Stop talking! Work faster!' She struggled to say these words clearly because of the cold: even though she was wearing a thick army coat, the collar was turned up high and held in place by a thick woollen scarf that covered her head and half of her face. She was walking backwards and forwards while occasionally stamping her feet on the ground. We guessed she had obtained the army coat from her husband who was a former soldier of the Ethnic Minorities Army. I stood looking at her, thinking, 'She is such a beautiful young woman and yet she's spending her life in such an unpleasant place year after year without knowing if she will ever leave. The prisoners leave this place when their term is ended, but her work has no final date. She will be spending all her life in this environment, suffering from its hardships.'

She noticed me looking and got annoyed, 'Hey, why are you looking at me like that?' I simply smiled back at her before quickly jumping down the hole with the bucket to retrieve some soil.

The men we had seen in the distance now walked past us. It was the postman. We couldn't wait to go back to the dormitory, restless with the thought of receiving a letter or a parcel from our families. I was daydreaming when Sewirnisa suddenly shouted, 'Hey girls, look! A truck is coming!' And all the girls rushed forward to look and screamed with joy. No one actually knew what excited them so much, but in a place where hardly any happiness was to be found in the day-to-day life, little things like this always made everyone emotional. I also felt very happy for no real reason. The truck passed us slowly with few people on board, all of whom had their arms folded in front of their chests, shivering in the cold.

'I think new prisoners have arrived', said Turnisa.

'Are you sure? Maybe someone came to visit us', said Helchem.

'Oh stop getting excited now. If someone comes to visit you, you will know who they are and what is going on when we go back', Turaxan said sarcastically while staring at Helchem.

Helchem was not impressed by Turaxan's comment and shouted at her, 'What did you say? Are you making fun of me? Who would ever come here to visit *you*?' Turaxan, enraged, pushed the basket to the side, as she ran and grabbed her. Ayshe punched Tilaxan furiously; Tilaxan pulled Ayshe's hair and knocked her down to the ground. They started kicking and punching one another, also pulling each others hair as they rolled on the ground on top of one another, neither was willing to give up. The team leader rushed over shouting, 'What is happening here, I order you stop immediately!' They finally letting go of each other before tidying up their hair and replacing their scarfs. They then dashed over to the field bringing back the baskets of earth.

We all carried on working as if nothing had happened. We were all used to this kind of behaviour, fights like this amongst some of the girls were commonplace and I had now learned not to pay any attention to it.

Suddenly, Ayshe Eyyup, who was standing on top of the reservoir wall, shouted –

'Team Leader, there is a wild boar coming our way!'

'Don't take any notice, carry on working', the team leader replied with indifference. Some of the girls put down their baskets and climbed on top of the wall to have a look in the direction where Ayshe pointed. I walked up the embankment to have a look, and saw a black animal walking in our direction about one kilometre away. It had short legs and wasn't as tall as a cow, I recognised that it was indeed a wild boar. Where was this beast coming from? What was it doing in the place like this? As a wild boar is a predator that is very dangerous. Maybe it is looking for food? I asked myself. The unexpected arrival of a wild animal worried me as I carried on working but we kept checking on it as it came closer. After a couple of minutes it turned off in another direction.

'Team Leader, the boar has now gone in another direction, shall I go and catch it?' Ayshe shouted.

'Don't bother, carry on with your work!' she replied impatiently.

I thought Ayshe was joking, but she then took the tamping tool from Turnisa's hand and jumped over the wall and started running towards the wild boar. Turaxan followed Ayshe carrying a bamboo pool in her hand, then Sadet, Sewrnisa, Manem, Zileyxa, Patem, Helchem and Ayshe Mahmut plus some other girls all followed. Turnisa suddenly ran passed me and grabbed my pole from my hand before running off after the other girls.

'Söyün, don't you dare move', team leader Gülnisa gave me a death stare. I stood still as she also ordered the rest of the girls not to move. We obeyed her orders and remained in our places. More than twenty girls had left the work place to chase the wild boar. We watched as they ran further and further away, we climbed on top of the reservoir wall to get a better view of what was happening. The day was closing and it was getting darker and colder. Soon everyone had disappeared from our view.

Half an hour later everyone reappeared. Having encircled the wild boar pointing whatever they were carrying towards it they forced it back in our direction. The animal looked terrified, surely it had never experienced such an incident in its life.

Gülnisa looked relieved and said, 'I thought they would have run away making excuse of trying to follow the pig. Now look at them – they have terrified the wild boar so much that it looked scared. Those girls are fearless!'

'Team leader, how would they even think of escaping from this wildness in the darkness and cold? They wouldn't even leave here if you ask them to', I said.

'What are you talking about? The last time this happened more than ten people ran away making the excuse about trying to catch a rabbit, some were rearrested but others are still on the loose!' she retorted.

Just as we arrived at the entrance at the dormitory Sadet came over to me saying, 'Two new girls have been brought here from prison, I heard they are both from Ürümchi and were studying medicine. One has been given a three-year and the other two years. It is possible you may know them.'

'Maybe they are from our University', said Sajide as she went inside. I followed her in.

The girls were sitting by the stove. One of them was petite, round-faced and fair-skinned and had beautiful dark eyes and natural pink cheeks; she was wearing a green cardigan with a black skirt. The other girl had an oval shaped face, a wide forehead and dark skin; she was slim and of medium height; she looked like a village girl.

We greeted them warmly before settling down in our own living areas. The petite girl came to see me and Sajide after dinner –

'Are you the girls who were arrested from the Medical University?'

'Yes we are.' Sajide and I replied simultaneously with a smile

'I am Zohre, from the Mal Bazar in Ürümchi', she introduced herself, 'My father's name is Emet, people called him Big Emet. I wonder if you have heard of him.'

'I am from Ürümchi but I don't know too many people there. I am sorry I don't think I have heard about him', I said.

'My father passed away many years ago, sadly', Zohre Emet continued, 'He was a well known businessman. He was very short, but people called him Big Emet. I look like my father'. She said with a smile.

Then Méhriban suddenly walked in shouting loudly, 'Zokre Emet, the team leader wants you to go to her office immediately!' Zohre stood up quickly, she looked at us and said before leaving, 'I am very happy to see you both, I feel as if I am seeing my own sisters. It could have been so difficult for me to be here without knowing you both, and I would like to spend the forthcoming difficult years in your company.'

23 February 1965
Moving to Shabahu

The piercing sound of the whistle yet again broke the peace of sleep. The girls, as usual, cursed Mahinur one after another. The team leader walked in as we were getting dressed. We were all surprised to see her come to the room so early.

'Pack all of your belongings before you go to breakfast as we will be leaving here immediately after breakfast. A tractor will come to collect you at about nine o'clock.' The girls started jumping up and down with joy.

'Where are we going?' Zeynep asked impatiently.

'You will find out when you get there', replied the team leader coldly.

Having packed our belongings and eaten breakfast, we were divided into two groups to be placed in the trailers of the two tractors. There wasn't enough room for so many of us so we were squeezed tightly together. An armed cadre sat next to the driver as we set off at eight thirty.

As we drove off I drifted into deep thoughts, gazing at the place we had left behind. The farm had become a shattered ghost town, looking creepy and unsettling out in the wild. I became more convinced that it was people that could add beauty to a desolate place, and turn a desert into an oasis.

'Söyün, What's the matter?' Sajide interrupted my thoughts, and said jokingly, 'Are you feeling sad that we are leaving this place?'

'Yes, actually. I am in a way. That place, no matter how much I've hated it, has become home to me. I am so used to it and am now finding it difficult to leave. We've left behind so many happy moments shared together', I said, half seriously and half sarcastically.

Everyone laughed at my words. Pashaxan had been sitting in the middle of the group, where she had been putting on some make up on her cheeks, which made them rosy red and her eyebrows extra dark in contrast. She looked very happy.

'Girls I feel like I have gained my freedom today!' Zeynep's voice came from behind.

'Zeynep, you have three months left and I have four months, we will soon be free, *inshallah*. Do you think the day of freedom will ever come? I wonder how we will feel on that day!' said Tilaxan, throwing her head back gazing up at the sky. The armed cadre shouted and told us off for being noisy, so everyone stopped laughing and started whispering to one another.

It was a beautiful and pleasant day. The sun was shining bright in the blue sky. It was as warm as spring. The tractor was running slowly due to the weight it was pulling. On some hilly roads we had to get off and push it up the hill, while in other places we walked in the mud through water and even snow. Finally we passed along a village road with thick trees on both sides and wide-open agricultural fields stretching as far as the eye could see.

Arriving at our destination at 3 pm, the tractor drove past a well through a gate into a large courtyard where five men came out of a building on the right hand side to help us unload our belongings. They then ordered us to stand in line as they opened a big iron gate to escort us inside. Once everyone was inside, the gate was closed and locked with a huge padlock. As we heard the sound of the gate closing behind us, all of our earlier excitement evaporated right away. Having been used to living in the wild open space of the old camp without chains and locks, the present situation made our hearts sink in despair. I feared that this new place could be more depressing compared to the one we had left. The walls surrounding the inner courtyard were approximately five metres high, with the building of three rooms facing the gate, plus another building of a similar size on the left hand side and a canteen next to the gate. We stood in a line as commanded, waiting for further instructions. Zohre Hoshur, who was standing right next to me, tapped my hand and pointed at the roofs, I noticed two angry-looking Chinese guards standing up there next to huge machine guns pointed at us. Then all the girls noticed them, and fear showed in their eyes. The team leader came with some documents in her hands. She allocated the Chinese prisoners to the building facing the gate and the rest of us were directed to other building. I was allocated to the dormitory next to the canteen along with thirty-nine women. The room was approximately seventy square metres and we had to squeeze our bedding next to one another in order to fit in.

There was hardly any space left for us to turn over when lying down.

24 February 1965
Life in Shabahu

Carrying our shovels, hoes and pickaxes, we lined up before setting off to the new work area. We walked along a country road lined with huge trees on both sides. After a while we crossed a bridge and arrived in a residential area made up of one-story office buildings with residential flats at the rear, behind which there were apple orchards. On the other side of the road was a hospital. All the residents of this area were staff from our labour camp. This area was developed and built by the prisoners of the labour camp. We proceeded a few kilometres further down the main road before turning onto a narrow path on the right. After one and half kilometres we finally reached our destination, which was a waterway. Our task was to excavate a waterway.

From that day onwards we were forced to work nonstop for over fourteen hours with very little food, by the end of each day we hardly had the strength to walk back. We managed to complete this task within a month.

28 February 1965
Baby Jélil's arrival

Jemile was already a few months pregnant before being interned in the labour camp. A couple of weeks ago she was taken to the Sanji hospital, suffering from labour pains. When we returned to the dormitory after completing the waterway task she was sitting in the dormitory with a baby in her arms. The girls screamed with excitement and ran to her side. They all took the baby from her one after another, kissing it with joy. The baby was a handsome little boy with cute and puffy cheeks. As well as being happy for Jemile everyone also felt sorry for both of them. It was the most horrible feeling of sadness to see a mother bringing an innocent child to the world in a deprived place.

Jemile was a tall, fair-skinned woman with warm brown eyes and short brown hair. Her appearance gave an outsider the impression of a quiet and timid lady, while in fact she had been arrested for prostitution, and she was two month pregnant upon her arrival here. Only God would know the truth behind someone like her being involved in such a lowly and horrible business.

'Is the baby a girl or a boy?' Turnisa asked as she lifted the baby from Jemile's arms.

'A boy', replied Jemile warmly, looking at the baby with motherly love.

'Does the baby's father know about the birth? If you inform him maybe he can get the baby out of this place', said Sajide sympathetically.

Jemile looked at the baby sadly and said, 'His father is in this very labour camp. He's been put in the male part, next to this one. His name is Ismail. Unfortunately he also can't do anything for the baby.' She looked away with a sigh.

'Does his father know about him?' asked Patime eagerly.

'Yes, he sent a towel and a bar of soap for the child.'

'Poor man... I guess that's all he can afford to offer in this place', said Zileyxa.

'Jemile, have you named the baby yet?' I asked out of curiosity.

'Not yet. I haven't thought about it.'

'Ok, let's name him Prison', Emine proposed.

Sajide gave her a 'what the hell are you thinking' stare and said firmly, 'No, we can't give him that name! The poor innocent soul, he is unfortunate enough to be born in prison. Why should he carry the name of such a horrible place for the rest of his life?'

Helchem suggested the name 'Tarim',[22] whereas Zohre preferred 'Israil', as it was similar to his father's name, Ismail. Other girls also came up with different names. I didn't like any of them. '

Why should we give him a name similar to his father's?' I said, 'If anything, his name should be closer to his mother's as she is the one who has suffered the most and who, for the time being, is the only person responsible for bringing him up. I suggest the name Abdujélil, Jélil for short. That's similar to Jemile.' Everyone immediately agreed. Jemile also liked the name, so he was named her son Jélil.

With a slight sense of pride, I took a look at the boy I just named. He was a beautiful baby with big, dark eyes and long eyelashes. His smooth skin was of milky colour, and his nose was long and straight, while his lips were pink and full. His dark and thick hair was dark poured down to his chiselled forehead.

We all adored him. As his only clothing right now was the piece of cloth that he was wrapped in, so everyone looked among their belongings to see what they could either give to his mother or make clothes for him. Mahinur made him a top and trousers, while I knitted him a hat and jumper with some wool I had. Patem made him a baggy trousers and socks. Our little boy was now beautifully dressed.

Jélil wasn't a quiet baby. He cried day and night because Jemile didn't have enough breast milk for him as she herself was constantly hungry due to the extremely limited

---

22   *A reference to the Tarim Basin in southern Xinjiang, through which flew the Tarim River. The six oasis cities, Kashgar, Maralbéshi, Aqsu, Yéngisar, Yarkand, and Khotan located around the basin have a long history of sedentary civilisation.*

food ration she received. Jélil would open his mouth to suck anything that touched his lips. We were very sad seeing our little angel suffer, but there was so little we could do. In the end we resorted to feeding him corn flour bread buns. We chewed the bun until it was very soft and then placed it in his mouth, he never refused to eat whatever he was given until he eventually fell asleep. We were all worried about his health, since the bread was hard to digest even for us, let alone a newborn baby.

12 March 1965
Jélil's agony

I have been ill for the last two days and could not work much with a fever. After being seen by the doctor I was allowed to rest for a day. I was desperate to rest as my body was in pain. The rest I longed for was short lived as Jélil never stopped crying and I spent all morning trying to calm him down. His agonising screams exhausted me physically, mentally and emotionally. Luckily Sajide was allowed to return early in the afternoon because she also didn't feel well. This allowed us to take turns in looking after the baby during the afternoon. We did everything we could to stop him from crying, but our efforts were in vain. He was hungry, but there was nothing we could feed him. Sajide and I always saved one of the wheat steam buns which we were given once a week for Jélil and shared the other one between us. We also gave him our corn steam bun, yet most of the time he would cry either of hunger or pain from indigestion.

Suddenly some cadres walked into the dormitory along with the director of the labour camp. 'Whose baby is this? Can he not stop crying?' asked the director, looking annoyed.

'This is Jemile's son. She's one of the women prisoners here', replied Sajide.

'Why is he crying so much? And where is his mother?' he asked impatiently.

'Jemile is at work digging the canal. He is left alone in the dormitory most days, we were off sick today so we are here looking after him', I replied.

'You didn't ask my question. *Why* he is crying so much? Is he ill?' The director came up to inspect Jélil, who was still crying on top of his voice.

'He is hungry I think, but we have nothing to feed him', said Sajide.

'Doesn't his mother breast feed him?'

What a ridiculous question! I answered him honestly, 'His mother does hard labour, Director. She works long hours and eats too little. She doesn't have enough milk. We often share our corn flour steam bun but the baby can't digest it.'

'Every new-born child is entitled to a ration of food under the Party's rules, aren't they? Can he be given his own ration?' he said, looking at the tall Chinese cadre standing next to him, 'Is the baby registered within the system? Where is his *hukou?*' he asked.

The tall cadre turned around to look at team leader Lai standing opposite them and said, 'I don't know where his *hukou* is, it maybe at the head office. I don't know what kind of arrangement was made by the team leaders.'

Team leader Lai looked embarrassed and said quicky, 'Let me ask the workers in the canteen.' He he rushed out, and the director also left not long after along with the other cadres. Jélil was still crying.

Later, team leader Lai came back to the room with a smile on his face. 'Good news', he said 'They have agreed to add the baby's ration to his mother's. His mother doesn't have to go to work from tomorrow. She is going to help in the kitchen.' We were delighted by the news. Our prayers had been answered.

13 March 1965
Conflict between ethnic minority and Chinese prisoners

Due to the constant rain disrupting our work of digging a cannel for a waterway we finished working one hour late. We returned to our dormitory exhausted and hungry. We were about to enter the canteen for dinner when Ayshe, who was standing at the entrance to the kitchen, scremed, 'Oh my God, they are cutting pork on the kitchen counter and weighing it in the same scales used for weighing flour. I can't believe my eyes!'

'What? Why have they brought pork into a halal canteen? This is such an insult!' Turahan shouted furiously as she rushed into the canteen, while everyone followed her. The whole place suddenly became chaotic, as the girls carried out various kitchen utensils such as the chopping boards, scales and knives into the court yard and threw them on the ground, shouting angrily, 'Why are you insulting us and our religion? You consider us criminals, that's fine, but why do you have to insult our religion?' Some of the girls also brought out the food and threw it on the ground while cursing the Chinese women. A fight immediately broke out between the Chinese and ethnic minority prisoners, and both sides were punching, kicking, and pulling one another's hair. Other female Muslim prisoners heard about this and came out of their dormitories rolling up their sleeves. They joined the fight shouting in solidarity, 'If we die we die together!' Sajide and I looked at each other in shock, but we stood aside trying to stay calm, as we didn't want to be the one's to be blamed for instigating this riot. We knew very well we could conveniently be accused of starting the disturbance because of our current political statuses.

I looked at Sajide and said jokingly, 'If we were called to war to liberate East Turkistan, these girls would definitely be on the front line', Sajide nodded and smiled.

Some of the girls carried buckets of food including the corn flour buns, which they threw into the sewage hole. Team leader Lai rushed to the scene, ordering the girls to stop, but no one paid any attention and carried on. He then left before returning with a number of senior cadres, who also tried to calm the situation by blowing their whistles and shouting at the girls at the top of their voices. No one paid heed. The courtyard had turned into a battlefield. Some of the Chinese women retaliated by collecting shovels, hoes and pickaxes from the tool store. The ethnic minorities women were about to do the same, when the prison governor walked in with other cadres and shouted, 'Stop! All of you stop immediately!' One of the prison guards standing on the wall fired into the sky, and threatened to shoot at the women if they carried on. Everyone stopped immediately; the courtyard suddenly became dead silent.

Pointing his pistols at the crowd, Governor Zhao shouted, 'Don't move, every single one of you! What the hell was going on here?' Then chaos started again as both sides replied loudly at the same time justifying their actions. 'Don't shout!' he yelled again, 'I will shoot you dead if you don't obey my orders!' He then picked roughly fifteen people from both sides and had them escorted to the head office with him.

Team leaders Gülnisa and Lai ordered the rest of us to go back to our dormitory. Less than half an hour later Patem came in and said, 'Söyün, Gülnisa wants to see you. She is waiting for you at the gate.'

I looked at Sajide. She was worried for me, 'Why has the team leader asked to see you?' I was wondering about the same myself.

Gülnisa took me to her office. I walked in, ready to bear the consequences of a fight I didn't even start. But to my great joy, I saw my mother and sister there waiting for me. I couldn't believe my eyes! My dear mother and sister, whom I'd been longing to see for so long! I ran towards them instantly but Gülnisa stopped me, 'Wait, stop! You aren't allowed to sit together. Come and sit over there.' She pointed at a chair for me to sit on.

My mother looked at me nervously and said, 'Why don't you reform yourself properly, my child?' I was surprised to hear this from her - after such a long separation, the first thing I heard from my dear mother was this! Perhaps it was the team leaders who had pressurised her to say it.

'Mother, what makes you think that I am not reforming myself? What have I done wrong?' I said in protest.

'Why didn't you inform the team leader about what's going on among the girls?'

'You know me mother, I don't like to tell tales.'

'This is not about telling tales', Gülnisa interrupted, 'You are responsible for their reformation and re-education. If you inform me with regards to their thoughts and bad behaviours, we could assist them better.'

'Their crimes have been written into their files already. What more would I know and do?' I replied defiantly.

'Don't be stubborn, my girl. You should always listen to the team leader's instructions.'

I was very upset, but said calmly, 'Mother, do you think it is fair for me to report every minor incident among the girls and every minute mistake they make? They are also people's dear daughters. They are already suffering so much in this place and I don't want my actions to cause more suffering to their lives.'

'Your daughter is good at everything, madam', Gülnisa spoke again, 'She is very capable and there is nothing that she can't do. She's got a good heart and a good personality. And everyone here respects her very much. However, her thoughts are problematic, and it is due to her incorrect thoughts that she came to this place. I like her, but if she doesn't change her ideas, I'm afraid her future will end here.'

'My girl, please listen to the team leader's advise for my sake, because what she is saying is for your own good', my mother started lecturing me.

'I will, mother. Please don't worry', I said reluctantly. I then asked about my father, siblings, and other relatives. I was also curious to know how they'd made their journey here under such terrible weather conditions, as there was not any public transport.

'We have walked for many hours carrying our stuff and the food which I have made specially for you', my mother said, 'It was difficult going in such terrible weather, with the snow mixed with rain today. The roads were very slippery and we had to walk on the side, in the mud. My winter boots were soaked and I was worried we would never make here. Luckily we got a lift here for the last part of the journey.'

My mother looked absolutely exhausted, and sadness was written all across her wrinkled face. I felt awful at the thought of her stumbling in the freezing cold weather just to see me. I wanted to hold her tight and cry on her shoulder, but I was banned from even touching her. All I could do was to look at her silently with intense emotions. Seeing a good opportunity for emotional blackmailing, Gülnisa looked at me and said,

'You see, you are making your whole family suffer. They don't deserve that. Were you not aware of their high expectations on you when they sent you to university? Instead you have ended up in this place due to your own wayward actions.'

She wasn't wrong. It was true that my parents had very high expectations on me and they had made great sacrifices in order for me to study at university. I felt deeply sorry for my mother, who had worked extremely hard in order to bring up eight children while working in the commune at the same time. Instead of sharing my parent's burden I had made life even more difficult for them.

'Mother, why did you have to endure such a long and difficult journey at this time of the year? We could have communicated by writing to each other', I said, my voice full of guilt.

'You are in our thoughts day and night. You are our biggest worry now. You have no idea how much we've missed you, so much that I'd be happy to travel millions of miles just to see you with my own eyes. How can my heart find any peace before I see with my own eyes that you are alright?' she said with tears in her eyes.

As if wanting to cheer up both of us, my little sister Sofiye asked how long I still had to serve and came over and hugged me.

'One year, my dear, I have just one more year left. Please take care of our mother while I'm away', I replied with a reassuring smile.

Just as I was savouring the moment, Gülnisa interrupted us again, 'Söyüngül, your time is up now, you have been with your family for half an hour. I am now going to arrange accommodation for them so they can rest before getting a lift home tomorrow morning.' She then inspected the things my mother had brought before passing them to me. I said my farewells to my mother and sister in deep sadness and left them reluctantly.

15 March 1965

We had been doing roadwork for three days, it was a job that normally requires at least a month's labour but we were told it had to be completed within a week.

Whatever the task, it was the same monotonous hard labour coupled with long hours, day after day. The fights among the girls continue daily, as though they had become mentally unstable as time went by. Any trivial matter would trigger a terrible fight, followed by relentless verbal assaults on one another. Perhaps that's their way of dealing with the daily hardships; everyone is too damaged psychologically.

The conflict with the Chinese prisoners has continued since the pork incident. Melike and Wang Shaopin brought lunch for us, and as soon as we finished eating,

Turnisa and Wang Xiaopin started shouting at each other. The Chinese women sided with Wang Xiaopin, whereas the ethnic minorities women backed Turnisa. The Chinese women came over and hit Turnisa, this angered our girls, who immediately hit back. The fight developed into a free-for-all and the workplace once again transformed into a battlefield where both sides fought aggressively. None of them was willing to give in.

Our team leader went home for lunch because she has young children. The Chinese team leader Lai was left in charge together with Mr Barat, who had been recently appointed as the leader for the work unit. Both of them tried to stop the fighting by ordering the girls to stop, while Sajide and I once again sat quietly on the side of the road with five or six other girls while it was happening.

No one took any notice as the brawl carried on. Mr Barat suddenly walked up to me and Sajide, shouting angrily, 'You girls are lucky that I didn't carry my pistol with me today. Otherwise I would have shot you two. Don't think I don't know. It is you who have instigated these women to fight each other.' He raised his fist as if ready to hit us. Sajide looked shocked and raised her arm in front of her face to defend herself.

'Leader Barat, think what you may, but we have nothing to do with this. You've seen all from the start: we have never been involved in anything!' I said firmly.

'You think I don't know? You pretend to be innocent but in fact you are the ones who started this and incited these girls to fight with each other', he shouted aggressively, pointing his finger at us.

'Leader, you should carry out some investigation before jumping to serious conclusions like this', said Sajide.

'Oh! So you are telling me now that *I* am making things up, huh? That I am wrong in accusing you of something you didn't do? Don't try to fool me. I know damn well that you two are the root of the problems right from the start!' He shouted at the top of his voice as he stood close to us, which caused his spit to splash on our faces. More cadres came to the workplace and managed to stop the fighting. Our workmates noticed that Mr Barat was shouting and gesturing at us and came close by to check what was going on.

Turaxan said, 'Mr Barat, don't blame them for this. They had nothing to do with it. If you want to know the truth you can ask me. You are a Muslim so you know how we feel. We all consider pork as haram. How was it our fault that they bring pork into our canteen? It's not like they don't know! Furthermore, we hardly ever see any halal meat prepared for us, but they often have pork to eat. Where are they getting it from? Not to mention that we aren't even allowed to have eggs in our canteen. Why are the rules so relaxed for them and so strict for us? We are deprived of so many things but they are not!'

Turnisa interrupted Turaxan, 'Leader, before trying to blame it all on us, perhaps you should investigate the case to find out the real problems which have caused the conflict.'

Emine stepped in and said, 'Even though we are criminals, we remain Muslims. we don't stain our religion by eating haram food. We respect our faith no matter where we are.'

Pashaxan joined in, shaking her head, 'Leader, you are a Muslim too. You don't eat pork, do you? What if someone sneakily put pork in your food? How would you feel? We felt insulted! They keep discriminating against us to the extent that we can't bear it any longer.' She raised her eyebrows so high that we found her face comical.

The girls made their complaints one after another. In the end Mr Barat yelled, 'Ok this is enough! Go back to your work!' After they all left, he turned around again and stared at Sajide threateningly, 'Listen, if this kind of incident happens again, *you two* will pay for it with your heads. I'll say it again: consider yourselves lucky today that I'm not carrying my gun with me. Otherwise I could have finished you already.'

My blood was boiling with fury. I couldn't stay silent any longer so I retorted, finally raising my voice, 'Leader, we are human beings and not sparrows. You can't kill us as you wish. The Party has rules and regulations, which should apply to everyone. Everybody has their own brain and they are capable of making their own decisions without any other individual's influence. None of these girls would have ended up here if they had listened to people!' I stormed away from him back to work.

At night I was woken up by a piercing scream. I jumped out of my bed and tried to see with my sleepy eyes in the darkness what was happening. I recognised the voices of Patem and Nuriye. They were fighting. In a crowded room like ours, it was not even possible to turn over without hitting someone, let alone to fight. I quickly woke Sajide up and led her to the door way.

Apparently the reason for their fighting was that Patem's hand had hit Nuriye's face when she turned over in her sleep. Nuriye retaliated by slapping Patem's hand very hard. This made Patem sit up, which gave Nuriye an excuse to slap her in the face. Patem couldn't understand why Nuriye was hitting her and instinctively struck back. During their struggles they stepped on other girls, and this in turn woke up other girls, who also started attacking each other. The room descended into chaos as more and more girls joined in the melee, screaming, punching, kicking, and pulling each other's hair. As we stood bewildered at the door, I said to Sajide, 'I hope they don't end up killing someone in the dark. This is getting out of control.' She turned her face away and said, 'I am *so* fed up with their fights, as if our lives were not hard already! We can't even have few hours of peaceful sleep because of these people. What did we do wrong to deserve this? Oh God, when this is going to end? When?' Sajide almost cried. As things started to get worse, we ran outside to avoid being hit.

Suddenly someone let out a scream so loud that it made the whole place tremble. A number of team leaders and cadres entered the courtyard carrying torches. They asked us what was going on. We said that we didn't know. They entered the room and we followed them. In the torchlight we saw that some girls were half naked, whilst others' faces were unrecognisable, their clothes in a miserable state. Dust was flying everywhere. As soon as they saw the torches, the girls ran looking for their bed sheets to cover themselves with.

I then saw Patem's face and hands covered in blood. Nuriye's hair looked like she had been dragged through a hedge backwards, and she was out of breath, gasping for air as if she had just finished a long race. Emine's hair was covered in straw, and one of her eyes was swollen, red and bruised, as she sat crying in a corner. Everyone was coughing and sputtering in the dusty room.

We quickly ran to our places. We managed to find our beddings with the help of torches, but our sheets were covered in straw and dust. The Chinese cadres stood at the entrance to the room, swearing and cursing us in the most obnoxious manner for a long time before leaving.

26 March 1965
Meeting with my father's old friend Ma Jingtang

Patem and I were sent to work at a Mill today where five or six men were working. While we were tying up bags of flour, I noticed a tall strong built man who kept staring at me. He looked like he could be either Chinese or Dungan.

'Söyün, does that man know you? He keeps looking at you', Patem whispered to me. Indeed, he looked familiar to me but I couldn't remember where I'd seen him before. As soon as the team leader left the room he came over to me immediately and said, 'You look like someone I know. What's your father's name?'

I paused for a moment before replying, 'My father's name is Salih. Why?'

'Oh! You are Salih's daughter! How is he? Is he all right? Where is he now?' he asked me warmly as his eyes lit up upon hearing my father's name. After I had answered all the questions he introduced himself as Ma Jingtang, from Chöchek, and his Islamic name[23] was Majid.

'Lao Ma,[24] it looks like you know her?' asked a tall big man next to him who introduced himself as Musa.

'Yes, her father was a good friend of mine, a brilliant man. He was the director of Qarashehir Local Goods Limited Company. I accompanied him to Qarashehir where we started the company. Salih was very young at that time but he was a very knowledgeable, intelligent, competent, and hard working. Above all he was a humanist. We also started an export business to Russia, which grew fast and was profitable. As the business expanded, he acquired land and designed the buildings to be built there. He became very successful and was transferred to Kashgar to set up a new company, which I learned was also a successful project. But later a Chinese guy replaced him as director and Salih was sent back to Ürümchi. I moved back to Chöchek that year and I haven't seen Salih since.'

Musa said, 'Such a small world! You never know who you cross path with every day. I bet you've never ever thought you would meet your old friend's daughter in this place.'

'It is true. I would never have expected to see Salih's daughter in a labour camp', He sighed.

I remembered that my father had mentioned Ma Jintang's name a long time ago when he told me about how he set up the business in Qarashehir, and said with excitement, 'Uncle Ma, my father has told me about you. He said you were from Chöchek. You used to go hunting with him, didn't you, and he'd bring his dog Palwan along.'

'Yes, that's right. Salih loved hunting. We used to go hunting on our days off with Palwan', he laughed cordially.

Just as we were enjoying our conversation when the team leader returned to the Mill, we quickly returned to our work. Mr Lao Ma treated me like his own daughter, helping me in every way, whenever he could during the time I worked in the Mill. One day the head office called all the prisoners to a meeting in the central square of the labour camp. They announced that Lao Ma was rearrested and to be sent to a security prison. He was chained up and taken away in a police van. I was devastated as the girls

---

23   *Dungan Muslims usually have two given names, one Chinese and one Perso-Arabic, i.e. Islamic.*
24   *In the Chinese language, elderly people are often informally addressed as 'lao' (old) plus their family name.*

looked at me sadly with tears in their eyes. That would be the last time I ever saw him.

When I told my father of his re-arrest after I was released from the prison he was very sad. He said to me that Lao Ma is a very kind considerate person with a generous nature whom he always had a very high respect for.

24 April 1965
Actress Merpu's arrival

It's been a beautiful day of spring. The day was warm and pleasant, and the endless blue seemed to be dripping from the cloudless sky. The green leaves had already appeared on the trees, and the fields were covered in a luscious green carpet. These kind of sunny days always cheer us up. We walked about six to seven kilometres to the wheat fields close to the men's accommodation. Our job was to pull out the weeds and the wild grass growing among the wheat. Having started very early in the morning, my legs and my back ached from the constant bending and squatting by midday. I wished to have a break but the team leader stood by us watching all the time so there was no chance for such luxury. At about two o'clock the team leader left us to go back home. As soon as she disappeared from view we ran to the edge of the field, throwing ourselves under a big tree to lie down and rest.

'Oh it's so beautiful! I hope no one comes to disturb us, I really need to stretch my legs', said Amine lying down next to me.

'Thank God the team leader has young children and has to go back for a while. Otherwise how would we get any chance to rest', said Sajide with a smirk. All the girls joined us one after another.

Suddenly, Helchem noticed that the team leader of the No. 2 Men's Group coming towards us. We quickly sat up.

'Hi girls, I have big news for you. The actress Merpu has just arrived. You won't be bored any more', he said with excitement.

'What? Wow! Merpu, the actress from the National Theatre?' the girls shouted, overjoyed. Some of them got up and started jumping up and down, impatient to meet her.

'Oh Team Leader, what time is it?' Turnisa asked softly raising her perfectly shaped eyebrows and flashing her big eyes almost in a seductive way.

He looked at his watch and said, 'You will finish in two hours. Anyway, I think you should return to work now.' He then made his way in the direction where his group was working.

'He looks very pleased today. He is definitely in a good mood now that Merpu is coming', Turnisa smiled with a wink. We all laughed with her.

'Poor man, I feel sorry for him. He must get so bored in this place', Bilqiz commented, 'Even we become excited each time a new woman arrives, let alone him. Obviously he is happy to know that Merpu is here. Oh poor him, forced to spend most of his life in such a place because of people like us.'

The girls were desperate to return to the dormitory to see Merpu. But I wasn't too bothered.

'Why are you so happy to see someone brought to this miserable place?' I asked, 'I personally wouldn't wish this sort of suffering upon anyone.'

'You are right. But don't you think that those privileged people should also experience hardships like ours, in places like this. Then they will have a better understanding about the lives of people like us?' said Mahire, justifying her excitement with a noble reason.

'An interesting point you have there. But they are not responsible for our suffering. They are not the people who imprisoned us', Sajide remarked.

'Oh are you feeling sorry for her now?' Saadet teased her with a grin, 'Prisons along with hardships are not only for poor people like us, but also for people who have positions in the society enjoying the high life. Let them come here, we will teach them good lessons while reforming them to become like us!' The other girls seemed to agree with her.

I was surprised by her comments. Both Sajide and I found it hard to understand their way of thinking. As soon as we reached the gate, the girls ran through into the dormitory. I was the last one to enter. As always I went over and picked baby Jélil off the floor to kiss his soft cheeks. Jélil was growing up fast; he gave us so much joy, whether by smiling like an angel, or crying like a devil.

I then went over to my place. There I saw the famous Merpu. She was relaxing near the stove, her legs stretched out. She looked like she was still acting in a play. The girls were all sat around her asking about her well-being. I watched Merpu's response to the girls' questions, some time she pretended to smile, other times she had tears in her big eyes. I didn't think she looked natural. She appeared as if she was on the stage. I didn't join them and went to mind my daily chores instead.

After the evening political studies, I returned to my room to make my bed. Merpu left the girls and came to my side. We greeted each other politely.

'I am so pleased to see you here', she said, 'At least I know that I am not alone.

A lot of rumours have spread among people since you were arrested. Members of our organisation were deeply affected by your situation. People still speak highly of you.'

I was surprised when she mentioned 'our organisation', so I asked curiously, 'Were you a member of an organisation?'

'Yes, I was a member of Mr Ötkür and Haji Yaqup's association. The association was investigated and I was turned in. I've been given three years. They brought me here', she said.

I was puzzled. I have seen Mr Ötkür in the Security Prison before. What kind of association could it have been if the leader was already in prison? Perhaps the association wasn't exposed at the time when he was imprisoned?

Sajide read my mind and said quickly, 'But we've seen Mr Ötkür in the prison. Would that that be the same Mr Ötkür you are talking about?'

'Yes, Haji Yaqup remained the person in charge after Mr Ötkür was taken away. He is out of prison now', she answered.

'But you said that the association was exposed. Have they been arrested again?' I asked nervously.

'No, I was the only one to be arrested so far.'

'That is interesting. They are the ones who set up and were running the assocation, yet they are free while you are here!' I said.

'Exactly, that is very strange indeed', Sajide added.

'Well, I have no idea', replied Merpu. Her words were suspiciously contradictory, so I decided to be very careful when talking to her.

She stayed quiet for a while before speaking again, 'Haji Yaqup is a very good man. He knows a lot about the history of Xinjiang. I had a role in a film on Lutpulla Mutellip.[25] According to him Lutpulla's wife betrayed him and handed him over to the police.'

'That's right. I also heard that it was Lutpulla's wife Nurnisa who betrayed him. Later Haji Yaqup married her after Lutpulla was executed', I said.

'Yes, that's true. I played Nurnisa in the film, but when we finished the film, Nurnisa complained about the plot, saying that the film would give her a bad name and ruin her relation with her son. In the end they changed the storyline and claimed that Lutpulla's friend Baqi betrayed him instead. For that reason my role was cut short', Merpu explained.

As she was talking, I imagined her role in the film. She's a real beauty: tall, elegant,

---

25   *One of the most influential Uyghur poets of the early 20th century.*

with big and charming eyes and silky fair skin. She always spoke playfully with a soft voice.

25 April 1965

Team leader Turnisa approached me when I was working in the field and asked curiously if I knew the reason why Merpu ended up here. I explained that she's here because the organisation she was involved in was denounced.

'Pah! What kind of organisation was she involve in? She is lying, that woman. Don't trust a single word she says. I hope you didn't say anything to her?'

'No, don't worry. We said nothing to her', I reassured her.

'Good, Merpu was brought to here but we haven't had any information about her criminal background. So be careful with her. I don't think she was involved in any sort of organisation at all', she warned. I was very surprised to hear this kind of warnings from a team leader.

Turnisa was moved from Bortala Labour Camp to Shabahu and has been working as our team leader since she arrived. She is a happy person who would joke and dance around the girls. She likes to chat with everyone when no one was around watching. Her husband, Atiq Hikmet, is a cadre in the labour camp. Her aged mother and a younger brother also lived with her. Her mother is a simple, kind-hearted religious lady. One day Turnisa punished us with one hour of extra work for not working fast enough. Half an hour later we saw Turnisa's mother rushing towards us, out of breath and shouting, 'My child, why don't you let the girls go? Why do you have to keep them so long in the field? They are also people's precious children, just like yourself!' We were all moved by her kindness, some of the girls even started crying. Turnisa was embarrassed and annoyed. She said, 'Oh mother, when will you understand the rules of this place? You shouldn't get involve in this.' And then she took us back to the dormitory quickly.

One day when we were labouring near Turnisa's house, her mother came to see us. She quickly looked around and, seeing no cadres around us, she took out five pieces of *nan* wrapped in a scarf, which she had carried under her arm. She said, 'Quick, quick, my poor girls, take them. I made these this morning at home. You must have missed this bread a lot!' The bread tasted so delicious that we finished it in a matter of a minute. It had been two years since I had a piece of homemade fresh *nan*. We all thanked her for her kindness. She then said a prayer for us, 'May God bless you girls, and keep you safe and well! May this hardship end soon!' I noticed she had tears in her eyes.

Team leader Gülnisa, on the other hand, was very different from Turnisa. She's always very serious and harsh. She often shouts at the girls but rarely uses abusive language, which sets her apart from most of the Chinese cadres, who are very rude and violent and like to abuse the prisoners verbally and physically. I've never seen any ethnic minority cadres hit any prisoners during my time in the labour camp.

29 April 1965
Sajide's prison term comes to an end

Today was the last day of Sajide's prison term and we decided to do something special to celebrate. Zohre offered some cooking oil and I had some flour and sugar my mum had brought me during her visit. We used the stove outside the kitchen to make a special dessert for dinner. Everyone was very happy for Sajide, and we made jokes and laughed during the dinner. Later Sajide was called to the head office to be informed officially that her term had ended and that she was going to start a new life. She was told to move to new accommodation. Seeing Sajide in such happy mood pleased me. It was almost too good to be true and deep inside, I was worried that something might go wrong. The dream I had last night kept flashing through my mind, and, no matter how much I tried to push it away, it kept coming back to disturb me.

In my dream Sajide and I were dressed up in our old traditional clothes as we left the prison happily. As soon as we walked out of the prison gate the sky turned dark and stormy. People were running all over the place. Armed police were everywhere, arresting anyone they encountered. There were four armed guards standing on top of the prison walls near the watchtowers firing machine guns at the people running below. Sajide and I were terrified, as we looked around for a place to hide. We found a big rock around the corner and quickly hid behind it to watch what was happening.

I saw black lorries driven out of the prison gate fully loaded with prisoners. The thundering sound of the people screaming as they were running for their lives echoed in the sky. Suddenly someone crawled quietly from behind to where we were squatting behind the rock. Startled, I turned around and found an old man with a long white beard.

'Where did you come from, my children?' he whispered.

'We came out of the prison over there, grandpa. I served three years and Sajide served two years. But as soon as we came out we saw the police were arresting everyone so we decided to hide ourselves here', I replied.

'I don't understand why they are beating, arresting, and shooting at people', said Sajide after me.

'My children, our world has changed. People's lives have become worthless. If we don't stay here until the situation calms down we will lose our lives.' He then mumbled to himself as if reminding himself of something before he continued to speak, taking out a book from under his arm, 'Did you say you have just been released from prison?'

'Yes. Which book are you holding?' asked Sajide.

'This is the Book of Fate, my child. Let me read your destiny.' Then he put the book on the ground and bent his head down to look closer at what it said. After an excruciating moment he lifted his head and said to us, 'You can't be free from prison in two to three years; it will take at least ten years. However even that is not certain.'

While he was explaining the readings to us, I looked around and realised that we had already been surrounded by police ready to handcuff us. The old man suddenly disappeared, leaving me in great shock. I was wondering who he was when the police twisted my hands behind my back to handcuff me. At that moment I woke up. My arm was in pain because Patem was lying on it.

Two days later I told Sajide of my dream. It worried her. She said, 'Dear Söyün, I don't know why you had such a terrible dream. May God save us from any more suffering. I hope your dream won't turn out to be real.' But as I feared, her release wasn't straightforward after all: one week later Sajide got permission to visit her sister in Ürümchi for a week, but didn't get the permission to leave the camp permanently despite her prison term having come to an end for some time. She had been notified that the leadership of the prison would discuss her case before they can allow her to return home.

20 September 1965
Sajide's return

I couldn't believe my eyes when I found Sajide sitting in the dormitory as I returned. I ran and hugged her with excitement. But she looked terribly sad, having been called back from her home by the leaders of the labour camp. No matter how much I tried to comfort her, she remained in an inconsolable sadness. We chatted for a long time, she told me about Abliz Sewirdin and Ahmet Toxti, who were both serving their sentences in the Tarim Labour Camp. Abliz had been sentenced to 19 years; along with a few other young prisoners, he had managed to escape the labour camp a year later, and he went to a remote village outside Tarim to live with a Uyghur family, helping them herd animals for a year. One night he suffered a heart attack and almost died. The couple he was living with were terrified and asked him to write a letter to say that he was dying of heart attack. Fortunately he survived and recovered well, and turned himself in at the labour camp. Now he is practicing as a doctor in the camp treating prisoners. As for Ahmet Toxti, he was sentenced to 13 years and working as a hard abourer like other ordinary prisoners. Sajide had heard their stories from prisoners who returned from Tarim who had known Abliz and Ahmet.

I was sad. How could they receive such long sentence for the same reasons that we have been imprisoned? They are going to spend all their youth in the hard labour camp now. I can't imagine Abliz, my handsome best friend, in the harsh prison condition. What will he look like after serving almost 20 years in Tarim, in the middle of the Taklimakan Desert?

'Aren't you worried about yourself? I wonder what is going to happen to us. I fear I may be put under surveillance outside prison… And to be honest with you the labour camp is better than being under surveillance. I just can't see any light at the end of the tunnel based on what's happening right now', said Sajide with despair.

I feared the same and prayed that God would save us from hardships. We talked until she was called to the office. She then returned and told me that she was leaving tomorrow, and someone from the head office was going to accompany me home.

'I don't think I will ever be able to regain my freedom. Söyün, the dream you had, the white bearded man, it still haunts me. Maybe is a sign. I am scared', She said with tears in her eyes.

'My dear sister, don't think too much right now. Let's hope nothing worse than this will happen. Perhaps it's a new rule that they have to accompany the prisoner in person to their home address?' I tried to be optimistic, trying to lift her worries. We didn't sleep all night, lying on the floor and chatting. Early in the morning she was called to leave. We parted with tears.

15 November 1965
Sopsun's arrest

There were about forty to fifty women standing in front of the office upon our return from work. As always the girls became very excited at the thought of so many women joining us. After the dinner the new comers were dispersed to their rooms. We welcomed those coming into our room, which was now heavily overcrowded. They were originally in Dadamtu Labour Camp; then they got transferred to Bajahu Labour Camp for a short period before being finally transferred to here. Those who had been sentenced to Reform Through Labour were kept in Bajahu, and the remainder, who had been sentenced to Education Through Labour, were brought here. We helped them to settle in as we got to know the girls slowly. During the study hour the team leader arrived to tell the girls the rules of the camp.

I was chatting with Zohre when one of the new girls came over and introduced herself as Ruqiye from Ghulja. We both introduced ourselves to her. Upon hearing my name, she said, 'Oh, that's beautiful name! I've never heard that name before,'

'She is Tatar that is why she has a special name', Zohre said with a smile.

'Oh are you Tatar? There was a Tatar girl called Seyde in Dadamtu Labour Camp. She was transferred to Bajahu as well. She'd been sentenced to 12 years for being a "rightist". She was blond, and I thought all Tatar people were blond, but you are not, you have dark hair.'

'Well, I guess in every ethnic group there are people who look different from others', I said.

Within days everybody got acquainted with each other. Among the new girls there was a tall beautiful Kazakh woman who did not interact as much with the group. She always looked angry while distancing herself from everyone. Once Mahire asked how she was, and she replied with astonishing rudeness – 'What the hell has it got to do with you, bitch?' So no one dared to speak to her after that. She looked constantly vigilant and nervous. I thought she must have gone through some horrible experiences in the past.

There was also a very pretty Mongol girl of slim build and small stature with beautiful big brown eyes and long hair down to her waist. She was intelligent with a good sense of humour. Within days we became soul mates. Her name was Sopsun.

One day Zohre Emet asked Sopsun, 'How did you end up here when you are so intelligent?'

'I am not sorry for being here', she replied with a smile, 'It relieves me from the pressure of my family life. My father had three brothers, having inherited land from their father they worked hard to earn money to purchase more land, animals, and goods and to build houses.

'They became well known and respected by the local people. One of my brothers worked at a news agency in Ürümchi. Late one night in 1951 he got home unexpectedly, looking very tense. As he sat down he started to talk to my father about the implementation of the government's land reform policy. He urged my father to give away all the land and the wealth as gifts to the government, and keep only the basic necessary things in the house. He said, "You must inform my uncles as well. Let them know Government's land reform policy, and try to persuade them to do the same. Otherwise everything will be confiscated and the consequences will be disastrous for their families. If you don't give up all the wealth voluntarily they will accuse you of being a "capitalist roader" and you could be executed in public." Three hours later he went back to Ürümchi.

'My father was in shock, and left immediately for his brother's house to inform them of my brother's visit. He told his brothers about the upcoming land policy, including the possible repercussions if they fail to comply. But no matter how he tried his brothers refused to listen to his warnings. They said, "We worked hard all our lives to build up all these wealth, and no one has the right to take it away from us. We will never give it up." My father did all he could but failed to make them change their mind.

'The next day my father handed over all his possessions including my mother's gold jewelleries to the government as my brother had advised. A meeting was held in the government office praising my father as a model citizen of the people. My father's brothers laughed at him and called him a coward.

'In less than two months the governmental land reform team arrived to implement the new policy. My three uncles were accused of being illegal land owners and capitalist roaders. Not only were everything they owned confiscated, but they also were subjected to violent public struggle meetings, during which they were verbally and physically abused for three days on end before being publicly executed. My father didn't escape the persecution despite the fact that he had given up all his wealth. He was also branded as an "evil landowner" and he was put under surveillance.

'I was seventeen when all this was happening. I was one of the most popular girls in the area and had a number of suitors.

'One day, a party secretary came for a visit with some of the cadres from the local council and asked my dad to marry me off to a thirty-year-old destitute man with mental disabilities, who would never have been a marriage candidate for any girl. This made us very nervous, as it was not a request but more of a demand, judging by the statement made. They said, "If you have reformed yourself to become a working class citizen then you would offer your daughter to a son of the poorest class." My father didn't know what to say, so he said that he needed to discuss the matter with rest of the family members before being able to give them an answer.

'When my father broke the news everyone were shocked by the demand, and all of us cried.

"I don't care what they do to me. I am not going to give my beautiful daughter to a man like that!" My father said to my mother. My parents called my brother back from Ürümchi to discuss what to do. Obviously no one was happy for me to be forced into marriage with someone like that. But at the same time time everyone was aware of the danger my father would face if he didn't give the Party a positive answer. We felt as if my father was sentenced to death. I cried and worried day and night and couldn't sleep for days.

'I couldn't let them take my father away to be executed like my uncles. So I decided to marry this Party-appointed groom as we had already been mourning the death of my uncles for two months. I didn't want to plunge my family into further darkness. It was my duty now to sacrifice my happiness to save my dear father and everyone else.

'One morning during breakfast I told everyone about my decision. They looked shocked. To convince my family, I said, "I know that he is not good looking or clever but at least he is not a bad person. Maybe the poverty and hopelessness has made him what he is, and I may be able to help him." After a long debate the family agreed with me. My father organised a big wedding to make me happy. I looked splendid in my traditional wedding gown. My family, friends and admirers looked as if a funeral had taken place, and their tears were not of joy but of sorrow. When the time came for me to leave my home to go to my husband's house I finally broke down. According to the tradition, male relatives followed me to my new home, shedding tears while singing love songs. I looked back at them in silence with tears running down my cheeks. The only thing that consoled me was the thought that my father would be safe.

'On the wedding night he showed no interest in me. He fell a sleep before I even went to bed. According to our tradition, male relatives would stay outside the house making cheeky remarks about the bride and groom. He paid no attention the noise outside and slept like a baby. My mother in law was a good lady. She treated me well and always kept saying to me, "My dear daughter, don't look down on my son, please try to love him." I'd say to her frankly, "You should look at your son, he doesn't understand anything about love, he works like a bull in the field, and comes home to eat and falls asleep. Sometimes he falls asleep while eating. There's very little I can do." She tried her best to teach him about love and affection, but he remained the same, he simply didn't seem to understand such emotions. I was with him for seven years, during which we had a son. Our relationship always remained cold. I felt lonely. In the end I couldn't bear the sight of him. So I decided to divorce him but the court turned down my request.

'I was depressed. My daily life was miserable. I desperately needed someone to lift my spirits and show me some hope in life. During this period a lot of young Chinese graduates came from Shanghai and settled in our area. One of them fell in love with me. He was good looking and full of life, so I liked him as well. Slowly an affair developed. As people became aware of our relationship, they reported it to the party leaders. Not long afterwards I was arrested by the police, accused of insulting my peasant class husband, and sentenced to three years. After that we were formally divorced. The official divorce statement was, "We can't allow our peasant class friend continue to be insulted by such a woman."

'The police handcuffed me and paraded me through the streets to shame me in front of everyone. I was not ashamed of myself and walked upright like a hero. People came out from their houses and watched me being led away. I could see in their eyes that they were sorry for me. I even saw some people crying for me. I was so happy to have my divorce that me feel I was free like a bird. I would rather spend three years in prison and get my freedom than live with a man who I have never loved and will never love. I have spent two years of my prison terms in Dadamtu Labour Camp already and now I have one year left.'

'So where is your son now?' I asked her after her long story.

'He lives with his father, and my mother-in-law is looking after him', she answered with sigh, 'I have to admit that the hardest part was to leave him behind. He had always been with me since he was born. He looks like me and even his character is similar to mine. He is everything to me but it has been two years since I saw him last. He is in my thoughts all the time, and I miss him terribly.' At that point she burst into tears. The happiness that had shown on her face when she talked about her freedom from her marriage fell apart as she thought about her boy. As we sat quietly in deep sympathy, yet not knowing how to comfort her.

As Sopsun spoke about her uncle's execution, I thought of a story told by Abliz about his father's execution, which he had shared with us in our university dormitory -

'I was in the primary school at the time of my father's death. That day we were taken to an open court hearing, some older children came to me saying that my father was going to be executed. You cannot imagine the panic I felt at that moment in time. My lips became dry, as my head spun with the thought of my father's demise, while my heart pulsed so fast that it made my chest ache. I said to myself that I must do something to stop them from killing my father. I thought if I could reach the person who is appointed to execute him, I could hold on to him begging for the freedom of my father. With these thoughts in my mind I ran towards the stage. But the stadium was full of people, so I kept tripping over their feet before I finally managed to get close to the stage.

'It was not long after reaching the front that my father was escorted to the centre of the stage by armed personnel. He was wearing a high pointed "dunce's hat", with the board hanging from his neck with the sign for execution. The crowd at that moment spat at him and shouted, "capitalist roader", "cruel rich landlord" and so on. It was difficult to recognise him as his face was covered in bruises and blood. I felt I was about to faint. I wanted to scream but I was unable to as if I was being strangled. I wanted to run to save my father but my legs were frozen. I don't remember what happened next. When I woke up I was at home. I heard that they had brought my father's body home. I passed out once again. When I woke up again, I was told that my father had been buried.

'I was ill for over a month, unable to go to school or eat properly. My childhood was over. I couldn't forget the image of my poor father when he was husked onto the stage. The trauma will stay with me forever. I will never forget and forgive those who killed him. The pain in my heart felt as if I was being stabbed and set on fire, which I still feel to this day.'

I saw his teardrops running down his face and fell onto the floor. He was covering his face as he was telling the story, the flood of emotions lasted for several minutes before calmness descended. During this time the girls in the dormitory cried in silence with him. Even now whenever I remember his story, my eyes glazes over with sadness.

At the time of my arrest, I was questioned about what Abliz said in relation to his father. I denied any knowledge of the story. The authorities were aware of the words he used: he swore to avenge his father's death. For this reason he was sentenced to nineteen years of hard labour, sixteen years longer than my own sentence for the same alleged crime.

13 March 1966
Removal of the female prisoners
to a new settlement in Maralbéshi, Kashgar

After breakfast we gathered in the courtyard as usual, waiting for the team leader to come and take us to work. Fifteen minutes had already passed but the team leader still hadn't showed up. We kept looking at the locked gate, hoping it would open any minute. Girls started asking each other what day it was and wondered if it was a special day for celebration. We always preferred to work in the fields rather than being locked up in this depressing tiny prison surrounded by its high five-metre walls.

The wait was agonising. About an hour later the gate opened. Team leader Gülnisa came through and blew the whistle. We picked up our tools quickly and lined up. We stood anxiously, knowing very well that she had come with some news. She quickly inspected us to make sure we were all present before reading out a list of names.

I expected my name to be called but she had finished with ethnic minority names and started reading out Chinese names. When she finished she ordered, 'All the girls I have called out must get ready within half an hour. You will be collected and transferred to the New Life Labour Camp in Qara Qilchin, located in Maralbéshi. You will participate in the development of the place and start a new life there. You will settle there permanently and start your families and build a bright future.' Jemile's name was on the list, but little Jélil would have to be dropped off at her mother's in Kucha on the way to the new camp. Everyone was saddened that baby Jélil was leaving, as he was source of our joy during these dark times.

None of the girls were happy about this decision and some of them started crying. On the list for transfer there were girls whose prison terms should have ended.

Among these girls there was Zohre, who looked stunned.

'Team Leader, did you say that I have to go there as well?' she asked, her voice trembling with disbelief.

'Yes, that is right', answered Gülnisa.

'But I have served my two-year sentence and I have been in the New Life Group for over two months. I am no longer a prisoner' Zohre protested in frustration.

'Well, that wasn't my decision and I can't do anything about it. You must obey the Party's decision. Go and get ready now', Gülnisa replied coldly.

Zohre looked shocked and angry. Her face turned red as she burst into tears. She was shaking. She turned around in fury and stormed to the dormitory. I felt very sorry for her.

All of us were devastated by this terrible news. Gülnisa repeatedly shouted at people to be ready in half an hour before she left. We assisted the girls to pack their belongings as fast as we could. Half an hour later the truck arrived and all the selected girls were forced onto it. We all waved goodbye to each other with eyes and cheeks soaked in tears. Poor souls, they were so fervently looking forward to starting a new life after serving their prison term, only to be banished forever to a life of hell in another labour camp.

17 March 1966
The brothers' escape

Ill with a high fever, I was unable to drag myself out of bed. The team leader saw my condition and allowed me to remain in the dormitory. Hejer Buwi was also in the room. She has been ill since her arrival From the Dadamtu Labour Camp. She looked depressed and sad all the time. We have always brought food for her from the canteen, hoping that she would recover soon and become a part of the social group. But she hardly ever spoke or smiled to anyone. I was concerned about her I wanted to speak to her, but I didn't know how to approach her. Today it's just me and her in the room, so I decided to try and strike a conversation.

I walked over to her bed and sat down next to her, asking, 'How are you feeling today? Have you been seen by a doctor? Do you know what your problem is?'

Adjusting her scarf, she slowly raised her head from the pillow to look at me and said, 'I have a... women's problem, I was given medication but it doesn't seem to have worked.' She sighed. I wanted to ask her more questions but I was worried my questions would upset her. I just sat next to her in silence. After a while, she started talking voluntarily -

'I was an only child in the family. Two years after I was married my mother became pregnant. Sadly she died giving birth to Abduqadir, my brother. I accepted the responsibilty of bringing him up, my husband loved him as much as I did, treating him as if he was our own son. He grew up to be a fine young man. One day he went to the market to buy vegetables. Not long after he left, my neighbour's daughter Peride rushed into the house screaming: "Sister Hejer Buwi, Sister Hejer Buwi..." Her face was pale and she was shaking. I asked what the matter was, and she told me that there had been a mass shooting in the city centre and apparently Abduqadir had been shot. I couldn't believe what I was hearing. We ran out of the house to the city centre, which was close by. Arriving at the scene of the shooting we found a sea of blood with bodies scattered everywhere. My mind was in tumoil, as I shouted frantically, "Abduqadir, my brother, my darling, my son, where are you? Answer me!"

'With most of the dead and wounded covered in blood, it was impossible to recognise anyone. Suddenly I heard Peride shout, "Sister Hejer Buwi, there is a young man lying over there who looks like brother Abduqadir." I went up close and dropped down to my knees to hug him, crying hysterically. A man close by tried to comfort me by saying, "Are you certain this is your brother? Have you looked carefully?" I steadied myself to look more closely, to find out that it was not my brother. I then stood up slowly to look around me before going over to look at other bodies. Peride shouted again, "There is an injured man over there calling for his sister." I went to look. As I got closer I could hear him calling, "Sister, sister!" He was maimed beyond recognition. When I knelt down by his side he opened his eyes - you could see and feel his pain by looking at his eyes. He took out a piece of paper from his shirt pocket murmuring, "Please, sister, take care of this." He stretched his arms towards me, and as soon as I took the document his hand dropped lifelessly. I knew he had died before I could speak to him.

'I held him in my arms, cried and cried, wishing I could bring him back with my body's warmth. Suddenly the gate of the city hall compound opened and hundreds of soldiers and policemen rushed out to secure the area, collecting all the injured and dead and moving them into the compound area as other military personal disperse the people who were looking for their loved ones.

'Not long after clearing the area, the whole place was hosed down to wash away the blood. Items of clothing were collected and disposed of, and within one hour it was impossible to tell that a blood bath has taken place there.'

'The police and the soldiers disappeared back into the compound closing the gate behind them, leaving us in a purgatory of emptiness and despair. No one dared to interfere by asking questions during the clean up. I stood outside the gate crying like a madwoman as I called my brother's name again and again. Peride was busy during this time asking questions to other people who were standing around near the gate. After a while she came to me and said, "Sister, I just heard that the wounded have been taken to the hospital. Shall we go and make enquiries there?"

'We rushed to the hospital. We asked doctors if there was anyone by the name of Abduqadir. After a while we were informed that there was indeed an Abduqadir, but I was not allowed to see him. I requested to have a look at his clothes to see if I could recognise them. The clothes were brought over and they were soaked in blood;

the trousers had bullet holes along the length of the legs, but they didn't belong to my brother. I asked the nurse if the owner of the trousers was still alive. She said yes, but his condition is critical and his legs had to be amputated in order to save his life.

'I was more and more shocked by horrors that I saw and the stories I heard in the hospital. It was hard to come to terms with the reality. I didn't know what to do next. Suddenly one of my neighbours, Mr Hüseyin, walked in and asked me what I was doing there. I told him everything that'd happened. Then he said that he'd seen Abduqadir getting on a truck with other young men about an hour before, and they were heading to the Russian border.

'I thanked and dashed out of the hospital to hire a horsecart to take me to the border. I got off halfway on the journey and flagged down a passing truck asking the driver to take me to Khorghas.[26] Arriving at the border crossing I found a sea of young people moving backwards and forwards. Worry and panic was written on everyone's face. The question on everyone's mind was, why is the border closed? There seemed to be some kind of serious tension between China and the Soviet Union.

'There were some people who had permission to cross the border but were now forbidden to cross. Others were fearful of returning to Ghulja because of the massacre. Suddenly we saw many military trucks approaching us; people's facial expressions went from those of worry to those of horror, as they now had nowhere to run or hide. It was just a case of waiting for the inevitable to happen.

'The trucks encircled the crowds before stopping, armed soldiers jumped of the vehicles to encircle the people at gunpoint. We were all chained up in groups before being searched. I had the letter from the dying man in my pocket, which I had not read. When I was questioned they asked me where the letter came from? I replied simply that it was from "a brother".

'I was panicking. I really didn't know what I was doing or what was the right thing to say. It turned out that the use of the words "brother" and "sister" was to cost me dearly. I still can't come to terms with what I have done. Only later was I to learn that the paper I carried was a permission to allow travel to the Soviet Union, which had been issued by one of the top officials in Ghulja. The man who had passed me the letter turned out to have been an organiser of the demonstration outside the city hall compound.

'We were loaded onto lorries and vans which took us to detention centres. I received a three-year sentence, accused of trying to flee the country illegally.

---

26   *A town bordering the Soviet Union.*

'My brother Abduqadir was indeed alive. He was given a two-year suspended death penalty as a suspected leader of the anti-government rebellion. I wasn't given any opportunity to clarify my statement with regards to the dead man's travel permit. No matter how much I pleaded, I was eventually denied courting hearing. That piece of paper and my initial statement to the soldiers became the undeniable evidence used against my innocent brother. Due to my stupidity my brother is suffering and his life is going to end in a most cruel way. This is eating my insides away and killing me slowly…'

Hejer Buwi started to cry uncontrollably as she finished her story. I didn't know what to do or say to comfort her. I held her close while she shed silent tears.

She stopped crying after a long while. Then I asked if she had seen her brother since his conviction.

'Yes, I saw him recently, when I was transferred from Dadamtu to here via Bajahu. On the way we stopped for two nights at Bajahu Labour Camp where my brother was imprisoned in a high security unit awaiting execution. Upon my arrival I requested permission to see him, the prison authorities agreed to this on condition that I would convince my brother to admit to his crimes. I accepted their terms in order to see him.

'He was in a tiny dark cell chained up in shackles. For a moment I thought I'd been taken to the wrong cell: the man I saw through the wired window looked like a skinny old man with saggy hair and a long dirty beard. I couldn't say a word. I couldn't believe that was him. I nearly fainted as my head spun at the sight of my brother's state. I couldn't control my tears, but I knew I have to control myself in order to speak to him.

"Is that you, Abdukadir?" I asked in denial.

"Yes, It is", he took a while to answer. The calmness in his hoarse voice was unbearable.

'Tears poured out of my eyes. I quickly told him about the events surrouding my arrest and the information leading up to his arrest before informing him of the offer of the prison authorities.

"Dearest brother, they said that you are not cooperating with them and have a bad attitude. They say that if you are willing to accept your responsibilities and reform, you could be spared from the death penalty. Please accept their offer even though it is unfair, at least you will live. I made a mistake but I need you to help me to put it right. You can't imagine the pain, the sorrow and the regret I am suffering from right now because of what's happened to you." I begged him sobbing uncontrollably.

"Sister, whatever happened has happened. There is no turning back. I have done nothing to confess to. I am an innocent man I will not plead guilty just so they can spare my life. I would rather die than live a life of lies. Don't worry about me any more! I will accept whatever Fate has written for me. Please go and take good care of yourself", he replied firmly.

'At this point the guards returned to take me back to my room. We were a simple happy family suddenly torn apart, and it's all my fault…' Her weeping distorted her voice. After a moment, she went quiet and fell asleep.

29 April 1966
The last day of my three-year prison term

Today is the last day of my prison term. I had been yearning for this day for the past three years and yet somehow, when it finally came, I still couldn't find the joy I had been longing for. I always imagined that this day would bring me so much happiness, that I could finally be able to live and put my past behind me. Yet deep inside me, fear was devouring my being and the news of my release was ominous, like a dark cloud ready to unleash a deluge.

In the morning my friends congratulated me and asked if I was happy. I simply smiled at them without saying a word.

I looked back at the past three years of my life in captivity. I had now learned patience and mental strength through terrible hardship. I felt I could now face any of life's adversities. I had been living with girls considered to be members of the lowest class of society. I now understood their way of life, their pain and the reasons behind their choices.

The Chinese government's policy had turned villages into controlled communes. People's basic living rights had been taken away, even the right to cook in their own homes. This had driven many young people to abandon their villages and go to big cities such as Ürümchi for these basic rights of living. They did not know the dangers that lay ahead. Innocent young beautiful village girls were forced to become thieves and prostitutes, which resulted in them being sent to prison, which in turn damaged them immensely physically, emotionally and psychologically. All these experiences had made me resent the system even more.

The fertile soil of our motherland has always provided us with everything we needed; it is rich in natural resources and abounded in farmlands; the air quality is pure and the water is sweet. Since the Chinese communist came into power all this has changed: people were now living in a man-made prison under the commune system; they have lost all their basic family lives; everything they owned and had made has been taken away by the government forces. They were no longer seen as human beings; instead, they have become tools of the system. Stripped of their personalities and individualities, they no longer have voices or choices and are not allowed to have their own thoughts and ideas. Even our own officials now only represented the voice of the Chinese Communist Party. It has now come to the point that only those who unconditionally accept the party rules and regulations and agree to sign any unfair treaties against their own people are kept in power; those who voice even the slightest concern are heavily persecuted.

I was working fast in the fields with all these thoughts in mind when Gülnisa came to my side and said, 'You are working very fast today. It seems like you are trying to complete all outstanding tasks on your last day.' She then smiled at me. I put the shovel down and smiled back.

At dinnertime, all the girls got together to celebrate my departure. Zohre Emet offered some snacks her mother brought when she came to see her and I also had some sweets from home which I had kept aside for today. This has become our tradition in the camp: when someone's term is due to finish we all get together to offer whatever we have to make a farewell dinner party. Gülnisa came over to me after dinner and informed me to move to the New Life Camp located outside of the prison compound.

Sopsun's uncle came yesterday to collect her. They left together this morning. I accompanied her to the gate to say goodbye. I felt deeply sad, as we had become close friends since her arrival here and I didn't know if I would ever see her again. On my way back I bumped into Uncle Seley, who congratulated me and wished me a bright future. He has been looking after Ismail since he had become paralysed during the horse accident and so I asked him about Ismail.

'Poor young man, he's in such a bad state. He is completely paralysed from the lower back down and there have been no improvements at all. He can't sit or move without my help and is suffering from depression. I am trying my best help him think positively but he's not taking in anything I say. Please come and visit him, he will be so pleased', he said, fully of emotion.

I promised him that I would. After lunch I bought some biscuits from the shop with the last pennies in my pocket and went to see Ismail. He tried to sit up as soon as he saw me but failed. He looked with the shaven head and blood shot eyes. Having lost so much weight, he now looked like a skeleton. It was hard to believe that such a strong and handsome young man like him could have changed so much in just a few months.

I was shocked but tried very hard not to show my emotions to avoid upsetting him any further. I went over to his bedside and greeted him, and he explained his situation to me.

To lift his spirits I said, 'Ismail, one day a miracle will happen, *inshallah*,[27] and that you will stand up and walk again.'

He thanked me with a smile and said, 'You know the only way I can now find comfort is by remembering God. I never had any chance to receive any type of religious education. I became an orphan from a very young age. There were no elders around me or in the family that could teach me anything about Islam. The communists had outlawed any form of religious education. Luckily Uncle Seley is teaching me some prayers and *sura*s from the Qur'an, I have learned quite a few *sura*s by heart now. Each day I recite them and give my prayers to God. I tell Him of my sorrows and ask Him to show me the *sirat al-mustaqim*.[28] Only by doing so can I find comfort and peace. Other than that there is nothing I can hope for in this life. I still feel lucky and grateful that uncle Seley is here looking after me like his own son. I dread to imagine what would have happened to me if he hadn't come to my life.' He was moved into tears by his own words. I spent half an hour talking to him. In the end, I wished him luck and hoped that one day he would recover. I learnt later that he passed away two months after my visit.

---

27   *A common Arabic expression used by Muslims, meaning 'If God wills it.'*
28   *Arabic for 'the way of the righteous', a Qur'anic expression.*

LIFE UNDER SURVEILLANCE REGIME:
THE CULTURAL REVOLUTION

12 May, 1966

I had been watering vegetables during the night until two in the morning. This has become a routine since I moved out from the old dormitory, since my prison sentence had come to an end. Today a heavy knock at the door woke me up. I quickly got up from my bed checking the time. It was only six.

'Who's there?' I shouted as I approached the door, which was suddenly flung open and a Chinese person walked in.

'Be quick and get yourself and your things ready! There's a truck waiting for you outside the gates. You're going home.' This was the message and words I had been longing for over the past three years. However, I was too sceptical to feel the joy.

I was restless. I felt as if I was going to be taken somewhere even worse than the places I had already experienced, as if there were more miseries and hardships waiting ahead. Yet I had missed my parents, siblings, relatives, friends and our beautiful city Ürümchi. I longed to see the exciting faces of everyone I loved.

I always suspected that they might put us under 'surveillance'. I was desperate to find out the if there was a possibility of this, so I went to see the team leader a few times, but she kept saying she was busy and would see me later. I was left in the dark, without knowing what the future had in stock for me. My gut feelings were not good.

My Chinese roommates helped me quickly pack my belongings; I only managed to wash my face before rushing out from the room, because the truck kept beeping its horn for me to hurry up. The Chinese girls then accompanied me to the gate, and I saw a few cadres sitting on top of the truck. As I was feeling sad that I could not say my farewells to my friends, I suddenly heard my name being called from the inner courtyard. I ran to the gate to look through the slats finding all my friends squeezed up against the gates looking through the slats. They all shouted their farewells and wished me well with tears in their eyes. I left them with a heavy heart and wished I could hug them for the last time. It was with reluctance that I climbed onto the truck while trying to hold my tears back as it drove away.

We left Shabahu behind and soon arrived at Sanji. I started feeling a little more positive, and desperate to see my parents and siblings. The patience I had all along vanished. I could not wait any longer. Oh my friends and classmates! – They would for sure all come to see me as soon as I had arrived home, to catch up on the past three years of our lives. The journey from Sanji to Ürümchi seemed endless. My heart started beating faster and faster as we entered Ürümchi. I was overwhelmed by the sight of every corner of this beautiful city, and realised how much I had missed it. I even started to fear that this was not real, that I would wake up to find out that I was only dreaming...

The truck stopped at Beimen.[29] Mr Ou, a Chinese person in charge of the truck, asked me to get off and follow him. Two other men also got off with us and went their own way. Mr Ou then called a tuk-tuk to take my baggage, and the driver agreed to take my stuff home for five yuan. He helped me to put my things in the cart and then turned around to me saying, 'You can pay him when you get home later. Before that we now need to go to the Municipal Public Security Bureau to register you before you can go home.'

My heart sank. My fears were now confirmed and dangerously real. I knew immediately that I was not free after all. They were now putting me under a surveillance regime, which practically meant house arrest. Plus, the system would allow anybody in the community from young children to the elderly to take advantage of me and order me to do any kind of work they needed me to, and I had no right to refuse. I feared how hard life would be under a surveillance regime in Nanshan. I knew for sure that my life now would be a lot more difficult than it had been in the labour camp. I followed Mr Ou quietly with deep sadness. If I had known this beforehand, I would have refused to come back and remain in the camp instead.

Once we had walked to the top of the hill Mr Ou stopped and asked the tuk-tuk man to wait there. He then led me to the County Public Security Bureau.

We walked through the gates and into an office opposite. A Chinese man came over to Mr Ou and shook his hand warmly. Mr Ou showed me a chair and asked me to sit down, while they went into a private office inside. I could see them through the door window: Mr Ou took out some papers from his bag and handed them over to the officer. They discussed things for a while and then finally came back.

'I am going now', said Mr Ou, 'If there is anything you need to know, it is the people in this office you need to contact from now on.' He walked out of the office quickly. Mr Ou was a tall, dark, haughty and serious-looking man. He was one of the well-known bullies amongst prison governors. I remained quiet and waited tensely for the officer to tell me what would happen next.

'Can you go back to Nanshan on your own or do you need us to take you?' the officer asked.

'I can go by myself. But why did you ask me this?'

He ignored my question completely and asked, 'Do you have any friends or family in Ürümchi that you can stay with? Just make sure you go back to Nanshan as soon as you can.'

29   Chinese name for 'the North Gate'.

'I have relatives in Ürümchi and I am going straight there', I replied.

'Good. Any problems, just contact us', his words were terse. I was puzzled and didn't understand what he really was getting at. I was relieved that he had not mentioned the surveillance regime. I decided not to think too much about the unknown and enjoy my newly gained freedom while I could. I had already resigned to the fact that I would have no power and control over my future, so I would accept whatever came my way and stay strong in all kinds of hardship: I was mentally prepared for the worst scenario possible.

I walked back to Beimen and saw the tuk-tuk man waiting for me. I told him to take my things to a bus stop on Ghalibiyet Road and wait there for me. I then got onto the bus. My heart was once again beating fast with excitement. I got off at the Xinhua Bookshop and was now at the most precious and familiar place in the world: Ghalibiyet Road, where I was born and brought up by my loving parents. I looked around eagerly to check if anyone I knew was around. There was no one to be seen.

The tuk-tuk man arrived shortly. I paid him the fees and led him to my uncle's house. He carried my luggage into the house courtyard ahead of me and I carried my bags following him. My mum, my auntie and all her family members were sitting in the courtyard when I walked into the house. They all ran to me and wrapped me in their arms and cried - so many years of desperate, frustrating wait compounded with the joy of finally seeing each other. I was overjoyed to see my mother – so much in fact that I somehow feared again all of this could eventually turn out to be a dream. She told me that she had come the previous day, as soon as news of my release had reached home. I quickly freshened myself up and changed my clothes before I sat down at the table. My auntie was busy preparing food, we chatted happily. Soon our other relatives and my mum and auntie's best friends arrived. One after another they greeted me, hugged me and kissed me. What a precious moment to be once again surrounded by people who had showed me so much love and support during those difficult times. It was like a special festival for everyone, especially for the children, who were jumping up and down with excitement in the courtyard.

I spend each day receiving guests and chatting with them. However none of my friends and classmates I had really longed to see came to visit me. I was perplexed, sad and hurt. On the fourth day my mum decided to go back to our home in Nanshan, whereas I decided to remain in my uncle's house for a few more days.

15 May 1966

It is doubtlessly the most beautiful season of the year in Nanshan. Endless rows of fir trees stand proudly along the hills; the mountaintops are covered in white snow. The wheat fields along the hilly roads were a thick and lush green. The colourful wild flowers stretched along the fields and streams all over the hills miles and miles away. The fresh smell of the various flowers and the pure transparent water running in the streams delight everyone's heart.

I didn't blink my eyes as I watched all the way to our home and could not have enough of the breathtakingly beautiful landscape. I didn't realise that I was already in front of my house, as I was so immersed in the magnificence of my surroundings all the way.

The bus stopped in front of the shop, I jumped out of the bus as fast as I could and saw my siblings running towards me screaming with excitement. I dropped everything on the floor and opened my arms to hug all of them at once. They gave me affectionate kisses, their tear-socked cheeks made mine wet. Then I saw my father walking towards me. I ran to him and threw myself into his arms. He held me tight for a while, then he kissed my forehead asking, 'How are you my girl? How is your health?' while looking at me from my head to toe with his tender, smiling eyes.

Our house was filled with joy. My siblings ran around the house screaming, laughing, jumping up and down, crying tears of joy and happiness. They kept check on me every now and then, saying how much they had missed me. I held every single one of them in my arms, kissing them again and again. They have all changed a lot over the past three years - they have grown taller and started to look like adults. There's so much that I have missed, so much of their lives that I haven't shared!

16 May 1966

A day after I came back home we got a phone call from Ürümchi, saying that my father's cousin, uncle Ehet Abliz, had passed away unexpectedly. My mother and my father immediately left for Uncle Ehet's funeral in Ürümchi. I was left behind with my siblings.

After all the excitement of yesterday I now have time to start thinking about my life, the commune and my future. I did have hopes of going back to university and completing my degree when I was serving in the labour camp. However it's now very clear that I've no chance at all. I've now been assigned to this commune system and will have to spend my life labouring here. I don't want to be a burden on my parents so I have prepared myself to go ahead and work in the commune as soon as they come back home.

My youngest sister Musherep and my little brother Riza stayed with me at home today while the rest of them had gone to school. I occupied myself with housework all morning. Just after lunch there was a heavy knock on the door, a well-built Kazakh man pushed the door open aggressively and walked straight in, frightening us all.

'Söyüngül, the village head has asked you to come to the commune meeting', he said coldly.

'Ok, I will be there soon', I answered. I could see clearly what was happening and felt a sharp pain in my chest, but I managed to stay calm, trying not to show my anxiety.

'No, I have been asked to come and collect you. You have to come with me right now.'

I told him to give me a minute. I went to tell my little brother and sister that I was going to a meeting, and asked them to lock the door from inside and stay inside. Then I grabbed my cardigan and walked out of the house with him.

The commune hall was full of people. It looked like they had all been waiting for me to arrive before they could start this meeting. I looked around at everyone with a smile and was ready to greet everyone before sitting down. To my surprise, I did not receive any warm welcomes: they all stared back at me with anger and hatred, as if ready to attack me at any minute. I collected myself quickly and went over to the seat that had been specially reserved for me.

The hall sank into a terrifying silence; a flat faced, malicious looking Kazakh man was sitting on the stage facing the crowd. He fiddled with the papers on the desk in front of him for a while and then cleared his voice before starting his speech:

'We have received a counter-revolutionary, revisionist and a bad, very bad element in our commune here with us today. I am now going to read out notes from her file.' Everyone turned to look at me immediately. I felt degraded; my face was burning with embarrassment. I tried hard to control my feelings and look relaxed. I did not move my eyes away from the speaker; I sat straight as normal and listened to him with all my attention. I wanted to give him the impression that his words could not affect me. I did my best to ignore all the people, whispering and gossiping around me.

The speaker then took out a piece of paper, which has a red stamp on it, and continued:

'This is to confirm that Söyüngül, a direct agent of Khrushchev and was the leader of the Ghulja and Chöchek Border Incident. She's a revisionist who had tried to flee over to the Soviet Union illegally. She is also a proven counter-revolutionist. For this, she has been formally handed over to the Nashan Commune and put under the surveillance regime. She must be reformed through labour. She shall henceforth be stripped of all her political rights, and shall perform hard labour under the leadership of the commune. She will not be allowed to go anywhere without the permission of her work unit. She will not be allowed to miss any labour work even for an hour without the approval of her work unit. This document in front of me is the legal document, approved and stamped by the Provincial Public Security Bureau and the County Public Security Bureau. I would like to stress again that she has been stripped from all her rights, and she has to do hard labour under the supervision of everyone in the commune.'

My head started spinning; I did not catch the rest of the words he said. I was so shocked by these false accusations against me that nothing else sank in. How could I be Khrushchev's direct agent, while I have never met this man, or have any connection to him? I was so confused and angry. For a moment, I thought and wanted to believe that they had made a mistake and sent someone else's file to the commune, but I accepted in the end that it would be naïve to be in denial.

I remembered then that there was a huge difference between Education Through Labour and Reform Through Labour. Someone sentenced to Education Through Labour keeps their political rights, whereas someone sentenced to Reform Through Labour is stripped of all their rights. This is to say that, after spending three years in the labour camp, my rights have now been taken away completely. I have, as they say, escaped from the monster only to be caught by the demon. I wanted to shout that nothing in his statement was true, that it was a huge lie, that I had never been convicted of such crimes when I was sentenced to prison three years ago. However, when I looked at all the malicious faces in the crowd, I fell silent. I knew there was no point for me to try to defend myself.

'She will start by working with the building construction team from tomorrow. She must work four extra hours compared to the rest of the workers: two in the morning and two in the afternoon. She must start work half an hour earlier than the rest of the workers during her lunch break. She will not be rewarded for her work, in other words she will be working on a voluntary basis. She has no right to refuse any type of work given to her by the team leaders or the members of the public. If she were to refuse work or disobey the rules, she will be denounced at public struggle meetings. If she does not repent and continues to rebel, then she will be arrested and sent back to prison.' The man carried on criticising me further for some time. My ears started buzzing and I could no longer hear what he was saying. I now clearly understood my fate in the commune: spending my life as a slave.

The speaker ended his speech by saying, 'We must always remember that we now have the most notorious class enemy among us. Therefore I ask all of you to remain vigilant and careful. We must watch every movement she makes cautiously at all times. We must not give her any opportunity to cause any damage to public properties. We must guard our Alataw, the buildings, and the fields from her. Class enemies are always ready to attack us at anytime and cause destruction within the community, therefore we must remember every minute to carry out class struggle. Now I order our class enemy Söyüngül to leave', he shouted passionately. The rest of the crowd repeated vociferously, 'Class Enemy Söyüngül, leave the hall now!'

I felt my cheek, no, my entire body, burning. I stood up from my seat slowly, trying hard not to show my feelings or any signs of emotion on my face, I held my head up high and walked out from the hall with the same facial expression I had walked in with, a friendly grin. Yet I felt as if I had a big lump in my throat, which almost caused me to choke and faint. I looked around to check that there was no one watching before stumbling back home.

I kept thinking about all the false accusations I had just received. Why had they distorted the charges on my file with which I had been sent to the labour camp? My real 'crime' was to be a separatist, to be the founder of the East Turkistan People's Party, to mastermind an anti-government party that aimed to establish the independence of East Turkistan. As I went through this in my mind again and again, I suddenly found the answer. They could not say this out to the public because they feared that people would show sympathy towards me. They needed to find a more effective way to turn the public against me, and that was why they called me a 'class enemy'. I remembered that when I was questioned at university after I had been exposed as a separatist, the interrogator said, 'You are a local ethnic factionist', to which I answered, 'No, let me correct you. We are not ethnic factionists. We want to establish an independent East Turkistan where all our people live freely and happily.' He then asked, 'In what way was that to benefit you if Xinjiang became independent? Only the Uyghur people would benefit and you are not even Uyghur!' I replied firmly, 'The majority of the people in East Turkistan are of the Turkic race, and I am one of them, we are all cousins and we share the same dream.' The Chinese interrogator was fuming with anger at that point, banging on the table with his fist and walking back and forth in the room, shouting, 'To hell with your dream! You will never achieve that! You'd better correct your thoughts if you don't want to bear severe consequences!' He lectured me for over an hour and then stormed out of the room. All these memories flashed through my mind.

The community have never been so convinced that I am a bad person, an enemy of the people who deserves to be punished. There's nothing I can do to turn things around. I have to face this calamity bravely and pray to God to protect me from any harm. I'm thinking about my parents and cannot imagine the pain they will suffer once again each day. This time, the leaders and bullies of the commune system will treat me even more brutally in front of my parents' eyes. I wished I had never come back from the labour camp, where, apart from hard labour and hunger, I never received harsh treatment from anyone there. Even the team leaders would treat me with respect. What I experienced today is unbearably painful.

As I reached home, I made the decision not to tell anyone about what had happened at the meeting. I stood outside the gate for a short while to take a deep breath before walking into the house with a smile. My siblings were sitting on the carpet quietly, looking distressed and very concerned. When they saw me smiling they all stood up and came over to me cheerfully.

'Why did they call you to that meeting? What happened?' my sister Sofiye asked.

'I have been assigned to work in the building construction team and they just wanted to inform me further about the job I will be doing', I answered, deliberately understating the reality.

'Oh that's alright then! When we heard that you were taken to the meeting, we were so, so worried!' said my little sister Gheyshe, hugging me.

'Don't worry about anything my sweetheart. Come on, let's have some tea!'

'So, which mountain is Alataw?[30] I have never heard of that mountain before', I asked them while preparing the table for tea.

They burst out laughing and said, 'Alataw is not the name of a mountain, dear sister. It's a cow. Dad brought it from Shanghai, and it is a very expensive special cow. The Kazakh people call that cow Alataw. Looks like you don't understand the Kazakh language very well, do you?'

They laughed innocently. I was surprised to learn that Alataw was a cow. It made no sense. Why do they want to guard the cow against me? Why would I hurt a cow? Living under the control of all these foolish people was going to be hard, I thought.

---

30   *The word taw means 'mountain' in Kazakh.*

17 May 1966

I went out to work carrying a shovel. My day had begun two hours before the normal working hours. As the other workers came one after another, I tried to look friendly but each and every one of them would stare back at me with hostile eyes. I felt very uncomfortable and didn't know how to react. People in the community who were on their way to work elsewhere behaved in the same manner, stopping in front of me and staring at me angrily for a while before continuing on their way. I realised that realistically I could not expect a friendly reaction from these brainwashed poor souls. I ignored them and tried not to be let down by their behaviours. To them, I was their enemy, a dangerous but powerless person who had no right to talk to them or explain her innocence.

The team leader arrived not long after the rest of the workers had gathered at the site. He was a middle-aged slim man with slanted dark brown eyes. He stood proudly in front of the team and stared at me aggressively (just like the rest of them) before giving orders. He ordered me to sieve sand. People of all came to watch me one after another. I was like an object being exhibited for the curious eye. Some of them stood not far from me staring at me for hours, I was nervous at first, my body trembling when I was sieving the sand. I tried to look away but they were everywhere around me. I kept telling myself to stay calm, strong and ignore these people - it was not worth feeling hurt by their actions.

18 May 1966
Mobilisation speech for the Cultural Revolution

My parents looked anxious and distressed when I came home for lunch. I went up and hugged my mother tight, and she broke down and started crying. They had sensed the seriousness of my situation and it was heart breaking for them to see me suffer again and again. I tried my best to comfort them, saying, 'I am still very young and things might change for the better soon. I will stay strong in any situation. Please don't worry too much.' I felt deeply sorry for my mother and father, for they had to endure all this suffering along with me.

I returned to work as soon as I had finished lunch. An hour later two broad-shouldered Kazakh *minbings*[31] came by horse and stopped in front of me. Their looks <u>gave me great fear.</u>

31   *A minbing, or 'citizen-soldier', is a member of the militia used in the period to implement policies of the Cultural Revolution.*

'Hey you', they yelled at me aggressively, 'Leave your shovel and come with us to the meeting at the commune. Hurry up!'

I followed their instruction immediately. I was herded all the way to the commune; I walked as fast as I could while they were following me on horses. People stopped to watch me as I passed by them. When I arrived at the commune, I saw many people already sitting on the ground on raw earth in the open air facing the commune administration building. Almost everyone turned around and looked at me. I was ordered to sit with a group of elderly people on the side; they looked terribly sad and vulnerable. Their clothes were dirty and faded, many of them had been unable to shave for a very long time - I could see one man's beard was down to his chest, and another man had a big lump on his forehead. They sat with their heads down, motionless and lifeless. I went over and sat alongside them.

The meeting had now begun. The speaker delivered a report from the Central Government stating the launch of the countrywide Cultural Revolution. 'The aim of launching the Cultural Revolution', he announced, 'is to remove the capitalists hidden within the Party. There are capitalist elements within every corner of the country, in the government and society at large, aiming to restore capitalism. The only way forward is to remove these revisionist through violent class struggle!' The speaker's chilling voice echoed in the air, followed by the slogan shouting lead by the *minbing*s: 'Wipe out the Class Enemies!' 'Drag out the hidden capitalist among the Party!' 'Down with Deng Tuo, Wu Han, Liao Mosha!' 'Long live Chairman Mao!'

We had only been told that Deng Tuo, Wu Han, and Liao Mosha were the 'anti-Party coterie', class enemies of the Party. I didn't really know who these people were apart from the fact that they were part of the central government in Beijing. Only years later did I learn that Deng Tuo was a Chinese poet, intellectual and journalist. He served as the editor-in-chief of the People's Daily, the Party's mouthpiece. Deng Tuo later committed suicide in prison, very same year they were dragged out and targeted during the Cultural Revolution.

Wu Han was one of the most important historians and a leading member of the Democratic League before 1949. After 1949, he was the Deputy Mayor of Beijing. In November 1965, at the start of the Cultural Revolution, he came under severe attack for the part he had played in the upright Ming Dynasty official. He was to die in prison in 1969.

Liao Mosha was also a well-known Chinese writer and former co-editor-in-chief of the Chinese Merchant Daily in Hong Kong before the communist came into power in

1949. After 1949, Liao was appointed as the deputy head of the Propaganda Department of the Beijing Municipal Party Committee, head of the Education Department and of the United Front Work Department affiliated with the Committee, Vice-Chairman of the Beijing People's Political Consultative Conference and a member of the Chinese People's Political Consultative Conference (CPPCC).

Deng Tuo, Wu Han and Liao Mo-sha had written for the column, called 'Sketches of a Village with Three Families'. Their writings raised controversial questions about contemporary life in China and therefore became vastly popular. It was these writings that became the far-fetched basis for an unfounded charge against them.

Fear was written over everyone's face. It was a disturbing experience for most people. I could sense that many of us were going to be the targets of this new political movement. I felt cold, my mouth became dry and my heart jumped to my throat with each slogan shouted out. I closed my eyes and prayed deep in my heart.

'Down with the Class Enemies! Get out of there now!' the *minbing*s shouted violently. 'Down with the Class Enemies! Get out of here now!' repeated the people in the meeting, throwing up their fist in the sky looking at us aggressively. Those who I was sitting with stood up immediately and rushed towards the gate, I quickly followed behind them.

I was left shell-shocked after this experience. How could humans be so cruel to one another and publicly, shamelessly abuse weak, elderly, and innocent souls? I wished that this wasn't real, that this was a nightmare I would soon wake up from. Yet I deceived myself. I had been living in an insane world for the last three years and things have only become worse: I am now in the hands of a mad crowd behaving like wild dogs ready to tear my fellow 'class enemies' apart. We all followed behind a *minbing*, he said nothing until we approached a mountain pass next to the school. He turned around and asked us to stand in a line, and ordered us to make mud bricks. All of us quickly followed his orders and picked up our tools and started working immediately. I picked up a shovel and went over to the mountain digging earth to make mud for the mud bricks. The earth was yellow, soft and sticky, perfect for the job that needed to be done. When no one was watching, they all poured me with questions one after another curiously, 'Where are you from? Why were you branded as a class enemy? What crime did you commit at such a young age?'

I briefly told them my story.

'Oh, how did you dare to involve yourself in such big political movements? Did you not think about the consequences? What a shame! You were on the way to becoming a professional doctor, and your beauty and youth will be ruined in this terrible place. It is heart breaking to see an intelligent pretty young girl like you being humiliated and destroyed by these mad mindless and soulless *minbing*s forever. We have been branded as class enemies for thirteen years now, we have been every waking moment working like slaves under their cruelty; we have prayed and hoped that a day will come and all these nightmares will end but from what we have experienced we can see no end to all this. We are getting very old. We don't think we will survive for too long. We feel so sad for you... How will you be able to handle these cruelties?' They showed their concerns and genuine care like I was a member of their own families.

'It is ok, whatever happens life will still go on. Nothing will last and nothing is permanent. I believe that these hard days will end one day', I said with a defiant smile.

Lao Ma, a Dungan with a long dark beard and wearing a black skullcap, came to my side as he dragged his left leg and said, 'My girl, God doesn't like this. I can't stand this slavery, I can't stand being treated less than an animal at my age. I'd rather give my life to God than suffer like this!' he spoke with heart-rending sincerity. Lao Yong, an elderly Chinese man in his seventies - the one with a big lump on his forehead and shaky hands - agreed with Lao Ma: 'Lao Ma is right, what good does a long life do if to live is to endure such cruelty. It is better to die than live a miserable life. Especially at our age, things are getting far too difficult.'

I was touched by what they said. Still wishing to remain optimistic, I replied, 'But what can you do, Lao Ma? When a disaster befalls us, we have no choice but to face it and try to overcome it as best as we can. God tests his people in different ways so they remember him and become even closer to him. Please try your best to find little joy in whatever you come across to cheer yourself up. Please try to stay positive even for a short while each day. I know there is no place for us to escape from this terrible situation, but please let us be patient and find a way to make the best of this life. Let's pray to God in the hope that our lives will change soon. There is no one around us to offer us any comfort, but as least we can comfort ourselves - if we support each other we will find happiness and peace.'

'You are absolutely right. You are an educated girl, and your mentality is different from us. We agree with you, yes we should, we should!' they responded happily one after the other.

Liu Yong was on his way back after diverting the water to mix the soil from the canal on the side of the mountain. He suddenly yelled at us, 'Hey you, stop talking! Black Dog is coming.' We all immediately got back to work. I saw a man in black coming towards us and realised who was being referred to.

We were preparing to make mud bricks when suddenly water started overflowing. Everyone tried to stop the flow of the water from running everywhere. I offered my help by throwing more soil into the water. The man dressed from head to toe in black had now arrived. The angry look through his narrow eyes reminded me of that of a predator.

'Oy, take off your shoes and jump into the mud and mixing it with your feet!' he screamed at me, 'Don't think you can fool me by holding a shovel pretending to be working hard while clearly you aren't. Do not forget who you are, you are a class enemy! And don't forget you are working under the glorious proletarian dictatorial regime. Don't play smart with me - there are eyes everywhere watching you. Understood?' He came towards me as if he was going to hit me. I stood my ground and did not move, but watched him calmly as he approached, which increased his frustration: 'Get into that mud, I am ordering you to mix the soil and water with your feet! Are you deaf?'

My labour camp experiences have made me strong enough to face this kind of situation with total calm. Had I been in my early school years I would have definitely burst into tears: I had never shown my bare feet or legs in front of men and felt embarrassed to be taking off my shoes in front of all these men. I felt helpless and humiliated, being unable to challenge him. Taking off my shoes and socks as fast as I could and rolling up my trousers above my knees, I jumped into the mud pit. He stayed next to me for half an hour shouting and gesticulating at everyone before finally took his leave.

'Who is this man? What is his position?' I asked those around me.

'That was Qadirbeg, head of the production unit. We call him Black Dog because there's no humanity in him. Don't take his words seriously. You will get used to it slowly as this is going to be the kind of words you will hear every day. Ignore him and stay strong!'

After the work finished at seven, I returned home exhausted to face my parents' melancholy faces. I guessed that they had heard that I had been labelled a class enemy and put to work with other 'class enemies'. I pretended to look happy as usual while trying my best to hide the cuts on my hands.

19 May 1966

I went to work at six o'clock today to find everyone else already there working hard. I quickly got ready and jumped into the freezing cold mud. This made my brain and my body numb. We prepared a mud pile nearly as high as a small hill. At eight o'clock thirty young men arrived to start making bricks.

A medium-built, dark-skinned Kazakh young man came and stood not far from me. He looked around and said, 'Wow, have you seen there is something new amongst the class enemies? Orazan, have you noticed it?'

Orazan was a stout man in his thirties. He had a round face, which appeared even rounder with his clean-shaven cheeks. He glanced over in my direction before shouting back to his colleague, 'Do you know who you are and why you are here? They did not bring us here because we are their guests. They brought us here because we are the children of the rich and wealthy "class enemies". These people's today is our tomorrow! Remember that.'

A man standing next to Orazan joined in and said, "It is true, didn't you realise why they have picked us to work here? There are many interesting games awaiting us; soon you will be invited to the middle of the crowd and ordered to dance for them.' He then started dancing, which made everyone laugh. Another young jolly young man joined in the traditional Kazakh dance, and the two of them with their dance enlivened this dismal work place. The atmosphere had barely changed to one of happiness when Black Dog arrived shouting. The dancing stopped and work was resumed. The hill of mud disappeared within two hours.

It indeed hard collecting soil from the base of the mud hill and mixing it to the right consistency for making the mud bricks. Nevertheless, immense pressure was placed upon us by the number of different supervisors giving contradictory orders, which resulted in the brick makers complaining that the mud we had mixed was too soft or too hard. Having been soaked in water and soil from six in the morning until noon, my legs and feet no longer had any feelings.

We finished working at eight in the evening. My body ached from head to toe. I didn't know if I had strength to walk home or not. I decided to go to the stream to tidy myself up, washing away the dirt from my face, legs and clothes before combing my hair. I made sure that I looked presentable before making my way home. Knowing that my parents' hearts were already aching for me, I tried my very best not to show them in any way that I was suffering. All the longing and joy my parents had for me upon my return from the labour camp had now disappeared completely to be replaced by more sadness and worries. However like all parents they tried to hide their true feelings while lifting my spirits.

I kept all my pains and sorrows to myself as I worked away for over a month in the same place from sunrise to sunset. Some times we were forced to work thirty-six hours nonstop once or twice a week. We were constantly bullied by team leaders and the brick makers who took out their frustrations on us with verbal abuse, but we have no choice but to persevere.

10 August 1966

We worked for another month building cowsheds near the school in the valley where we were forced to work two days without break most of the time. The skin on my legs and feet have gone dry from being exposed to the mud and dust for so long, and my hands have cracked and bled, and I can't even hold a cup of tea due to the pain. But since I'm barred from any medical attention, I've been putting Vaseline on my hands and wrapped them in strips of white cloth serving as rudimentary bandage.

After completing the cowshed, we started to work at a new construction site. All the women in the commune have been forced to work on the building sites, and as there are no nurseries, mothers with babies and young children are forced to take them along. The babies often cry for food or water, but the mothers are not allowed to stop to breast-feed their babies.

Meetings are organised in the evenings for everyone. The families have to bring along their children, who often end up falling asleep on the concrete floor. The cadres, however, having spent their day eating and drinking, tend to keep the meetings lasting late into the night.

This has serious implications on the family traditions of the Kazakhs. Most of the women are ethnically Kazakh; according to tradition, they are the ones who usually look after the house, animals, and children, and tend to their husbands' needs. Now, despite the exhaustion from the heavy labour they are subjected to during the day, they are still expected to serve their husbands once they return home.

15 August 1966

After working for thirty-six hours I went home completely drained. All I wanted to do was go to bed, but dinner was on the table, so I sat down to eat with my family. Suddenly two *minbing*s stormed in and shouted, 'Class Enemy Söyüngül, the commune leader Qadirbeg wants to see you.'

'What for?' I asked.

'He is ordering you to go back to work immediately.'

'Let me eat something. Then I will return to work', I replied.

'Well I'm not sure he's going to wait. Get out right now!' they said angrily.

My parents and siblings looked at me anxiously as I got up to leave. I gave them a reassuring smile as I quickly put on my jacked and left.

I was escorted outside the commune to where over ten muscular Kazakh men were standing around a large concrete tube. From their appearances I knew they were *minbing*s. As soon as I arrived, Qadirbeg passed a long thick wooden pole through the concrete tube. He told the men to lift one end and for me to lift the other. The concrete pipe was extremely heavy and even the men struggled to lift it up. It was impossible for me try and move the other end on my own, so I shook my head and said, 'I am sorry. It's too heavy.'

'Well why not?' he approached me menacingly, 'You were powerful enough to commit such a big crime, and too weak to lift this up?'

'What you are saying are two different things. One is the ideology and the other is physical strength. People that have committed these so called big crimes are not necessarily physically strong', I stepped back and tried to reason with him.

He turned around facing the *minbing* and let out a malicious laugh. 'Liston to her! Just listen to her. Did you hear what she said?' The men burst out laughing. I found it odd to see these cold-faced bullies laughing, especially when I wasn't sure what had made them laugh. After that they carried the tube away. I had to remain standing there awaiting further orders.

A truck arrived later. The driver was a tall and skinny manwearing a blue hat. Qadirbeg ordered me to get on truck to go to Genggu Valley to bring back timber for the building sites. I did as I was instructed and the truck drove to the canteen to pick up other 'class enemies'.

Genggu is one of the most beautiful valleys with the most stunning scenery. The southern side of the valley is covered in wild flowers and green wheat fields, while on the northern side grew thick emerald-green spruce trees. Tinkling streams provided beautiful oasis a pretty touch at the foot of the mountains. I always loved and enjoyed the striking beauty of this land with the fragrance of its wild flowers, and the burbling of the streams running from valley to valley. This place always reminds me of freedom.

As a child I loved to listen to the birds singing while lying under the spruce trees gazing up at the blue sky, I would sit along the streams listening to the tinkling of the water running over the stones. I would sing songs, running among the wild flowers and picking my favourite ones to make garlands. All of these childhood memories flashed into my mind while sitting in the darkness of the rear of the truck with my fellow 'class enemies', overwhelmed by nostalgia. I am now no longer the free girl I used to be, but a captive of these mountains.

The roads were slippery due to the rain of the last few days. As a result it took two hours to reach Genggu Valley. The full moon was shining among the twinkling stars, brightening up our surroundings. It was truly a magical sight. I jumped off the truck to breath in and to feel the magnificent nature. My peace was only to be shattered by the voices coming behind me, urging me to go back to work.

Looking in the direction of the voice I saw two *minbing*s standing next to a large pile of timber. Immediately everyone started loading the truck. The timber planks were huge and heavy; two old men carried the thinner end and I lifted the thicker end onto my shoulder and loaded them onto the truck. The weight almost crushed my shoulders. By the time we finished loading, the skin on my shoulders had bloody blisters, and my blouse was stuck onto my damaged skin, causing more pain. We climbed and held onto the timber precariously for the return journey. After a long bumpy drive we arrived back at the commune after two in the morning. There were no lights as the commune's electricity generator had stopped working. We unloaded the timber in the pitch darkness. We were then given half an hour to go home for something to eat before returning to work at the bottom of the mountain to move earth to the commune school.

When I went home everyone was already fast asleep. Not wanting to disturb them, I left as quietly as I could. It was my third night without sleep, and I could sense that my body was about to give up. I walked straight to the mountain where I had been instructed to dig earth. Upon arrival, I saw a small pile of straw on the ground and it looked as if it had been left for me. I immediately lay down and fell into a deep sleep.

I don't know how much time had elapsed when I was suddenly woken up by the noise of people shouting and the piercing sound of truck horns in the distance. The noises became louder and louder and came closer and closer. I tried opening my eyes to find out what was happening but I couldn't; I tried to move my body but it remained rigid and immobile. After I finally managed to open my eyes, I could see the stars in the sky, and for a moment I was confused not being able to figure out where I was. I sat up and looked in the direction of the beeping lorries. The blinding lights on the lorries lit up the entire place, and I saw my fellow 'class enemies' digging up the ground and throwing earth and dust onto the rear of a truck. Realising that I had fallen asleep, I jumped up in panic. I quickly shook off the straw from my clothes and ran to join them.

A *minbing* was startled by my arrival and shouted, 'Who is there?' I went over to him to show my face.

'Where the hell have you been?' he interrogated. '

'I sat on the straw over there and fell asleep because I arrived early', I replied.

'For goodness' sake! Do you see all the people on the hillsides? They've been looking for you!' he sounded extremely annoyed. I looked up at the hills and could see torchlights everywhere, and along the valley. Without uttering a word I picked up a shovel to start working. The guard told the man standing next to him to go and call off the search.

'Where have you been? They said you had run away and even ordered a search of the area. We've all been very worried about you!' Luo Jun said quietly.

'Well, where could I escape to? We all know that they are everywhere. There is no safe place to go', I said.

Not long after my two younger sisters Sofiye and Gheyshe came running. 'Sister, what happened? Where have you been? We were so scared! Thank God you are safe!' they said out of breath. I explained to them what had happened. They left hurriedly to tell my parents that I was safe and well.

20 September 1966

We, the 'class enemies', along with some skilled builders were deployed to build a large farm in Tujan Commune. After being tossed about on the back of the truck we were finally dropped off in the valley on the bank of Tutunhu River, which we walked along to reach the commune. Barren mountains stood on either side of the valley, which was wide with trees and flowers shielding both sides of the river.

Tujan was a commune with less than twenty families. All the female residents, including girls as young as twelve, had been called to work at the site. None of the male residents of the commune were on site when we arrived. They had gone to cut hay on the valley sides of the mountains. I was allocated the task of bringing water from the river located at the foot of the mountain. Once again we had to make earth bricks. The men's task was to build walls while the women's was to carry the dried bricks to the men's working area.

We worked incessantly under the watchful and bullying eyes of three *minbing*s from Nanshan Commune, who, as I happened to notice, even tried to encourage the younger girls into smoking and harassment sexually. Frustrated by the girls' refusal, one *minbing* said, 'You must obey what we have asked you to do! Anyone who refuses to smoke cigarettes will be dragged to the denunciation meetings. We are undertaking the Glorious Proletariat Cultural Revolution. We are fighting to eradicate your old traditions and establish a new modern way of life. Understood? To hell with your religious beliefs!'

The girls were terrified with the thought of being dragged to a denunciation meeting, but at the same time they did not dare to smoke a cigarette. Later I heard that their mothers, who must have heard about their misadventure, were furious about the behaviour of these men. The *minbing*s, intrepid with their self-proclaimed ideological superiority, hustled the girls in front of their mothers and forced them to smoke. The women rebelled and stood together protesting against this behaviour. The *minbing*s then shamelessly responded, 'You silly, backward people, ignorant of the glorious social changes in this country. You are no longer allowed to hold on to your traditional beliefs. You can say no today, but just wait and see: the Party will soon forbid you to wear even your traditional clothes, let alone your traditional way of life and your religion!'

An elderly lady couldn't hold back her anger any more and shouted, 'What are you trying to say? Are we being forced into dressing like the Chinese? Never! I would rather die than have to give up my dress!' Then everyone joined her and a huge quarrel broke out.

I was shocked when I heard about this. I worry about the chaos that will ensue if such an extreme plan is implemented.

19 November 1966
Vandalism

As soon as I walked through the door my sisters and brothers ran up to me, shouting in excitement. My mother and father came out of the house and hugged me. I had been away for two months.

Entering the house I noticed that something was missing. Also I could sense a feeling of sadness in everyone. I looked around and asked everyone if everything was alright. Despite their affirmative answers, I was convinced that they were hiding something from me.

While my mother was getting the table ready for tea I went to the courtyard to wash my hands. My little brother Ahmet confessed while pouring water over my hands from the kettle.

'Sister, a lot of bad men have visited our house. It nearly collapsed when they were digging up the floor. They smashed all the windows and daddy had to replace them. They acted like animals forcing us to stand in the snow in our bare feet. I was so cold and upset but I didn't dare to cry, so I cried quietly.'

My younger sister, who was standing next to Ahmet, added, 'Yes, they took a lot of things away from our house. They yelled as daddy as if they were going to hit him. They ordered him to stand still for hours. Daddy couldn't do anything, so they went and took away mummy's things. She didn't say anything until her Quran dropped on the floor. She was so angry and shouted at them, "Don't you dare drop the Holly Quran on the floor!"

Dinner was ready and I went back in with a heavy heart. Once more we sat around table together as a family. This should be one of the most happy and precious moments of life, but after what I'd heard from my siblings, I feared how long we'd be allowed to have such happiness.

After dinner, Gheyshe told me about her experiences in Ürümchi, where she went for treatment for her tonsillitis.

'On the day I arrived in Ürümchi, there was a huge demonstration in the streets. The people at the front were waiving red flags, while people behind them held lofty portraits of Chairman Mao. At the rear there were people banging drums and metal plates, making the most horrendous loud noises. In the front of all these demonstrators I saw probably one hundred men and women wearing tall dunce's hats with placards hanging from their necks. They stopped walking now and then, each time they stopped metal plates were passed to those wearing the dunce's hat who would bang the plates before shouting out their names and the crimes they were accused of.

'When we reached Ittipaq Road, I saw people standing in a circle with an elderly man banging metal plates loudly with his hands and swirling around fast in the centre of the crowd shouting, "I am Emet Ömer. I am a rightist." He acted like a clown pulling funny faces despite being a victim of humiliation. Children in the crowd laughed out loud clapping their hands in merriment. An angry looking man came and chased the children away.

'As I walked past Xinhua Bookshop two men emerged, at the same time a group of demonstrators on Yanan Road approached a group of man. They placed a very tall dunce's hat on one man's head. The man looked helpless and terrified by what was happening. He was then dragged into the middle of the crowd before being beaten badly. I witnessed similar scenes everywhere and was terrified that something might happen to me and I could not return home.

'I stayed one week in Ürümchi, going to the hospital twice a day, where only a few doctors remained as others had been accused of various crimes such as: rightist, nationalist, Guomintang scum, collaborators with foreign countries... With the shortage of doctors the sick and seriously ill had to wait for a long time to be treated.

'A day before I returned to Nanshan, a group of teenagers wearing red armbands and carrying sticks raided our uncle's neighbour Ismail's house. A number of them entered the house forcing the family into the street where they were met by a mob of angry youth chanting slogans. Back in the house, they confiscated everything, including their clothes, furniture, pots and pans, as well as cash. The flowerpots were smashed as they removed the tiles from the floor in search of further valuables. They dug up their courtyard and the shed as well.'

Zekiye, who visited the city after Gheyshe returned, also told me about what she had seen there:

'I went to visit my uncle the day after Gheyshe had returned home. The *minbing*s were terrorising the citizens using physical violence without justification. Law and order had collapsed. Loudspeakers had been installed everywhere, screaming intimidating slogans from dawn to dusk - Mao's quotations, you know: "All revolutions are violent by definition. We must break up the Four Olds: old culture, old ideals, old customs, and old traditions!" From time to time the loudspeakers would broadcast revolutionary songs mostly in praise of Mao being the saviour of the people of the New China.

'One morning we heard the banging of metal plates, along with the drum rolls and people shouting slogans outside. Our cousin Xalide ran to the gate and looked through the gap between the doors and shouted, "Mum, they are coming towards our house!" We all jumped up and ran to the gates to look: there were approximately a hundred people brandishing flags, some carrying banners, many of them were twelve to seventeen-year-old kids! They pushed opened the gates shouting, "Don't move!" and we were all scared. Then they searched us. The little *minbing* who searched me took my food vouchers and thirty yuan, which he placed in his pocket. I stood silently in fear. My auntie saw the boy putting the money and vouchers in his pocket and screamed, "Give back the girl's money and food vouchers. She's a peasant. How do you want her to survive without any money or food vouchers?" One of the older men heard my auntie's scream and came forward to tell the boy to return the money and voucher. The boy reluctantly returned them to me. After we'd been searched, we were herded out of the house as it was being ransacked. Everything valuable was confiscated, including my auntie's jewellery. As usual the floor and courtyard were dug up and whatever was left smashed into pieces…

'The next day I went to see Uncle Zeikin, and saw his house in the middle of a house raid. One of the *minbing*s saw me and questioned me They ordered me to stand aside with the rest of the family. I told him that Zeiki is my uncle, so he turned to Uncle Zeikin and said, "So you have a brother, where does he live?" and he answered "Nanshan." Three *minbing*s left the house in a hurry. I was worried that they might organise people to raid our house as well. Uncle Zeikin's house raid lasted until midnight. They confiscated everything they judged valuable, and destroyed whatever was left.

'Over a hundred houses were raided that day and the families were left devastated. That wasn't all – a huge number of people were arrested and accused of being involved in illegal trading, because they had more valuable items in their homes than others. Everyone was ordered to hand over all the books related to history and religion - they threatened to torture us in public and then throw us into prison if we didn't. This was announced over the loud speakers, also posted on the walls in every corner of the city. And it did happen: some people didn't hand in books and were beaten to death, and many were arrested and taken to labour camps!

'Books were being burnt everywhere, and I still can't believe they were burning the Quran! Activists and troublemakers calling themselves revolutionists joined the *minbing*s to stir up more trouble. They looted the houses, taking revenge on their colleagues and neighbours they don't get along, branding them as 'class enemies' in order to justify and cover up their personal revenge. The dead were buried without any religious proceedings as mosques were closed down and religious figures were arrested being accused of poisoning the people's minds.

'I also saw Uncle Musabay on a truck one day. He was wearing a tall white dunce's hat with 'Capitalist Musabay' written on it. They draped a chain made of golden bangles hanging down to his knees. I had tears in my eyes when I saw him, and then he saw me and smiled at me. Poor man, he was going through so much, and he still wanted me to believe everything was ok! I asked Uncle Zeikin later about the golden bangles. He said they were made of bronze, and they made him wear them because he had been accused of possessing too much wealth…'

Gheyshe suddenly remembered something and interrupted Zekiye, 'I also heard from Uncle Zeikin that his brother Abliz's youngest son suddenly lost the ability to speak from the shock of their house being raided by the *minbing*s. Apparently he was having a nap when they broke in. The city of Ürümchi was in a mess: torture and looting spread throughout the city like a wild fire.'

My mother, who had been doing the dishes, joined us after having heard our conversation, and started telling me about the house raid at ours.

'On the same day as your uncle Abliz's house got raided, over fifty people stormed into our home carrying shovels and pickaxes. Some came from the Department of Commerce in Ürümchi where your father has worked, and the rest were from the commune led by Salik. He ordered us to leave the house as soon as he entered, so we were forced to stand in the courtyard. It was a very cold and snowy day. Twenty or more people went into the house to search while the rest rifled through the stockroom, coal and animal sheds. A number of them climbed onto the roof, looking to see if anything was hidden there. Finding nothing they partly dismantled the structure. I was worried about the children who were shaking and shivering from the cold. So I shouted, "Can you please bring some clothes for my children, they are going to catch their death of cold?" "Don't you dare to speak! You are the people's enemy and have no rights to speak!' Salik shouted angrily. One of the men from the Department of Commerce indicated to a young man to bring some clothes for the children.

'One of the *minbing*s brought out Ahmet's toy machine gun, the one that your grandfather bought for his circumcision ceremony and said, "Look, they are hiding weapons in the house." He started examining the toy gun carefully, pointing it at the *minbing* who was standing opposite him. The man moved aside, shouting angrily, "Don't point that gun at me." One of the cadres from the Department of Commerce took the toy gun away from the man saying, "Leave it alone, this is just a child's toy." One of the *minbing*s who was searching in the house took out the electric iron from underneath the bed, shouting, "Look, this is the kit they use to communicate with the Soviets." All the other *minbing*s rushed to his side excitedly, eager to see his important find. "Oh yes, we found it", they said, and looked satisfied.

'They then turned to look at us in rage. As if they have found iron evidence to prove that all of us were guilty. It was funny but I found it disheartening that these naïve *minbing*s had lived all their lives in the mountains, never seeing any toy machine guns or electric irons. They held the long electric cable and started heated discussion about how it must be used to communicating etc. An elderly man from the Department of Commerce from Ürümchi took the iron away from these men saying, "Don't waste your time on this, it is just an iron for ironing clothes."

Having completed searching the house, they decided to check underneath the floor boarding which was completely removed to see if there was anything hidden beneath. I stood nervously thinking about them finding my Quran, which I had hidden in the storeroom. After long search Salik came out from the storeroom dragging a sack on the floor, I immediately saw my Quran in the sack. It angered me seeing my Quran being dragged across the dirt. It was like the biggest crime I have ever seen. I shouted angrily, "Don't drag my Quran across the floor!" But Salik ignored me as he continued to drag the sack out of the house. I felt as if my heart has been removed, tears fell like rain. A young man from the Department of Commerce came over to me and the cheek to ask, "What is wrong in dragging the Quran across the floor? Why are you crying about it?" I asked what his name was, and he said he was called Suleyman. I then said, staring into his eyes, "Your father named you Sulayman for a reason, ask your father why it is wrong to drag The Holy Quran across the floor. He will tell you, if he's a Muslim!"

'Having removed all the floorboards and five tons of coal, nothing had been found or left untouched. At this time they started questioning your father – "Where did you hide the cartload of silver? Refusal to cooperate will lead to your arrest."

Your father asked in surprise, "What silver are you talking about?"

"Don't pretend" they said, "Where did you hide the silver? Salik screamed at him in rage. Your father turned pale at that moment. An official pulled Salik away and said to us, "We are talking about the silver that Aqsaqal Hesen brought from Chöchek." Your father thought for a moment before replying, "He sold it at that time and returned home with the money as I was not part of his business." They insisted that he was lying, but your father calmly repeated that we didn't have silver, or gold, or cash. The officers then went back into the house to discuss something, and Saliq along with other *minbing*s took the opportunity bully your father by shouting political slogans at him – "Let's eliminate Salih! Let's eliminate the saboteur with foreign connections! Let's eliminate rich landlord Salih! Let's eliminate capitalist-roader Salih! Let's eliminate the Kuomintang scum Salih." They branded him with seven different criminal titles, telling him that he would be kept under surveillance from that moment onwards. In the end they took away all my jewellery including my wedding ring and having smashed the windows and everything in the house they left. It took us until midnight to get the house back to a somewhat habitable state.'

My little brother Ahmet put his spoon back onto his plate and looked at me eagerly. I could see from his expression that he was thinking of the something seriously. His long thin eyebrows were pulled together, his eyes were sharp, and his lips pressed together before he opened his mouth –

'When we heard the shouting in the house we were all very frightened, we thought they might be hitting mum and dad. We ran to the house screaming, but the *minbing*s stopped us from getting in. I tried to get loose by pulling hard but they held on to me, so I bit the man's hand as hard as I could, and he screamed in pain as I pulled away from his grasp. Then I ran past everyone and saw Salik shouting at dad. I went over to kick his leg hard from behind then dashed to hide in the crowd. He stopped shouting and turned around looking to check but couldn't find out who did it. Then he turned to dad again and continued shouting slogans, I went over and kicked him again and hid myself.' He spoke with great enthusiasm, like a hero who has just won a battle, when he finished he looked around at us all with a grin of satisfaction. He looked so adorable and handsome with his beautiful curly hair falling onto his forehead.

'Dad, why was the man so angry with you?' I asked curiously.

He sighed deeply before replying, 'How would I know? I dedicated so much time teaching him accountancy, and with my help he became a qualified accountant in the commune within one year. I taught him everything I know up to today. I am finding it hard to understand why he is suddenly treating me like an enemy.'

'Dad, don't be upset. It's not worth it. That man is an opportunist who is trying to take advantage of the current situation, finding excuses to put you down so he can obtain the position of head accountant. He will then be in the position of great power. I'm sure of that', I said.

'Let it be. I may have sinned in the eyes of God, but I have never done anything bad or wrong to anyone; I have never betrayed anyone's trust or misused public money. I am clean in the eyes of God and my people', he said.

'Bless you, dad', I said in admiration of his calmness. Then I remembered not quite understanding the story of the silver, so I asked again my father about it.

'It is a long story, my child. You know, I spoke to Brother Zeki afterwards and find out that it was Hemze who provided the information about a cart of silver to the Department of Commerce', my father explained.

'Hemze and Erin were raised by my parents. We all grew up together. Their parents were herdsman and lived in the mountains. One day a group of wolves attacked their farm, killing the parents and other siblings. Hemze, Zamza and Erin survived the attack by hiding inside their yurt. Later other herdsmen stumbled across the devastated farm while passing by. They went to the yurt and found the three terrified children. The community came together to bury the dead and discussed the children's welfare. The elders of the community asked my father to raise Hemze and Erin, and he agreed. Zamza was given for adoption by someone else. My parents adored them and took extra care of them because of their tragic fate. They tried their best to provide them with a comfortable living environment and a good education. When Burhan Shehidi imported cars from Germany in 1929 for the first time to East Turkistan, my father sent them to learn how to drive. It was very expensive in those days. They were among the first of the younger generation to learn to drive. When the Department of Transport was established in the country, Hemze was appointed to it. But since the start of the Cultural Revolution, he has been denounced as a "capitalist roader" and publicly punished. Apparently he exposed the silver business to the interrogators in order to save himself', My father sighed deeply as he finished speaking.

'Thank goodness we are alive. Look around every corner in the country innocent people are being killed everyday in the name of senseless crimes. New policies with conflicting rules are coming out all the time and causing confusion and chaos. I wonder where all this is going to lead. If we can survive this madness everything will be ok', mother added while serving the tea.

My sister Sofiye added, 'I heard that In Turpan and Toqsun, the *minbing*s set fire to the *doppa*s[32] they had confiscated. An old man said to them, "You can burn all *doppa*s easily, but you will never be able to change the thoughts in one's head. And they arrested the old man and called him an anti-revolutionary. And, can you believe they even took away calligraphy works, paintings, traditional clothes, musical records to be burned? They even took away mum's embroidered boots, the ones that grandfather brought from Kazan! I felt sorry for Kazakh girls who started embroidery work and knitting at the age of ten, most of the work was for their dowry. It was beyond belief that they should even target these things!'

'I didn't mind too much about my other stuff. What I missed most is my Quran and the two boxes of books', said my mother with deep emotion.

My father spoke of his sadness over the loss of his dictionaries of a variety of languages, including Russian, English, Uyghur, Chinese, and also French, and said with frustration, 'They have no respect whatsoever for learning and for tradition. Where else in the world does this happen - a bunch of illiterate people punishing the intellectuals for being intellectual? It's completely out of order.'

30 November 1966
Denunciation parade in the commune

It was one of the coldest days of the winter, with everything covered in snow and ice. I was ordered to clean out the stables, which are located in the heart of the

---

32   *Traditional embroidered hats worn by Central Asian men and women of many ethnicities.*

mountains. The manure at the stables was mixed with wet and soggy snow to become solid ice approximately half a metre thick, and to remove this mess I had to make use of a pickaxe.

After two hours Su Wenqing and Ahmad joined me. Resting their shovels on the ice they started chatting.

'Do you think they are organising another parade today?' Ahmad asked Su Wenqing.

'It seems like it, some people are very passionate about this so-called "revolution". These illiterate nomadic people are very naïve; if asked to bring someone's hat, they would bring their head as well in order to please their master. I don't know what will happen next, I am very worried', said Su Wenqing in a low voice.

'I believe things are getting worse, I am scared. I am worried they may come for me next and I don't know what to do', Ahmad said nervously.

'Has your mother left yet?' Su Wenqing asked.

'Yes, I have sent her to Enenchu.'

'How about your sister Zaynab?'

'She has gone with my mother.' Ahmad replied.

'You are eighteen now, if you are branded like your father you will be finished, It would be better for you to leave here as quick as possible.' Su Wenqing suggested. Ahmad's face turned pale at her words as he was shaking with fear.

Ahmad is a young Dungan man from a wealthy family. In the 1950s during the land reform period, his parents were branded as 'repressive landlords'. His father died from torture ten years ago. Like other families with similar backgrounds, his family have been suffering from cruelty at the hands of the government and the local bullies. Since turning 18 and becoming an adult this year, he's been worried about whether he will be branded like his father. I think his childhood experiences have traumatised him. Compared to other young men of his age he is weak and fearful of others.

While they were whispering their conversation, I heard intimidating slogans accompanied by the clashing of metal plates along with the beating drums. I raised my head to listen carefully as Ahmad ran to find a place to hide in.

'Oh my God', he screamed, 'There are many people coming this way! Look, some have placards on their chests. Oh, no, they are coming towards us!' at that point he almost burst into tears as he turned around to look at me, saying, 'Are they coming for you? Are they? You should go outside. Please go quickly!' His eyes were full of fear.

I couldn't help but laugh, seeing the state that he was in and said, 'Why do you want me to go to them? If they call my name, I will go and it won't have anything to do with you', I said.

He was in such a state of panic that he ran around the stables like a frightened dog. He then entered one of the stalls and climbed into a feed trough to hide under the hay, which disturbed the horses. Feeling sorry for him, I said, 'Ahmad, please don't do that, if you are found there then you will be in serious trouble. Listen to me: if they call your name, don't just go to them, stand up and reason with them. Ask them, "What do you want me for? What offence have I commited?" If they say that you are an "oppressive landlord", then tell them that you were born after the Liberation,[33] therefore you have nothing to do with so called "tyrant landlords." They can't do anything to you. You must learn to stand up for yourself and be a man!' My words lifted his spirits, the fear in his eyes disappeared. He grasped my hand and thanked me repeatedly.

The shouting of slogans got louder as the group of people reached the stables. We continued to brake up the frozen manure trying to drown out the noise from outside. We didn't dare to look up or take the waste outside. After a short while I realised that they were moving away. I looked through a gap in the wall to see my father in the front line with a slogan board hung around his neck. There were at least forty people escorting the board carriers. Some were waving Chairman Mao's portrait, while others banging metal plates or drums. My heart was heavy with the thought of what my father going through at this time.

Besides my father's normal accountancy job, he worked hard to help others. People used to walk long distances to fetch water to their homes; to save them the trouble, my father and his brother Wahit worked months in their spare time digging canals along the mountains to bring water to people's doorsteps. He then went to Ghulja and Bortala areas and bought an electric generator, which he installed for the community. Later he travelled to Ürümchi where through his contacts he was able to source a breed of cow that could be interbred with local animals in the commune to produce more milk, after which he set up a factory in the commune to produce powdered milk. Also setting up an accountancy training school for the young people. He worked tirelessly without asking for an extra penny. Every single family in the area has benefited from his hard work. How could anyone denounce someone like my father? There are no words to express the anger I felt.

I noticed that Ahmad's face had turned pale again and he started to shake and was close to tears. I found it strange that a young man should show so much fear, so I said,

33 *In official Chinese historiography, the incorporation of Xinjiang into the territory of the People's Republic of China in 1949 is referred to as the 'Peaceful Liberation of Xinjiang', or simply the 'Liberation', or jiefang, in Chinese.*

'Hey, you are 18, you are a man now, remember! Why are you so scared? No one has come to take you yet. If they came and placed a dunce's hat on your head, do you think that would kill you? Show some strength! Don't be afraid of these idiots!'

'Sister, I don't understand how you've managed to cope with all the cruelty for so long? I don't think I could cope even for one day', he replied.

'She was educated in university, so she is able to understand things better than us. University graduates have no fear, even when faced with death. There are not many such people around us', said Su Wenqing in response to Ahmad's question.

From that day I never saw Ahmad again. He disappeared.

13 December 1966

Today my mother was dragged out by the rebels. She was branded as a revisionist and a saboteur, because my grandmother and my mother's sister, as well as my uncle's three daughters all migrated to the Soviet Union. Anyone who has relatives abroad was branded as revisionist. When the cadres of the commune tried to put large wooden placard around my mother's neck, she managed to grab it from their hands throwing it into air with all her strength. To everyone's astonishment it landed on the roof of the warehouse.

My mother recited some of the quotations Mao's Red Book, such as: 'The target of the Cultural Revolution is those persons in authority taking the capitalist road.' In the end she pointed to the cadres in front of her, quoting, 'The target of this revolution is people like you who are in authority, not housewives like me. You must first understand this revolution by studying Chairman Mao's Red Book by heart to find the right targets!' She walked out of the crowd and went straight back to the house. No one tried to stop her because she quoted Mao's words correctly.

My mother showed extraordinary courage and intelligence and I'm extremely proud of her. I know my family is one of the biggest targets in the commune because of me, apart from having 'connection' with the Soviet Union. Not long after this incident my younger sister Musherrep was attacked by Salik's daughter, Meghribe, along with the teacher's daughter Mehpuze. Musherrep tried to run away but they chased her, shouting, 'Let us eliminate counter-revolutionary families!' She ran so fast that she lost her balance on the slopes and fell rolling three metres down the hill and broke her hip. There was no doctor in the commune to treat her. She was in a great deal of pain until my mother finally managed to obtain a referral letter from the commune to take her to

Ürümchi where she was hospitalised for a week. She returned with the plaster cast on her hip and upper leg had to stay in bed for three more months. I felt guilty and sad. It broke my heart to see my sister, my mother, and my entire family suffering because of me.

January 1967

The new wave of crackdown on intellectuals started at the start of the new year, and all schools were shut down at Mao's order. Intellectuals have been given a new insulting nickname, the 'Stinking Ninth Caste'.[34] Those who used to work in the cities have been forcibly dispersed to the villages to work on the farms and in the fields. Leadership changes have taken place everywhere from the cities to the villages. The positions of the 'Stinking Ninth Caste' have been taken up by ordinary workers and peasants,[35] and the poor have become the Party's favourite and were given positions of the responsibility in the communes. In our commune, for instance, a blacksmith named Nokte has been appointed to the position of Commune Leader, while Mukash, a horse cart driver, who have received no education, has replaced the former headmaster of the secondary school, Moldash. Not only them, but most of those appointed into positions of importance have had little education. The entire East Turkistan is in chaos. People wonder what has happened to common sense throughout China, where educated people, especially teachers, have always been the most respected within the community, and one would ever disrespect them or their authority. Now they are under attack, and being called names by their own students.

This new development has affected my father physically and emotionally. He has suffered from asthma for sometime and it has now got worse. The doctors advised my father to seek treatment in Ürümchi, so my family asked for permission from the commune authorities, who allowed him move to our house in Ürümchi.

I worked outdoors with a Production Corp for over two months, digging wells, with water up to my waist most of the time. Afterwards I was directed to cut bushes on

34   *The Chinese term, chou laojiu, widely attributed to Mao, has encountered various English translations, such as 'the old stinky ones' and 'the stinky ninth social category', portrays Mao's perception of intellectuals as the lowest social class during the Cultural Revolution.*

35   *The ideology underlying the Cultural Revolution saw ordinary workers and peasants as the highest, most ideologically advanced social class that was to lead the revolution itself. Intellectuals, along with others who used to occupy the higher social classes, were ordered to learn from ordinary workers and peasants in order to reform themselves.*

the north side of the mountains until the beginning of May. The snow in the mountains was still quite deep as I worked with half of my body immersed in the snow, cutting down the thorn bushes. Other members of the commune did not work for over three months due to the lack of work within the commune. Despite this I didn't have any free time, as I kept being ordered to work in the mountains regardless of the weather conditions.

People were now split into two different factions: 1 – 3 Commando who supported Wang Enmao;[36] and Red 2-Commando who supported Wu Gang. Each group occupied different areas of the region with people from one group not daring to step onto the other group's territory. The East Turkistan people were now divided into two separate factions opposing each other.

The leadership of our commune supported the views of the 1 – 3 Commando. They were always loyal, having devoted themselves to its' principles and worked very hard to achieve its goals. They recruited one hundred of the fittest and the most hot-blooded young men as their *minbing*s. These young men were given uniforms, arms, and horses, and named the 'Horseback Soldiers'.

They were often sent into the city to 'clean up' places, which included confiscating people's properties or fighting rival factions. There were also rumours of them being involved in killings.

Different factions were often in conflict with each other, which became more and more intense as people within work units, factories, schools and family members divided between different factions thus becoming enemies. In many families children were left without a mother or a father. Loudspeakers were installed in various public places where people would shout intimidating slogans 24 hours a day, quoting Chairman Mao or broadcasting revolutionary operas, such as Shajabang and Red Azalea. They were played on the radio so often that the public became fed up, but there was nothing they could do to stop this. People couldn't sleep at night as the two groups fought for control over the loudspeaker system nonstop. Some used cotton wool to plug their ears in order to find some peace, but this had little effect, and they were left mentally exhausted.

My family home in Ürümchi was located in Yanhang, an area controlled by the Red 2-Commando. People in our commune therefore believed that my family supported the Red 2-Commando and watched our house day and night.

---

36 *People's Liberation Army lieutenant general, who was twice the Chinese Communist Party's Committee Secretary of Xinjiang.*

June 1967
The atomic bomb

When I returned home for lunch, and I found out that my auntie Mehpuze from Ürümchi had come to visit us. We all sat down to lunch happily laughing and joking. Just as we were about to start enjoying our meal, everything in the house started shaking; dishes and pots fell to the floor and the mirror came off the wall and smashed on the floor. Then a mighty bang ensued.

We jumped up and rushed outside in panic to find that the sky was dark and the sun had disappeared behind thick cloud. I looked around and saw all our neighbours in the street looking in the same direction: a dark mushroom cloud rose in the distance where the bang came from, spreading quickly in our direction bringing sand and dust.

My heart sank. The shape of the cloud was clearly the result of an atomic explosion.

'They threw a bomb! An atomic bomb!!' I shouted in despair to the panicking crowd.

'My girl, are you sure? How do you know that?' Antie Mehpuze asked.

'I studied about this at university. That is exactly what it is - an atomic explosion!' I screamed

'Speak quietly, will you?' my mother warned me with a stare, 'If they hear you, you will get us all into trouble!'

'Oh God! I must go home immediately', said Auntie Mehpuze, who looked sick, having witnessed something terrifying that she couldn't fully comprehend.

It would be many years later after I had left my country that I would find out I had witnessed one of the biggest atomic air detonation carried out by Chinese state in East Turkistan, these didn't stop until 1996. As a result there has been a dramatic rise in stillborn babies, birth defects, various forms of cancer and unexplainable death.

15 June 1967
The denunciation meetings at the Production Corp

Everyone in the Production Corp had finished their work for the day. As always I had to continue working along with other 'class enemies' until I was given permission to leave. Among us, some were former landowners or rich peasants. We all wore different 'dunce's hats'. People called us *qalpaqliqlar*, which means 'the hatted ones', in other words, the 'branded criminals'. I was stacking up dried bricks when six armed *minbing*s came and surrounded us with their guns pointed at us. There was a chilling look on their faces, as if they were ready to kill us at any time.

'Why are they here?' I asked Lao Li quietly.

'Don't speak, my girl, or they will shoot you!' he whispered. I sensed something terrible was about to happen. Half an hour later we were called to stand in a straight line before being herded into the hall of the Production Team.

The hall was already crowded with people. There were roughly fifty *minbing*s from the age of sixteen to twenty-one with hand grenades and ammunition pouches tied around their waists and guns slung on their shoulders. They were marching noisily back and forth. The sound of their army boots instilled fear. They looked proud and impatient to utilise their energy and strength in an explosive demonstration of power.

'Let's wipe out the Four Types of Enemies!' 'Down with the class enemies!' - they shouted their slogans as soon as we entered the hall.

Then everyone followed, repeating these slogans and shouting blood-curdling menaces, their fists punching angrily in the air as we were being paraded in front of them. My heart was pumping faster and faster as I was being assaulted by so many slogans and insults. For a brief moment, I actually started questioning myself: am I really a bad person? Have I done such terrible deeds to make the whole world so angry? What have I done? I didn't steal, I haven't killed anyone, I haven't done anything to offend these people or our society. I wish no harm on these people despite being humiliated by them daily. All I wanted was freedom and independence for my own nation to stand up on its own feet. Is that such a terrible crime? No, it is not! I am an innocent person and I have nothing to be ashamed of! I reassured myself and calmed down a little.

I stood upright while trying to look proud, and then suddenly I felt a kind of inner strength growing rapidly within my body. I lifted my chin and looked at everyone with a smile. This antagonised the *minbing*s, and one of them ran up to me with fury. With no hesitation, he started kicking and punching me, and hitting my head, yelling, 'Head down! Keep your fucking head down!' He pressed my head down aggressively. He then dragged both my hands down until I was touching my toes. 'Do not move, do you understand?' he shouted while pulling my scarf from my head, which he threw into the crowd. I glanced up to see some children catching my scarf, which they threw onto the floor before they started spitting and stamping on it. I felt humiliated as if it was my soul that was being torn apart, trampled and mocked.

My younger sister Sofiye who was amongst the crowd squeezed through the screaming mob to pick up my scarf. It didn't take long for two *minbing*s to drag her out of the hall. Her screams made my heart bleed. A *minbing* grabbed me by the neck, dragged me forward and shouted to the crowd while pointing his finger at me, 'Listen to me, people, do you know who this is? She is the counter-revolutionary Söyüngül. She is a traitor. She tried to sell Xinjiang to the United States, Japan and the Soviet Union!' Other *minbing*s came up and encircled me, shouting one after another aggressively, 'How much did you sell Xinjiang for? Come on, confess your crime now!'

One tried to strangle me before pushing me away violently. I lost my balance but managed not to fall, stopping right in front of the *minbing*s on the other side of the circle. They interrogated me relentlessly, and, receiving no answer, they started punching me. The punches fell like raindrops. My hair clips came undone and my long hair fell onto my shoulders. They carried on kicking and punching me, knocking me in all directions. They then grabbed me once again while shouting straight into my ear – 'Tell us, how much did you sell Xinjiang for? Did you hide the money? Give the money back now!' This was repeated one after another by those in the circle. Every punch I received made my head spin, to the point where I was about to black out.

After a while they dragged me to the side so that the others could be displayed and subjected to the same torture. I was about to part my hair covering my face so as to see what was going on when a *minbing* hit my hand with a bat so hard that it could have smashed my bones. They then pushed my head down to the lowest point my neck would allow, and ordered me to stay in that position, before proceeding to torture Luo Jun, who was branded a 'capitalist roader'. They tortured him for quite a while before dragging a third man up on stage, who was from the Tutunhu Mill Production Corp.

'Now this one, he's a rebel from the Paddock Village, and he is a member of the No. 2 Commandos. He instigated people in the city to rebel against the government. Confess and redeem yourself in front of the people now!' With my head down, I couldn't see what they were doing to him, but I knew exactly what the *minbing*s were doing to him, from the punches, kicks and the painful screams of the man pleading for mercy. He screamed hysterically, 'Yes I was in the city! I was! I had overheard people saying that all the students who had held a hunger strike in the People's Square had been killed. So I went to visit the scene of the massacre…'

'Shut your mouth you fucking liar!' yelled the guards, 'Who killed whom?' and they starting to beat him again.

The man who in charge of the denunciation meeting finally spoke up, 'Stop! Let Qurban explain himself first!'

Qurban's voice continued, 'I went to visit People's Square where the students had been on a hunger strike for three days, but they disappeared overnight.'

'How did they disappear?' someone interrupted.

'I don't know. Like I said I just went to the square and when I arrived there I saw a lot of blood all over a bus, which had broken windows and shattered glass all in and around it...'

'Oh what are you trying to say, huh? Who are you accusing of killings the students? He is making an accusation against the government!' Qurban was interrupted again, and the beating started all over. I could hear him begging them for mercy as he shrieked in agony.

The crowd carried on shouting slogans all evening. For over five hours I was forced to bend my neck and keep my head down while listening to the terrifying screams of the *minbing*s. It's impossible to describe the mental and physical torture I endured during those five hours. At midnight, the commander of the *minbing*s finally announced over the loud speaker, 'The Four Types of Enemies, leave now, get out of the hall!' As soon as I heard it was over, I dashed out of the doors before any one could reach me with their thrusting fists. However, my other fellow friends didn't manage to escape the renewed punching or kicking of the mad crowd.

I spent a little time tidying up my hair and calming myself from all the emotional horrors tormenting mind before I entered the house. I felt sad to have to put my younger siblings through the mental torture of seeing their sister in such a miserable state, so I walked into the house humming a song with a big smile on my face.

My sister looked at me in shock, 'Söyün, are you ok? Why you are singing and smiling after they have been torturing you all evening?' I nodded and went to sit down as all my siblings came to sit near me. They looked at me intensely with their tender eyes examining my face. I patted their heads, trying to reassure them.

'It is ok. Don't worry. In this world there are good things as well as bad things, but all will go by in time. We haven't done anything bad to anyone. We live with a clear conscience.'

My cousin Muqeddes, who lives in the city and is visiting us at the moment, said, 'Now I understand what's helping you cope with all the unfair treatment you are put through every day.' I smiled.

Then I suddenly remembered something. Did they beat my sister Sofiye when they dragged her out?

'Yes!' she answered, 'One of the *minbing* dragged me outside from the meeting and kicked me so hard that I fell into a ditch. He then came over punching me hard in the back many times. Have they got no shame?! They have so much hatred, sister! They even beat up children! He said that I had sided with the counter-revolutionary, and I deserved to be taught a lesson for my actions. If Gheyshe hadn't been there at that time I think he would have killed me.'

Gheyshe sat close to Sofiye with teary eyes and gave her a hug. She said, 'I was so furious when I saw that animal beating Sofiye that I had to do something. I jumped into the ditch and pulled his belt from behind with all my energy, thankfully he lost his balance and fell backwards onto the ground before he could attack me. At that moment two men who worked with you on the building sites came out from the hall and saw us. They took us back home and told us angrily that we shouldn't have been at the meeting, that there was nothing we could have done, that our presence would not only bring trouble to ourselves, but also make things worse for you. They said, "There is no law and order out there, and those people have the power and will to kill anyone, anytime without question or punishment for their actions, in the future you must be very careful!"'

16 June 1967

Gheyshe fell ill last night. She woke up complaining of nightmares and a high fever.

I went back to work at daybreak. The *minbing*s brought in Qurban to join the team of 'class enemies'. Like the rest of us, he jumped into the mud mixing the water and the earth with a shovel. As soon as the supervisor left, he approached me and said in a low voice, 'I have heard a lot of good things about you from other people. There are people writing songs about your resilience and bravery. I always hoped to meet you in person one day that has finally happened. I truly admire you. You are the most dignified, courageous, a heroic young woman I have ever met. I have two daughters and I hope they will grow up to be like you.'

His warm words comforted me; I was so overwhelmed that I didn't know what to say. He continued speaking while mixing the mud, 'It is a very strange world indeed. Did you see there was a slim man in the front line who shouted slogans non-stop at the top of his voice? Do you happen to know his name?

'Yes, I saw the man. I don't think he is from this commune, though', I replied.

'When he left the denunciation meeting, he complained about his throat and chest. He was taken to the doctors who said that his tonsils were damaged. He had a serious heart problem, too, and they were going to take him to see a specialist in Ürümchi. Poor man, he died before an ambulance could be arranged to take him. May God bless his soul! You see, life is so, so short and fragile. Yet there are people who still live as if they will never die while taking pleasure in causing misery to others!'

29 June 1967

In addition to 'class enemies', we have now a new nickname: the 'Four Criminal Elements', which refers to landlords, rich peasants, counter-revolutionaries and the ambiguously named 'bad elements'. The commune leader summoned us, the 'Four Criminal Elements' to gather at the commune courtyard in half an hour. I rushed home, got changed quickly, and rushed back to the commune courtyard. We were ordered to stand in line. The party secretary of the production unit, Ghabdal, started shouting at me all of a sudden, 'How dare you dress up as if you are going to a wedding? You are a counter-revolutionary! You have no right to dress up or hold your head high. Don't you know that you should present yourself humbly before the public? Don't you understand?' He jumped in front of me as if he was going to hit me. I was surprised by his remarks regarding my clothes because I wasn't 'dressed up' at all: I was wearing an ordinary dress, which was clean and ironed.

We travelled on foot for over three hours carrying our belongings before finally reaching our destination. I was placed in the girls' dormitory next to the door. There was no accommodation left for my fellow male 'class enemies', so they had no choice but to sleep outdoors. I went to the canteen for food; it was crowded with people from different production units who were brought in for the harvesting.

We were ordered to stand in the middle of the canteen. People walked past us and didn't miss the chance of verbally abusing us with degrading words. We were ordered to stand aside until everyone finished their meal. When it was our turn, there was very little food left apart from some burned bread. In the end I returned to the dormitory with an empty stomach, and I swore never to go back to the canteen again. My sister Gheyshe and Sofiye, who joined me there later to work in other groups, helped me out by bringing food from the canteen.

As usual, the 'class enemies' were separated from the other labourers. We were given the fields cursed with the lowest grain yields in order to harvest from them twice as much as other groups. In some parts of the fields it was impossible to use a sickle and having to pull the wheat by hand. To reach the target we had to work from two in the morning till ten or eleven at night. After two months of slavery we miraculously finished the harvesting.

1 September 1967
Hardship in Qizilsay

We walked for hours from the wheat fields to reach home – my sweet home that I had been longing for over the last two months. But upon our arrival, the commune leader informed us that we would be leaving next morning for Qizilsay to build a road.

Qizilsay is barren place. The rocks on the hills are bright red, from which it gets its name, which means 'Red Valley'. They informed us that our task was to build a road across the mountains and down the valleys to the entrance of the coalmine. The commune leaders held a mobilisation meeting for all the workers except us, the 'class enemies', who were usually banned from such meetings.

I was ordered to pick wood from the hillside. I was wondering around picking up wood when suddenly a stone fell in front of me. Startled, I looked upwards to see where the stone came from, and I saw a frail old man with white hair and long grey beard resting on a stick. He was traditionally dressed in a *tumaq*[37] *and a long green gown with soft leather boots. I first thought he was a xizir,*[38] and my jaw dropped as I gazed at him with amazement. I said to myself, 'This can't be an ordinary man. It is impossible for a man his age to be so high in the mountains.' I smiled at him.

'My child, whose daughter are you?' he asked, staring at me.

'My father's name is Salih', I answered.

'Oh, I know your parents very well! We are old acquaintances. Are they well?'

'Yes, they are. God be praised.'

He then came down in front of me and said, 'I am Meydar Molla. I was accused of poisoning people with religion, for which I was ordered to Reform Through Labour under heavy surveillance. Of course, it was difficult at my age. My child, you are very young, may God help you through hardships and give you abundant blessings!' The sadness in his eyes was hard to ignore. It was painful for me to see respected elders of our community being forced to work under such harsh and dangerous conditions.

We started the roadwork early next day; as usual we were given twice the workload compared to others. There were about ten old men who joined our 'class enemy' group,

37   *A traditional hat from Kashgar.*
38   *A type of spirit.*

most of them being rich Kazakh herdsmen aged between 65 and 80. Meydar Mollar was among them.

Building the road on the steep mountainside without any safety equipment was a dangerous task. We were allocated to the most dangerous parts of the mountains to work. To start the construction process we first had to clear out the rocks. As usual there were *minbing*s stood over our heads with whips. They kept urging us to work faster, and wouldn't allow us to roll the rocks away, but would force us to carry them to a place they picked in the distance. The elderly workers suffered the most, and as they repeatedly failed to carry the heavy rocks, they were constantly whipped. The mental torture of witnessing such cruelty exhausted me more than the actual work itself. Having worked non-stop since the early morning, I suddenly felt dizzy. I couldn't stop my body from trembling. Fearing that I might collapse and end up being whipped by these cruel *minbing*s. I pulled myself together and quietly prayed to God to give me strength. My prayer was answered: at that very moment, the bell rang for lunch break! I was so relieved and quickly sat down on the ground. My colleagues came over to me at once asking if I was alright, and I reassured them, saying that I was.

After lunch we were taken to the coalmine, which had been abandoned since 1957 - the year that the country was mobilised into steel manufacturing. Giving each of us a heavy pickaxe, the *minbing*s ordered us to bring the coal from inside the mine to the entrance, and told us that they'd be back at three o'clock, and that we'd better have collected plenty of coal by that time. It was dark inside and we didn't have a torch, so we had to walk like blind people using our hands and feet to feel the surroundings before moving on. The group leader Zhongyin Li was leading us and kept warning us against potential dangers.

I remembered the time when I injured my head in the coalmine tunnel while running chasing the donkey a few years ago. So I started walking very cautiously within the outcrops of rocks and coal in the tunnel. Before long, I reached a big rock, where I had to lower my head to crawl through the tiny opening just about one metre long. Suddenly I heard someone shout from behind, 'Meydar Molla has collapsed! He can't breathe! Come back and do something!' I asked the group leader Zhongyin Li if we could leave the elders outside until we locate the coalface. He agreed with me and said, 'Let them wait at the entrance by the big rock. We will carry the coal there and they can move the coal out to the entrance.' The elders were relieved by Li's decision.

We continued walking down the shaft until I caught a glimpse of some lights. We con, lntinued in that direction until we saw that the light was coming from a large hole in the roof allowing the air to come through. We examined the whole place carefully. After a short moment, Zhongyin Li commented, 'Guys, it is very dangerous here. See the cracks in the walls? That's the reason why this mine was abandoned. It can collapse at anytime! We can't use pickaxes to dig out the coal. Let's collect the coal on the ground and carry it outside. We need proper mining equipment and experienced engineers to examine the site before we can start digging.' He's a very experienced coal miner, having worked in the mines for many years. We listened to his advice.

As we were busy looking for coal all over the place, we heard noises from outside. The *minbing*s had come back and shouted, 'Class Enemies, bring the coal outside!'

'Just ignore them and stay quiet. Let them look for us. Then we can show them the risks in here', Zhongyi Li suggested.

We quickly passed the message to all of workers and everyone stayed silent. The *minbing*s called us again and again from the entrance of the mine, 'Hey! What's going on? Speak up! Are you dead or something?'

We thought they'd come in, so we could show him what the dangers we were faced with inside the mine. However, they stood outside shouting for over an hour and none of them dared to enter. In the end we carried the coal we had collected out of the mine, and told them of the dangerous condition of the mine.

'I'm sorry, but this is all we could manage to get. It's impossible to mine any coal without proper equipment', explained Zhongyin Li.

'Well go and get whatever you need from the mine nearby and go back to work!' the *minbing*s ordered impatiently.

As we didn't make much progress, we were told to build the road during the day and mine coal at night.

5 October 1967

My workmates moved to the site of the coalmine after dinner. A mining technician named Sedu was appointed as the team leader. The elderly men were placed in a roofless deserted mud house not far from the mine after being cleaned out. The rest of men were place in a Kazakh yurt used by the shepherds from the other side of the mountains. Being the only female in the 'class enemies' group, I remained at the central accommodation with the other female workers, which was over one hours walk from the mine.

On my return to the mine we decided to light a fire near to the entrance. Some of my workmates went into the mine to collect some coal, they emerged very quickly, looking frightened.

'The roof of the mine where we were at yesterday has collapsed. We were lucky it didn't fall while we were there yesterday!'

We were directed to a safer work area where we stayed until midnight before bringing out all the coal we had dug out. Then we called it a day.

My workmates were concerned about me walking alone in the darkness over the dangerous mountain track back to my dormitory. I told them that I would be fine and continued my journey. I soon realised, however, what it meant to be walking in the steep terrain in the pitch darkness: rocks and boulders were everywhere, and I could fall over them and rolled down the mountain with nothing for me to hold onto. Fear and panic started to get the better of me, and I felt isolated and helpless. I wanted to scream for help, yet I knew no one would hear me. Who would and who could come to rescue me if something happened? I stopped to take a deep breath and said to myself, 'Come on, Söyüngül, there is nothing for you to be afraid of. You have promised that you would overcome all the difficulties and fear, and God is always with you. You are not alone!' I felt better and started slowly walking down the mountain.

Gradually my eyes were adjusted to the darkness, and I could see my surroundings better. I kept reminding myself that there were three very dangerous inclines ahead of me, and I must not fall over and die. I still managed to trip over several times, and each time my heart would leap to my throat. Fortunately I'd always manage to hold onto something to save myself from falling. After tripping over some unknown obstacle for the last time, I reached a flatter part of the mountain. Knowing the worst was behind me, I started to walk faster, and finally reached my destination. It took me about one and a half hours.

I was walking pass the canteen when I heard a familiar voice, 'So you are finally here, my girl. Gheyshe told me that you'd be back after midnight and asked me to keep some food for you.' It was Lao Ma.

'Sorry, I don't feel like eating now. Please just give me a cup of tea, uncle.'

'I'm so sorry for you, my girl. I wish I could do more to help', he said while passing me the tea. I thanked him for his kindness; his warm words gave me a great deal of comfort.

Having had some warm tea, I went to my dormitory and lay down before getting up again at 3 am, as I had to be back at the coalmine by 4 am. But no one had an alarm clock. I managed to wake up one time, wondering if I had actually been used to the routine. I washed my face quickly and made my way back to the coalmine when Lao

Ma stopped me again, offering me some tea. I refused politely as I didn't want to be punished by the *minbing*s for being late.

I walked as fast and careful as I could in the darkness. When I arrived at the mine when the first rays of the sun had lit up the sky in the east. I saw my teammates standing outside waiting for me. I was glad to know that I wasn't late. Everyone greeted warmly and welcomed me like a returning hero from a battle. 'Well done, Söyün, we all are very proud of you! We were so worried last night that you might not make it. We are so happy to see you back safe and sound!' they cheered.

The *minbing*s ordered us to bring coal to the canteen every time when we went there.

'But we don't have anything to carry the coal with', we protested.

'Well it's none of our business. You have to find a way to transport the coal to the canteen, otherwise you will be punished', they said coldly.

I wrapped my jacket around my waist, so I could I carry the coal inside it. The rest of my workmates did the same. On our way to the canteen we normally have to cross a steep ascent. When we got there, I led the group walking slowly and steadily upwards. I turned around to check on them when I reached half way. Meydar Molla was last, he was out of breath but he was still trying to keep up with the others. Before I could go down and help him, he lost his balance and rolled down to the bottom of the hill, the coal he was carrying spilled everywhere. I was worried that that he might not be able to stand up again, but he got up with trembling legs. Unable to bear the sight of him suffering, I said to Sedu, 'Team Leader, look, he is clearly too old to do this. Please let him get some rest and bring him some food, will you?' Everyone else agreed, and Sedu hesitantly accepted my request to leave Meydar Molla behind.

Being the first to reach the top, I waited for the rest to arrive. Once everyone had arrived we stood in a line before descending. When I was on the top of the mountain, the Internationale was being played on the loud speakers, which were on top of the canteen roof. This was followed by the song 'Jilikchi Atbaqit Qiz'.[39] I didn't pay much attention in the beginning but I realised that this music starts whenever we come to the top of the rise, and I know it isn't just a coincidence, because there are days when we finish work late, yet the music always starts as we pass over the rise. I've heard this song played in many films as the heroes are tortured or taken away for execution. I'm always curious to know who is in control of the radio. I know this person is our friend and against the regime.

---

39   'The Singing Shepherdess'

11 November 1967

As the days are turning colder, we have started work in the new mine, which is located on the southern side of the mountain. Having conquered my fear of darkness completely, walking at night is no longer a psychological burden to me. I sometimes come across wild animals such as foxes, rabbits and goats; some nights I could hear the wolves howling in the distance. Ignoring all these dangers I carried on my journey regardless. I learned from Gheyshe that people were talking about me with admiration. Even Sedu came over to me once and said he admired my courage.

Today after the dinner, Sedu picked up some left over cow bones (the meat had been consumed by the cadres) from the ground outside the back of the canteen and put them all into a bag. He asked Orazan to carry it to the mine. Sedu then took two buckts out of the canteen and filled them with the rain water from a ditch.

'What are you going to do with that?' I asked him curiously.

'We are going to make some delicious soup later', he said with a wink.

'But are you sure rainwater is clean? It has been in the ditch for months and there are worms in it.'

'No, it will be ok. All the worms or germs will die once the water is boiled. I could not remember the last time I had full stomach. At least the soup will give us some energy', he answered, and I looked at him with disbelief.

At the coalmine, huge rocks were put together with coal placed in the middle and lit; a large pot was placed above the coal resting on the rocks. The pot had been left there by the previous miners and had been rinsed thoroughly. All the bones were thrown into the pot, submerged in the dirty rainwater.

After working inside the mine for two hours we came out for a break to find that it was snowing. Sedu rushed to the pot and shouted excitedly, 'Guys! Our delicious cow bone soup is ready! Hurry up, and bring your bowls before it gets cold!' All my teammates then picked up their bowls and hurried to the stove. I stood to one side watching them. Sedu filled each person's bowl, laughing and joking with joy. After he passed the soup to the last person in the line he looked at me and insisted I should try some. I thanked him for his kind offer and told him that I was not hungry. Everyone was happy as if they just had a big feast. The hot soup brought comfort to their empty stomachs, aching from the hunger and the cold. Most of these 'class enemies' were branded as such because they had wealthy backgrounds. I wondered if they had ever thought that they would one day end up in such misery when they still lived comfortable lives.

'Things change in life all the time and nothing lasts forever. So whatever we are experiencing now will not last forever', I said to myself.

We came out of the mine at midnight. A blanket of glistening white snow covered everywhere our eyesight could reach. I quickly cleaned my face with the snow before saying goodbye to my workmates and headed over the mountain. The path was icy and slippery. Meydar Molla and other workmates expressed their concerns about me walking on such a perilous terrain. I assured them that I would be extremely careful. Wishing them a good night, I set off towards the crest of the mountain confidently. I knew they would be watching me as always until I disappeared from their sight.

I slipped constantly from the minute I started going up the slope. No mater how careful I tried, it was like skating on ice upwards. I managed to get half way up the path and was thrilled by the thought of conquering yet another difficult task when I slipped rolling all the way down the hill passing the coal mine before stopping in the valley.

'SÖYÜNGÜÜÜÜL!!!!' my workmates shouted in panic, 'Please listen to us for once! You are going to kill yourself. Come back here!' I rose up slowly and walk towards them.

'Söyüngül, don't torment yourself. We are your family and we know your parents. Please come and stay with us!' they said to me caringly. Medyar Molla lent me his sheepskin coat, as Sedu gave me his dog skin rug before turning to walk to their hut. The fire was in the middle of the room, making the place warm and cosy. I climbed onto the sleeping platform, spreading a dog skin rug near the wall before sitting down against the wall and covering myself with a sheepskin coat. Watching the snow as it fell to disappear from the heat of the fire and listening to my friends' snoring, I sank deep in my thoughts as I slipped into sleep.

3 December 1967

Having finished the road, we started working at a new coal mine after two shafts were opened up to the coalface through the old mine. Sedu kept a number of strong men to continue working in the previous mine after telling the rest of us to return home with the main group. Leaving the site after breakfast, we arrived home in the dark. Gheyshe and I walked and entered our empty cold house to find out that one of the windows had been removed. The house has been ransacked. Nearly everything is gone, including the coal and potatoes we had kept for winter.

We were devastated, having walked all day in the cold without eating we were looking forward to getting home, sitting by the warm stove and cooking something to eat. We tidied up the house quickly, gathered some wood to light a fire in the stove to keep us warm. As we wondered what we could eat, our cousin Hajiye Banu entered the house carrying some food and tea. She told us that it was Nokte's gang who looted the house.

'Our neighbours saw his wife Zeynep and her children in your cloths and asked them about it. She said, "It is our right to rob the rich. They are the "class enemies"; we are the poor and we have power over our enemies. They don't deserve anything."' Hajiye told us angrily.

What Hajiye told us left us speechless. After a moment of silence, she tried to comfort us –

'My dear sisters, people like Zeynep have no shame. Why let her bother you? Don't be sad. We will get through hardship together. You will not starve. Look, I am here!' She looked at us with sincerity, and her words made us feel better.

By the time Gheyshe and I finished washing ourselves, it was already 11 pm. I went to bed and immediately fell asleep.

4 December 1967

A knock on the window woke me up. At first I thought I was dreaming, then I heard it again and opened my heavy eyelids reluctantly.

'Who is it?' I shouted.

'The sun is up. Why are you still sleeping? Go and clean up the snow on the roof of the cowshed!' team leader Qenighet shouted.

I had no idea which sun he was talking about. It was still dark outside, and my clock said it was midnight.

'It's only midnight, Team Leader! I will start the job at dawn making sure it is finished in the morning', I said grumpily.

'Ok, I just wanted to make sure you know. Throw the snow into the street not in the courtyard. You will be in trouble if you don't finish the job before I start work in the morning!' he warned me before leaving.

This upset me immensely. How did he find out I'd returned home? For the first time I let negative emotions flow free. How dare he? How dare they?! I was constantly being treated worse than an animal. Isn't this enough?!

I dragged myself up at four to start cleaning the snow of the roof of the cowshed, managing to finish everything by eight o'clock. The roof was made of bamboo, so it was extremely slippery. Oh God, when will these miserable days end? My life here is worse than the times I spent in the labour camp! What did I do to deserve this? When can I be free from this life I am living? I am sick of being enslaved. My longing for freedom grows stronger every day. Oh God, brighten up my life like the sunbeams light up the sky! I need my freedom to live!

I prayed while I scooped up the snow and piled it up on one side before throwing it into the street. My hands were numb, my arms were in pain and my legs were loosing their strength because I was constantly deprived of food and sleep. I could barely stand the cold: the temperature in the morning was -30 degrees…

21 March 1968

It was another cold day with a mixture of snow and sleet. I was working in the cowshed placing manure into bags. Suddenly the secretary Ömerbeg's wife, Nurile, shouted angrily from the other side of the shed, 'Oh I can't believe the world is falling into the hands of the *fangeming*!'[40] Hearing her screaming the word '*fangeming*', I felt as if she was slapping my face. Since my nickname was changed to '*fangeming*', everyone takes pleasure in calling me by it, so I knew immediately that it was me that she was referring to.

Upon my arrival in Nanshan, everyone everywhere has talked about me. I have become the main object of the Cultural Revolution in the area and the focus of the denunciation meetings. My name has been used in all of the slogans and on local newspaper articles plastered all over house walls and commune buildings. The headlines always begin with 'The Counter-Revolutionary Söyüngül, The East Turkistan Separatist…' and are always full of an array of accusations criticising me along with other people. I'm now seen as the most dangerous individual in Nanshan. What is more, my family has also been labelled 'The Counter Revolutionary Family' and blacklisted. People have drawn a clear line between themselves and us in order not to look as if they are revolutionaries ready to condemn and attack my family at all times. The most painful reality for us to accept is that some of our relatives and those we used to consider as good friends have all turned against us while protecting themselves from being implicated in my family's 'crimes'. People have been avoiding walking past our house. It has brought us much misery to be ostracised by society.

---

40   Chinese for '*counter-revolutionary*'.

I can't believe what a dangerous person I've become in the eyes of so many. Hardly anyone looks at me in a friendly way since I arrived in Nanshan. I'm not surprised to have the name *fangeming* shouted in my face, but I sometimes still hope they are referring to someone else. But who? Who else but me is *fangeming*? I was eager to know, but it is impossible to ask anyone such a sensitive question. Everyone is scared to talk about anything as whatever is said can be twisted and turned into something else before they realise it's too late. The atmosphere in Nanshan is tense. I haven't heard laughter in a long time. All I see is misery and anger on people's faces.

I went home for lunch with all questions in my mind. On my return to work after lunch, I found no other woman but Mukajan andtwo other Han Chinese 'Class Enimies'. Mukajan came to my side whispering quietly – "Do you know why that woman was shouting thie morning?" I have no idea." I replied. The secondary teacher Kibek's wife, Reshide, was given the 'Model Woman Worker' award last night. She received thirty yuan from the commune as a reward. The commune secretary's wife, Nurile is angry that it was Reshide but not her that got the rewards. Now she is accusing Reshide of being a *fangeming*. Why does she call Reshide a *fengeming* ? I asked out of curiosity. "Well apparently, nine month ago, someone falsely announced on the loudspeakers – 'We are liberated! We are free from the current oppressive regime!" And then some women went ecstatic, jumping up and down. One of them shouted, 'Down with Premier Zhou!' Another, 'Down with Liu Shaoqi!' And Reshide apparently shouted, 'Down with Chairman Mao!' Soon they all realised that the announcement was false, they all became frightened. There weren't many people around to hear what had been shouted, so they all promised one another to keep this outburst among themselves, well, until last night, when Reshide receiving the award, Nurile got so bitter that she is exposing her now. I fear that there is going to be a big trouble…" said Mukajan. The next day, all the women involved in the incident related by Mukajan were dragged out at the commune assembly to stand with Reshide, all of them branded a counter-revolutionary before being put under surveillance.

13 April 1968

The team leader ordered me to sieve sand near the river behind the Nokte's wooden house. Normally the riverbed would be dry but since it's the rain season, the river has overflown its banks today.

Mukajan's wife lives very close to the river. I noticed while I was working that she kept opening the door and popping her head out to look in my direction, and then disappearing again. I found this hilarious and wondered why she was doing that, but didn't give it too much thought and carried on working. About one hour later she popped her head out once again, and looked around her house before running towards me. Then, shockingly, she squatted down two metres away from me as if she was about go to the toilet. I felt she was trying to insult me by this, so I turned my back to her and continued with my work.

'My child, listen to me carefully', she whispered from behind me, 'I have learned that last night there was a meeting for all the *minbing*s. They had arranged a jeep to go and collect your parents for a denunciation meeting. They have been ordered to parade them from Totobos[41] on foot all the way to the commune. They are going to be brutal. I heard they've even been given permission to kill them! My child, I'm worried sick that once in the hands of those beasts your parents may not survive. I pray that this madness can be avoided. I've been desperate to tell you about this. Forgive me of the indecency, my child. This is the only way I could pass on the information. You must find a way to inform them today before it is too late!' she then stood up quickly and ran back to her house before I could even thank her.

Oh, my poor parents! Angered and frightened, I was determined to find a way to save them. With everyone away in the city, only my younger sister Firdews was at home. I must send Firdews and Hajiye Banu to the city, but I could not leave my work to go home myself. Just as I was worried I might not be able to do anything, I suddenly saw my sister walking towards me. It was as if God had sent her to me. I told her everything I had heard. She started shaking with fear.

'Sister! What shall we do?' She asked with a trembling voice.

'The best thing you can do of course is to head for the city straight away. But how could you travel there…?' I could hardly hide my frustration.

She thought for a moment before replying, 'Ok let me do this: when I walked past the commune earlier I saw an army jeep. It may be going back to the city later. I am going to ask them right now if they can give me a lift to the city. I'll be back!' Then she ran of like gust of wind. She returned before long beaming with joy to tell me that they would be leaving in half an hour.

They returned the next morning telling me that they had told my parents of the *minbing*s' crazy plan. My parents called friends and relatives to the house to discuss the problem, and they decided to do everything to keep my parents away from the commune for the sake of safety. I am so relieved and thankful to Mukajan's wife for

41   *A mountain about 7 km from the commune.*

taking such a great risk in giving me such crucial information. Thanks to her kindness my parents escaped death.

28 April 1968

Reshide's nightmare had begun two days ago in the central Commune meeting hall. A sand bag filled with heavy stones was hung on a thin wire around her neck; she was physically and mentally tormented for two days and nights. She was forced to confess her 'crime', but she couldn't tell them much and only managed to say, 'I don't have any bad thoughts within me. It was my mouth to blame. I said a very inappropriate thing. I accept fully that it was a mistake it should never have happened and will never happen again!' On the second day at the denunciation meeting the students protested outside the meeting hall, shouting, 'You can fight to change people's thoughts by education and communication, not by physical abuse! We demand that you remove the bag from Reshide's neck right now! If you don't remove it we will storm the building and attack you!' Under such pressure the *minbing*s removed the bag and let her go home. Then a fight ensued between the *minbing*ss, the cadres and the students. It lasted all night.

Reshide was three months pregnant and suffered a miscarriage during the violent ordeal. The doctors told her that she would never be able to have children again…

29 April 1968

One of the young *minbing*s, Qenighet, came to see me at home. He came to my side saying in a quiet and gentle tone, 'I've come to tell you that they are planning to take you to the denunciation meeting tomorrow. I thought I'd better let you know in advance.' He looked at me nervously before leaving. I have never expected such kindness from any of the *minbing*s; my daily experience with them has made me think that all of them are bad. I was in shock, but at the same time very pleased to see that not everyone is bad.

After work I went home I quickly washed myself. I changed my cloths before sitting down for dinner. Two *minbing*s stormed in and summoned me to the meeting in the commune courtyard.

The courtyard was full of people and many didn't have seats, so they crowded around the corners. People started shouting slogans all as soon as I walked in. As I walk past people they pushed and heckled me. Some *minbing*s as well as the commune leaders

Qajay, Saliq, and their chauffer Ahmet were standing on the stage. They hoisted me up onto the bench facing the public. When the public stopped chanting slogans, Qajay gave a speech explaining the significance of the denouncing meeting. He said that the intension of bringing everyone to the meeting was to give public the opportunity for retaliation. He finished his speech with a resounding 'Down with Söyüngül!' Everyone present followed suit.

Then Qajay immediately grabbed my scarf from my head and throw it onto the floor angrily. It fell near Nokte's family. His three young children stood up immediately and started spitting on the scarf while stepping and trampling on it. My beautiful scarf was ruined within minutes. I felt upset seeing young children behaving in such a beastly way, encouraged by their parents and relatives.

'Bow your head!' screamed one of the *minbing*s. He then brought the same bag of stones that they had used on Reshide and place it around my neck. It wasn't long before the thin wire started digging into my neck, causing excruciating pain. The weight of the stones kept pulling my head downwards. I tried to hold my body upright with all my strength to stop from falling off the bench, but my body started shaking uncontrollably with pain. I couldn't hear a thing, only the sounds of screams and slogans, only noise and not words. Half an hour passed like half a year as blood dripped down onto my blouse from my neck. I wanted to touch my neck to feel how bad the wound was, but I clenched my teeth hard and told myself not to. 'This will pass. Everything will be alright', I thought to myself.

After a while, I heard a number of loud noises coming from outside. The people in charge of the denunciation meeting were called to go outside. Two *minbing*s came in and took the bag off my neck. The wire having cut deep into my skin, and removing the wire caused more pain than carrying it - it felt as if someone was rubbing salt into the wound. I didn't want to show my misery in front of so many people. So I bravely composed myself and stood up straight and held my chin up as if nothing had ever happened. Salik, the party leader, jumped up in front of me pointing his fingers towards my eyes, I quickly moved my head to avoid his fingers poking into my eyes. 'Keep your head down! Bow to us!' He shouted as he moved towards me, but because I was standing on a bench he couldn't reach my head, which frustrated him a great deal, and he kept yelling, 'Head down, head down!' but he still couldn't reach.

After everyone had stopped shouting slogans Salik took the opportunity to come up close shouting angrily into my ear, 'Tell me, what kind of person your father Salih is!'

I answered back calmly and firmly, 'My father is a kind-hearted, humanitarian, and generous person. He's very hardworking man who has dedicated his entire life to the people.'

'Ha! You see, she is praising and defending her father in front of everyone', Salik shouted to the crowd, but no one paid any attention to what he was saying. He looked around the courtyard, hoping that someone would say something, but everyone remained silent. Frustrated again, he turned to me, pointed his finger at me and said, 'Your father Salih worked for the Kuomintang. He is part of those scums. Why didn't you mention this to the people? Huh?'

'My father worked for Trade Inspection Office during the Kuomintang era. He didn't do anything wrong', I said.

'Oh look at this!' he said, turning to the crowd, 'How is he a good person then, if he had worked for Kuomintang? He is a Kuomintang scum!' he screamed hysterically.

'People have to work to make a living under any government. I'm sure you of all people are aware of this fact. No one would give you bread money if you didn't work for them', I replied.

'Oh we've got a smart one here, haven't we?' Ahmet joined in to prove his prowess in denunciation, 'Don't you fucking dare argue with me! Who do you think you are? You a stinking counter-revolutionary!' Then he jumped in front of me, pulled me off the bench and started punching me. People started cheering and shouting slogans again.

Qajay took out a piece of paper from his pocket, shjouting, 'Silence! Now I need the public to authorise something. Listen to this!' Everyone stopped shouting at once.

'As everyone is already aware, we needed Söyüngül's parents to come to the commune for questioning. But when we sent our *minbings* to bring them here, their family promised that her parents would return the next day. Our *minbings* waited for them to return for three days, but they failed to turn up and wasted our time. Therefore Söyüngül herself is liable to pay the fine of 400 yuan. Secondly, Söyüngül worked along the river sieving sand, but the sand was washed away by the flood because she didn't do her job properly, so she has to pay for the loss of the sand, which is 80 yuan. The total amount she owes to the commune is 480 yuan. We need to authorise this decision in front of the public. Do we have your consent?' Before anyone even answered, Qajay took the paper for Salik, Ahmet and a number of other leaders to sign. I was shocked that the sand washed away by the flood should be worth 80 yuan, and was taken aback by the ghastly decision that, having been exploited all these years without receiving a penny, I should now be shamelessly asked to pay back something I didn't even owe.

After the paper was signed, Salik shouted, 'Now everyone listen, this stinking counter-revolutionary will never be able to get married as she doesn't have the right!' He then came to me and said, 'If you want to get married, you have to register with us, but we will never give you permission. Is that understood?'

Shameless bully! As if all the methods he used to torture me were not enough, he had to disgrace me publicly by interfering with my private life. Having been fighting each day just to survive, marriage or relationships have never crossed my mind. Why did he have to mention such a thing? These cruel people are trying all the evil ways in order to break me.

I heard the public shouting slogans again. This time they were ordering at me to leave. I walked out of the gate as fast as I could heading towards home. Some children followed me behind throwing stones at me; luckily I reached home without being hurt.

12 May 1968
Reshide's arrest

It was a beautiful sunny day of May, with the sun shining high and bright. The hills were covered in colourful flowers and the fields full of green growing crops. The fragrance of the flowers gave me immense joy in my heart.

The leaders of the commune mobilised all the citizens to build a concrete road along the valley. Mukajan and I were assigned to dig the sand from Haba and load it onto the truck. Several *minbing*s stood over us kept shouting, 'Work faster! Faster!' We were not even allowed to stop for a second or wipe off the sweat on our foreheads. After filling two lorries with sand, Mukajan sat on the floor complaining of an upset stomach. He was taken to hospital and I was left alone to continue the task. I worked as fast as I could, not wanting to attract any criticism from the *minbing*s; I was amazed by my own resilience. Having managed to complete numerous difficult tasks within the time limit, I felt that I was even stronger than many young men.

By midday my throat was parched, so I carried my jug and went to get some water. The production unit leader Qadirbeg's wife was in charge of water. When she saw me coming she started shouting, 'Go away, there is no water for a counter-revolutionary like you!' I was hurt. The most spiteful people are now in charge in this commune. There is not a single trace of humanity left in their hearts! I managed to hold on to my last breath until the working period was over, and returned home exhausted.

Gheyshe and Hajiye Banu were at home. They looked sad, and I sensed some bad news was waiting for me. As I was too tired and drained to take in any sad news and needed peace and tranquillity to recover from the hardships of the day, I didn't ask them anything and sat down for dinner quietly.

'Sister, did you know Reshide was arrested this morning?' Gheyshe finally broke the silence after dinner.

'Poor Reshide, she has two-year-old child… What are they going to do?' Hajiye Banu added.

May God help her! I said to myself.

'Sister, I saw various types of dunce's hats in the commune', Gheyshe said with a trembling voice, 'I don't understand why they need so many dunce's hats. I am afraid that more people are going to be dragged out for denunciation. I am really worried…'

I took her hand and held it firmly.

'Just stay calm. You won't change anything by worrying. Let's just wait and see', I said.

17 May 1968

It was another lovely sunny day. They ordered me to dig sand at the mountain pass opposite to the stable alone.

The atmosphere was tense today. People were busy running between the commune building and the production unit's office. The *minbing*s who were on horseback rode back and forth with whips in their hands, creating an atmosphere of fear. They shouted intimidating slogans every time they passed by me. A new stage had been erected in the courtyard of the warehouse. I guessed that the next denunciation meeting would take place there, and, judging from the size of the stage and the venue, it was going to be a big one. I knew that I would be the lead 'actress' on that stage. Trying my best to stay positive I carried on the working as normal reminding myself again and again that all the terror would pass one day, because nothing last forever. My eyelids kept twitching and I gave in to the superstition that this meant something terrible was about to happen.

The morning was quiet, but the afternoon started with the familiar sounds of slogans in the distance. I saw people being herded by the *minbing*s towards the commune, many of them wearing dunce's hats. The numbers increased as they got close to the commune gate. About an hour later I saw a group of people coming in my direction from the residential area, they carried flags along with portraits of Chainman Mao.

Then I heard the familiar slogan, 'Down with Söyüngül!' As they approached where I was working, they shouted, 'Come down here, and bring your tools with you!' I swiftly tidied myself up, combing my hair before putting my scarf on securely. I quickly walked down the hill to join them.

They placed me in the middle of the first line as we headed to the commune. There were a lot of new faces, including new *minbing*s whom whom I'd never seen before; I guessed that they had come from nearby villages. I was ordered to join the approximately one hundred 'class enemies' who were working on the hill near the commune.

People were picked up in every street and accused of being 'capitalist roaders' before being herded to the commune courtyard. I was surprised at seeing my uncle Mijit and Hajiye Banu among the 'capitalist roaders'. I know Hajiye Banu very well: she is a timid, fragile person, and the present situation was not helping her: Her face was pale, and her lips were trembling as if she could burst into tears any minute. When she noticed me, I smiled at her trying to show support and courage. As for Uncle Mijit, he was visibly nervous, as he looked around frantically at people with wide-open eyes, wondering why he had been dragged into this.

I bumped into Luo Jun as I was carrying earth down the hill; he was wearing a funny dunces' hat made of paper, which resembled a Chinese emperor's throne. He was also forced to wear his jacket back to the front in order to carry earth in it.

I almost burst out laughing at his new look. I walked up to him and whispered jokingly, 'Hey Luo Jun, you look like a real emperor today.'

'My friend, that's not funny at all. We are not going to survive in this time. They are planning to finish all of us off, and they will! Our families will soon receive our corpses.'

I felt a cold chill run down my back, but still tried to sound normal, 'Oh Lao Jun, you are not serious, are you? You are scared. We are not going to die. We are going to live! We must believe this in order to survive!' Then I noticed we were being watched and we parted quickly.

Lao Jung's pessimism affected me deeply. I tried to stay positive but I couldn't stop thinking of death. The *minbing*s constantly shouted aggressive slogans while cracking their whips over our heads, urging us to work faster. We finished at ten in the evening and were told to return at four the next morning.

18 May 1968

We started our day at three in the morning, in pure darkness. The atmosphere was dismal, and although we had been through so many painful experiences lately, so much torture and death, I sensed something even worse was about to happen, and my heart was heavy in my chest. There were over two hundred of us working out in the fields, and over the sounds of the shovels, hoes and pickaxes, we could hear the *minbing*s shouting – 'Work faster. Hurry up, Get on with it!'

We carried on in silence.

I stopped at six o'clock and went home for breakfast. Only Gheyshe and Firdews were there, and both of them were panicking. Firdews couldn't stop crying, 'Sister, what is going to happen? I'm scared!'

'Nothing will happen, my dear, don't panic. They are creating this atmosphere to terrorise people. It will end soon — God will protect us. I'll live through this, don't worry!'

My reassurance seemed to have worked.

I went to my room to plait my hair. I threaded a needle with cotton and stitched the hair up tight so that it wouldn't fall onto my face easily if it was pulled. I looked in the mirror to see if it suited me, and was surprised to find that it did — my face was beautifully framed. I saw a pretty, youthful girl in front of me.

'How awful to watch my precious youth being violated', I said to myself, 'These are supposed to be the loveliest days of my life. And here I am spending them in hardship and brutality, facing threats and torture. My youth is being trampled under their feet.'

Hajiye Banu burst in as I was contemplating my life.

'Oh Söyün! They have beaten a man to death, and now they're approaching the commune dragging the dead body with them!' Her face was pale with fright. I threw my jacket on and headed out. As I walked towards the commune, I saw a group of men dragging the corpse by its feet. There were a lot of women with them too, kicking the dead man and shouting as they went by. I felt a sharp pain in my chest just at the sight of it and couldn't stop shaking.

Luo Jun's words yesterday were echoing in my ears. I could sense death in the air now. I rushed out to the work area, picked up my shovel and started digging. Crowds of people were heading towards where we were. Teachers had been dragged out from primary and secondary schools by the *minbing*s and were being ordered to join us. Some refused; arguments broke out. It was a chaotic scene, and in order to restore some sort of calm, people were asked to line up according their production groups.

As always, I was placed in the first line of the 'class enemy group. The teachers were lined up separately.

They placed a pointed three-foot dunce's hat on my head. It was decorated with coloured strings, and my face almost disappeared underneath it. Others were forced to wear them too. I had been forced to wear the dunce's hat in countless public struggle meetings. At first it was hard to take, but after being forced to wear it so many times, somehow I became inured to it.

I stood straight, head up, as if nothing had happened. One of the *minbing*s brought out some machine lubricant and began smearing my face with it. I felt degraded, hurt in the deepest way. What have I done for them to paint my face black? Time after time they tried to break me, to shame me in front of the public, but I had nothing to be ashamed of. I was fighting for our people's freedom. I have sacrificed my career and my youth, and I'm even prepared to sacrifice my life for the dreams we have as a people. The desire for freedom and political independence burned in me like a fire, and even after all the humiliation, hardship, torture and death, the dream is still worth fighting for. From the minute I got involved in the movement for freedom, I knew that there would be immense obstacles to overcome. I prepared myself for every kind of danger and have no regrets.

I was taking strength from these thoughts, and trying to tie up the colourful strings hanging from the hat so they wouldn't fall in my face. At that moment, they punched my right hand viciously. I felt like it had been crushed, the bones broken into hundreds of pieces.

I heard the teachers screaming, and guessed that the *minbing*s were trying to paint their faces black too. I heard the voice of one of the teachers, Ghalim –

'It's the people like you, the people who snuck inside our party and betrayed all the rules, who should be shamed before the public. Not us! Wait and see – you will pay for your mistakes and for what you did to all those innocent people. Qadirbek, Qabdal, Salik, all of you, listen carefully: you are the criminals in this community. You are the ones who need to pay for your crimes, not us!' As he shouted, a group of *minbing*s dragged him out of the line and to the front. Then we heard another teacher Eliqan's voice – 'You are making a big mistake; I always helped you with everything you asked of me. I am one of you!'

He pleaded as if he himself were facing execution. The *minbing*s called their leader Qabdal to make a decision. As soon as Eliqan saw Qabdal, he continued, 'Oh my brother, you know me well. I helped you with that job, remember? Please don't do this to me!' Qabdal was relishing the power he held over him. He held his head up high and immediately ordered the *minbing*s to release their captive.

The other teachers stared at Eliqan with disgust. But Eliqan was so relieved he almost burst into tears, and as he left the group he raised both hands to the sky, shouting, 'Long live Chairman Mao! May Mao live for many millions of years!' He ran to the stream and washed off the black paint; but when he came back he wasn't sure where to stand, as he knew he couldn't go and rejoin the rest of the teachers. He stood as far away from them as he could.

We were all taken in strict order to the courtyards, one group after another. As soon as the first group was in, a thunder of slogans arose. To my horror I saw Meyder Molla on the raw earth floor, lying unconscious in a pool of blood. He was the eldest, kindest and most respected figure in the community. Seeing him like that filled my heart with rage. Then for a terrible moment I began to fear he was dead. I felt an overwhelming desire to cry, but I held back my tears.

As I was walking towards the stage, ten *minbing*s, as well as Qalay, Salik and Qenighet, jumped in front of me like lions ready to tear at their prey. They dragged me into the middle of the circle of people and started attacking me. Punches came from all different directions, landing on my face, head, ribs and chest. I felt heavy boots kicking me.

'Bow to Chairman Mao, Bow to the people!' They screamed as they beat me. 'Tell us – do you know who Chairman Mao is? Do you respect him?'

They clearly weren't waiting for any answer. Blood covered my face, and the duance's hat lay forgotten under their feet. I cannot remember how many times I must have fallen to the floor and got up again — the fear of being trampled and killed made me leap back up every time I fell. After a while, they dragged me on to a bench and pushed my head forward, forcing me to stand in a bowing position. For a long time, blood poured quietly from my nose.

As well as the *minbing*s, there were many revolutionary rebels from the different regions. They were trying to break into the courtyard. After standing in a bowing position for some time, I raised my head slowly and saw more than ten solidly built men coming towards me. The commander of the *minbing*, Séyitqan, who was standing on the roof, shouted, 'Stop them from coming into the hall!' But the rebels didn't seem to listen to him and replied, 'Leader, leave the counter-revolutionaries to us. We will slash their noses, tongues and ears. We will gouge their eyes out.' They flashed their knives in the air as they approached me.

I closed my eyes and started praying, 'Oh God, protect me from their torment, you are the only protector I have! Please don't let me suffer under their feet. Oh merciful God, you have heard what they are saying, please don't place me in their hands!' I prayed from a place deep within myself, again and again.

Séyitqan shouted loudly from the roof again. 'Comrades, revolutionaries, don't act rashly. Let us teach them a lesson first. We'll ask them to repent for their crimes, and to give us information about their criminal acts. Teach them a lesson first, then you'll be free to do whatever you wish with them.'

The denunciation meeting lasted the whole day, from nine in the morning until five in the afternoon, I stood bowing on the bench for the whole time. The pain from the beating was unbearable, and my legs were almost giving up. Just as I felt that my body was on the verge of collapsing, we were ordered to leave the venue.

I said to myself that I should get out from the crowds as soon as possible. I gathered all my strength, but I could hardly put one foot before the other. People ignored the orders, and were already flooding towards the gates before us. Just as I was struggling to move, five or six thugs got hold of me and started punching and kicking me in their turn. They wanted me to fall to the ground, but I clung on to the people in front of me, and managed to move forward with the others.

The crowd surged towards the gate like waves trying to find the shore. The thugs were standing on both sides of the crowd, kicking, punching, and whipping the 'class enemies' as they went through. The victims held one another to keep moving.

Then, to our astonishment, the radio started playing the Internationale through loudspeakers that had been rigged up everywhere. The *minbings*, cadres, and activists looked equally bewildered; stunned momentarily into the silence of disbelief. Of course the quiet didn't last long and Say Tung, a member of the army personnel, screeched at the top of his lungs, 'Stop, Stop! Whoever is playing this must stop it right now!' His eyes were bulging with fury. They all ran towards the commune where the radio had been placed, but the song had finished by the time they reached it.

At times like this, I felt happy. The spirit of resistance was a tonic - giving me not just hope, but the strength to carry on. Finally I managed to get through the gate alive.

Just as I felt myself free of danger, I was attacked yet again by thugs and fell to the ground immediately. I moaned in pain as they kicked me with their heavy boots. After a while, I heard someone shouting over the loudspeaker, 'No one is allowed to leave; all of you go back to the courtyard right now!' I could hear people's screams and the sound of horses' hooves everywhere. It was the *minbings* on the horses trying to herd people back to the courtyard from all directions.

They were kicking me harder now, trampling all over me and shouting aggressively: 'Get up, I am telling you to get up!' I was trying to get up; no matter how hard I tried my body had finally given up. I couldn't do it. Soldiers also came by on horses and ordered the people who were attacking me to go back to the courtyard. Then out of nowhere two strangers gave me their hands, so I grabbed them tightly. They helped me to stand up, and we rushed into the courtyard.

'Oh God, help me! If I do die, let my faith be my companion!' I prayed as I walked back to the courtyard. I could no longer see those who had been lying unconscious on the floor earlier. Even their blood had been cleaned up. I wondered where they had been taken.

All those that had been subjected to the public struggle meetings were now herded on to the stage one by one. Say Tung started his speech. Duysabay's son Kalybay grabbed my hair from behind and started punching me. He snatched my jacket and ripped it into pieces. I held on the people next to me tightly. Qabdal joined him, grabbed me from behind and threw my jacket on the floor. Teacher Ghalip, who was standing in front of me, turned around and stared at them with rage. When they noticed him, they left me and moved on to attack him instead.

Finally Say Tung finished his speech and ordered the 'class enemies' to leave. I hardly had any strength left to walk; I could not see how I would manage to pass through the gate again. Then, unexpectedly, I heard my name being called. I turned my head in the direction the voice came from; I saw those who had been subjected to the public struggle meeting today had gathered in one place. The group had locked themselves in a circle by placing their heads in between the legs of the person in front and holding onto their knees. The *minbing*s were trying to untangle them. My workmates were calling me, 'Come this way, join us here quickly!' I was about to move and join them when suddenly someone opened the back door near where I was standing, I got out from the back door to the square by grabbing whatever I could. All of us gathered in the square. About two hundred people had been subjected to this struggle meeting, and about half of us were left.

Suddenly, a woman's shriek froze my blood. I looked up and saw a man and woman being whipped and dragged along by two horsemen. They were heading in our direction. The poor woman couldn't bear the pain, and screamed and begged the men –

'My brother, please stop whipping me, please, please! I belong to the poor class. Please, I beg you, we are all brothers and sisters, don't do this to me!' They didn't show any mercy to the lady's imploration, and continued to both of them with all the strength they could muster. When they stopped in front of us, other riders who were already there joined in - soon the man fainted, leaving the woma's screaming and pleading echoing from the Nanshan Mountains…

I struggled but finally reached home. I felt like I was fighting to hold on to my last breath - if it is not one's turn to die, one can survive in any condition.

I looked at myself in the hallway mirror. My face was black with tar. Whole clumps of my hair, which I had so neatly done up that morning, had been pulled out from the roots. My face was badly swollen and there were cuts around my eyes and lips. My summer jacket was in tatters, with only the collar and front hanging from my neck and the rest gone. My white blouse was stained with red blood.

The image I saw in the mirror frightened me — I looked ghoulish, like something from a horror film. I almost cried. I wanted to screamm but somehow I found the strength to control myself again. And I was grateful to God that I had come out alive. I don't know how many of my fellow sufferers had been killed, but I prayed for their souls to rest in peace and for God to grant them paradise.

'We are heroes', I said quietly to myself, 'They can never break us! We live with a good conscience, and if we die, we die with honour.'

Both of my younger sisters Gheyshe and Firdews were in the courtyard when I walked in. My appearance shocked them. They stared at me in horror for a few seconds. Then they ran to me, held me tight and wept uncontrollably. I tried very hard not to break down as they hugged me, and told them that everything would be all right.

I went over to the kettle for some warm water and washed my face.

I was my parents' precious daughter, and had always been the star pupil of all my teachers. I was very popular in my university, respected by my classmates and loved by my friends. I had never once been bullied in all that time, but my life turned upside down the day I was arrested.

I feel sadness at my own suffering, of course, but what was truly unbearable was to witness so much horror inflicted on others by these cruel, mindless thugs, not to mention that most of their victims were men above seventy years of age.

19 May 1968

I felt very weak as if I have been sick for years. I wished I could rest in bed just for a day, however that was not possible. I had to be at the field by 4 am. I washed my face gently as I could feel lumps all over it. I didn't want look at myself in the mirror, knowing that it would frighten me. As I combed my hair it came out in lumps in my hand; and my scalp hurt when the comb touched it. My body ached all over, especially my legs. The kicking inflicted on my body from heavy boots had left black and purple bruises all over.

It had been raining all night and the road had become muddy and slippery. Walking carefully I dragged myself slowly to the field in the rain. The *minbing*s in charge today were not as aggressive as the ones yesterday. We carried grit from the hillside to the commune's courtyard where the restoration was being undertaken in preparation for the forthcoming denunciation meeting. As soon as we finished laying the grit, we were ordered to clean out the toilets with our bare hands. In other words we had to use our hands to remove the excrement into buckets before carrying it to the fields. I was completey soaked in rain.

In the afternoon people from different production teams started arriving at the commune courtyard. The *minbing*s quickly closed the gates placing guards outside to stop people from going in. I saw people climbing on top of the walls calling people's names nervously. Every time someone replied they would cry out loud, 'Oh thank God I found you!'

Soon I realised that those were the family members of the people who were denounced yesterday. Later I also found out that when we were told to leave the courtyard first time many young men had managed to run away to inform the families of those who were tortured during the denunciation that their loved ones' lives were in danger. The families waited nervously all night for their return, and when they failed to return home, they came to look for them in the commune. Those who found their relatives cried emotionally with relief, and those who didn't demanded to know of their where abouts. The angry crowd tried to break into the commune, however the armed *minbing*s encircled the courtyard in no time, dispersing the people at gunpoint.

The air was heavy with grief; it was clear that everyone was suffering from the wounds of yesterday's brutal beatings. Most people's faces were disfigured like mine, I noticed that many of them were limping, whilst others were suffering from broken ribs. Furthermore, many familiar faces were missing today: Meydar Molla, Luo Jun, Yaqup Axun and Bibish the last two were the new members of our 'class enemy' group.

I was told later that in fact Meydar Molla wasn't dead immediatley, but regained consciousness and asked for water. Children playing near the toilets heard him; they dripped urine into his mouth using a branch of a tree, whilst some forced earth into his mouth for fun. The poor man died tragically as a result of that. His two sons along with family friends buried him quietly the very evening. His stepdaughter Mediye told me that on the eve of 18 May, Meydar Molla didn't sleep and prayed all night. In the morning as he sat having tea with his wife he said, 'My dearest, I know I won't survive today. I have prepared myself for the next life. You have been a good wife to me and I want to thank you for supporting me over all these years. My last request from you is to stay strong. Don't cry for me, instead pray for my soul.'

As for Luo Jun, he was taken back to his production unit that night, having been unconscious for many hours. The head of the unit thought he was dead and ordered the *minbing*s to bury him. As he was being carried to the burial ground his wife appeared after receiving a tip off. She threw herself onto him crying; as she stroked his face to say goodbye, she realised his body was still warm, and, much to her surprise, he was still breathing. She begged the *minbing*s to let her take him home, and after they checked him again, permission was granted. He regained consciousness in the evening today.

Yaqup Axun's son Qurban joined the No. 2 Red Commandos in opposition to Commando 3 – a unit supported by the commune. Qurban's support for the opposition infuriated the leader of the commune and they decided to denounce him. However Qurban disappeared over night. In order to get him back they dragged Yaqup Axun to the denunciation meeting instead. Yaqup Axun was brutally tortured by the *minbing*s and thugs during the denunciation meeting. His family took him home after he was left unconscious; he died a week later from the injuries. I heard that Qurban secretly went home one night to record details of the people who had beaten his father to death.

20 May 1968

Today all the 'class enemies' from other production units were taken back to their own unit. I was assigned to work with my old construction unit to make mud bricks. The people in charge were brutal as usual – they never stopped shouting or swearing at us. The other workers were nasty too - they did their best to show their loyalty to the leaders in order to avoid being branded as 'class enemies'. Even the children playing in the fields shouted abuse and threw stones at us for fun. No words could describe the feelings of sadness and pain in us, but there was nothing we could do apart from trying to ignore the cruelty around us and get on with life.

My job was to take mud in a three-wheeled cart to the brick workshop over the hill. It was the hardest task pushing a fully loaded cart over the grassy hill with all the injuries I had endured; my left side under my rib cage hurt the most, and every breath I took felt as if a sharp knife was being plunged into me. It hurt even more when I coughed, and I couldn't stop coughing as I was stumbling uphill. Despite all this, I had to push heavy loads on the handcart back and forth, again and again, and by the end of the day I found it difficult to breath.

After work I went straight to the clinic. Doctor Sarkitbeg was seeing other patients when I arrived, so I waited for him to be free. When all the patients had left his office, he raised his head looking at me and said, 'I am really sorry, but I can't see you. I've been told not to treat any "class enemies" suffering from the beatings.' I coughed badly as I pressed my hand against my left side trying to control the coughing. He could clearly see that I was ill. I stood there without saying a word, my cough painfully echoing in the doctor's office.

'Leave my office now, will you? I can't see you even if you are dying', he said coldly after a while.

I was terribly hurt. Terribly. He was once one of my father's closest friends, and his wife Meziye, a regular visitor in our house, was very close to my mother, who treated her like a sister. It is hard to accept insults from people who were once close to you. Why did he have to be so cruel as if there was someone watching him?

I stood up and left his office immediately. In the corridor I bump into Dr Wu, who heard me coughing and asked me gently how I was. I explained to him my symptoms and how Dr Sarkitbeg had refused to treat me. Appalled by my misadventure, he asked me to follow him to his office. He checked me thoroughly and told me there was a blood clot between my lungs and my ribs in addition to some severe damage to the diaphragm.

'I can't prescribe medicine in your name. Please send your sister Gheyshe to me so I can prescribe the medicine for her. You must take the medication continuously for a month. Normally people in your condition shouldn't do any labouring work at all and should rest in bed until they've recovered. Unfortunately they won't allow you to take a sick leave. All I can say is: please take care of yourself very, very well.'

I was moved by his caring words. I would have never thought this Chinese man would help me. All the way from hospital to home I couldn't stop comparing the heartless Dr Sarkitbeg and the kind Dr Wu. Doctor Wu is from Sichuan Province and graduated from Sichuan Medical University. He has always treated me like an old classmate, despite me being branded as a 'class enemy', and he is the only person right now who hasn't changed his attitude towards me and always speaks to me with respect, unlike many of my 'own people' whom were once close to my family yet have turned their backs on me.

Gheyshe, Firdews and Hajiye Banu were in the house when I got back. Gheyshe was putting a cream on Hajiye Banu's hand, which was severely swollen and oozing pus. I asked Hajiye what had happened, she replied with a sigh:

'We were forced to clean the toilet using our bare hands. An open wound of the beating the other day became infected. Those people are so cruel that they won't allow us use a shovel to remove the excrement from the toilets into the buckets. It was unbelievably disgusting and we felt sick and couldn't stop vomiting. Oh what kind of life is this? What can we do?' She burst into tears.

'And Hajiye, what reason did they give you when they came to your house?' I asked.

'I have been suffering from gynaecological diseases for sometime now. About a month ago I went to see the doctor. The doctor wrote me a letter suggesting I should see a specialist in Ürümchi. I went to the commune office with the letter, hoping to get some cash for my treatment. But Qenighet, the leader, showed no sympathy with regards to my illness, saying that there was no money in the commune account. I was about to walk out from his office as Qajay's wife entered asking for some money to go to town. Qenighet wrote out a chitty of sixty yuan immediately and right in front of me! This upset me greatly. I said to him, "You are a racist! You have money for your own Kazakh people but don't have money for a non-Kazakh who urgently needs medical treatment. I have been working in this commune for the last ten years without one day off or a single penny in payment. This is the first time I've ever asked for help, and this is how you treat me?

'Qenighet was surprised that I dared to challenge him. He screamed in my face, calling *me* a racist and saying that he'd teach me a lesson. I left the commune angrily. I didn't go for treatment and I have never been back to the commune for money since. On the day that people came to the house we were having lunch, they shouted as they entered the house, "Denounce the racist Hajiye Banu!" Qenighet was leading the mob; he came straight up to me and tried to drag me away from the table, but I held onto the head of the metal bed next to the table. I shouted, "I am not a racist, *you* are! You have no right to denounce me!" Then six or seven men joined Qenighet and tried to pull me away, the bed moved with the force of all these people trying to take my hand off the metal bar. My three-year-old daughter Ilghire was so scared – she was screaming the whole time. But my coward of a husband picked her up saying, "Hajiye, please obey their orders and go with them." I was so disappointed with him, instead of standing up for me and telling the people to get out, he asked me to follow their orders despite knowing that they were wrong!'

Hajiye's lips twitched and she started crying again. I held her hand and said, 'Don't take it too hard, the whole country is suffering from this political madness as people in power take advantage of the situations for personal revenge. You are not alone; we must stay strong in order get through these hardships. One day all this will be over, so now all we need is to survive!' I waited until she calmed down before asking –

'Do you know why Uncle Xeyrulla was among those denounced?'

'Oh poor uncle, he was beaten up so badly, so terribly! I saw his head bleeding from the beating. I haven't seen him since we were sent away from the meeting. I hope he is still alive... oh God help us!' Hajiye said tearfully.

'But do you know the reason he was denounced?' I repeated my question but didn't know if I should have asked.

'Well', said she, clearing her throat and wiping her tears, 'I heard from others that when he was working in the mine during the Iron Refining Movement in 1959, when the whole country was starving.[42] One day one of his colleagues complained of hunger and said sarcastically, "I wonder what Chairman Mao eats for dinner?" And uncle jokingly said, "Surely the Emperor's stomach is full; he doesn't care about his slaves." Recently one of his colleagues reported what he had said nine years ago to the commune officials, and uncle got into big trouble...'

I wasn't surprised, having heard many similar stories. But I still find it difficult to understand what benefits people get from reporting friends and colleagues to the authorities. We both sat silently, drowned in our own thoughts.

Gheyshe returned with my medicine, to our surprise Sadiq walked in after her. Firdews jumped from her seat, ran to Sadiq, hugged him tightly and kissed his cheeks.

'Did you come back alone?' she asked him.

'Yes, Sofiye helped me get on an army truck', He said with a smile.

Sadiq gave us the news from Ürümchi. The 18 of May was a blood bath in Ürümchi as denunciation took place in all the work units, from government departments to primary schools, hospitals, and factories. Many people were tortured to death. Work units shamelessly claiming they had committed suicide despite the obvious visible injuries shown on their bodies.

My father's elder brother, Uncle Zeki, was targeted by his work unit as well. He was branded as a 'capitalist roader' and was almost beaten to death. My uncle was one of the founding members of the Home-Grown Product Company, which had business links with companies abroad since the governor Sheng Shicai[43] came to power. He worked

---

42   *The economic policies during the Great Leap Forward, namely the rapid industrialisation mentioned above and the agriculturalisation, which required fields to produce more than they realistically could, resulted in a large-scale famine.*

43   *Warlord who ruled Xinjiang from 1933 to 1944. As a result of his rule, Xinjiang was a de facto separate entity from Mainland China, rule at the time by the Chinese Nationalist Party and under the name of Republic of China.*

as an accountant for several years before being promoted managing director of the company. In addition to his job he also set up training course for aspiring accountants in the country. He was a kind man who was almost beaten to death, if it was not for his families in Ürümchi who managed to get him out and send him to hospital, he would have died. I was devastated to hear this terrible news. My heart ached for days at the thought of my loving uncle being trampled under those beasts.

11 June 1968

Qajay sent me to prepare mud for making bricks in the square next to the commune courtyard. Pointing at the mountains of earth placed all over the square, Qajay said to me, 'You must finish mixing all the earth with water by the end of today! Make sure the mud is ready for tomorrow, otherwise you will be in trouble!' before heading back to the commune. The work I was asked to perform is normally a one-day job for four to five people, but I had to finish it by myself in one day. I started immediately to work as fast as I could.

In the afternoon I heard the painful screams coming from the commune's courtyard. There was another denunciation taking place. I couldn't stop thinking about the people who were suffering, and prayed for God to help them while running in the mud from one side to another trying to get my work done as fast as I could. Then about two hours after the meeting started, Qajay came out from the commune courtyard with the party Secretary Ömerbeg's wife Nurile, and instructed me to supervise her work today.

Looking at Nurile, I was shocked to see the damage on her face: there were bruises everywhere, under her left eye there was a dark purple bump and the eye itself was red as if it was bleeding. Tears came running down her face. I felt terrible.

'Oh Nurile, can you see with your left eye?' I asked.

Covering her right eye with her hand and looking around, she said sobbing, 'Yes, I can; but I am worried about my husband, he was beaten so badly that he can't stand up, he is lying on the floor. I'm so scared that he is going to die.' She started crying.

I gave her a hug and said, 'Oh Nurile, stay strong and pray to God that everything will be fine! You don't need to come into the mud. Stand where you are and if you see someone coming, just pretend to be moving the mud with the shovel. Deal?'

It is interesting how things changed so quickly, Nurile's husband Ömerbeg was the vice secretary of the Party at the commune, but for some reason he was also dragged out to be denounced as a 'class enemy' on the 18. When I was displayed on the bench in the bowing position he shared the same bench with me, also being forced to stand in a bowing position.

I remember when my prison term ended, my parents were worried that I would be sent far away. They petitioned to the commune leaders to accept me as a resident. On one occasion my father went to Ömerbeg's house to talk about me, he was in the middle of the party with friends. He became very angry with my father and even organised a meeting in the commune to denounce my father in public, accusing him of disturbing his family's peace. He tried to shame my father in public by saying, 'This man wants us to register his counter-revolutionary daughter in our commune, I refused categorically. There is no place for a counter-revolutionary in our commune. We don't want his corruptive daughter to contaminate our residents' thoughts!' His actions hurt my parents badly. Later, despite the commune leaders opposition to my father's application, the provincial government allocated me a place within the commune under the surveillance regime, which my parents never expected. I am sure Ömerbeg never anticipated that he himself would fall to the "class enemies' group to suffer the most humiliating insults from his most trusted people within the commune. His wife, who always regarded herself a head above such a 'class enemy' like me, ended up today being ordered to do forced labour under my supervision. What an interesting turn of events![44]

21 June 1968
The prison camp of No.2 Squad, South Wind Commune

It was a beautiful day of summer. The sun was shining gloriously, and the wild flowers spread their rich aroma throughout the Nanshan Mountains. At dawn, all the birds started singing as a new day started. As all the *minbing*s went into the commune courtyard, I took this rare opportunity to relax from the draining work. I was gazing at the mountains and enjoying the picturesque scenery when suddenly I heard a disturbing scream. Turning in the direction from where the noise coming from, I saw four men on horseback dragging a man along the ground as they approached the commune.

This ugly scene shocked me as well as everyone around me. People were terrified; those who were chatting picked up their tools in a hurry and started working. They didn't dare to raise their heads to look when the *minbing*s stopped right in front of us. The *minbing*s dismounted from their horses and untied the man's wrist, to our

---

44   *The author revealed that Ömerbeg never recovered from the injuries of two denunciation meetings and died two years later; she became close friends with his wife Nurile and supported her through the most difficult period of her life. – the translator*

surprise the man stood up immediately - we had initially thought he was dead. It was Abdulhemit who had disappeared on 18 May. He picked up a shovel next to me and started to work. We all got on with our jobs in silence.

As soon as the *minbing*s left us, Orazan broke the silence, asking Abdulhemit where he'd been hiding.

'I was in my Uncle Abdulhey's house in Sarichoqa Farm', Abdulhemit calmly replied with a smile as if nothing had happened.

'So how did you escape? I remember you didn't have any strength left after the beatings. How did you manage?' Selimjan asked curiously.

'When the *minbing* were busy organising people to work in the field I crawled outside slowly before quietly walking down the valley and hiding under the thick bushes. After midnight when everyone had gone to sleep I walked through the hills all night to my uncle's house. My uncle hid me in a cavity under the bed. He gave me the most nutritious food until I recovered from my wounds. Today I was having lunch at the table when two *minbing*s walked in and arrested me straight away.'

'So did they drag you all the way with the horses from Sarichoqa?!' I asked.

'Oh no, they only did that when we were passed by people. They walked with me when no one was around', he replied with a grin as if it was funny.

We worked as pairs carrying a *zembil*[45] full of bricks. Meriye who worked with me had also been denounced on the 18th as a class enemy. As we put the *zembil* on the ground she covered the left side of her face with the palm of her hand, saying, 'Oh, the left side of my face has been twitching constantly for days. It is getting worse and worse and I am so fed up!' I looked at her face carefully noticing that it was visibly twitching.

'Maybe you should calm down a bit', I said to her, 'God knows if something good is on it's way. The twitching could be a good sign', I said jokingly in order to cheer her up.

'Oh how can you expect anything good to ever come?! I have always had twitching problems on this side of my face, and whenever I'm stressed it always gets worse. Since the 18th when all my family suffered beatings during the denounciation meeting, the left-hand side of my left face started twitching and got much worse today. It's become uncontrollable. You may not know, but we have been called to the commune many times since that day to be tortured by the bloody *minbing*s!' she said angrily, clearly unable to take my joke well.

---

45   *A basket suspended between two poles, it was carried by a person at the front and rear.*

'I'm sorry Meriye. What happened? Why is your family being targeted?' I asked.

'Well, do you know that reckless guy called Kaylar, who always hangs around the main production unit?'

I immediately had a mental image of the person she was talking about and asked, 'Do you mean that puppy-eyed Kalay?'

Hearing the word 'puppy-eyed', Meriye burst out laughing.

'Oh my dear Söyün, that's such a good nickname! His eyes look exactly like those of a puppy: small, dark and deep, and he always stares at people in a sort of aimless way. Yes, so it was not long after the big denunciation meeting that we were called to another one where the *minbing*s displayed all of us on a bench. The head of the commune stated that my daughter should marry Kalay. They said to her, "Kalay is from the poorest class, you should be honoured to have someone like him wanting to marry you." Then Kalay approached my daughter with a document in his hand. He proposed to her and asked her to sign the document. Of course my daughter said no. The *minbing* then started kicking and punching my husband to the ground. Kalay went back to my daughter again and forced a pen into her hand to sign the document. My daughter threw the pen away and shouted a resounding "no". The *minbing*s became angry, and their response to the rejection was to beat up all of us. My husband was pushed to the ground where he was kicked, punched and trampled on. They looke like they really wanted him to die! My seven-year-old son held onto my legs tightly and screamed, "Don't hurt my father. Don't hurt my father!" but the cold-hearted beasts dragged my son out of the commune and continued to beat us. We were detained in the commune until midnight. When they had stopped beating my husband he was unconscious. My two eldest sons carried him out. We feel like we are living in limbo, agonising every day...' she finished her story with tears in her eyes.

23 June 1968
Roadwork again in Qizilsay

Yesterday we were told that we were going to build roads in Qizilsay, and most of the class enemies left that day. Today we set out at 8 am on foot, escorted by four heavily armed *minbing*s on horseback. It was a two-hour drive by truck from our commune. On the way we pass two production teams, called Qizilbayraq and Tengri Tagh,[46] which are located in Chewchizi Valley. As usual the *minbing* shouted loudly at us cracking thier whips in the air – 'Walk faster! Stop being lazy!' They always enjoyed showing the

---

46   *Uyghur for 'Red Banner' and 'The Heavenly Mountains' (or 'Tianshan', the famed mountain range between Xinjiang, Kazakhstan and Kyrgyzstan).*

power that they had over us in front of the people. Everyone would come out of their houses to watch us being forcibly driven along the streets. We walked all day without food or water, carrying heavy bags on our back in the heat, crossing over many hills and mountain passes before finally arriving at Qizilsay after sunset.

Having dropped our belongings in a yurt specially set up for the new labourers, we went to the canteen for dinner. Unsurprisingly, there was no food left, so we drank some cold water before returning to the yurt with empty stomachs. My head was spinning as I wobbled back with sore legs. I wished I could get in bed straight away and sleep late into the morning. However there would be no such luxury, as we were soon called to attend a meeting in the large yurt, which was located in the centre of the living area. That yurt was packed with people. The *minbing* ordered some people to bring some gravel and lay it in the centre of the floor and ordered Orazan to be dragged into the centre and kneel on the gravel, while a few other 'class enemies' were paraded behind him. The *minbing*s screamed one after another, 'Orazan, it is time for you to confess your crimes!' But he remained silent as always, while a rain of punches and kicks fell on him. He rolled on the floor in pain. THE *minbing*s asked him to confess his 'crime' over and over again while continued hitting him. One of them sat on his back and started hitting his bald head viciously, while two others kicked him with heavy boots from either side. Poor Orazan groaned, 'Oh God, oh God!' throughout his ordeal.

It was a very hot evening. The air inside of the yurt was oppressive with the body heat and body odour from so many people. I felt sick and could faint any minute. Suddenly I heard a gunshot in the distance, and a row broke out outside. A man rushed in shouting, 'Those men who confronted us yesterday are back! They are asking us to stop the denunciation meeting immediately or they will attack us!'

The *minbing*s who were beating Orazan stopped immediately and dashed outside. A momentary silence settled in the yurt as everyone looked at each other. The rumble of noises outside got louder, and before long, the *minbing*s came in the yurt again, saying, 'This meeting is over! Go back and sleep now!' We left the yurt, leaving Orazan behind lying unconscious and covered in blood in the middle of the yurt.

In the middle of the night we were told to get up and go to expand the road. Having done this type of work before I was aware of the hardships and dangers it encompasses. It is now summer with temperatures rising easily above forty degrees. Unlike other areas in the mountains, which have lush vegetation, Qizilsay is barren and rocky, which increases the temperature and unbearable to stand in the sun at midday. As expected, we had to work without water or rest.

Just after midday I heard the sound of galloping horses in the valley. Looking down from the hill, I saw approximately twelve horsemen approaching our work place. They didn't appear to be *minbing*s. I was wondering who they were when I heard the *minbing*s whispering to one another nervously, 'Oh damn it! They are back again, the men from last night!'

The horsemen stopped not far from us. Dismounting their horses, they stood watching us for a while as they conversing with one another. The *minbing*s went up, shook hands with them and offered them cigarettes. It was obvious that they were talking about me as they were staring at me. I was used to people staring at me with hostility, however, the horsemen looked at me in a friendly way. They remained until we were called for lunch.

After the lunch Orazan asked me if I knew who the visitors were. I told him that I had never seen any of them before. Then he said, 'I noticed that they were looking and talking about you. From their eyes I could see admiration, respect and friendship; they didn't look at you as a beautiful girl working among a bunch of old men. I think they were here because of you and I thought you knew them. I heard that they were here last night making threats that they would come back with more men to fight the *minbing*s if the denunciation meeting wasn't stopped. This made the *minbing*s promise them that they wouldn't inflict punishment on anyone in the future. Thanks to them, I wasn't killed. We are lucky to have their protection.'

15 June 1968

We travelled on foot, crossing many mountains and walking through many forests, carrying all our belongings on our backs all day in the scorching heat, escorted by the armed *minbing* on horseback. As always the weak elders were constantly flogged for not walking fast enough. Some of them fell to the ground towards the end of the journey, crawling to the destination. It was agonising to see them suffer so much, my heart ached for all of them, and it almost made me forget my own troubles.

All the men settled in the shade of the tractor shed roof. Since we were only four women – Meriyem, two Chinese women, and myself, we were given a small grass hut for sleeping. The floor of the hut was covered by animal manure so we scraped the floor before placing our bedding down. Exhausted, hungry and thirsty we headed to the canteen, hoping to have something to eat. Half way there we saw men coming back from the canteen and, with their grumpy faces, complaining that there was nothing left.

So this would be another night we would be go to bed with an empty stomach. My elderly friends were on my mind as I fell asleep. In my dreams I heard noises, they became louder and louder, I struggled for some time before I could open my eyes. I then heard the *minbing*s shouting, 'It is time for work! Get up quickly!' Gathering all my strength I sat up. It was still dark outside, and my roommates were still fast a sleep.

Finding it hard to keep my eyes open, I laid down hoping to be left alone for a little longer. Murmuring angrily, 'You cruel murderers, why can't you wait until day break? Why can't you let us sleep a little longer?'

Then I heard the disturbing sounds of people being flogged, followed by the screaming of the men who were sleeping outside. Jumping out of bed, I shouted at the girls, 'Get up, please! The *minbing*s are flogging the guys!' They woke up one after the other groaning and cursing the *minbing*s, having now heard the men's painful screams, they all jumped out of their beds. They put on their clothes in anyway that came to hand and rushed out of the hut in all haste.

We all lined up in strict order before setting out for the wheat fields in the darkness. Walking along hilly roads in the darkness was especially difficult when there were men cracking whips above your head and urging you to walk faster. Once again the poor weak elderly men fell victims of the whips. I kept looking at the people around me who were walking faster than those falling behind. My heart and mind were tormented by the fact that I couldn't help them in any way. Being annoyed with those walking too fast, I shouted, 'Guys, please consider the poor older men who are trailing behind us. Why do you have to walk so fast? They are being flogged because of you!'

'Do you want to be beaten to death? If not, you'd better hurry up!' replied one of them.

'But those poor men are suffering so much. Can't you see? If you walk a little slower maybe that would help them.'

'No, you are too naïve. You think that could stop the *minbing*s from beating the weak? They'd kill us all one by one if we didn't listen. You'd better saving yourself than dreaming of saving others', Orazan said sarcastically as he speeded up.

I followed them reluctantly, but still couldn't stop checking behind. How could they be so cruel towards defenceless old men who are like their own fathers or grandfathers? – I was murmuring to myself repeatedly before finally arriving at the wheat fields just before daybreak. The fields were laid out along the mountain valley. The *minbing* allocated our harvesting area. We started work immediately with no one daring to speak a word. The whole of the mountain fields were depressingly quiet apart from the sounds of our sickles cutting through the wheat stems. Soon we heard screaming as the *minbing* flogging the elderly men who were groaning from the pain. Finally they all arrived at the fields with blooded injuries.

About ten thirty we were called for breakfast, I went down to the canteen collecting a piece of burnt bread along with a cup of water. The old men were sitting in one corner in silence, I walked over to sit with them and saw their heads and faces covered in blood and wounds, making them almost unrecognizable.

'Oh God! This is a disgrace!' I couldn't hide my shock.

Shoqash did a 'hush' sign with his finger on his lips and checked around us before saying, 'They flogged us all the way from the dormitory to the fields for not walking fast enough.' His voice was trembling as tears rolled down his cheeks. I also broke down in tears. 'I feel so terribly sorry for you all. You don't deserve anything like this at your age.' I said as I wiped the tears away with my hand.

'Orazan is very ill, he didn't slept last night, he couldn't even stand up but they dragged him all along', Jursun said as all of them shook their heads and sighed.

Suddenly the whistle blew; everyone looked at each other in surprise. It was unusual, because we had just sat down for breakfast.

A number of *minbing*s arrived on horseback shouting, 'All of you, climb up to the top of the mountain, quickly!' They pointed to the mountain opposite us.

I placed the bread and my mug in my bag in a hurry before heading towards the mountain. Cracking their whips in the sky, the *minbing*s shouted nonstop, 'Quick, run fast! Walk fast! Don't be lazy!' I knew from experience that something terrible was about to happen. I ran as fast as I could but it still didn't spare me from the lashing whips. The *minbing*s were everywhere; some were on foot while others on horsebacks bellowing as they whipped people. As usual the older 'class enemies' suffered the most; those who had no sthength to walk crawled in the end to the top while being flogged, their heart-wrentching screams shaking the peaceful mountains.

On the top of the mountain, I saw others who had come for harvesting from different communes already lined up in their own production teams. It looked like another denunciation meeting. Everyone's eyes were on us, the 'class enemies'.

With everyone reaching the top of the hill, Qabdal, the party secretary, known to be the nastiest man in the world, shouted, 'Now, time to bring the class enemies out here!' Two armed *minbing*s ran up to us and dragged us to the front. They lined us up behind a meeting table, which was placed in the front of the crowd.

The people all shouted slogans at once, 'Let's finish the 'class enemies'! Let's take revenge on the 'class enemies'! Long live the dictatorships of the proletariat!' Their thundering slogans echoed in the hills and travelled far far away.

Qabdal came to Kerembay Molla's side, shouting, 'Kerembay, you have been hiding yourself behind a religious mask, poisoning the public all these years, do you accept your crime? You are an enemy to the public and communism.' He poked Kerembay's head with his index finger so viciously that the old man lost his balance and fell few steps backwards to lean on a pole near him.

Leaders from different communes walked to the front and sat down around the big table to give speeches one after another, telling people how to follow the rules of the revolution as well as how to show their loyalty to the party and to take revenge on the 'class enemies'. After all of the speakers had finished their lectures, we, the 'class enemies', were called to the front one by one. As usual, my name was on top of the list. I calmly walked up to the front to receive a piece of white cloth with large black letters written on it: 'I am Counter-Revolutionary Söyüngül'. My other workmates received the cloth showing their names and 'crimes'. We had to wear it all the time unless we wanted to be punished.

As soon as I returned to the standing line, Kerembay, who was standing not far from me collapsed to the ground and didn't move. Two *minbing*s dragged his body by his feet to the front and left him on the ground. I felt sad to see such a respectable man being handled in this way. Kerembay Molla was an erudite elder well educated in the Islamic tradition. He always spoke softly with kindness and was always ready to help people.

Kerembay Molla regained consciousness not long after. He opened his eyes, looked around him in confusion, and raised himself from the ground with great difficulty. At the same time, the *minbing*s blew the whistle for work, and we went straight to the wheat fields.

I sewed the white cloth with my name and crime onto my summer jacket during the break. I noticed that Ahmet was sitting not too far from me, looking terribly sad, so I went over to him.

'Do you need any help?' Would you like me to stitch the banner on your jacket?' I asked.

'I watched the way you collected the banner with your head up, looking so proud. Is this something we should be proud of?' he replied crossly.

'Ahmet, it is not worth wasting our energy getting upset about everything. You are new so you are finding it hard to adjust. There is a saying, which I'm sure you know: "If you scare the coward often, he will eventually become a hero." You will slowly get used to everything. We face good and evil in this world everyday, but all will be in the past one day. You are a man who has seen a lot in life, and I'm sure you will agree with me that everything apart from death is a joke. Don't get too serious about all this madness', I said in an attempt to comfort him, but he remained silent with his head down.

During the afternoon he was taken away with Abdulhemit to a denunciation rally within the commune. The following day I didn't see him, so I asked Jursun about him.

'We won't see him again, I am afraid', Jusun replied, holding back his tears.

'What do you mean?' I asked him nervously.

'He's gone. Before going to the denunciation meeting he went to his mother-in-law's house, hoping to see his children. You may not know that his wife left him for another man after he was denounced. His mother-in-law, Fatihe, has been looking after his three children ever since. She is a very harsh woman. She threw him out of the house as he turned up and refused to let him to see the children. At the rally he was badly injured, and they say that after the meeting he went back and hanged himself in the stable. I heard that two men from the commune buried him in a ditch on the hill this morning…'

This news shocked me. I knew he had been depressed for sometime but never thought he would take his own life. I am still suspicious about the claims of his suicide; I believe he may have died from the injuries he sustained during the rally, as it was common practice for the abusers to claim the victims have committed suicide thus covering up the killings. When I heard about his death, I felt terribly sad all day; my mind kept drifting back to our conversation the day before and the overwhelming sadness in his eyes. I couldn't believe he was gone forever and I prayed for God to rest his soul in peace.

20 Jul 1968

Our elderly colleagues were kept behind today. I thought the *minbing*s might take them to work in the orchards nearby, so I was pleased that they didn't have to walk the long distance to the wheat fields under the threats of the whip.

It was such a hot day. Sweat ran like water soaking my clothes. The dust from the wheat mixed with the sweat caused my body to itch all over: it was another day of hell. I noticed many Kazakhs around me were wearing clothes made from animal skin despite the heat. I asked them curiously the reason why they were wearing such thick clothes.

'We love warmth. We Kazakhs live in the mountains where we don't really have hot weather even in summer. So we are enjoying this heat', one of them said jokingly.

Suddenly some *minbing*s arrived in the field on horseback. They started to flog people for not working fast enough. I increased my working pace to avoid being hit. After the *minbing*s left, some Kazakhs laughed and said, 'And, as you've seen, our magical animal skin clothes saved our skin from being hurt by the whips. As the powerful lashes touch the skin you can imagine what happens to your body - your skin would be torn apart as your tiny waist breaks in two!'

Having spent one month of terrible suffering, the wheat harvest finally came to an end. Everyone, including our elderly workmates, was in a much better mood. Workers left the camp one group after the other happily. We also packed our belongings, eagerly waiting to set out on our journey home. At the last minute we, the 'class enemies', were told that we are going to the No.4 Production Unit to harvest wheat. Saddened and disappointed, we carried all our belongings escorted by eight fully armed and uniformed *minbing*s on horsebacks. As usual when we passed by residential areas they showed off their supremacy over us by shouting and flogging us. People came out from their houses to watch as we passed by. Children followed behind shouting and throwing stones. We walked over thirty kilometres to finally reach the No.4 Production Unit just before sunset. As we placed our belongings on the floor the *minbing*s ordered that we went straight to work in the fields, we did this until it was too dark to see.

Our male workmates were placed in the warehouse, as we settled in the tractor shed. The place was covered in dust and grease and had strong musty odour. We cleaned up the sleeping area as fast as we could before spreading out our bedding. Just as our heads reached the pillow, a loud bang maked everyone jump back up. This was followed by another loud bang. We heard children swearing loudly outside the tractor shed, so went to have a look. It turned out that approximately forty to fifty children were calling us all sorts of names while putting fireworks and throwing them through the door of the shed. Our bedding almost caught fire but we have managed to stop it in time.

These dreadful acts carried out by the children continued for many nights. In the end one of the team leaders came and took them away.

24 August 1968

I brought lunch from the canteen to the dormitory and was about to start eating when I heard someone mumbling next door. I sat quietly listening for a while before going to check on it.

I opened the door and popped my head through. Ten lots of bedding laid on the floor, on which a man was crying in agony. His face was swollen with open wounds. I went over to see who he was, and to my surprise, it was Uncle Mijit Abliz. He was breathing heavily and with great difficulty.

'I am sorry to see you like this. How are you feeling?' I asked with a heavy heart.

'My child, I am in so much pain that my body can't take any more beatings. It feels as if all my bones are broke. When will they stop? Oh God, when will they stop?' he replied with a sobbing voice.

'Uncle, I will try to find a way to inform Eziz. He must come to take you home!' I promised before leaving.

'That would be so wonderful, my child', he murmured.

'I will do whatever it takes, uncle', I said confidently.

I came out of the room, thinking about what I had promised and felt heavy with this responsibility. It was easy to say but difficult to fulfil – how would it possible for me to contact anyone while in captivity? I prayed to God for help.

I was lost in my own thoughts as a horse-drawn cart stopped not far from me. My sister Gheyshe jumped off the cart, carrying her two months old baby in one arm and a bag in the other. I quickly ran over to her, grabbed the baby for a hug then kissed her.

'Why did you bring the baby? You must be so tired!'

'Sister, we were worried about you and missed you terribly.'

Then I told her about Mijit Abliz's situation before taking her to see him. We only managed to spend fifteen minutes together before I returned to work.

The next day Mijit Abliz's son, Eziz, came to collect him, I asked Eziz to take him out of Nanshan to somewhere else safe.

The rest of August 1968

I have been placed to work in the kitchen. At first I was happy that I didn't have to work in the fields under the scorching sun, thinking I might have bit more freedom in the kitchen. This joy vanished when I learned that *minbing* Shaymerdan was appointed to watch over me. Starting at four in the morning, my job is to bring water from the river in the valley to the kitchen before breakfast. After thatI have to go and dig four barrows of potatoes from the field and take them to the kitchen using a handcart. Shaymerdan is a typical bully and constantly shouts at me. This makes me more tired than the job itself.

The *minbing*s have received new privileges since we moved to the No. 4 Production

Unit. They have received new uniforms, new army boots, new machine guns, new grenades which they wear around their waists, and new belts of bullets to drape over their shoulders. Many now have a whip sticking out of the top of one boot as they ride on the best saddles on horses. These are the most powerful and and most privileged tormenters in Nanshan. They hold unrestricted power over all the 'class enemies', and have the authority to kill anyone who doesn't obey their orders - even the head of the production unit doesn't have control of them. What surprises me is that many girls worship them and feel proud to acompany them. I regularly see the head of the *minbing*s, Qani, with a young girl, who proudly struts around. My workmates are surprised that a cruel person like him could possibly have human feelings.

I was struggling to pull the cart loaded with four big sacks of potatoes over the hill. I felt the weight of the cart becoming heavier as I went, but I didn't to stop to check as I could easily lose control on the slope and roll down the hill. So I tried to pull the cart with all my strength, my head almost touching the ground in the end. When I reached the plain I was completely out of breath and I stopped. As I turned around, the girl who's always around Shaymerdan jumped off the cart with a grin on her face. I looked at her with disgust, but she giggled and said to Shaymerdan, 'Oh, I must say that she is stronger than a man!'

After lunch I went down to the river to fetch water. Two horsemen appeared from the main road and stopped not far from me. I noticed that they kept looking at me while talking. I didn't pay much attention to them as I carried the water with shoulder poles heading towards the kitchen. When I returned they were at the riverside holding the reins as they watered their horses. I felt uneasy but had to go and get the water from the same spot. As I approached the river one of them spoke –

'Are you Söyüngül? All of the supporters of the East Turkistan Association send you their warmest regards and greetings. We have come here to see how you are. We want to let you know that you are not alone, you are in our thoughts and we hold the highest respect for you as you are one of the bravest daughters of this nation.'

I was overjoyed, my heart jumped with excitement. I felt the warmth of love in my heart, my face blushed, and my soul was filled with eternal happiness when I heard the name 'East Turkistan Association'. I wanted to jump up and down crying out loud, 'Yes! The East Turkistan Association exists!'

However, my excitement disappeared in a matter of seconds like a passing storm because of my doubts. I didn't know who these people were. I didn't know if I could trust them. I didn't know if it was a trap. My mind was in turmoil when I saw Shaymerdan in the distance, running towards me. I smiled at these men friendly and quickly lifted the water buckets with the shoulder poles to proceed to the kitchen.

The next day we completed the work at the No. 4 Production Unit. Everyone was happy with the thought of going home, however we received an order to work at the No. 6 Production Unit. As usual we were herded there under armed guards. Upon arriving we were taken straight to the wheat fields where we worked until it was dark.

I was again called to work in the kitchen, my task was the same, bring water from the river, and to dig potatoes, which I transported by hand cart to the kitchen where I prepared them for cooking. Every day I was the first to start work and the last to finish.

One day I was told to work in the potato fields, loading potatoes in bags before placing them onto trucks to be taken to the city. As we were running backwards and forwards with bags of potatoes, a bus arrived from Ürümchi carrying new workers. I saw a middle-aged Uyghur woman among them who joined us working in the fields. It was not long afterwards that a fight broke out. To my shock, I saw some men were hitting the woman. The *minbing*s joined in and started flogging her. It started raining heavily as we continued loading the seven trucks. By the end of the day, we were all soaked through and I had no energy left to move my legs.

The following day the woman joined us as a 'class enemy'. She became a new target for the denunciation meeting that evening. She came up to me and asked in a hushed voice if I was Uyghur and why I was among the 'class enemies'. I told her about myself briefly, the story put her in tears.

'Oh, how terrible it must be to be exploited in such a harsh way when you are so young. I feel so sorry for you and your family.'

I thanked her for her kind words and thoughts. But I was also curious about her background, so I asked her directly.

'Disasters may come at anytime from nowhere without notice', she sighed deeply before continuing, 'I live in a village and my sister lives in the city. I went to visit her two days ago. She gave me some bread, meat, eggs and vegetables in a basket to take home. Upon my arrival home I was told to come here to work. I quickly emptied the basket and carried it here with me for use in the fields. There was a newspaper lining inside, which my sister had used to keep it clean from the items she placed there. When I emptied the potatoes from the basket onto the truck, the paper fell out with them. There was a picture of Chairman Mao at the back, and it was torn where Chainman Mao's eyes were. The *minbing*s who saw that went nuts. They accused me of deliberately poking out Chairman Mao's eyes. I tried to explain to them that I had no knowledge of

Mao's picture in the newspaper, but the *minbing*s branded me as a counter-revolutionary all the same. What could I say? I can't believe what has happened to me. Why would I ever deliberately do something like that and get myself in trouble? These mad *minbing*s think everyone is crazy like themselves. I saw you yesterday toiling alongside the old men, my heart ached for you, but you didn't seem to be so sad. How do you do it? How long have you been branded a class enemy?'

'Five years it has been, but I've tried to stay positive', I replied.

'Oh, that is a long time. You know, you stand out like a beautiful red rose among the weeds in the fields. I was in despair until I saw you. You've inspired me so much and I think that maybe I shouldn't feel so sorry for myself any more!' she said sincerely.

A *minbing* was coming our way, so we stopped talking.

25 September 1968

Having completed wheat harvesting in the No.6 Production Unit, we left in two trailers pulled by two tractors early in the morning. The drivers and the *minbing*s stopped a few times during the journey for food, leaving us in the trailers. People didn't abuse us as much as before, however. Instead, they offered us bread, yogurt and other homemade snacks. In spite of the large banner stitched on the back of my blouse, which read: 'Counter-Revolutionary Söyüngül', some people greeted warmly and asked how I was and how my parents were. It made me happy to see that people's attitude towards us is changing as they realise the truth behind all the brutal political games.

Arriving at the commune at dusk, the driver drove us straight inside the commune courtyard. There was excitement on everyone's face with the thought of going home. After all the hardships, we all missed home terribly, and we got off the trailer eagerly waiting for Qani to let us go. To everyone's disappointment he ordered us to stay in the commune hall. There were over seventy 'class enemies', among them four were women, including myself. We spread our bedsheets on the floor and sat down. Later in the evening the *minbing* brought a man and his son to the hall then left, locking the gate behind them. The father and son were clearly scared and confused, looking at us with wondering eyes.

It was awkward to be kept with so many men in the same place at night. After having been away for so long, I was dying to wash myself properly and get some rest at home. Some men started snoring as soon as their heads hit the pillow, whilse others were chatting. I took off my shoes and sat on my bedding.

Orazan asked the new comers in Kazakh, 'Where did you come from?' They didn't understand him, I realised that they were Uyghur as the father asked the son what Orazan said. I repeated his question in Uyghur.

'We are from Kashgar. We left Kashgar to look for work. We heard that labour was needed in this region so we came. The *minbing*s made us work all day long without a break then they brought us here. They didn't tell us anything, so we have no idea what is going on. I can hardly understand these people's accent', the father replied.

'That's strange. They already have plenty slaves like us, how can there still be work left for others? Why would they need you for anything? If you ask me, I'd say you are asking for trouble by coming here, but you're very well welcome', Orazan said.

The old men didn't understand Orazan but sensed the unfriendliness in his tone.

'My child, who are these people?' He asked me.

'Hey old man, who do you think we are? We are cursed people by God. We are beaten every single day before getting locked up. Didn't you see the big metal lock on the door?' Orazan said angrily.

'My child, I couldn't catch what he said. Could you explain it to me?' the old man asked me sincerely.

'Uncle, all the people in this hall are accused criminals. We were put under the surveillance regime, that is why we were locked up in this place', I replied.

'Oh, but yourself are also locked up for the same reason? I can't believe this, I have never seen or heard that young woman like you been locked up like this', the old man said with disbelief.

'If you stay quiet they will keep you here, and later accuse you of some sort of crime and put you under surveillance, too', Orazan said, 'But once you get out of here, offer you thanks to God. Don't go to unfamiliar places for work; there is no work for anyone because there are plenty free slaves like us everywhere so you'd better go home as soon as you can.'

'Thank you, my child', the old man said with a trembling voice and looked terrified and desperate to get out of the place. Half an hour later a *minbing* came and let the father and son out of the hall.

I was about to fall asleep when I heard someone banging on the door. It was the elderly men who needed to go to the toilet and shouted at the *minbing* to open the door for them, but there wasn't anyone outside. They shouted desperately, 'Let us out! We need the toilet!' and woke everyone up. Some suggested getting out from the window, but the window were all firmly sealed off and no one managed to open them.

'Oh God, what should I do? I can't hold any longer!' one of them screamed.

'Go and do it in the corner', someone suggested.

'Oh no, I don't want to smell the piss. Please don't piss in the room for everyone's sake', another person yelled.

The whole place turned noisy. In the end those desperate old men had no choice but to piss in the corner of the hall. Many people complained with disgust, and I hid my head inside my duvet cover.

Most of us hadn't washed ourselves properly since we left home four months ago, and many of us were wearing cloth made of animal skin - one can imagine the stinking smell, which made the room already unbearable to breath. On top of that now people have to urinate inside the room. I can't really blame these people, what can they do otherwise. I didn't sleep for a long time in discomfort.

Late September – late October 1968

We had been working three days in the commune cleaning out the area and preparing for the National Day celebration on 1 October. On the 28th of September, we were taken by truck to Torjan Production Unit where we'd spend two weeks cutting weeds in the fields. People there treated us with respect and some even brought us home made food regularly in secret. One of the ladies who brought us food told me that she knew my great-grandfather and that he was a well-respected generous man who cared about everyone in the village. She visited me regularly giving me food when the *minbing*s were not around. But we didn't stay in this place for long; we completed the entire task in two weeks and made our way on foot back to the central commune.

Initially we were told that we would be spending whole winter in this place, so we had brought a lot of winter clothes and heavy quilts with us, now we had to carry them all back unused. The journey was hard, with many dangerous mountain paths along the way. With the heavy loads on our backs it was difficult to keep the balance when climbing the stiff cliffs. I kept reminding myself that I must walk very carefully when we were passing the dangerous cliff. The path was very narrow, so we walked in a line. When I reached the top of the cliff suddenly my feet slipped, lost my balance and fell. The heavy weight on my back pulled me down towards the Tutunhu River about 30 to 40 metres below the cliff, I thought I was finished as there wasn't anything that I could hold onto to stop myself from falling. I heard my friends screaming in shock, there was nothing they could do to help me either. I reached on the edge of the cliff in a matter of seconds and my heart almost jumped out of my chest. I managed to stop myself by holding onto some plants and placing my foot onto a big rock along the cliff. Jorsun and Lao Ma came quickly and got hold of my hands. They pulled me out of danger. I thanked God for saving my life. I felt like escaping from the jaws of death.

We carried all our belongings all the way to Topdirek Valley where they were picked up by two horsecarts. We walked much faster on the rest of the journey and reached the commune just before the day got dark. We were placed in the same commune hall.

Early next morning Meriye and I were assigned to build a gate in the middle of the road with mud bricks to write Mao's quotations on. We carried mud-bricks all day long from the commune square to the roadside outside the commune where the gate was planned. Teenagers stood along the road and threw at us sand, stones and earth all day while we were working. Meriye couldn't cope with the bullying and started crying while I tried very hard to persuade her to ignore them. Before finishing work I saw my siblings watching me from a distance, I wished I could run to them and hold them in my arms as I missed them so much but I could only wave my hands to greet them because the *minbing*s were watching us closely all the time.

Suddenly I heard a scream from the men's group who were repairing the roof of the commune buildings. The *minbing*s rushed out, Zekiye and Gheyshe took the opportunity to come to me immediately. She quickly updated me with the news about our family members, and fortunately they were all safe and sound.

'It hurt us so much to see children throw sand and stones at you all day long, it is frustrating not being able to stand up for you', Zekiye said with tears in her eyes.

'What can we do? We just have to cope with whatever we face each day and try to survive.'

'Oh yes, I have a good news for you actually. Our neighbour Hüsen came to visit us last night. He said that Radio Free Motherland in Tashkent broadcasted a special programme about Sajide and you. It said that you are spending your golden youth in prison for the freedom of the nation, being forced to carry out hard labour in the most dangerous jobs in the mountains. However you have never surrendered to the occupying regime, but exemplify the spirit, resilience and courage of our people against the oppressors. They said you are the most precious daughters of this nation, and you will live in the heart of people forever. I was so happy to hear this broadcast that I couldn't wait to tell you. You see, whatever you have been gone through, it's not in vain. People know the truth and recognise your sacrifices. Being broadcast on the Soviet Radio is not a small thing. We are so proud of you!' Zekiye said excitedly. I was so happy to see the joy on my sister's face, as the news of our injustice imprisonment was recognised within and outside our country.

Standing behind Kalay in the queue for dinner, I noticed that his neck was covered in lice, particularly along the wrinkle lines, which indicated that the bugs had been sucking his blood. I felt sorry for him, sorry for this old man who had to endure the constant beatings, hard labour and the misery of lice sucking his blood just to be able to survive. I called one of the *minbing*s to show him the lice on Kalay's neck, but the beast grimaced with disgust and spat on the floor.

'Well, could you please allow him to go home to wash himself and change his clothes at least?' I asked. Other friends also supported what I said. In the end our demand was accepted, and he was allowed to go home.

Kalay came back the next day looking like a different person. Having washed shaved and changed into clean clothes. He said to us, 'My wife burst out crying in horror when I walked into the house looking in such a terrible state. But I feel much better now. Thank you for speaking out for me!'

Late October – December 1968

We worked in the commune for five days before being told we were being sent to dig a canal in the mountains near Chewchiz Village. All our belongings were transported by horsecarts, as we ourselves travelled on foot across the mountains and dangerous gorges before arriving at our destination. All the men and women were accommodated in a large wooden shack located on the outskirt of Chewchiz village.

The digging was to last for two months, working from daybreak until dusk with little food. Each day during our return from work the *minbing*s forced the men to crawl up the mountain path on their hands and knees, cracking their whips above their heads as they sat on the men's backs shouting relentlessly, urging them to work faster. My elderly workmates cried for mercy, as they were too weak to carry the heavy thugs. However the heartless *minbing*s repeated this cruel act everyday.

One day all the men were lined up and had their hair, moustaches, and beards shaved off. All the men begged for their not to do so, but the *minbing*s took pleasure from their emotional and physical suffering. I overheard them groaing, 'Oh what now? What dignity do I have left? How will I be to look into the eyes of others now that I look like an old woman without my beard? Where in this world can you find an act of such cruelty towards helpless elders? Do I still live among humans?'

Every evening when we returned to the dormitory the *minbing*s would lock the room from the inside before ordering us sit in a circle, they then ordered the men to crawl on the floor while in turn riding them like dogs and slapping their bold heads and laughing until the men collapsed and were unable to move. Only then the tormentors would leave. No words could describe the cruelty and the suffering of the helpless men as they became more suicidal with each passing day.

As soon as we finished the canal we were ordered to remove trees, grasses and flowers growing in between the two mountains in order for it to be turned into farmland. On the last day working with three men we had to fell a huge tree, which was over one hundred years old. Digging around the roots of the tree to a depth over two metres then we cut the roots but the tree remained upright. It was getting dark, as I struggled to dig out a large rock from under one of the main roots. I heard people shouting, 'Run, quick, the tree is falling!' I looked up to see it was toppling over. I tried to crawl out of the way as fast as I could but the tree fell and I was trapped. In that split second I thought my life would end, but as I lay trapped I heard people screaming in panic and distress, 'She is dead, oh my God, she is dead!' At that moment I was so confused that I didn't know where I was, or if I was dead or having a bad dream. I gathered all my strength and started to move; people realised that I was still alive and crawled back to the branches to drag me out. I stood up and saw many people looking on in horror as they thought I was dead.

'It is a miracle! God saved you!' they yelled with joy as I staggered towards them. I was shocked that that I wasn't hurt at all - it was truly a miracle. One after another my colleagues asked with deep concern in their voices: "Are you in pain? How do you feel?"

'God sent his angels to support the tree while you were trapped beneath it. It was truly amazing how you emerged from that huge tree without being crushed. You must have performed good deeds during your lifetime to have God's special protection, Söyüngül!' said Kerembay Molla as he wiped tears from his eyes.

Minbing Ibray said, 'Söyüngül, God saved you today, so you must donate something to show your gratitude to God. Give you dinner to Orazan!' His remark surprised everyone. As he was directly involved in the beating of Kerembay Molla almost to death accusing him of poisoning people with religion. Now suddenly he was referring to God.

January 1969

On the 17th of January we move into Qizilbayraq Production Team to do roadworks. It was freezing cold but as there was nowhere for us to stay, so we were ordered to dig out a cavern for living and sleeping in the side of the mountain.it was 20 metres by 5 and 2.5 metres high. We were able to settle in the damp cave that evening as the freezing temperature dropped to minus 30 degrees. It was impossible to light a fire or close off the damp cave entrance, so we shivered all night without being able to sleep.

We lost Noruz brother during this time on one of the coldest nights. Upon his return from work, he flopped onto his bed and died shortly afterwards. He had been complaining of feeling unwell for sometime but being denied time off from his hard labour duties. I had heard him praying to God to take his life away. Four men went to prepare a rustic grave and he was buried without a proper Islamic ritual. I pray that his soul is now at peace!

27 February – end of March 1969

The road we were building had now reached the Charwa Production Team area. Residents often came to watch us as if we were animals in the zoo.

The *minbing*s always enjoy their power over us and make sure to show it when people are present. They have no shame in shouting the most obscene words while flogging us. When Shoqash was working next in line to me on 27 February, he said quietly, 'Those beasts have nothing else to show off so they impose their brutality and take great pleasure and joy from it.' The *minbing* noticed that he was talking, they approached him at once to flog him viciously, Shoqash collapsed not long afterwards. They kicked his motionless body violently before leaving. Zekiriye and I helped him to his feet, he tried to remain upright but he collapsed in agony holding his back. 'Oh my back, it feels broken', he moaned.

Shoqash has never managed to stand up or walk since his beating, suffering severe pain day and night. He wasn't allowed to go home and died one month later in the cave.

On the 2nd of March we moved to the Tianshan Production Team to dig a canal. Many elderly men were too ill to work so the workload fell on the shoulders of the few of us that were fit.

We resumed work on the 27th of March and were told to return to our own production teams. Having spent almost one year with so many unfortunate people who were also persecuted by the regime, it was difficult to say goodbye, as we had become more like an extended family. We said our farewells with tears in our eyes not knowing if we would ever meet again, for many were weak and ill from the harsh punishment they had received from their captors over the past year.

I never did see them again, but years later I made enquiries about their whereabouts only to find out that many of them had died within months of being moved.

Not feeling well for a long time, I woke up one morning to find my body was swollen all over so I went to see the commune doctor. He suspected that I might be suffering from a liver problem and immediately referred me to the No.2 Hospital in Ürümchi for a check up. After travelling to the hospital for my appointment I was immediately admitted as I had a serious liver disease. I remained there for one and half months receiving treatment. During this period my friend Zohre, whom I had met in Xigobi labour camp visited me daily to check on my recovery. She had a number of good contacts among the doctors at the hospital so she was able to persuade them to give me the best possible treatment. I was discharged as an outpatient with instructions to attend daily for treatment for one month, during which time I stayed in our family home in Ürümchi.

During this period I decided to meet with the head of my university Ayim Eziz to discuss my current political accusations in order to see if I it is possible to rectify the situation. At the university I was informed that she was on leave, so I went to the senior cadres' luxury compound where she lived, but there were two security guards at the gate who stopped me, saying that I needed permission from the person whom I intended to visit. I told them that I had come to see Ayim Eziz, who was my relative - I lied in order to obtain entry. One of the guards went into the small office next to the gate and telephoned her as I waited nervously. About half an hour later I was given permission to enter the compound. I had to pass two more security gates before reaching her house.

I was greated by the maid who led me through a spacious wooden corridor, where a beautiful patterned rug ran through on the floor at the entrance to the reception room, which was laid out and beautifully decorated like a luxury conference hall with a large oblong table in the middle of the room where I was asked to sit and wait. Some women and children passed through the room as I entered. I presumed they might be checking who I was. Approximately half an hour later Professor Ayim appeared, after exchanging greetings she looked at me warmly saying, 'I can hardly recognise you, how come you are related to me?' I introduced myself briefly and said, 'I am sorry but I lied in order to see you. I was one of your students from the Medical University. I was one of the four students who was arrested in 1963 and given a three-year prison sentence as a counter-revolutionary.'

She welcomed me once again with warmth and compassion. We talked like friends for over an hour, during which I learned that she was also subjected to denunciation meetings at the start of the Cultural Revolution. She said, 'I was paraded in the streets of Ürümchi during the hot summer days with dirty shoes hanging around my neck, in a paper dress with large insulting slogans.'

She listened to my story attentively while looking at me with sympathy. When I finished speaking she said warmly, 'I am going to speak to Seypidin Eziz and will ask him to write you a special letter in which it would stated that every assistance should be given to you when requested. I will be in the office on Wednesday, so please come to see me then.'

I went to Professor Ayim's office on Wednesday as requested, She gave the letter written by Mr Seypidin Eziz. The letter was addressed to the Provincial Public Security Bureau stating that they should follow the party's principles of Education Through Labour to correct and review the unjust information of my case. Ayim Eziz comforted me with positive words, insisting that Governor's letter would assist in the removal of the unjust accusation made by the Public Security Bureau. She asked me to stay positive.

Overwhelmed by such encouraging words and armed with the newly gained confidence, I went straight to the Public Security Bureau with the letter. I presented the letter to the official in the case management department explaining my situation, he looked at the letter briefly before throwing it into my face and said coldly, 'This is not valid regardless of the person or his position. We do not accept anyone's proposals.'

The letter hit my face and fell on the floor, as I remained frozen with shock, having realised that all the power was in the hands of others and the governor was nothing but a puppet. I picked up the letter before leaving the office without saying a word.

The following day I returned to Nanshan to resume work in the commune. A week later one of my sisters who went to visit our parents in Ürümchi returned, telling me that a lady from Kashgar had visited the family home to deliver a message to me from the people of the Kashgar region. When told that I had returned to Nanshan, the lady said she would come here to see me, but our mother told her about my situation and said that her visit might cause further trouble for me. In the end she said that comrades in Kashgar want me to know that they hold me in highest esteem, and that the people of Kashgar had realised that Ablikim was a traitor and dragged him out of his home and paraded him in the streets. It made me very happy to hear now that people living far away were thinking about me. I was comforted by the fact that many people all over of my country shared the same ideals and dreams as myself.

28 March 1969

Not long after returning to Nanshan, my health deteriorated and I had to go for treatment again in Ürümchi. I was on my way home from the hospital after my injection, when suddenly I saw a crowd of people, including screaming children, following a man in what looked like a street parade. I was curious to know what was going on.

An old man walking past me said, 'Did you see that? There was no place for him to live within our own society so he existed by living in the wilderness of the Tarim Basin. There he lost his humanity and turned into a wild man of the Taklamakan Desert. What miseries haven't our people experience under the rule of the Chinese? It makes your heartache when you think about it.' He sighed before walking on with his walking stick. I was curious to see the 'wild man', so I walked faster to catch up with the crowd. But by the time reached them they had turned and disappeared into Ittipaq Road. I went home instead.

My parents were about to have lunch when I arrived so I joined them. My mother asked how I was and if there was any news. I told her about the 'wild man of the Taklimakan Desert' who was being followed by so many people in the street.

'Oh, looks like you saw Jappar Axun then', my mother explained keenly, 'He is from Turpan, a relative of a well-known family named Esseydulla. He was a soldier under the command of General Mahmud Sijan. When the general was defeated and fled, his army was captured by the troops of Sheng Shicai. They were tortured and treated in the most inhumane way before being exiled to the Taklamakan Desert, where they were shot by Sheng's soldiers. Thousands were left dead in the desert, which has been kept secret until this day.

'Jappar was among these soldiers, but he was lucky to escape death with minor injury. When he woke up, he didn't know where he was at first. Sitting up slowly he looked around and realised that he was in the middle of mountain of dead bodies in the desert. He called out the names of his friends and for help to see if anyone else was alive, unfortunately no one answered. He then slowly crawled to each of the young men who had become brothers to him over time, but they were all dead, lying in a pool of blood. Realising he had lost all his fellow companions, he broke down and wept inconsolably for a long time. The overwhelming sadness of the scene before him made him numb from the physical pain he suffered. It was only after he returned to his normal senses did he start to feel the pain of his shoulder and also of the terrible thirst he had. He slowly dragged himself out of the pile of dead bodies into the open desert as he aimlessly walked leaving his beloved, dead friends behind. He sat down behind a rock closing his eyes in order to figure out what to do next. After a long, long time, he was suddenly woken up from his thoughts by the sound of animals. Opening his eyes, he founnd himself encircled by a herd of wild goats. They were gazing at him with soft gentle eyes as if feeling his pain and loss. They looked sad too. He thought looking back at them with tears in his eyes. He felt comforted by their presence. He felt hope, and convinced himself that he could survive as long as there is life in this wild place. He stood up to touch the animals, they didn't run away; instead, they allowed him to embrace them gently as he caressed their hair with his hands and telling them his painful story.

'Hungry and thirsty, he struggled to think of what he could eat or drink. As he stroke the goat he saw milk dripping from the breast of one of the animals. He slowly approached the goat, speaking gently to her with soothing words. He then gently milked the goat into the cup of one hand, which he then drank repeating this until his thirst was quenched. The goat accepted him and followed him wherever he went. Although there were other animals, such as camels, he survived with the help of the goats as well as the eggs from wild birds. He made clothes from dead animals along with leaves and bark from the trees. He lived this way for over thirty years until 1967 when the Chinese government sent a survey team to the area. The survey of the Talamakan desert was to explore and report on the underground and topical resources of the region so that more Chinese immigrants from the mainland could be moved there, it was during an arial survey that they saw the figure of a man running with wild goats and camels. This was immediately reported to Beijing. The Party, obviously, suspected the man was suspected of being a spy from the Soviet Union, so ordered that me had to be captured alive. They chased him with a helicopter and two motorcycles and finally caught him. He was immediately transported to Beijing for interrogation. Having tried to converse with him in different languages and dialects, it was finally established that he was Uyghur. He spoke and convinced them of his tragic experiences of over thirty years ago. Having listened to his story the government decided that he should be released to a place of his choice to which he chose Ürümchi.'

'What a legend! Where did you hear all this, mum? Have you met this man personally?' I asked.

'Yes of course my child! I have met him and heard his story myself, as he lives next door to Zohre in Ittipak Road. His story is so intriguing that he has been receiving visitors every day since his return to this so-called civilisation.'

My father, who had been gazing at the sky through the window, commented,

'Sheng Shicai was one of the most brutal rulers in the history of East Turkistan. He committed mass genocide during his rule. He killed almost everyone who dared to challenge his brutal authoritarian policies and silenced those who dared to speak up against his orders. He brought so much misery to so many families, and disappeared many, many intellectuals and wealthy business people. Many students, teachers and the heads of the Military Institute at that time, which he helped to establish, would fall under his persecution for no obvious reason. He employed most brutal methods of torture, one of the which was squeezing prisoners' heads with metal band that was connected to an electrical power system, when switched on, the eyes of the prisoners would pop out of their sockets and cause unimaginable agony. Hundreds and thousands of brave men and women were either shot or tortured to death as he turned East Turkistan into the largest prison on Earth. Today history is repeating itself once more.'

'Hey, by the way, do you remember our neighbour, teacher Zeynep, and her husband Heyder?' my mother interrupted, 'Heyder was one of the most well-known Tatar scholars in literature and history – such a refined and erudite writer and poet, who was arrested by Sheng and accused of treason. Before his arrest he had given some of his writings and poems to his eighteen-year-old son Rustem for safekeeping, but not long after his arrest Sheng's men also took his son away. They demanded Rustem to release the documents. One week later, Rustem was tortured to death in prison. Zeynep was warned not to view the corpse by those who brought him home. But she couldn't control herself and took a look and collapsed immediately. Poor Rustem was unrecognisable! His eyes had popped out of his face, his nose was broken, and all his nails were pulled out, his arms, legs and ribs were all broken! Zeynep never recovered from the sight of seeing the tragic way that death had taken her son. Her tears never stopped falling since that terrible day.' My mother said struggling to hold back her sadness and tears.

'Not surprised', continued my father, 'Tens of thousands of people were murdered under that brute's inhuman rule. Some were killed using a hay guillotine, others were thrown into deep wells, and many others were pushed off high cliffs. He also put people in sealed bags and dumped them in desolate places left them to die. Many were thrown on the railway tracks. But the majority were taken to Taklimakan Desert to be shot and left for the wild animal to devour.

'My uncle Hemidulla was one of the victims who were burnt to death in Tarim. He was in the army and was captured by Shen's men and taken away, never to return. His family travelled all over East Turkistan in the search of his whereabouts. Word gradually spread from the villages in Tarim that the shepherds had witnessed the massacre of many people. People who lived close to the desert boundaries spoke of a shepherd who had spoken to my dying uncle. He said that one day, while tending his flock, he heard terrifying screams coming across the desert. He crawled up to a high point to see what was happening; to his horror, he witnessed soldiers setting fire to prisoners then leaving on the empty trucks. The shepherd went to the scene of the devastation to see if there were any survivors, and on the way he heard one man moaning in agony. He quickly approached the man to give him water. The man managed to tell him his name, Hemidulla, and that he was a Tatar from Ürümchi. Uncle Hemidulla asked the sheperd boy to tell the world what he had witnessed that day, and also to pass on his name to anyone he knew that was going to or coming from to Ürümchi, before he finally died. Years later my uncle's family learned of this massacre his death from people who had travelled from that region to the capital. It was after hearing this story that they travelled to Tarim to confirm where the massacre occurred and the final resting place of my uncle.'

Silence fell onto the house. After a long while, my father continued, 'There was a rumour circulating in 1944 that, when Shen left Xinjiang, he was going to take a higher position in the Chiang Kai-shek adminstration. At the time his personal belongings and wealth, which was believed to be pure gold, and other precious artifacts were loaded onto a convoy of 50 vehicles escorted by heavily armed military personnel. He later fled to Taiwan of course, after Kuomintang fell in 1949.'

My mother then related another event: there was a lady named Niyaz Buwi, who, according to rumours, was taken away by the spirits before being returned. She had somehow gained special spiritual healing powers and became well known and respected in the community for these powers. People would travel long distances to seek her help, and she would visit the very sick in their homes. One morning Niyaz Buwi came to our house to greet my mother, and, when asked what she had been up to, told her the following story –

'I was in Hangching along with six other *buwis*[47] on the invitation by a widow to perform special prayers for her son. The son had been chosen by government officials for a special job in the prison service and as such was escorted to and from the prison during the periods he was allowed to visit his mother for more than thirty minutes once a month. But his mother was very proud at the thought of his important position along with the rewards it brought her, food and cloth for making clothes. It was on one of his visits accompanied by the usual two guards that he told his mother quietly, while

47   *Female psychics.*

changing his clothes, of the spiritual problem that he was involved in, asking her to pray for his spiritual release from the dark side of the world. She feared for her son's sanity, and invited herself along with six other *buwi*s to the house in order to pray and cast aside the evil spirits from their home and the prison where her son worked. We stayed in the house for seven days, praying and chanting *sura*s from the Holy Quran with the mother to drive away all that was evil and for her son to be returned safely to the arms of his mother at home.

'It was not long after we left that the son returned in an agitated state to tell his mother what he got himself into in prison: he was employed by the prison governor, a cannibal called Bi ZhiDung, who once forced him to cut open the chest of young living men and remove the fresh beating heart, which was immediately taken to Bi who sucked the fresh warm blood from the heart as he performed cannibalistic rites. The son had managed to escape from the prison because there was a riot and Bi ZhiDung fled. He and his mother remained in the house that day before fleeing during the night to Turpan as it was dangerous for them to remain at the family home due to the activities he had been involved in. This is only one of the many shocking things that are occurring everywhere. Bi ZhiDun was captured later by an official, who had him transported to Ürümchi and had him paraded through the streets in a cage. During the parade he was stoned and spat on by the people for his hideous crimes and was eventually killed.'

Abliz, who was a year below me at university and who I hadn't seen since our time working in the Mechanical Engineering labour Camp came to visit me one day.

'Whatever you have suffered won't go invain, Söyüngül!' he said, 'Rest assured that there are people out there who are carrying on the fight you started for the freedom of East Turkistan. There are organisations secretly operating in many places.' His uplifting words gave me great comfort as well as hope for the future. I was so happy - it was as if I had found the fortune for which I have been searching all my life.

'Is it true, Abliz?' I asked him eagerly.

'Of course it is true! Why would I make up stories about such a serious matter?' said Abliz with a sincere friendly smile.

'So, are you a member of one these organisations?' I enquired.

'No, but whether I am member or not I am a staunch believer in the cause', he replied.

'That's great. Please introduce me to one of those people one day, as I wish to become involved again.'

'But you are under surveillance. It is a very big risk under such circumstances at the present time', he warned.

I thought for a while and admitted that he was right. If I was caught being a member of such an organisation, I could face the death penalty. Yet at the same time, if I took a step backwards for my safety what would be the future for my people in danger? I would rather take a risk to realise my dream of independence. And what hardship hadn't I experience so far. I knew that nothing could stop my desire to fight for the freedom of my country and people. So I said to Abliz, 'I can and will deal with any kind of danger or problem. So sign me up.'

'Ok, let me speak to Yasin. He can introduce you to one of them', said Abliz before leaving.

I was in completely different mood from that moment on, as I started to see hope again in life.

Not long afterwards Yasin came to visit me, he is related to my family and we had worked together in Mechanical Repair Labour Camp for over a month, so I was no stranger to him. We discussed a wide range of subjects from history to the future, and at the end of our conversation, he agreed to introduce me to members of the organisation.

I eagerly waited for a reply from Yasin. He returned a week later saying that they had agreed to meet me. We went to a jujube Orchard at five in the evening. While we sat talking, I saw two men appear in the distance.

'Here they are!' said Yasin, waving at them. Looking in their direction I saw one of the men was tall and broad-shouldered; his deep and intense eyes gave an air of mystery to his personality. The other was slim of medium height, fair skinned, and from his appearance he looked like a typical cadre. After the formal greetings, the tall man introduced himself warmly as Malik, a factory worker, whereas the shorter man introduced himself as Qeyyum, a schoolteacher.

Then they asked to tell them about myself. I briefly explained about my involvement in my old organisation, my subsequent imprisonment and my current situation. We exchanged views on the current political situation. In the end, Qeyyum said before leaving, 'We share the same ideology, and the name of our organisation is also the East Turkistan Association. Let's meet again soon, Yasin will inform you about our next meeting.'

The next day Yasin took me to a small house located near the back of the No.2 Hospital. He lead me into a dark room on the left hand side of the house. This was the main family reception room with a small window next to the door, the adjoining room

318 THE LAND DRENCHED IN TEARS

being a guest room with traditional raised seating and sleeping platform. As I entered, Malik appeared from the inner room hurriedly to welcome me.

The guest room was traditional with its raised platform covered with a traditionally designed wool rug. The main wall had a large traditional hand-made carpet adorning the wall. The room's decoration was simple and tasteful, giving of a feeling of warmth and comfort.

Tearcher Qeyyum was sitting on a chair next to the window; I took a seat on the edge of the platform. Malik left soon to return with a pot of tea and some fresh *nan*. After talking casually for a while, Malik said –

'We have decided to accept you as a member of our organisation, so we would like to enroll you today. He then placed a Quran next to my right hand, I place my hand on the Quran and swore, "I, Söyüngül, hereby solemnly declare that I have joined the East Turkistan Association of my own free will. I swear in the name of God that I will not betray the organisation or my comrades under any circumstance. Were I to break my promise, I would be punished severely.'

Qeyyum said in a deep voice as I finished taking the oath, 'I congratulate you on becoming a member of the East Turkistan Association. You must obey all the rules and regulations of our organisation and carry out the orders you are given by the leadership.'

I was over the moon. I felt a deep happiness within me. I have finally found the people I had been looking for all my life, which gave me a powerful feeling of strength.

Speaking directly to them both, I asked, 'So, gentlemen, what are my duties?'

'You will influence people and recruit members from Nanshan. That will be your task for now', Malik replied.

I felt the weight of the new responsibility. I asked myself - will I be able to carry out such a task? I've been classed as an enemy of the people and the villagers of Nanshan are extremely naïve with very little education. I have suffered discrimination, hostility and ill treatment for years from these very people. I wondered if I would be able to approach anyone and influence them to become a member of such an organisation. It is possible they might turn me in straight away in order to receive favourable treatment from the government. The thought of the tough reality troubled me greatly, and I didn't know what to say to them.

'Nothing is impossible, I am sure I can find a way forward', I reassured myself before saying to them –

'Yes, I will do my best to influence and recruit people from Nanshan. I can and will fulfill the task that you have given me!'

'Good, I will inform you of other activities at our next meeting, which will be held near Central Bridge behind the No. 2 Hospital on Sunday 29 June', Qeyyum said warmly.

29 June – 1 July 1969
First military curfew

My mother's best friend Selime invited her to lunch, to which I also went along with my sisters Sofiye, Gheyshe and Zekiye. After lunch I told mother that we were going out shopping.

It was a pleasant day. Three of us chatted happily as we passed by the shops. It was not long before I realised that we reached Central Bridge. I looked around but didn't see any of my friends, so we waited at the designated place for over half an hour, but no one showed up. While standing there, we realised that the busy street was gradually becoming very quiet.

'This is strange. There are fewer and fewer people in the street compared to when we arrived. What is happening?' said Zeikye.

Gheyshe also looked around and said in a troubled voice, 'You are right, something is wrong. The whole area looks very chilling. I'm scared.'

I also sensed the ominous change in the area, realising that we were the only people on the street. I suggested hesitantly that we should go home.

Just as we started to make our way home, I saw a man walking towards us in the distance. I was pleased to see at least someone in the street. As he approached I recognised that it was Yasin. He was carrying a *dutar*.[48]

'*Salam*, Yasin, nice to see you here. Do you know why the streets have suddenly become empty?'

'I have no idea, Söyüngül. I am also finding it a bit strange.'

'What's the *dutar* for, brother? Are you on your way to a wedding?' Gheyshe said jokingly.

'Oh no, I had it repaired and have just got it back.'

By this time we had reached the middle of the shopping district, which would normally be crowded with people all day long, but now there were only the four of us. We walked as fast as we could, the only sound being that of our own footsteps which echoed around us. Poor Gheyshe looked terrified and was running as if escaping

---

48   *A traditional musical instrument popular in Iran, Afghanistan, and Central Asia.*

a catastrophe; it was difficult to catch up with her.

As we turned into Baihua Road, we saw some Chinese *minbing*s who were wearing white arm bands stopping people as they walked along the road. As we approached the crowd, one of the men shouted, 'Hey beautiful, come over here and join us.' 'Are you returning from a wedding?' another one asked. We ignored them and walked straight ahead hoping that we would not be stopped. Two *minbing*s jumped in front of us and ordered aggressively, 'Go and stand over there with those people. No one is allowed to go anywhere! Wait there quietly for further instructions.' We had no choice but to join the group standing at the side of the road. I quietly asked an old man next to me about what was happening. He told me that a military curfew was imposed today.

'Has anything happened? Why they have imposed a military curfew?' I asked.

'We don't know. There have been so many different things happening all at the same time!' other people replied.

More and more people were stopped and forced to join the growing crowd. Before long two black trucks arrived and stopped near us. The *minbing*s immediately ordered everyone to board the vehicles. I asked a Uyghur policeman on a motorcycle next to one of the trucks –

'Could you tell us where we are going?'

'You will be taken to the local police station first, after which you will be send to different detention centres', he said with a cold voice.

'Will we be allowed to go home tonight?' I asked.

'No, that is not allowed.'

'My father is seriously ill with a heart problem. We are just three sisters who came to do some shopping. If he doesn't hear from us today he may die of a heart attack as he is very weak. You can't just arrest us for no reason. We are going home!' I said while jumping out of the truck with my sisters following me. Yasin also got off the truck. The rest of the people on the truck followed us very quickly out of the truck.

The *minbing*s became nervous. They encircled us immediately, yelling, 'Get back onto the truck now! No one is allowed to leave!' Then they push everyone back to the truck again, but the four of us refused to get onto it, saying that we had to go home to take care of our father.

More and more people were being brought from different areas of the town and told to stand in the same place that we had occupied earlier. An argument soon broke out between the people and the *minbing*s, and I was surprised to see Brother Hesenjan among the crowd shouting at the *minbing*s. Quickly the police and the *minbing*s herded them close to us. I learned that his son Iminjan was practicing bicycle riding in the street outside their apartment block when the police arrived suddenly to take him away. The children who were playing saw what had happened went straight into the apartment block informing people that Iminjan had been taken away by the police. Everyone in the apartment block rushed into the street to see what was happening. Immediately a police car arrived arresting everyone including the children before bringing them to this place.

A busload of people arrived and stopped next to us, the *minbing*s pushes us onto the bus, and I noticed that everyone was beautifully dressed. I learnt that they were arrested at a wedding party. They didn't seem to be bothered about what was going on: as we were pushed onto the bus, some men whistled at then clapped to welcome us; a young man took the *dutar* from Yasin and started playing; men and women joined the music of the *dutar* singing joyfully. It was like a typical Uyghur wedding where the bride is transported by her friends and musicians to the groom's home.

The driver drove us straight to the Sanshi Hanzi Local Police Station, where we were ordered to get off the bus. The courtyard was crowded, and soldiers were sitting at the desks taking registration information. Half an hour later, black trucks arrived to collect us, who had been organised into groups before being ordered to climb into the trucks one group after another.

The truck I was in turned into the Ittipak Road then drove to the No.14 Middle School, which was the former No.2 Girls' Middle School where I had studied, before entering the Medical University. Entering the school, the truck stopped at the rear of the school's main building. Soldiers lined us up before herding us into the school building. That was the first time visiting the school since completing my education here. As I entered the building I was overwhelmed by emotions. The familiar stairs along with the classrooms brought back a lot of beautiful memories of my teenage years: the images of myself as a happy girl running up and down the stairs, of the teachers and classmates, flashed in front of my eyes one after another like a film. For a few moments I felt relaxed as I travelled back to those years when I could still breathe freely. I felt so very happy. I quickly went to take a look at the classrooms: the rooms were empty without desks or chairs, and the lonesome blackboards hung deserted, and sadness rose from my heart, devouring the momentary happiness I had just felt.

This was the place I had studied and learned so much. This is the place where children are supposed to be educated, but has now turned into a detention centre, bringing misery and tears to so many families who have been brought here against their own free will. How I wished I could go back in time! Where were all my good friends and caring teachers? I have lost those friends just like the lost years - they won't even say hello to me even when we come face to face in the street.

The man played *dutar* and sang songs until 10 o'clock that evening. At about 11 o'clock Mr Turaxun, who used to be a chef at the Medical University, entered the room carrying a heavy bag. I recognised him immediately, and he also noticed me among the crowds and shouted my name while pushing his way through the people in my direction.

'Söyüngül! How are you? How did you end up here? Oh God is great, I never expected to meet you in a place like this. I hope you are well!'

I briefly explained to him what had happened. He said, 'I left the university soon after you were taken away. I started my own business to support my family. I went to the villages buying dry fruits to sell it in the city. I was on my way back from Turpan after purchasing raisins. But as soon as I got off the bus the *minbing*s arrested all the people and brought us here. The world is turning upside down. It's trouble everywhere…' He sighed while offering me some raisins, insisting that I eat some.

I suddenly heard a woman sobbing on the other side of the room. I walked over to her to see what had happened. She was crying uncontrollably with an unconscious baby in her arms.

'What is wrong, sister?' I asked.

'My baby is very ill with such a high fever. I was on my way to hospital when we were stopped by the Chinese *minbing*s, who brought us straight here.'

'Didn't you tell them that your baby was seriously ill?'

'I can't speak Chinese but I pointed and showed them the baby with tears running down my face. But all they did was to force us onto the truck. Oh my poor child, he is going to die! His temperature is so high and he is not moving. Look at him, he won't even open his eyes now. What shall I do?' She cried at the top of her voice. I rushed through the crowded room to approach a soldier, I explained to him about the seriousness of the situation regarding the baby's health. I told him that if they didn't allow the woman to take the baby to the hospital immediately he would die. The soldier went over to look at the baby and said, 'I am going to get a doctor.' He returned with a doctor two hours later. The doctor checked the baby immediately and requested permission from the soldier to take the mother and the baby to the hospital.

Just as I felt relieved for them, the loud screaming of a woman in the next room pierced through the air. I immediately went to see what was happening, and saw a heavily pregnant woman screaming in pain.

'She was suffering from labour pains and was on her way to the hospital with her sister when she was stopped by the *minbings*', said an old lady standing next to her.

'Oh for God's sake! This is ridiculous, this poor woman should be taken to hospital immediately!' said one of the men said angrily, before shouting, 'Soldier! Soldier! Come here to help this woman! She's giving birth!' More people joined in his call. One of the soldiers hurried over and shouted one after another, 'Look at this poor woman - she is in labour! She should be in hospital! What if something happens to her and the baby? What crime has she commited to be treated and suffer this way? Don't you have mothers or sisters? There is no justice or value in this life any more!' More and more people complained and petitioned for the woman and her sister to be allowed to go to the hospital, and the *minbing*s had no option but to arrange transport for them to the maternity hospital.

I stood leaning by the window as a lady approached sobbing. She had passed through the room full of people to where I was standing. Her eyes were red and swollen and soaked in tears.

'What is the matter?' I said, reaching out to caress her shoulder gently.

'Oh my sister, I have three young children, and my husband collects wood from mountains and sells it in the city to support our family. He was out in the mountains when someone from the local council called at my home to tell me to fill in a registration form. I thought it wouldn't take long so I locked my children in the house and went, but when they learned that I didn't have a city *hukou* I was detained and brought here. I am so worried about my children. They were sleeping when I left. What will happen when they wake up to find out their mummy isn't at home? What if the little one falls from the sleeping platform to the floor and dies? Oh, what shall do? I'm worried sick!' She cried inconsolably.

'Didn't you explain your situation to them?' I asked but I could already guess the answer.

'I tried of course, but they won't listen to someone who doesn't speak Chinese. I feel so helpless, so worried!'

A man who was standing near us overheard and said, 'Come sister, let's go and talk to the *minbing*s. They might let you go.' Contrary to the first two ladies, this one wasn't so lucky: she and the man returned not long afterwards telling me that the *minbing* snapped at them, saying, 'This is not our problem, let them die! You must stay here!'

Trucks kept coming and going all night with people. By the morning the two-storey building was completely full of young and old people including children. Just after dawn a truck full of elderly men arrived; they had been detained at the mosque while performing dawn prayers. Looking around, I realised there was not a single Chinese person present. If the government was carrying out a *hukou* check, it was reasonable to assume that there must be some Chinese living in the city without a residence permit, so why were they not detained like us? It was obvious that this so called curfew targeted at the ethnic minorities only. It's most absurd that the so-called 'ethnic minorities' of East Turkistan, who actually actually outnumbered the Chinese living here, should be forced to register in a Chinese system in order to live on our own lands while migrants from Mainland China can live anywhere of their choosing without restriction and able to obtain *hukou* anywhere! My own people are restricted from seeking a better lifestyle in the growing urban centres filled with Chinese people and are now being locked up in closed schools, colleges, work units and other makeshift detention centres as all the prisons now are overflowing with non-Chinese detainees.

Yasin turned up and asked me to go out to the balcony with him from where I could see hundreds of people outside the school gates calling the names of their loved ones. Being away from the eyes and ears of the *minbing*s, he said to me, 'My brother is on his way to collect me with my sister Rabiye Hoshur's *hukou* booklet. He's getting you out of there too. When he comes and asks for my sister Rabiye, you must say that you are Rabiye. Do you understand?' I said yes, and he left. Around lunchtime his brother returned with Rabiye's *hukou* booklet and I pretended I was Rabiye. Luckily all went well and I was allowed to leave. My sisters too managed to leave with the help of other family friends.

My parents were relieved when we all returned home safely. My father said, 'Thank God, you all came out of that without being hurt! The situation is getting worse and we don't know what is going to happen next. The Chinese are creating chaos in this country by making various excuses to detain innocent people and send them to prisons or labour camps. You must go back to Nanshan tomorrow morning and stay there till the situation has calmed down.'

The next morning as I was waiting for the bus to Nanshan, I bumped into the team leader at Xigobi, Gülnisa. She hugged me tight and greeted me as if I was her best friend.

'We missed you so much, she said. The cadres often talk about you and Sajide. They all have the greatest respect for you girls and admire your courage. We all wish that we had foreseen what is happening now like you did. We would have done things so differently…'

Her words surprised me, but I did not make any comment. Instead I asked her where she was going.

'My mother has been very ill for many years and I was not allowed to have time off to visit her until my prison unit received an official document saying that she was in critical condition. Only then was I allowed to go home to visit her. I don't know if I will see her alive.' She said with tears in her eyes. As I was trying to comfort her I heard the call for the bus to Nanshan, so I hurriedly said my farewell to Gülnisa and dashed onto the bus. All the way to Nanshan, Guülnisa's words played in my mind again and again, and wondered if the cadres and officials really realised that independence was the only option for our people, and if they'd support any indenepdence movement.

Later I learned that during the military curfew in Ürümchi, over thirty thousand people were arrested, those who didn't have a Ürümchi residence permit were either imprisoned or sent to various labour camps.

July and the rest of 1969

Gheyshe one day told me that she had met Token, who told her that he was coming to visit me that evening. I last saw Token two or three days prior to the curfew, so I was excited to see him.

Token and I first met when I was a patient in No.2 Hospital. He was a graduate of Xinjiang University; his younger brother Kajay was my construction team leader. Both of them were members of the new East Turkistan Association. During our last meeting he had two other men with him; he recommended that I should flee to Soviet Union via Ghulja, saying that he could make the necessary arrangements. But I declined his offer because it would subject my parents and my siblings to severe punishment. I told him that I would rather suffer in the hands of these people than put my family in danger. He accepted my decision before telling me that he was going to Ghulja the following day. I was now surprised of his quick return.

I waited for him all evening. He finally arrived after midnight when electricity had been switched off. He was always very cautious of how and when he visited me, as he feared getting into trouble if others caught him visiting me. We had our conversation in the dark.

'I met our organisation's leaders before travelling to Ghulja', said Token, 'I explained to them your present situation saying that you would not be able to recruit any members. They agreed with my observations and asked me to tell you to keep a low profile and do nothing, as the political situation is getting worse. During the military curfew a large number of our people were turned in by traitors with the organisation, and were arrested and sent to prison. It has been decided that all the members of the organisation would stop further activities for the time being.' He repeatedly asked me to be careful and take care of myself before he finally left.

Two weeks later Sofiye brought a message from Yasin saying that Malik had been arrested along with many key members of our group. At this time members were being arrested everyday, exposed by people under interrogation and severe torture. Yasin also warned Sofiye that Malik might give them my name and said that I should prepare myself for the worst. I was devastated upon hearing such terrible news. Having thought that I had finally found the organisation I had been looking for all my life, the feelings of inspiration and motivation were now disappearing again. I couldn't imagine what would happen to me if they found out that I was a member. They would very possibly execute me this time. I shivered at the thought of this and said to myself, 'I will keep my promise no matter what happens. I will never admit anything even under the worst torture possible.' I prayed for God to protect me and all the people in the same predicament.

It was during this period that I learnt the events which occurred in Ghulja in April 1969. Iminov's two daughters travelled to Ghulja in a truck full of people in order to flee cross the border to the Soviet Union. It was rumoured that the Provincial Public Security Bureau was directly involved in arranging their defection. After arriving in Ghulja, the girls separated from the group and after some time, they managed to slip across the border. However ,the rest of the group who followed them in the truck at a later time were arrested during the military curfew; this also included the people who had looked after the girls while they stayed in Ghulja. Also, my future brother-in-law Igemberdi, who married my sister in 1979, was one of the many men who followed this route attempting to enter the Soviet Union. He was also arrested during the curfew and was subsequently imprisoned for 10 years. After serving his sentence he met my sister again and got married shortly afterwards. When my family and I immigrated to Australia in 1981, it took five years for my family to obtain permission for my sister and husband to immigrate because of his criminal record.

5 March 1970

I had a letter from a doctor at No.2 Hospital of Ürümchi stating that I was incapable of any manual labour work, and that I must attend the hospital for a check-up once every three months. As requested, I went to Ürümchi for a check-up and further treatment. But after two weeks I was summoned to return to Nanshan to attend a political studies programmeme. Having no choice I returned immediately. Not long after arriving home, the leader of the new working group Yang Zuorong came to my house, and his presence worried everyone.

'I want you to come with me to my office', he said, 'as there are some important matters that I need to discuss with you.' We left immediately. My heart jumped with the suspicions that he might have obtained some information with regard to my political involvement.

As soon as we arrived at the commune, Yang led me to his office and closed the door before sitting down behind his desk. I sat opposite him as he took out a notebook from the desk drawer. He started questioning me while reading the notes, asking me my name and the school I went to. I answered honestly. He then asked me the reason for my first arrest.

'I was involved in setting up an organisation to fight for the independence of East Turkistan.' I said it loud and clear, expecting him to become angry with me.

However, he showed no reaction to what I said. Moving his eyes from the notebook to look at me calmly, he said, 'There is some information I have received recently regarding your involvement in planning and organising people in this commune to flee to the Soviet Union. Is that true?'

I was shocked to hear this accusation and denied it categorically - 'No, that is not true! To be honest with you, I have never even thought about running away from here or assisting others to do that. I have my loving parents and beautiful siblings living here with me and they mean the whole world to me. If I flee, what would happen to them? My parents might be beaten to death, while my siblings would end up in deeper trouble. I'm a responsible person and I wouldn't do anything to harm the people who love me and whom I love. Think for yourself, do you know anyone in their right mind who would do such a stupid thing so as to put their own family at risk? Also how is it possible for me to organise anything like that in my current situation? Furthermore, how would it ever be possible to flee the country with so many people?'

Yang turned his chair around to rest his arms on the backrest. Leaning towards me and looking into my eyes, he asked, 'Are you a member of the East Turkistan Association?'

My heart started to beat faster as I tried my best to look and remain relaxed. Before I had even opened my mouth to reply, he said, 'If I were you, I would stick to my own decision. If I decide not to say certain things to people, I would never say it. If you don't want to say anything I will not ask this question again.'

I was puzzled by what meant and was uncertain how to interpret his words. The tactics he was using made me uneasy.

'Apart from the organisation that we set up at university, I have never attended or being aware of any other East Turkistan Association', I replied calmly.

He looked at me for a while before saying, 'Well, I have received a number of documents regarding your involvement in such organisation. If what you have said is true then I am going to destroy them. I repeated my answer once more. He didn't question me any further, but treated me respectfully instead and spoke to me in a very friendly manner for the rest of the meeting.

April and May 1970

After dinner I was talking with my sisters when two *minbing*s suddenly entered the house with my father following them. This was a big surprise. All of us ran to him and hugged him with joy. The house was filled with the sound of happiness. After the *minbing*s left I asked my father what had happened and why the *minbing*s had escorted him home.

'Two days ago I was at home alone, little Musherrep (my youngest sister) who was out playing rushed in to tell me that two policemen had arrived by motorcycle and sidecar outside our gate. The girl was so terrified that she was shaking like an autum leaf. The policemen came in and asked me to go with them. When the motocycle set off, Musherrep jumped onto my lap, one of the police got off the motocycle and dragged Musherrep off, got back on the motocycle and drove away. I was taken to the Petroleum Institute in Nurbagh and locked up for two days. The institute has been turned into a detention centre, overcrowded with detainees. Many of them have been there for over a year. The conditions were so poor that there was no begging, no food and no washing or toilet facilities. People are there for no reason at all.' We listened to him attentively. Our father noticed the nervousness on our faces and said, 'Don't worry about me, my children, they are not going to do anything to me. I arrived in the commune two hours ago to be questioned by the leaders who are investigating Qabdal and Salik. They spoke to me hoping I could provide information regarding their criminal activities but I told them that I didn't know anything. That's all.'

'Dad, why didn't you expose them? It's about time they were punished! We all know they have exploited people and bullied many families. You should have told them everything!' We said one after another in frustration.

My father said, 'My children, you don't know anything about politics. One can be right one day and the next day everything changes and you are wrong. It is better not to get involved with these power-hugry people. Let them find the answerers and deal with the problem themselves. Remember the saying: "When they ask - Have you seen a camel? You answer – no!" Avoid trouble, my children. No let's forget these unpleasant things, have some tea, and enjoy our family reunion.'

One day not long after I had returned home from work, Ablimit, whose father is the head of the production team, entered our courtyard where I was collecting some water. Although he is friends with my brothers and sisters, he has always kept his distance from me and I had never spoken to him. He looked around the courtyard nervously to check if anyone else was there, and was relieved to see there were only two of us. Feeling more relaxed, he said, 'Söyüngül, I am here to discuss something with you.'

'And what would that be?' I asked.

'Orazan has sent me to see you as we need your help. We want you to tell the investigators that you are solely responsible for all the illegal activities that have taken place in this commune in order to save everyone else from punishment. As you are a branded criminal so it will not change anything in your case, at the same time it will save many people from imprisonment or hard labour.'

What a shameless bastard! What a bunch of cowards! They wanted me to be the scapegoat for their actions? No way!

'No, I will not accept or take any responsibility for your actions', I said angrily, 'People must be responsible for any action they have taken and believe in their just cause. I am not willing to pay the price for something I have not done. Excuse me, my brother, but I cannot help you.'

Looking extremely embarrassed, Ablimit left the house immediately in a hurry. I was totally taken aback by his approach - how could people even consider opening their mouth to ask such a 'favour'?

Two weeks later I was summoned and told to stay in the school near the commune, there were already about eighty people who had been brought there from different production units to attend a political studies meeting which was to run day and night, aiming at forcing people to confess their 'crimes'. I was the only woman among so many men who had been detained as suspected members of the East Turkistan Association. The key target of this meeting was Mr Hamit, the dead teacher of the Chewchizi Primary School, who was accused of being a member of the East Turkistan Association and responsible for recruiting new members.

We were divided into two groups; each group had to interact and declare their crimes individually during the day time meetings while in the evening the two groups would join together to criticize the key members. In our group the targeted person was Mamakan; he was forced to reveal his relation with the head of the Forestry Department, Abliz, who was detained in the Ürümchi head office, accused of being a member of the Association. Mamakan's families were very close friends with Abliz's family, and for that reason alone he was pressurised into revealing information about Abliz.

Mamakan a funny man in his fifties. His wife was the daughter of the midwife Reshide, so everyone in the commune knew them. Each time when he was asked about his relationship with Abliz he always answered with the same response which made everyone burst into laughter –

'What relationship could we possibly have? I have over forty chickens and my wife collects all the eggs in a basket and takes them to the Forestry Department for sale to the families there. She uses this money to buy groceries. Abliz's wife is Uyghur, my wife is also Uyghur. When Abliz's wife asks my wife to visit her home, she happily goes there. He has five boys and I have five daughters. That is our possible relationship.' In the same fashion, no one provided anything about the Association during the meeting. When people were forced to confess their crimes they only talked about their everyday routine.

In the third week of the political studies programmeme, the head of the investigation group Tang Zurong was suddenly taken by the police to Ürümchi. We later learned that he was imprisoned for being a member of the Free China Movement. A new investigation team replaced the old one, and this new team was extremely aggressive. However, no matter how much they tried to force people into confessing their crimes, they had nothing to say.

One morning we entered the classroom and saw a large poster hanging on the wall; it was a list of the names of the criminals who have received death penalty. There were seventy of them in total, over sixty of whom were non-Chinese names whose crimes ranged from being anti-revolutionary to simply being a 'traitor'. The few Chinese names on the list were declared to be 'murderers'.

That was the third poster we had seen over the recent weeks. The number of people being given the death penalty shocked me, as only a few weeks ago they had sentenced 19 people to death to be followed by 29 more a few days later. All those were of ethnic minority origins, the youngest being only eighteen years old. Teacher Gheni's son Dolqun from Ürümchi, and Hemze, an elderly religious man from the commune were among the 29. Teacher Gheni was one of the most respected teachers in the community; his son Dolqun's crime was being a key member of the East Turkistan Association. I heard that Dolqun's brother and his friends secretly moved his body from the criminal graveyard to the Yanan Road Graveyard one night. Soon after Dolqun's execution, Teacher Gheni fell ill and passed away.

Hemze was originally from Kazan, Tataristan. He moved to Turpan, where he helped build schools with Heyder Sayrani and taught there for a few years before moving to Ürümchi. He had spent all his life teaching in East Turkistan, but ended up as an 'anti-revolutionary': one day the *minbing*s raided his home and hung a huge portrait of Chairman Mao above the *mihrab*. After the *minbing*s left the house Hemze removed Mao's Portrait because he was unable to perform his prayers under the eyes of Mao. The *minbing*s returned the next morning to find the portrait of Mao had been removed, so they arrested Hemze and took him away. The next thing we knew was that he had been sentenced to death for being an anti-Maoist.

One month later another poster appeared with the names from the last poster who were sentenced to death. Only this time had the court changed their charges from being members of the illegal East Turkistan Association or anti-revolutionary to violation of state regulations or robbery.

Countless men and women disappeared during this period after being taken away from their home or work places, and no one knows what's happened to them. Rumour has it that the majority were killed during the detention or after being sent to labour camps.

The political study and denunciation meetings lasted well over a month. Unable to find any evidence against the accused, we were all allowed to go home in the end. No one questioned myself regarding the East Turkistan Association, and I was very relieved.

10 June 1970

At lunchtime I asked permission to go back home quickly to see my father. On arrival I found my sister's son sitting on my father's lap in the middle of the courtyard; my father looked very sad and subdued. I asked him if he was alright and if my sisters had returned for lunch.

'I don't know, my child, I don't know', he said slowly, 'I've been having this very bad feeling today. I can sense something very bad is about to happen. The neighbour's chicken called out like a crow at our gate this morning, I chased it away but it made me feel anxious. It was the same chicken I saw acting in the same way the day Musabeg was detained and taken to the detention centre; you remember he committed suicide three days later. This is not a good sign, I am worried and not feeling well.'

'Dad, it's just a chicken. Everything will be alright. Try not to think too much about it', I said trying to make him feel better. But deep down I was unsettled and worried as well, and his words echoed in my ears the entire afternoon.

After everyone returned from work, we were sitting at the table and about to have dinner when a black jeep stopped in front of our house. We all got up from the table and went outside as my uncle's wife Mehpuze and her daughter plus two other relatives got out of the vehicle looking gloomy and quiet.

'What's happened?' we asked anxiously in unison.

'It was your Uncle Zeki Abliz. He died today', said Auntie Mehpuze with tears in her eyes, 'He was beaten so badly yesterday and was taken home unconscious by officials from his work unit.'

I felt dizzy for a moment. I remembered when we were working together, he used to say, 'Hopefully this government will change it's policies for the better. I pray that you and I will see better days.' Now he will not live to see the changes and the better days he'd hoped and prayed for. I prayed in my heart that he'd rest in peace in heaven.

I was very upset thinking about how an innocent man who had lived his life giving to others could be so brutally murdered. It hit my father harder as he was the only brother he had left, we all felt the grief for my father's loss and the pain he has feeling so deeply at this moment.

His funeral took place in Ürümchi, attended by all our relatives, friends and associates. His sudden tragic death left a huge hole in our hearts.

20 June 1970
The 'Down to the Countryside' Movement

I returned to Nanshan three days after Uncle Zeki's funeral. My father and my sister Firdews returned ten days later. My father looked thin and pale; he was a broken man. Seeing him in such a sad state of mind and health made my heart bleed.

When he saw me he updated me with the latest political situation before I asked –

'Ürümchi is in chaos today, my child. The central government issued new orders forcing families to leave their homes within days to go to the countryside. "Leave the City! Develop the Countryside!" is the new slogan', said my father with a shaky voice.

'They are taking away the cities from the ethnic minorities, forcing them to the rural countryside in order to make more room for the new migrants from Mainland China! They are now occupying our homes and our cities. What a good strategy!' I said angrily.

The Chinese authorities had achieved its goal conveniently by launching the so-called Cultural Revolution, which the goal of enforcing communism in the country by removing capitalist and traditional elements from within the Chinese society. In East Turkistan, however, the revolution made it convenient for the Chinese authorities to victimise all the ethnic minority officials who had power to implement minority-specific policies and protect people of non-Chinese origins. Teachers, doctors, artists, and all those with an independent business or business background, along with religious scholars and successful farmers had all been targeted. The majority of these were being killed during the numerous denunciation meetings, through detentions, labour camps and high security prisons. These government policies made it easy for the Chinese to fill all the empty positions with their own indoctrinated people.

The 'Down to Countryside' Movement was implemented throughout China but in East Turkistan it was an excuse to remove 'ethnic minorities' people from the cities and replace them with Chinese people from Mainland China. Young graduates, along with students who were still in the process of finishing their education, were exiled to remote villages and mountain areas to 'learn from peasants' – the most advanced social class in Mao's eyes – as if people hadn't experienced enough hardship under all the unfair and brutal policies implemented. With people now out of their homes, the government confiscated their properties without giving them a penny of compensation. There was no housing where people were exiled to, so they had to put up with living in camps under severe weather conditions as they struggled to build somewhere to live. Furthermore, the influx of people from the cities into poor rural areas put a strain on the limited resources. In the meantime, the authorities encouraged and forced more Chinese to go and settle in East Turkistan, where they were housed and employed within the cities, receiving a 'Subsidy for Living on the Frontier'.[49] These new settlers were ordered to take all of East Turkistan's natural resources, over- and underground, and to transport them to Mainland China.

---

49   *The Chinese name for the territory referred to by many as East Turkistan, 'Xinjiang', literally means the 'New Frontier'.*

February 1971

I went back to No.2 Hospital for treatment. My health was deteriorating again as a result of the extensive heavy labour work I was involved in. After finishing treatment I went home. Seley Abliz was visiting my parents. He greeted me warmly and said, 'I've come here to tell your parents what I had heard about you and I am so glad that you are here. I heard a very interesting story about you today. I was walking in the street when I noticed a large crowd opposite a building, listening to a story-teller, so I joined them out of curiosity. He was first speaking about the double-bladed sword of Ali – "The sword was so sharp that one touch could shove off the head of his enemies." He talked about Islam and bravery of Ali, but in the end he said, "At this present time we have brave girls like Söyüngül, a Tatar girl who has survived so much torture and mistreatment. When the enemy trampled on her until she couldn't move, and they believed that she was dead, she would arise and stand up as if nothing had ever happened. God is protecting her like an angel. Once she was trapped under a large tree which had fallen over, everyone thought that she was dead, but to the people's astonishment, she walked out alive." I was surprised to hear people praising you and talking about you as a legend in the street, and thought I must tell you!'

'Stop making fun of me!' I laughed.

'Seriously! I wouldn't have believed about this story if someone had told me about it, but I heard it with my own ears!' Seley Abliz said with a sincere look in his eyes, and continued, 'Let me tell you something else. When you were working in Qizilsay, did you not see twelve horsemen that visited the place where you were working?'

'Oh yes, I remember them.'

'Exactly. They went there because they had heard that you had been beaten to death. Also, while you were working for the No.5 Production Unit, two men visited you there to see how you were doing, it that not correct?'

'Yes, it is correct', I replied.

'That's it then. I know that you are going through a time of tremendous hardship but please remember, you have a special place in people's hearts. You should be proud of yourself. Nothing will be in vain. You are an inspiration to whole nation, especially women. I also heard that one man from Dongsen was beaten up by some mysterious men, and the man was questioned about your welfare. They asked him if he was involved in your being beaten to death. He told them that he had never heard of you. After they let him go, and was too scared to go out for days.'

After hearing Seley's words, I suddenly remembered Kenjitay's recent visit:

Kenjitay is one of the most active pro-communist members in the commune. Normally he always keeps as much distance from me as possible, and won't even walk past our house. He is illiterate, and doesn't even understand the meaning of the phrase 'Cultural Revolution'. Despite all these, he's active in carrying out the orders of the commune leaders without questioning them. One day he visited my home. I was so surprised to see him. After entering the house he sat down on the edge of the wooden platform looking at me in embarrassment and said –

'I have come to you to apologise for my behaviour in the past. Our people are like cattle - wherever you lead them they follow. I used to follow every order given by the authorities and have been involved in torturing you and many others. I sincerely ask for your forgiveness and promise that from this day on I will not harm you. The authorities always told us that you and your friends were the enemies of the people, and if any of you were beaten to death we didn't have to worry about the consequences. I believed it stupidly. We were consistently urged to be brutal. So I carried out what I had been instructed to do and that is why I inflicted such pain upon you. I beg for your forgiveness. Please forgive me!'

I didn't know what to say at the time, I was completely speechless as what he said was so unexpected. Since my arrival in Nanshan I had hardly seen any friendly faces or heard any kind words spoken. His apology really shocked me. I said to Kenjtay, 'It is just like as you said you are also a victim of the system, but you are still one of my own people and I will not blame you for what has happened.'

Kenjitay continued, 'Thank you, Söyüngül, this means a lot to me! You know that I am a very simple person with very little education. I carried out the orders without thinking or questioning them. When I was ordered to beat someone, I did, because I thought I was doing the right thing. When I last visited Ürümchi I was kidnapped by a group of people and taken to a room where I was tied to a chair before getting beaten up by them. They were shouting, "Were you involve in beating Söyüguül to death?" I said, "No, she is not dead, she is alive!" And they went on, "Can you swear on your life that what you said is true?" I said, "Yes, I promise." But they asked again, "Were you involved in beating her?" I replied, "No." And they said, "You are a liar, we know you did. You a lying bastard!" Then they kicked and punched me one after another.

'I couldn't stand the pain and shouted, "I was told to beat her, so I carried out the order. They said she was an enemy of the people so I didn't know I was doing anything wrong. Please understand and forgive me." I begged and begged for their mercy, but they wouldn't stop.

'I thought I was going to die but they stopped and said, "Don't ever lay your hands on her again! Also you must pass on our message to your masters – if anyone dares to harm her, we will come after them one by one and finish them in the night." I promised them that I would do everything they told me to do and begged them to give me one last chance. I also promised to ask for your forgiveness. When they let me go, I only managed to walk to my relative's house which was nearby where I spent two weeks in bed recovering from my injuries.'

I didn't know whether I should believe him or not at that time, but after what Seley told me, I believed he was sincere. It was and still is comforting to know that there are people protecting me without my knowledge.

On the night of arriving in Ürümchi for medical treatment, I was about to go to bed when I heard a heavy knock on the door. My mother answered the door nervously –

'Who are you? What is the matter?'

'We have come for your daughter, the one who lives in Nanshan.' I heard a woman's voice reply.

I quickly put on my clothes and walked to the doorway. I saw Meriyemnisaxan and Tursunay in the door opening, as soon as they saw me they said to the Chinese official, 'This is her.' The two women were known to everyone as the most active communists within the commune. Like Kenjitay, they had not been to school. I always knew that they watched me closely and reported all of my movements to the commune officials. They had little idea about the world except for life in a tiny mountain village. There were many illiterate naïve people in this society who are easily manipulated by the state to become useful tools in achieving their political goals. When the same naïve people are given the temporary power and incentive to go against their own people, they use the power violently without any hesitation. Some pro-communist activists pulled down the minarets of the mosques, forcing people out of the mosques and confiscating the Holy Quran from the people and their homes before setting fire to other religious books. None of the Chinese were involved in any of these incidents. If all of us had united as one and refused to do anything against our religion, the state policy would not have been pushed through. If they had wished to implement religious controls they would have had to carry it out themselves instead of using my fellow muslim brothers and sisters.

Two Chinese officials escorted me to the local committee compound; the courtyard was full of people, and I had to squeeze through the crowds to enter the office. The cadre's faces were like blocks of ice; as I walked in they demanded my name and my crime. I tried to explain to them that I had a medical appointment at the hospital and that I was returning to Nanshan the next day, however, they didn't pay any attention but shouted at me aggressively.

Approximately one hour later, twenty armed soldiers forced us into the back of a truck at gun point, ordering us to bow our heads to the floor and threatening to kills us if we dared to move.

After driving for a while, the truck stopped and the soldiers jumped out to surround the truck once again. With their heavy machine guns pointed at us, they ordered us to get out. We were herded into a large courtyard where we were ordered to stand in a straight line against the wall. Looking around to check where we were, I managed to read 'Art School' on the wall. As there was no lamp near where we stood, we remained by the wall silently in darkness. No one noticed us as I watched people passing in group after group escorted by some fourteen to fifteen-year-old Chinese *minbing*s who acted like thugs, pushing and kicking innocent people while shouting obscene words at them.

Another truckful of people arrived. They were quickly disembarked and taken into the building. An old couple fell behind the group looking confused. The old woman looked around and asked in a loud and frightened voice, 'Darling, where are we?' Her husband replied, 'I have no idea. It is dark, I can't see the place properly.' Then the old woman complained, 'My dear, I need the toilet and I can't hold it any longer. Please keep a look out for me.' Then she squatted down to carry out her business. They were about two metres from us. One of the men in our group suddenly coughed, which startled the poor old woman who stood up quickly, saying, 'Oh dear, there are people near us! How terrible!' Her husband tried to reassure her, saying, 'Don't worry. I can't see anyone.' Just at that moment a guard came out from the building and shouted at the old couple to hurry up. The old man held the woman's hand as they slowly walked up to the building. At that moment I realised that the woman couldn't see properly and the old man had hearing difficulties. It upset me so much to see the disabled and elderly were treated in such a way.

Fully loaded trucks were arriving one after another, I wondered if there was enough space for so many people. I then heard screans of agony coming from inside the building, it was clear that people were being beaten by *minbing* thugs. My heart sank.

We remained where we were in the dark silently until someone in the group coughed, which drew the attention of one the Chinese guards who were passing by. He came closer and saw us, and immediately ordered the *minbing*s to take us towards the buildings in the inner courtyard. As I was the only woman in the group, a guard escorted me to a large hall on the left hand side of the building while the men were escorted to right hand side.

The hall was filled with women and children and was very cold. Many armed guards were pacing back and forth in the middle of the room and were constantly shouting at the women for them to sit down on the floor made of bare concrete. It was very uncomfortable to sit on it, as the cold from the concrete got soaked immediately into your body.

There were quite a lot of women in the room with two or three young children. The poor children, who had been standing with the adults in the cold, looked tired and hungry, and as a result they would not stop crying. One soldier could not stand the noise any longer and ordered the children to stop crying. The children did not understand his language or listen so he kicked one of the children aggressively, which upset the mother a great deal. She stood up and shouted at him, 'What kind of soldier are you? Why is this innocent little child here and what has he done to you? I don't believe you have ever studied the Party's policy.'

'Ha! I will teach you the Party's policy right now!' the soldier responded with a terrifying roar and started hitting the woman with the butt of his machine gun until she fell unconscious. The children were so frightened that they did not dare to cry out loud, but sobbed quietly. Some women came forward to shout at the soldier to stop; they tried to reason with him but he responded by hitting them. In the end, many women were bleeding from cuts in their heads while others from their noses.

'That was a lesson for all of you. If you dare to move or moan one more time I will shoot all of you dead!' the soldier shouted triumphantly.

Ayshemxan, who was sitting next to me, spoke quietly –

'Look, Söyüngül, there isn't even a single Chinese person here. But if you look at the ones who have so much power over us they are all Chinese! We, the owners of this land from ancient times in history are becoming homeless. They can now herd us anywhere they wish like cattle whenever they want. They are turning this beautiful land of ours into the biggest prison on earth and we are their prisoners. Where is the justice in this?' I remained silent, not knowing what to say.

I spent three nights in the cold hall with screaming children. In the end, I was allowed to leave after my family brought the doctor's note and the permission letter from the commune allowing me to travel to Ürümchi for medical treatment. I was told to leave Ürümchi on the same day. I went to the coach station to find no coach to Nanshan, so I took the last coach to District 5, from there I got a lift to my sister's house in Sarichoqa.

When I arrived they were about to have dinner, everyone was very excited to see me. After dinner my sister and her husband Sabit went to attend the evening political meeting, leaving the children with me. I fell asleep with children and didn't even wake up when my sister and husband returned.

'What shall we do?' I heard my sister saying quietly and timidly.

'I am going to have to tell them everything. I must reveal everything, otherwise we will be in great trouble', Sabit replied.

I sensed something serious had happened. So I got up from my bed and asked, 'What is the matter?'

Sabit sighed before answering my question in a shaky voice –

'The meetings are becoming very serious. We were told today that they already have knowledge about the organisation we have been involved in, they are asking everyone to come forward and reveal everything, otherwise they will arrest us and put us in prison. I think the only way for us to get out of this problem is to confess everything.'

'Which organisation are you talking about? Are you involved in one?' I asked, astonished.

'Yes, I have no choice but to tell them what I know. Zeki Hoshur's son was arrested a few days ago, accused of being a member of the organisation. We were later told that he had hanged himself in the detention cell but we know clearly that he was tortured to death. I am very worried that the same thing will happen to us', Sabit said in distress.

I noticed that both my sister and Sabit were shaking with fear. I brought some hot water in a pot with some cups for them to drink and said, 'Calm down, don't be afraid. Confessing is not the way to save yourselves. You will only put other people's lives in danger. Also, by confessing you will admit that you have done something illegal, which in the end will be used against you. My advice to you is if you have joined an organisation you must not admit anything even if they say that they know. They may know nothing but say they know something - it is one of their usual tactics to get people to admit they are guilty. Don't fall into this kind of trap. Stay calm and act as if you know nothing. If they already knew everything they wouldn't have asked you to reveal what you've done. I personally believe that they don't know anything, but only suspect something. That said, even if they do have information against you, you should still never admit anything or reveal other people's names. Revealing others' involvement will not do you any good.' I tried my best to talk sensibly in order to stop them from doing anything irresponsible.

After listening to what I had said they both promised to remain silent. Not long afterwards they were called to go back to the meeting. Returning two hours later, they looked far more relaxed.

'Söyün, God sent you to us at right time to give us the right advice and guidance. Otherwise I would have made the biggest mistake of my life and caused so much misery to many families. Thank you. You were right - they don't have a clue about anything', said Sabit happily.

My sister said, 'I can't stop thinking of Zeki Hoshur's family, I can't imagine what they have been through at the moment. No one dares to visit them since Hüsen's death. They buried him on their own, without a proper funeral.' My heart ached so much when I heard about the brutal killing of Hüsen and the unfair treatment the family had received from the people around them. So I decided to visit them straigh away; it was late, but much safer compared to the day.

They welcomed me warmly, offering me tea before they started to tell me about what happened to Hüsen during his detention –

'My son was tortured so badly that his legs, arms and ribs were all broken. Bruises and blood covered all his body and his skin was torn apart. He was beyond recognition. It was impossible that he could hang himself. They killed him!' Zeki Hoshor said sobbing. There were no words to describe their pains. They were in such a state of sadness that I knew any words of comfort from me would be powerless. I simply sat and listened to them, and left their home just after midnight.

I left my sister's house early the next morning to make my way on foot to Gangu, the commune where I was residing.

30 December 1971

It was another long and hard day. I returned home exhausted after work. Gheyshe walked in smiling - it was a pleasant surprise to see my sister as she had been staying in Ürümchi for sometime.

'I've brought you the most precious gift', she hugged me, then pointed at the door, saying, 'Look!'

I looked at the door as Sajide walked in. I couldn't believe my eyes! I was completely petrified with joy and stared at her before opening my arms wide and ran to her. Unable to control our emotions we both cried holding each other. She looked frail, and fatigue was written all over her face. I could tell she had been going through a tough time.

We chatted the night away, Sajide told me about her miseries while being under the surveillance regime as a 'class enemy'. She had suffered all these years exactly the same way as I had. When I asked her about the scar on her left eyelid and the red spots in her left eye, she explained that on one occasion, when she was paraded on the streets of Chöchek along with many others branded as 'class enemies', she was beaten fecrociously by thugs; one of them slashed the left side of her face so violently that she nearly lost her sight in the left eye; it took many months before she could see clearly. Her mother was also branded as a 'class enemy' at the same time and detained in her work unit.

My heart ached as I listened to her experience. In the end, I took her into my arms and said, 'My dear friend, whatever has happened is now all buried in the past. I believe the worst is over. The important thing is that we both have survived. So I am still grateful to God, who has preserved us with our great dreams and goals. It is most wonderful to be alive and to see each other again!' We then discussed the future and both agreed to start seeking justice for the unfair treatment we had received over the years.

Sajide stayed with us for three days. On her departure she asked me to meet her in Ürümchi as soon as possible. I promised her that I would find a way to meet her at the earliest opportunity.

1972

I went to see Dr Oysing to get a referral letter to the hospital in Ürümchi. That was the only way I could ask for time off. After carrying out some basic checks, Dr Oysing said, 'I know you have been treated very badly over many years, it is now time for you to find a way out of this misery. You are the only person who can do this. The government's policies are now changing and things are returning back to normal. They are correcting many unjust cases; a lot of cadres who were imprisoned or sent to labour camps unfairly are now returning to their old positions. My advice to you is, don't return immediately after your hospital treatments, stay in Ürümchi and take the opportunity to lodge appeals. You must go to all the relevant departments to tell them your story and try to seek justice. If you don't do that you will be treated as a slave forever.' He then wrote me a sick note to take to the commute officials.

I was so grateful to have met such a kind-hearted doctor. He had come to Nanshan after graduating from Sichuan Medical University three years before I was placed under the surveillance regime. He was kind and compassionate young doctor - despite me being a 'class enemy', he treated me with respect as if I had once been his classmate. He helped me whenever he could. He married a Chinese girl in 1970, but was later removed from Nanshan clinic to a different clinic far away.

It took one month for the commune officials to make a decision on whether to allow me to travel to Ürümchi for treatment or not. I was lucky to be given one week off, so I immediately left for Ürümchi.

As planned, I met up with Sajide the next day and went to the Public Security Bureau. Sajide told me that she has been to the Public Security Bureau a few times but was thrown out of the office by a Uyghur officer named Musa Isa, who was in charge of the Department of Investigation.

We knocked at the door; it was no other than Musa Isa who opened the door to let us in. he was a short, fat, and angry-looking man. He looked at Sajide with annoyance before saying –

'I told you not to come to this office again. Why are you here?'

I spoke before Sajide could answer, 'Brother Musa, we were told that you are the person who is in charge of investigation of criminal cases, and that is the sole reason we've come here to see you. We need your help with our cases, if you please. We were wrongly accused of crimes that we were not involved in.'

Musa Isa looked at me coldly and said, 'Are you here to try to clear your names? Your ideas haven't changed. Go back to the commune and work under the surveillance of the masses.'

I was angered by his dismissive attitude. Raising my voice a little, I said, 'Brother Musa, You officials taught us that there are fundamental differences between Reform Through Labour and Education Through Labour. Those who were given Education Through Labour won't lose their rights. However I have lost all my rights over the past ten years. You placed us under the surveillance regime, and we were treated worse than animals.'

'Pah! Are you here to question the Party's policies? Or are you here to rebel against the Party's decisions?' Musa Isa shouted furiously.

'No, it is exactly because we respect the Party's policies that we are here to ask you to overthrow our cases. Are you going to punish us for that?' Sajide said.

Hitting the desk with his fist furiously, Musa shouted, 'Don't play smart with me! I can send you to prison right now without trial!'

'Good, we'd be pleased if you could do that. At least we would be free from the endless suffering, which we have endured all these years under your so called surveillance regime. It's a good decision, we are going to go and bring our belongings to your office right now', I said while standing up and walking towards the door.

'Stop! There is no place for you in the prison right now. Go back to where you've come from!' he shouted.

We visited Musa Isa's office daily to try to get him to review our case. He remained arrogant and rude, of course. We visited other departments that dealt with Education Through Labour, but we were told that our case belonged to the Department of Investigation, of which Musa Isa was in charge. In one of the departments one of the officials said, 'There are too many cases like yours, where people have been locked up for many years behind bars without charge. We know it is very unfair but there is nothing we can do.'

Having been unable to resolve anything with the Public Security Bureau, we went to the Medical University to get some advice. First we went to the Public Security Office of the university, where we were received warmly by Isa Rozi and Mr Ma, a Dungan officer. They listened to our stories patiently and with great interest without interrupting us, both of them were very sympathetic towards our experiences. They both agreed with us that it was wrong for the Public Security Bureau to place us under the surveillance regime. They said they needed to review the documents from the Public Security Bureau before they could advice us any further and asked us to return in two days.

Upon returning, Musa Rozi and Mr Ma said, 'We have checked all the documents. There was no official statement that ordered you to be placed under surveillance regime. This is good news, as you can now go to the Public Security Bureau and pressure them to review your case. Don't be afraid because you are not doing anything wrong.' Sajide and I were so pleased with the news.

It has been two months since I had arrived in Ürümchi, but I decided to remain here until I could see some progress regarding our cases. Sajide and I discussed different options on how to approach relevant people who could deal with this matter. We decided also to go to the Shabahu Labour Camp – the last camp we were in before being released.

We were about to leave the house for Shabahu, when Zohre, our former prison friend suddenly came to visit us. We told Zohre of our plans, and she said that the former team leader Turnisa and the governor of the camp Mr Atiq, were transferred to work in Bajahu Labour Camp. So we decided to go to Bajahu instead, which was located on the outskirts of the city, unlike Shabahu, which was far away from Ürümchi. We felt extremely lucky that Zohre was able to give us such vital information.

Upon our arrival, we managed to get inside the camp pretending to be Turnisa's relatives. Turnisa invited us to her house, where her kind-hearted mother greeted us and made us a delicious dinner. Turnisa also invited the prison governor Mr Atek to her home, where we told them of our experiences and the mistreatment that we have received since leaving the camp. We told them that there was proof of our innocence. Turnisa's mother cried when I told them of some of my near death experiences.

Mr Atiq said, 'I would like to help you but your files are in Shabahu. I will have to contact Shabahu first in order to review your files before I can proceed further.' We returned home without achieving anything.

The next morning we went back to the university to see Isa Rozi to seek further advice. He was standing at the door of his office when we arrived. He looked at us with a big smile and said, 'Girls, It is good that you have come. I was just wondering how to get in touch with you. An investigation team has arrived from Beijing to deal with similar cases as yours. Go and speak to them. They've given us permission to deal with your cases.'

Arriving at the Public Security Bureau's compound, we waited by the gate while Isa Rozi explained the reason of our visit. The guard at the gate took us to a red brick bungalow sited near the gate. The first room was a waiting room full of people. Isa Rozi went into the office next door and came out very quickly, saying, 'The officer has agreed to see us very soon.'

The door to the office was open, so I took a sneaky peak inside: it was full of people who had come to complain about the mistreatment they have experienced over the recent years. The office is surprisingly quiet despite the number of people in it; it looked as if everyone had sunken deep in their own thoughts. Their faces were blank and sad. I overheard a woman saying, 'My son was innocent, he was detained by his work unit and tortured to death…' She burst into tears before she could finish her story. Someone said, 'Sister, don't cry. Please try to stay strong. Take this letter to the People's Intermediate Court and hand it to [I didn't catch the name]. He is a very kind man and will definitely help you.' A minute or so later a teary middle-aged woman emerged from the office holding an envelop in her hand.

Isa Rozi then took Sajide and myself into office where a young Uyghur man was sitting at a desk listening to someone's complaint. Isa Rozi went up to the desk and whispered to the man before introducing me and Sajide to him and briefly explaining our situation. He turned to us and introduced the man in charge, 'This is Abliz, he is going to help you with your complaint. I'm sorry but I must leave now, but I want you to wait here until he calls your names.'

We waited as instructed, listening to other people's stories. Some complained about their forced removal from the city to villages where they have suffered great hardship; they were here requesting for the restoration of their city *hukou*. Others complained about their work unit and how they were unfairly removed from their posts. Some others told of how the work units unfairly branded them with a criminal title and how, as a result, they suffered many years of hardship.

Then it was a Kazakh man's turn to relate his story: 'My child, I have never owned a herd of animals, never been rich in my life. At the start of the Cultural Revolution I was wrongly accused of being the owner of a herd of animals. I've been through hell because of that. There are no words to express my sorrow and pain. I was branded a *muzhu*,[50] and you know, this was branded with hot iron onto our backs just as if we were animals. You can see the brand now.' Then he took off his shirt to expose his back. I saw the burn marks on his skin, which clearly showed the Chinese word *muzhu*. Everyone felt sorry for this old Kazakh man, and some in the audience could not hold back their tears. Abliz stood up to walked over to the old man feeling his scar and looked distressed and affected by what he was seeing and hearing.

The old man slipped on his shirt and said, 'I was only too happy that the word *muzhu* was short. I can't begin to describe the pain some of the others endured when burned with the long words of their criminal titles. They suffered from their burns for months and many of them became infected, which made it more difficult to heal. One of my friends died from the infections caused by the wound...'

His son added, 'Brother Abliz, the branding didn't stop with my father but was imposed upon all our family. Because of this we became outcast and were blacklisted. As a result we were not accepted by schools and couldn't find any job. We were restricted in everything we wanted to do. Still now I can't even find a wife, as all the girls are frightened of being married to the son of a *muzhu*.' His son added.

The room went quiet. Abliz looked exhausted – he must have heard enough of all sorts of terrible heart-breaking stories. He sat silently for a while after they finishing registering their case. Looking at the man with deep sympathy, he said, 'Uncle, please take this letter to the provincial committee. Someone will assist you there.' The old man

---

50   *Chinese for 'cattle owner'.*

took the letter from Abliz and thanked him before leaving.

A woman who was sitting not far from me spoke out of her turn –

'When I went to the regional government offices in Ghulja file a complaint, there was a middle-aged Kazakh man who had come with his father, who looked very ill. They were from Mongol Kure. The old man was there to make a complaint with regard to his son who was brutally murdered during the Cultural Revolution for his involvement in the Eastern Tukistan anti-communist movement. He said, "My 22-year-old son was arrested by the authorities, and while in detention he was tortured to death. He was tied up tightly with a thin flax rope and beaten ruthlessly. The following day when the rope was untied his body was scarred by the indentations of the rope. His flesh was puffed and damaged to the extent that he was unable to sit or lie down. When he was restrained with the rope the second time and tortured, he died in agony. My wife was unable to cope with the brutal death of our son and died within a year. My health has also become worse ever since the tragic loss of my wife and son." I had no control over my mind as I pictured the suffering of this family. I felt sick. How cruel can human beings be to others! What haven't we experienced while fighting for our very basic human rights. My heart ached for all those who had suffered and then being murdered in such brutal ways.' Abliz then told her that the people she talked about had been there to see him, and he had referred them to the People's Intermediate Court.

It was now our turn. After we finished telling him of our experiences, Abliz said, 'I am going to refer your case to the Public Security Bureau where all your files will be reviewed before they make a decision. A lot of files went missing during the Cultural Revolution, so it may take some time before you can hear anything from them. If you don't hear from them, you must go and make enquiries there.' We thanked Abliz and left.

Two weeks later we went back to see Abliz, the waiting room and his office were packed with people as usual. We were in the waiting room for two hours, and one more hour in his office before it was our turn to speak to him. While waiting in the office we heard many similar cases, but one couple's story really shocked me –

They were sitting at the front, the woman looked to be in her forties and the man in his sixties. When it was their turn to speak the lady introduced the man next to her as her husband. I was shocked as I thought he was her father because of how old he looked. I looked at the man very carefully and realised that it was his long beard and clothes that made him look much older than his age.

She continued, 'During the Cultural Revolution my husband was arrested and tortured daily. They forced him to confess his crimes, although there there was no crime he was guilty of. He was detained in his workplace. I made many attempts to visit him in vain. One night when I was sleeping I heard a knock on the door. At first I thought it was my husband and thought he might have been released and come home. But I started shaking with fear as at the same time, thinking it could be someone who had come to tell me that he had been tortured to death – at the time I'd hear everyday from friends and family that so and so had been tortured to death.

'I walked to the door and asked who was there. It turned out to be Ahmet, who worked at my husband's work unit, 'Sister, please open the door!' he said in a very distressing voice. I opened the door and asked, 'Brother Ahmet, what has happened? Has it got something to do wih my husband? Is he safe?' He said, 'Sister, they beat him so badly that he fell unconscious. They thought he was dead so they took him to the graveyard and buried him alive!' When I heard those words I lost my balance but managed to lean against the door. At this point, my 15-year-old son woke up because of the noise and came running to grab hold of me asking what had happened. Ahmet said to him, 'Listen to me my son, they have ordered us to bury your father, but I know that he is not dead. I purposely did not place too much soil over him and because it was dark they could not see what I had done clearly. If we go now we can still get him out alive. However remember one thing, you must keep absolutely quiet about what I have told you. Don't ever mention to anyone that I brought you the news about your father.

'It took me a while to think straight as I was in complete shock. My son quickly got dressed and was holding the spade ready to go. I quickly put on some clothes and rushed to the graveyard where my son dug with the spade and I used my hands. There wasn't a lot of earth so it didn't take us long to get him out of the hole. Oh, he was still breathing, thank God! We replaced all the earth to make it look like a grave again before leaving. We carried my husband home in the dark and have kept this a secret from everyone around us. I looked after him for a month at home until he recovered. We didn't dare to keep him in the house long, as it was too much of a risk. So we travelled to Turpan overnight by train to my husband's sister's house. He changed his appearance and his name to look like this. My husband has lived secretly in various remote villages in Turpan, Toqsun and Pichan for over two and half years. We used to visit him once a month to provide him with living expenses. Later as time passed by I managed to make up a story about my husband's older brother coming over from a village to have treatment at a nearby hospital so that he could come and stay with us at home. We have been through a lot of hardship over the last four years. I am here now to make a complaint against his work unit. I want an investigation conducted into what they did to my husband and why. I was told that my husband had run away from the detention centre and they could not find him!'

Abliz asked the man, 'What crime did you commit which made them want to kill you?'

'I didn't commit any crime. But they accused me of being a 'capitalist-roader' and of fraud; also I had a cousin and some other relatives who lived in Ghulja that had fled to the Soviet Union during the Ghulja Border Incident, so they interrogated me in order to provide them with information about our relationship. They then repeated all the crimes I had been labelled with and they forced me to confess by torture.'

'So were you ever involved in fraud?' asked Abliz.

'No, never!' replied the man firmly.

'Alright. We are going to send an investigation group to your work unit to obtain more information before we can do anything about your case', Abliz said and asked them to come back to see him in two days time.

It was now our turn to speak to Abliz who told us that he handed our complaint Isa Musa at the Department of Investigation – the very same man who asked us to go away on day one of our odessey to seek assistance.

Sajide and I visited Isa Musa's office almost daily for six weeks but we didn't receive any information. During this period I was asked to go back to Nanshan on two occasiosns, but luckily this was refused by the chief of police, Haris Abliz, of the County Public Security Bureau. He told them that I needed to remain in Ürümchi while the current investigation was being carried out.

One day in June, I went to see Musa Isa again, he said, 'Sister Söyüngül, we have failed to locate your files in the Public Security Bureau, so we've ordered Shabahu Labour Camp to forward us your files, which I have finally received. After reviewing your files, I have concluded that you weren't branded as a criminal and as such you were not ordered to be placed under the government's surveillance regime, but under public watch instead. I am going to send your files to the County Public Security Bureau.'

It was the first time that Musa Isa had spoken to me in a friendly manner, calling me 'sister' with a smile on his face. Unlike the first time when he threw me and Sajide out of his office like dogs with the most hostile attitude. During this recent month his bullying attitude had changed dramatically.

I was so excited upon hearing the good news after all this time that I couldn't sit still. I said to him, 'I am going to the County Public Security Bureau now, so can I take the files to them in person?' He looked at me with a smile saying, 'I am sorry, but that is not allowed. They must be delivered by a trusted member of the police force. But don't worry, your files will be delivered this afternoon. You can go to the County Public Security Bureau tomorrow.'

I went to the County Public Security Bureau early next morning, hoping that they would now confirm the good news. As I entered the office the Chinese police officer looked at me and said in a cold voice, 'Why are you here?'

My excitement from the previous day's news vanished at once. It was like a bucket of icy water had been pour all over me. I was convinced that my name would never be cleared.

Looking into his eyes I asked, 'Yesterday when I visited the Public Security Bureau, they told me that they would send my files to your office, have you received them?'

'Yes, we have received them. But we have sent the files to the Provincial Public Security Bureau because, although in the current files it said that you were branded as a class enemiy, the files we received about when you came out from prison was different. It clearly stated that you *were* a class enemy, so we placed you under the surveillance regime according to the information we had at that time. The Provincial Public Security Bureau should find the original files, which they have to send us for review them ordering us to correct anything. We only recognise the original files and not the new ones', he answered coldly.

I left the office with a heavy heart and returned home feeling downcast. I remained in Ürümchi for another six month, going from one department to another trying to find a solution to the problem. Just before 1 October, China's National Day, we received a warning that the government was going to impose another military curfew in Ürümchi, and anyone who was not a resident of the city would be detained. Sajide and I discussed the options of possible places to go. In the end we decided to go to Turpan because we both had relatives there and also it was far away from Ürümchi.

We packed some clothes and went to the main market area to find a way to go to Turpan. After making many enquiries, we managed to find a truck going to Turpan. The driver agreed to take us for a very cheap price. We got into the back of the vehicle which had already accommodated twenty more people, of whom six were young children. It was so crowded that there was no space to stretch out our legs.

We left Ürümchi early in the evening, as we drove along the valleys the wind became stronger. I immediately felt the biting cold. We had forgotten to bring any blanket with us, as we didn't realise how cold it would get on the back of an open truck as it travelled through the night. The children cried constantly throughout the journey, adding additional agony to the hardship we were enduring.

Arriving at Turpan located about 150 kilometres southeast of Ürümchi the next morning, we received a warm welcome from our relatives. On our first day we rested and enjoyed the freshmade food and the famed fruits of the region. The following day we visited the Emin Minaret built in late 18th century. At 44 metres, it was the tallest minaret in China. The next day we were taken to see the Bezeklik Thousand Buddha Caves – a complex of Buddhist grottos dating from the 5th to 14th century between the cities of Turpan and Shanshan[51], north-east of the Taklamakan Desert in Mutou Valley, a gorge in the Flaming Mountains. Most of the surviving caves date from the West Uyghur Kingdom around the 10th to 13th centuries. We also visited the *karez* water system,[52] which was built about 800 years ago. We remained in Turpan for a week before returning to Ürümchi. Upon our return I learned that a large number of people were arrested and detained during the military curfew, which took place two days before the National Day.

October 1972
The man of my life

One day Sajide asked me to go with her to her sister's house for dinner in Shandongbei where she was staying. When we walked into the house I saw a young tall slender man sitting at the table, he was fair skinned with deep black eyes, thick eyebrows, and volumous dark hair. He immediately stood up and greeted Sajide in a very friendly way. Sajide introduced us, saying, 'This is Latif from Chöchek and this is my friend Söyüngül.' We exchanged some pleasantries before sitting down to dinner. After dinner I spent some time talking to Sajide's sister in the kitchen, leaving Sajide and Latif talking in the dining room. It started getting dark so I said to Sajide, 'It's getting late now. I think I'd better leave before it gets too dark.'

'We're going to accompany you home', Sajide said cheerfully. The three of us set off chatting, when we reached Shandongbei, Sajide said, 'Söyün, would you mind if I went back home now? Latif is going past No.3 Hospital so he will be able to accompany you from now on.' I told her that it was fine with me.

It was a bit awkward to be left with a stranger, but he started a conversation, which

51   *Near the famous ruins of the ancient Kroran (Loulan) Kingdom, the earliest residents of which were the Tocharians, an Indo-European people.*
52   *A canal-based irrigation system invented in Achaemenid Iran and spread to Central Asia.*

made me feel that I had known him for a long time.

'My stepmother is in hospital. She was injured by the *minbing*s at the height of the cultural revolution. Now she's been looked after for some time and her health is slowly improving. She's the only close family I have left apart from a cousin. My mother died in 1960 in hospital after being given the wrong medication. In March 1969 my father fell ill and was diagnosed with terminal stomach cancer. They tried to treat him but it was too late. I took him home to Chöchek and he passed away on the 1st of October...'

'I'm sorry to hear that', I said in order to comfort him.

He sighed before continuing, 'We were a large family. My father's got six brothers and one sister, and my mother has two sisters and two brothers. Now all of them are living in the Soviet Union, including my only brother. They fled during the time of the Chöchek Border Incident in 1962.'

He stopped talking for a while and looked at me with a smile.

'I am so pleased to have met you, Söyüngül.' His compassion and sincerity for his family touched me deeply as I thought about his losses. I didn't reply to him and simply smiled back.

We walked in silence for a while, then he looked at me shyly and said very softly, 'To be honest, I really like you.'

I looked into his face with shock as he continued, 'I don't want to offend you, but... I would like to walk the road of life with you till the end.'

This unexpected request shocked me into saying, 'No, no, no! That is not possible! I have been in prison, you know. Also I am a class enemy living under the surveillance regime. In the present circumstances it is not possible for me to marry now... or in future.'

He just looked at me, relaxed and smiling, 'Yes, I know all of that and have known it for a long time. But I would like to be with you during theses difficult times and support you regardless of what may happen. If they send you to to prison again, I will go as well!.'

I was moved by his sincerity.

1973 – 1976
A marriage in the family

It wasn't long before I introduced Latif to my family, who liked and accepted him. When he asked my parents for my hand in marriage they were over the moon and agreed. Latif returned to Chöchek to apply for permission to marry and hoped to return in January but he returned at the end of March. His work unit had refused his marriage request, stating that I was not a suitable person for him to marry, as I was a criminal against the state. Our marriage was only made possible when one of his old friends who worked in administration obtained a blank stamped letterhead from the work unit and wrote him a permission letter in Chinese, which allowed him to obtain the marriage certificate. In April we had a traditional wedding where all our family came together to celebrate.

On the 29th of April I went to the County Public Security Bureau to enquire about my case review. On entering the office I saw Mr Haris Abliz, the official who had intervened the year before for me not to be sent back to Nanshan while I was waiting anxiousy to hear from Musa Isa in Ürümchi. I heard that he was an acquaintance of my father's, but had never had a chance to meet him till now.

He looked at me with a smile and said, 'Söyüngül, great news for you – we have heard from the Provincial Security Bureau. They issued a statement saying that you and Sajide are not convicted criminals and therefore you are no longer under the surveillance regime. I have destroyed all the compromising documents, so there's only this one document left in your file. Also Nanshan Commune has been informed to this effect. From now on you are a free person. Let's forget the hardships of the past and look forward to a happy future. I wish you all the best!'

My face lit up as my heart beat with joy. I smiled and thanked him as I left the office before running home as quickly as possible to tell my family this wonderful news that all of us had waited so long for. The day turned into a festival for Sajide and my family.

Sajide had been married to Rabin Shakirov, a Tatar from Ghulja who had brought love and happiness into her life like Latif had for me. Now they are expecting their first child, which brought immense happiness to myself and made me think that one day I would have a child, too.

On the 23rd of May, my husband Latif, my sister Zekiye and I left for Chöchek. We were able to get a lift from Latif's friend. The journey took us three days as we stopped at various places on the way. On the final day we stopped at the Dark Cave on the border with the Chöchek region, where we washed our hands and faces in the river before exploring the area. We followed the flowing water down into the valley, as we walked along its banks. The water was crystal clear and we could see through to the bottom. We were surrounded by a luxious dense forest, which the sunrays could hardly penetrate, which is how the area got its name. The forest extended for miles and miles, and the valley was a huge rug made of a multitude of coloured flowers; the birds sang their happy songs around us, and as the light fell, the nightingales broke into a chorus of lovesong. I was completely charmed by the beauty, but, although I wished to linger, we had to set off again since we had promised to be at Latif's home before the night settled.

Arriving at Chöchek, I noticed that the town was largely a place of single-storey buildings. With the exception of one building nicknamed the 'Red Tower', which belonged to the wealthy family of Hesenbay Janishif, there was no other attractive construction within the city. There was only one main road in the city and the rest were all mud tracks.

The city give the impression that it had been deserted after a war as there were very few people in the streets, although it was only dusk. We arrived at what was called Liberty Road. As we entered the road, a number of girls and women came out from the first house of the street and stopped us, cheering and shouting in a singing tone, 'Where is the bride? Where's the bride?' I looked on in amazement: out of the crowd two women and one man came and asked us to stop while they went to get the bridal money; we remained there as people from other streets gathered calling for the new bride to be seen by the folks of the town, as it was the tradition of our people. After ten minutes or so we started to move off slowly but this time we had people hanging on to the vehicle, so that we moved as if we were being pulled at the speed of a handcart, while other people followed on behind. Upon reaching a small bridge I heard melodies being played on accordions and people singing softly, which rose to a crescendo as they saw the car approaching them.

Latif looked at me and smiled, 'Söyün, welcome home. Look at all those people over there - they are our extended family and relatives. They are all here to welcome you.'

I felt an undescribable joy. The people's greetings and music made my heart beat faster, and I felt shy about not knowing anyone. Latif noticed my awkwardness and said, 'Söyuün, don't be shy. They are all family. Relax and smile as you usually do.'

The vehicle stopped close to the large wooden gate as the musicians led the crowd of people over to the vehicle. Latif's cousin Raziye opened the door to hug me with teary eyes; she escorted me to the courtyard where people greeted me while others threw flowers and sweets, singing as the musicians played wedding songs. The atmosphere was that of absolute bliss.

The courtyard was quite large; I was led across it to find the traditional two-metre wide white cloth laid on the floor which the bride must walk on to enter the groom's house. I crossed over the cloth, fulfilling the wedding tradition to enter my new home. The inside of the house was crowded with people who once more threw sweets and flowers. Then I was led into a room next door, where food had been laid out for our guests. We sat down to eat and talk, while I was introduced to everybody before our guests left later that evening.

I was to be come close to Raziye as well as her husband, who was a spiritual, kind-hearted man. They had three children, two boys and one girl; the girl was preparing to enter the Medical University while the boys were still attending primary school and high school. It was with the help of Raziye, who quickly became like my own sister, as well as her family, that I settled so quickly into my new home and married life. The worries I had before the marriage, that I would not be able to get used to my new life, was quickly dissipated, as Latif and I shared the same values and dreams. We were always able to understand each other's opinions and settle differences in a way that pleased both of us.

Chöchek was a small place in which an easy-going community. Gossip, unlike elsewhere, was nearly non-existent. People enjoyed helping each other, and it was this kindred spirit that helped us establish a good family life at this early stage of marriage. The simple and straightforward locals were always ready to afford assistance and advice. By the end of two weeks I had already made friends with all my neighbours. Although some of them were from different ethnic backgrounds and spoke different languages, they all spoke in the Chöchek dialect of Uyghur and accepted by the local people as their friends and companions, unlike other areas in the country such as Nanshan, where suspicion, rejection, and conflict were common.

Then our first child, a boy, came to the world. We named him Azat, a request made by my father because it meant 'freedom'. My father said the name would encourage common people to embrace the political ambition of East Turkistan. As soon as he was born, my husband telegraphed the news to my family so that they too could share our happiness. Azat's arrival brought great joy as he fulfilled our lives, which was to be complemented by the arrival of his sister two and half years later. Our children saw endless love and were growing up beautiful and healthy, and those days were some of the happiest memories of our married life.

In 1975, I asked Latif why he had not fled to the Soviet Union in 1962 like many others. He replied, 'That is a long story, but let me tell you what happened at that time, starting with my family and relatives –

'On the 5th of April, Sajide's brother, along with a few other friends crossed the border. He was followed a few days later by his uncle, his uncle's his family, plus a few other friends. In the beginning people would take few possessions with them and in some cases would get up from a meal and just leave. Later, however, people would try to take all of their possessions. A trickle at night became a flood during all times of the day – the number of people fleeing soared as defectors started to come from other regions.

'The local government initially turned a blind eye to this, but was now finding it hard to tolerate the situation. Therefore the regional government of Chöchek imposed restrictions on the movement of people, saying that all illegal immigrants crossing the borders would be forcibly repatriated. This information was distributed throughout the region. Before this change of attitude, my father had decided to follow the government unwritten rule, which was basically, "take all your possessions if you can and if not we will assist you, as long as you don't come back". At that time my father was encouraged by others to join them in the exodus, and told the family that we were leaving. My brother and I, along with members of our extended family, accompanied him on what turned out to be a nightmare journey from Chöchek to the Soviet Border. We had all our belongings with us, including the animals we owned, and we set off on horseback. The seven-kilometre trip took an entire day.

'At the border, we waited for three days for our documents to be checked as there were thousands of people in the queue. It was at this point that my father said, 'I must go to Tuli for your stepmother.' – as you know, he had remarried after my mother passed away. I worried about him travelling on his own, so I said I'd go with him. He agreed and told my brother to cross the border with the rest of the family and we would join them later. We set off on our journey immediately on horseback with a spare horse for my stepmother. On the way we stopped at Dorbojun, there my father noticed we were being followed. He immediately made the decision of going on the main roads, which were more populated.

'When we finally arrived at my stepmother's house, the police arrived to tell us that we could not leave until they give us their permission. This was granted in May after the regional auothorities imposed new rules on the 30th of April forbidding the border crossing. We had no choice but to travel back to Chöchek, which was now a ghost town with so many families having left – you could walk the street in bright daylight and see or hear no one. It was at that moment that I realised it was the people who made Chöchek the warm place that I remembered, and I started crying and missing my family members who had left. Of the many Tatar families who had live here, only 13 remained among the handful of Uyghur, Kazakh, Dungan, and local Chinese families. It was now a broken community. Our large wooden family house with its three bedrooms was eerily quiet.

'With those families that stayed behind, we arranged to meet regularly in order to support each other. My cousin Rabiye was so distraught by the loss of family and friends that she would constantly break into tears, but life was indeed miserable – we had nothing but the few families left behind in Chöchek to come to our aid, giving us bedding and cooking utensils along with any other necessities they could manage to spare.

'During this time students who were studying in Ürümchi and other cities were sent back to Chöchek or other places if their families had gone to the Soviet Union. They were told that they would be reunited with their families by the Soviet government, but sadly this never happened. We still wonder if it was because the Russians refused to accept them or if it was a ploy of the Chinese government to get them out of the universities before they were able to finish their studies – you know, many of them were forcibly relocated to the Shihezi Construction Corps. At the same time, Chinese families were brought from other regions of China to be settled in the empty houses here, which had been abandoned by their owners and requisitioned by the government, and this was a common policy throughout East Turkistan.

'The Chinese peasants who arrived with nothing found that they now owned spacious houses with ready-made orchards. But they were so badly informed about the region that they placed breaks over the wooden floors and made the windows smaller, believing that it would make the houses warmer. Orchards were also chopped down to make way for vegetable plots. Opposite my home there used to be one of the largest orchards that had belong to Taji Osman, one of the richest locals; but after the family had left, it was divided between ten Chinese families who removed all the fruit trees to make way for vegetables which they then sold. The city became quiet as the birds left as a result of the loss of their habitat. I was lucky to find work in the local tractor factory, which kept me busy and helped distract my mind from what was happening. And then the Cultural Revolution started, and our lives were turned upside down. A lot of the locals of non-Chinese backgrounds were being accused of being dissidents or Soviet spies. As in other parts of East Turkistan, public denunciations, torture and imprisonment also took place all across Chöchek and no family was left unaffected.

'In 1969 I was reassigned to go to work in Shihezi Construction Corps, about 500 kilometres away. At that time my stepmother was sick after the ill treatment she had received at the hands of the tormentors at work, and my father had just been diagnosed with stomach cancer. My father immediately wrote a letter to the Tractor Factory, stating that he was terminally ill and didn't have long to live. In the same letter he also questioned why our family was being punished for *not* having fled to the Soviet Union. He said that he would like my transfer to Shihezi to be cancelled so he could have me close by during the last days of his life. They agreed and decided to transfer me to the blacksmiths department instead. This would entail me having to work twelve-hour shifts, seven days a week. On the 1st of October, my father passed away, which affected me greatly. My stepmother sank into a state of depression after the loss of her husband, coupled with the constant pressure at work.

'One day I returned home for lunch to find chickens in the forecourt and the house door left open with the table still set for breakfast. Looking around, I couldn't see my stepmother and started to worry. I sensed that something wasn't quite right. I rushed out to the street to look for my stepmother. I saw Ms Merheb's son Hemit running in my direction out of breath. He said, "Brother Latif, I have just seen your stepmother in the street wearing only her nightgown and without her shoes or headscarf. People were kicking and punching her and dragged her by her hair all the way to her work unit. We must do something!"

'I ran into the house and grabbed my mother's clothes and headed off to her work unit as quickly as possible to find my stepmother tied to a chair in a room; her hair was everywhere and her face was badly bruised and swollen. Her pyjamas that she had been wearing were in shreds and you could see bruises all over her body. She was crying uncontrollably. I broke down and shouted at them, asking them why she had been beaten so savagely. Their answer was: "This traitor wanted to run away; she was running in the direction of the boarder when we caught her." I said, "How could this have been possible? How could she have run away in bright daylight without even being dressed properly while everyone was watching her every move? Don't you see that she is not well? Didn't you stop and think that if she were her normal self she would never go out in just her pyjamas and certainly not without her headscarf and shoes? She has not slept for days and as a result she's exhausted and has lost her mind. She needs to see a doctor for treatment instead of being locked up here!" And then they accused me of "siding with the traitor". They shouted at me and started punching my stepmother again. I ran over to her and tried to protect her from the violence, but they dragged me out of the room. It was unbearable to witness such cruelty from these young thugs against a weak elderly woman. I wished I could stop it, but it was impossible, and it pained me not to be able to stop this injustice. The image of my stepmother being tortured has haunted me for many, many years.

'I was told the following day that my stepmother had been imprisoned. I immediately took to her some clothes and bedsheets. I visited her weekly with nutritious food for the entire year that she was there. My stepmother's mental state deteriorated so quickly that she finally ended up in No. 1 Mental Health Hospital of Ürümchi. It was there that she slowly recovered before being sent home a year later.

'During that period a distant relative of mine, Ahmet Abliz, was arrested for telling a dream he had to his next-door neighbour. The dream was that a bolt of lightening struck East Turkistan burning all the portraits of Chairman Mao and destroying all his statues. He commented that this was a sign that change would finally happen and Mao's downfall was imminent. Within twenty-four hours the security police arrived at his home and beat him up in the most brutal way. He was then taken to the local police station where he was sentenced to ten years hard labour. His family was forcibly removed to Shihu and his home, together with the fruit orchard with a hundred apple trees was confiscated by the Security Bureau, which proceeded to cut all the trees down and built accommodation for its own personnel.'

Latif stopped for a moment and sank into deep thoughts before continuing his monologue –

'The border incident and the Cultural Revolution have destroyed not only what was a beautiful city but the lives of so many people. The fragrance of the city has been lost to the smell of vegetable plots and the use of human excrement waste. The cultural change has destroyed what had been an idyllic urban landscape built over many centuries. The fruits and flowers along with the singing birds are gone. Forever...'

My husband's story reminded me of what, Ms Mehbube, an acquaintance of mine from Mongol Kure, a town on the Soviet Border, had told me about the Ghulja Border Incident –

'One morning we woke up to find out that all our neighbours were gone. About fifty families had disappeared overnight. We could only guess that they had fled to the Soviet Union. Our house was located along the river, which is the only thing that separates us from the Soviet Union. Three days later I woke up in the morning to be surprised at seeing one of my neighbours in their yard milking the cow. So I got dressed in a hurry and went to see the family.

'I was invited into their home where they told me what had happened: after crossing the border, they were very happy about having managed to escape, but they were stopped by Soviet Border Guards and told to return. They begged the Soviet Guards to show mercy for their children but the guards were very harsh and paid no attention to their plea. For two days and nights they negotiated with the Soviets and on the third day, they were told by the guards to get in a truck used to transport coal, heading to Almaty, and they felt relieved. However it was a trap – before they realised, the truck had driven them back to the border and dumped them there. They screamed and started running after the truck in desperation, but the guards released the dogs to chase after them. They were frightened and ran towards the river seeking safety. A number of old men and children were attacked by the dogs as the rest of them jumped into the river and tried to swim across. Some people drowned in the process. The ones who survived finally arrived on the opposite bank in the dark.

'We all know from our experience that the Soviets can not be trusted and there is no one in the world willing to help us.'

Later we learned about what did happen to those who fled to the Soviet Union: when they passed the boarder the Soviet Guards searched them and took away anything valuable. They took away their children and housed them in orphanages in the remote regions of Russia and sent the adults out in the hills and mountainous areas to look after their cattle. These people were forced to live nomadic lifestyles for over five years before being allowed to settle within the local community. Some parents were eventually able to find their children. Latif's older brother was sent to a remote mountain alone and he lived there as a herdsman for over three years; later his uncle found him and married him to one of his neighbours. They had three children while living in that remote mountainous area before they managed to move to Tashkent and settle there.

Summer 1976
Mao's death

After lunch my parents who were visiting us went for a nap while I was in the kitchen trying to make my son Azat go to sleep. The radio was on and suddenly, it started to play mournful music; at the same time outside the communal loud speakers in our compound started playing the same tune.

I went outside to see what was happening. The streets were empty. I looked over the wall to my neighbours and saw their daughter.

'Have you heard that Charman Mao has died?' she asked me, shocked and confused.

'Well, I'm glad', I replied.

Not long afterwards one of my other neighbours came by my house asking if I heard that Mao was dead. I said yes. She then asked if I had black material with which to make an arm-band as it everyone had been ordered to wear one and to cry and not laugh.

Two days after Mao's death, all the people were called upon to gather on the town square for a memorial service in honour of Chairman Mao. It was hottest summer day I can remember, and many people collapsed due to the heat and the length of time they had to stand without moving. The crowds and lack hydration only made the matter worse. The local radio and the public notices stated that the people passed out due to 'their sadness at the tragic loss of Chairman Mao'.

1977

I went to Ürümchi to see my family. During the third week of my stay I was called to the local party office immediately. This was worrying for my family and me, as we didn't know the reason why.

Arriving at the office, I was met by two women. After a brief exchange of greetings they said, 'We are from the No.5 Primary School.' My heart missed a beat at that moment because Qeyyum was a teacher there. One of the women carried on talking, 'We are here to investigate Teacher Qeyyum and his involvement with the East Turkistan Association.' Then the other woman interrupted, 'According to the information supplied by him, you were recruited into the organisation by him approximately six years ago.'

I looked at them both in a relaxed manner before replying, 'I know nothing of what you are saying, nor do I know anyone called Qeyyum. I've never heard of such an organisation. Are you sure you got the right person?'

The women looked at each other before turning towards me saying, 'But Qeyyum knows you!'

'Well, that is completely untrue. Let me go and meet him and confront him now', I said firmly.

'No, there's no need', they quickly said, 'So you really don't know him. That's fine. We will go and make further enquiries and then we may talk to you again. In the mean time you can go.'

Luckily, I was never to hear from them again.

Since my siblings moved from Nanshan to Ürümchi, Sofiye had worked at No.5 Primary School. A few days after my interrogation, the school's head teacher spoke to Sofiye privately, saying that she had heard of my imprisonment, my suffering, and the praise given by others to my name, and he was saddened by what Qeyyum had done.

'Rest assured that all the documents and notes appertaining to your sister have been destroyed to spare her of any further hardship and suffering', she said.

I have lost all my respect for the weak-willed Qeyyum, but could not help but pity him as I learnt later that he had been removed from his post and sent to a remote farming village, where he is assigned to tend to the pig sheds.

Winter 1978

Latif had been unwell for a while and he went to Ürümchi for a medical check-up at the hospital. While he was away rumours started to spread that the Soviet Union was going to invade East Turkistan. These rumours were later confirmed by the government, and we were informed that the residents of Chöchek would have to move to other parts of the country.

One day I was visited by a group of officials from my husband's work unit, who informed me that all the workers and the families were to be relocated to Tömür Tam. They also said that, if I needed any assistance in packing and getting the children ready to travel that day, they would send someone to help me. I replied that I would not go anywhere with the children in this cold weather, and I must also wait for my husband to return home before we could move as a family.

This message was being passed down to all the families. A number of them started evacuating immediately. In preparation for moving, people started to make *talkan*.[53] Panic started to spread as Chinese families fled back to Mainland China with some Chinese officials sending their children away unaccompanied, only for them to end up in other towns and cities suffering from frostbites and hunger and requiring medical attention. In the commune near Chöchek, one family left with their two eldest sons leaving, their five younger children behind. During this period many abandoned Chinese children were taken in and looked after by local families of ethnic minority origins, while other Chinese families approached their ethnic minority friends with expensive gifts, asking if they would hide them if the Soviets shuld invade the country.

I also started to prepare for the move by making some cotton-padded clothing for the children. I went to see Raziye's house to use her sawing machine and saw that she was making winter clothes.

'Are you getting ready for war, too?' she said with a laugh, 'This reminds me of the Three Districts Revolution when I made padded gloves for the soldiers.' She then went on to tell me about that period of time.

---

53   *A flour and oil mixture, which is fried and preserved and can be eaten later by mixing with hot water.*

All the young men and young women went to the front to prepare for fighting while in Chöchek those that were left behind were allocated support work. The young mothers and girls knitted socks and made winter clothes, while the elder woman baked bread and did the soldiers' laundry. Old men were responsible for delivering the goods by horse and cart to the war zone. Although the work and hours were hard and long we all felt like one large family in trying to support each other. We hoped that by this concerted effort, one day would be free forever as the entire population of East Turkistan longed for that victorious day.

Everyone was worried about what the outcome would be if the war broke out in the depth of this cold dark winter. The war never broke out, but the people suffered mentally and physically at a time when life was extremely difficult.

In the same year, Latif visited a neighbouring village. Upon his return he asked me –

'Do you know anything about the 'Nanshan Massacre' which had taken place in 1973, when a Dungan soldier called Hushan shot and injured a lot of people? I met his mother today who lives in the village that I visited.'

This reminded me of what my sister Firdews had told me about a heroic Muslim soldier, as she was living in Nanshan in 1973.

At that time, there were four Chinese military units in Nanshan, one of which had four Muslim soldiers who had requested that they be given halal food. However this was refused and they were forced to eat from the Chinese canteen while being ridiculed by other soldiers. One night, the only Dungan soldier, Hushan was performing his duty as a night guard in the observation tower. Once left alone, he went to the armoury and removed guns and ammunitions from the building to the base of the tower. When it was time to change his guard duty, he told the oncoming Chinese soldier that he was not tired and that he would remain on duty and Chinese soldier went back to bed. Hushan then continued to empty the armoury and, at daybreak, he armed himself with a heavy machine gun before going to the officers' compound where he shot dead all nine officers. Returning to the observation tower he proceeded to shoot at anyone leaving the accommodation buildings, leaving dead, dying and wounded people everywhere. Although an urgent phone call was made to other army units and the three other Muslim soldiers were asked to stop Hushan from shooting further, they all failed to stop the massacre and to stop Hushan committing suicide afterwards. Afterwards, Hushan's body was publically displayed for people to vent their anger by stabbing it with a bayonet. The seriously injured from the massacre were transported to hospitals in Ürümchi, while the less seriously injured crowded the corridors of the Commune Hospital in Nanshan. It took days to bury the dead.

After the death of Mao, prisoners who had been sentenced to twenty to twenty five years for political reasons began returning to Chochek in small numbers. The once handsome teenage heroes had now become grey haired, grey bearded weak old men. Yet they were only in their early forties or even younger. It broke everyone's heart to see such dramatic changes in these courageous extraordinary young men, who with talent and courage had dared to stand up for their beliefs. They were the ones who put the future of East Turkistan before their own lives and for which they paid dearly.

The evil abusive system damaged a whole generation, which included the victims as well as those who were the power behind the barbaric policies. They now lived completely damaged, both mentally and physically after spending so many years in forced hard labour slaving in a harsh environment without receiving a penny. On welcoming their return, people found it difficult to hold back their tears as some managed to comfort them and make them believe that there is still hope in this life. In some cases, there was nothing for them in Chochek as their families had fled to the Soviet Union to avoid persecution during the darkest period of repression and victimization. There was nowhere for them to go or live, as their homes had been confiscated by the state. They were now homeless with a lost youth, health, and in a poor mental state. Along with these problems was the lack of financial support or a state house or a daily allowance. Also, they were unable to find employment having been labeled criminals and as such, it was believed they deserved nothing. At this time normal families were already struggling financially to support themselves.

One day Latif and I were on our way to do some shopping when we overheard someone cursing the Chinese Communists and Mao. We turned around to look back and Latif suddenly spoke saying, "hey, that is Heyrullam who has just returned from Tarim Prison, one of the harshest institutional prisons." As we waited for Heyrullam to catch up to us, my husband explained a little of his background. He used to work in a company as an accountant and was known for being conscientious, hard-working young man. But he was suddenly arrested being accused of fraud. His family home along with all his valuables and savings were confiscated by the state. And at the age of eighteen, he was sent to Tarim prison in the Taklamakan Desert before he was later cleared of all charges. The government repaid half the money they had confiscated from him but they refused to release him from prison. His parents fled to the Soviet Union and Heyrullm's case was left in abeyance.

As my husband finished telling me his story, he was now within speaking distance.

He was a medium built man who walked with the aid of a stick as one of his legs was deformed. He had a wrinkled face and grey hair. He was drunk and had the facial expression of a walking corpse. It was clear that he was sick of his present life and was using obnoxious and foul words as my husband tried to speak to him. My husband tried to calm him down saying, "you should not curse the Chinese and government policies, and certainly not Chairman Mao as this will bring about your return to prison." "That's what I am waiting for, I have nothing left to live for here! My parents have gone, I have no wife or children. I have nowhere to stay or a job to go to. And without money or health, how am I supposed to live! So what do I have to live for? tell me. They have taken everything I had and those cared about me the most." He replied bitterly as he sobbed like a child. I felt terribly sad for him and could not hold back my tears. No words could comfort him as we stood silently by.

One day Ahmet Abliz said to me, 'I went to see my musician friend Hüsen who had just come out from prison. He's now staying at an old Tatar shoemaker's place in Kardung. You know him? He's the accordionist. When I met him he looked old and in bad health, so I have invited him for dinner tomorrow. I would say that he is the greatest accordionist in the world. His music makes your heart sing!'

Before Ahmet finished speaking, Jaghar walked in and said while unbuttoning his coat, 'There has been a terrible accident in Kardung. Hüsen, the accordionist has been run over by a horsecart when the horse got out of control. I carried him along with others to where he was staying...'

'What? I was just telling Söyüngül that I met him and invited him to dinner!' said Ahmet in complete shock, 'Is he alive and where about was he injured?'

'Yes, he is alive. The cart passed over his stomach', Jaghat replied.

'I must go and see him now', said Ahmet, grabbing his coat and running out of the house.

The next day we have received the tragic news that Accordionist Hüsen had passed away. His friends and neighbours arranged his funeral, which many people attended to show their respects.

'Such a tragedy to come out of prison after 25 years only to die one week after under such terrible circumstances. It is almost as if he was meant to stay permanently in Chöchek. We will never forget the sound of his music. Ever.'

Hüsen was a well-educated and talented musician who was asked to perform for every wedding in the area. He was married to a beautiful woman and had two children, a boy and a girl. But then he was given to alcoholism. During the early years of communist reform, he was arrested for being an alcoholic, for which he was sent to the Tarim Labour Camp and stayed there for 25 years. His parents and wife appealed for his release but, failing to secure his release, they fled to the Soviet Union. During those long years of hard labour he must have longed to see his family only to return from one of the hardest labour camp to Chöchek, his hometown, to find that no one had stayed for him. He was not alone in that situation, however, as thousands of innocent people were wrongly imprisoned for extremely long periods and, upon being released, found only emptiness and loneliness in a strange society, having lost their youth, health, and families. In Chöchek, like in many other towns and cities in East Turkistan, the community worked together in trying to assist these poor souls sharing whatever they had such as giving them a room in their homes. The government, on the other hand, washed its hands of any responsibility for these people whom they wrongly imprisoned.

Also in the same year, Gheyshe came to visit us bringing the news that my parents and the rest of the family were going to emigrate to Australia. She explained that Seghit Abliz, a Tatar whom I had met while in prison, was now living in Autralia and was a part of a close knit community. Seghit had written to our father suggesting that with his help in processing the paper work through Hong Kong and Australia we should be able to emigrate successfully.

Gheyshe said, 'Mum and dad asked me to visit you to ask you also go to Australia with us as a family.' My mind was racing at this point as I thought about my country and it's people. How could I help them if I left? What would I be able to do for them a far-away land?

'I can't. Why should I leave my country and its people for a land in which I don't speak the language of and to start a life without any money?' I replied, a bit upset.

However, Latif's face was glowing with excitement as he looked at me saying, 'Well I think it's a good idea, as you are always being perceucted for your beliefs here.'

'Please, sister, look around you at what is happening. It's never going to change!' Gheyshe saw the opportunity and tried to convince me that the move would be good for me and the entire family.

I told them both that I would think about it seriously. Over the next few days I thought about the many times I had tried to find a job only to be refused, the last being the job of a street cleaner. I thought about the bureaucratic nightmare I had encountered in trying to change my *hukou* from Ürümchi to Chöchek after my marriage and how, failing miserably at this, I could only stay in one place for six month before having to move to the other. I also realised that I was unable to do anything for my people and my country here, but if I moved overseas there was a possibility I could write and publish a book about my experiences to reveal to the world the problems of East Turkistan and its people, calling on the UN and Free World for their assistance. Having considered all of these facts I decided it was the right course of action for us to take.

I said yes to my family. We proceeded to fill out the forms brought by my sister, and had passport-size photographs taken, which she took back to my father. After she left, it was the long wait – we lived in a state of uncertainty, not knowing if the outcome would be favourable.

May 1979

Having returned to Ürümchi I was invited to a party by some of my old medical school colleagues who were now doctors at local hospitals. While I was there I overheard a conversation by three of them who worked in the maternity unit.

'You are lucky to have developed high blood pressure. It will make it easier for you to retire earlier', one girl, Adalet, said to another, Kerime. 'Unlike me I can't find any reason to ask for early retirement, I might have to try bribing some officials.'

'Well to tell you the truth, I actually bribed some officials into issuing a fake document to say I had high blood pressure and, if God is willing I will receive my retirement documents on Monday', Kerime replied with a wink.

As I did not fully understand their conversation, I looked at them in a confused way. They turned around to me and said seriously –

'You know, Söyün, you are very lucky, having made the decision you did back at university you live with a clear conscience and people respect you. If you wonder what we are talking about, well, we are murderers; we are forced to kill one new born baby every day and carry that guilt with us is unbearable, and that is why we are seeking ways in which we can quit our jobs. Every hospital has been given a task of ensuring that one newborn child's life is taken everyday. A maternity unit which doesn't do that will suffer severe consequences, but if more than one child is eliminated, extra rewards would be given to that hospital as a whole…'

Their words sent shivers through my body.

'Oh my dear Lord! I can't believe what you just told me! How come the parents of the children don't know what is happening?' I asked.

Helime, the short chuby one of the three replied with a heavy sigh, 'Look, there is a notice at the entrance to the maternity unit saying: "No man allowed inside". So they must stay in the waiting room. And when the child has just been delivered and the mother has not recovered from the birth that is the time we've been told to administer the fatal injection. At that moment we inform the mother that the baby is stillborn. But the pain and guilt is so unbearable that we often can't sleep at night. If we don't fulfill their orders we will only be forced to kill more. That is why we are seeking retirement at under the age of forty. There are no other options for us...' As Halime finished talking she looked at the floor as if she was guilty of a crime.

At that point I asked, 'Are you told to only kill the non-Chinese babies?'

'No, as it doesn't matter what ethnicity they are. We just have to get on and do the job.'

'But hasn't there any compaints from the baby's parents, given that this happens regularly?' I asked.

'Once they are told by the doctor that the baby was dead they will normally leave the hospital in tears with the body of the baby and do not ask any more questions', replied Kerime.

The fact that our future generation was being destroyed by a heartless government shocked me profoundly.

June 1979

On the way back to Chöchek the coach driver stopped at Tuli to have lunch at a café. I remained on the coach along with some other women who didn't want to eat. As we were talking I looked out of the window and surprised to see Kamalbeg walking alongside the road towards the bus. I leaned out of the window and waved, and he looked at me in amazement before starting to cross over the road. I got off the bus to greet him. His eyes were shining bright as he greeted me warmly.

'I am so surprised to see you looking so well, Söyüngül! I have thought of you and Sajide every day, worried that both of you might not have survived the cruelty of the Cultural Revolution. I can't even begin to imagine what you girls must have been through.' There were tears in his eyes as he spoke.

'Thank you Kamalbeg, we are very well!' I said, before asking how he was and what had happened to him during the Cultural Revolution.

'I don't know where to start, because during the dark days of Cultural Revolution I was taken to the denunciation meetings where I was severely beaten and in some cases I was kicked so terribly and I collapsed. Once I regained consciousness I would be taken to the prison as the commune committee said they could not accept counter-revolutionaries in the commune. This happened in total 27 times. On the last occasion, my wife who was due to give birth to our child went to the hospital, but the doctors refused to treat her and she died giving birth. I was allowed out of prison for the funeral. Upon returning to the prison I had a mental breakdown and the prison authorities transferred me to a mental hospital where I stayed for a long time getting treated. When they saw I got better, I was discharged and sent home to find that it was not only I that had suffered but also my six children who had to fend for themselves because the commune wouldn't help them. We Kazakh people don't have education and are easily misled. To save our people we must educate them first! I've learnt that lesson the hard way, Söyüngül!' As he was saying this people stated get back onto the bus, so we quickly said our goodbyes as I rushed onto the bus before it drove off.

1980

In early 1980 we received news that our application for emigration to Australia had been accepted. Instead of rejoicing, my heart was sad at the thought of leaving my beloved country and its people.

We now had to arrange to sell our house, for which we needed permission from the local government. My husband made many visits to the Land Registry where he was told that, because the house belonged to us and the land belonged to the government, the property was only worth five thousand yuan in total. He refused to sell it at such a meagre price and therefore we remained in Chöchek while my husband visited the officials regularly to persuade them of the real value of the property before finally agreeing on the price of seven thousand yuan. We sold the house in late autumn and immediately prepared to leave. On our day of departure to Ürümchi all our friends and relations came to say their farewells. Our sorrow was beyond description.

Upon our arrival in Ürümchi, I was informed that some officials of the People's Intermediate Court had visited my family and wished to speak to me. I was deeply concerned in that they might bar me from leaving the country. Two days later, a man and a woman from the People's Court came again and walked in my house.

I welcomed them with a smile and asked them to sit down at the table. They responded to my greeting in a friendly manner.

'Are you Söyüngül, who was imprisoned in 1963 for setting up what was judged to be an illegal organisation?'

'Yes.'

The man then placed his briefcase on the table in front of him. He looked like a very experienced and knowledgeable person.

'So, as you may have become aware, there has been a change in government policy recently with regards to political prisoners who have received long term sentences. A number of your classmates who were imprisoned at the same time as you have appealed to the People's Intermediate Court regarding their unjust conviction which we are now reviewing and investigating. And that is why we've come here to speak to you.'

'I am aware. Go ahead.'

'Ok, are you the one who kept the organisation's documents?'

'Yes.'

'What documents did you give to Public Security Bureau?'

'A book - A Brief History of East Turkistan Up to 1912. It was printed in 1949 in Tashkent and used as a textbook while I was at primary school.'

The man turned his head to look at the woman in surprise and asked, 'Is that all that the Security Bureau has?'

'Yes, that is all they found after ransacking the house', I said calmly before the woman.

The man looked at the woman once again and then turned to me and said, 'That's good. This makes things much easier for us now. Do you remember there was a number of Kazakh students arrested just before you? They are still in prison and they appealed to us for our assistance. We tried to help them, but unfortunately all the documents appertaining to their organisation were in the hands of the Security Bureau. Therefore we were unable to effect their release given the evidence against them. As there is no written evidence against your organisation, we could immediately reverse all the decisions already made. Abliz who is still in Tarim Labour Camp has appealed recently, and it is his case we are dealing with right now. It is possible that we'll get him released within two weeks.' He then enquired why on my release from prison I had not appealed against my prison sentence and against being placed under surveillance regime.

I told him that I was worried about being punished for standing against the state. And that is why I pursued a course of action through the Security Bureau in trying to clear my name. I told him about being rejected from the Security Bureau's many times and treated worse than an animal for many years. I also told him about being threatened to be thrown into prison again if I kept 'harrassing' them, and that, when I urged them to send me to prison, my request was refused with the ridiculous answer that the prisons were full. I also told him that it was only with the help of university officials was I finally freed from the Nanshan 'commune', but it didn't stop the constant harassment, nor had it clearned my name enough for me to find employment.

'That's why I am emigrating to Australia', I said in the end.

At that point the lady, who hadn't spoken during the entire converstion, raised her head and looked at me in shock –

'Are you really leaving the country?'

'Yes. There's no other option for me left', I replied.

Two weeks later I was called to the office of the People's Intermediate Court to be informed that they had obtained all the necessary documents of the case and a letter had been sent to Tarim Labour Camp requesting the immediate release of my friends. They said to me, 'Once their release has been successful and they have returned to Ürümchi, we will take your case before the judge, where we will clear your criminal record completely and redress your grievances caused by misjudgement on the part of the Security Bureau. We hope that we will be able to assist you in getting back to what you were trained for as a free person you will able to get on with your normal life. We have written to the Public Security Bureau regarding the mistakes they have made, however as of today they have refused to accept their mistakes stating that their actions were implemented as your were deemed criminals against the state. Therefore we recommend that you and Sajide continue putting pressure on the Security Bureau with regard to this or we will take court proceedings against the Public Security Bureau.' I was extremely surprised at the last statement, as it sounded too good to be true.

Sajide and I visited the Security Bureau many times as advised, however it seemed impossible to change their minds. Finally on the day before I was due to leave for Australia I visited them once more and said –

'For 18 years we have worn the dunce's hat. It never goes away as it doesn't sag in the rain, doesn't get blown off by the wind, doesn't wear out or tear or fade over time in the scotching sun. It doesn't give us peace of mind or allow us a normal peaceful life. If you don't remove it I will have no choice but to leave this country wearing it, and I will not come back to you again!' I left the office with those words.[54]

---

54   *It was not until two years after the author's departure that her grievances were finally redressed by the Public Security Bureau. – the translator.*

Departure

As predicted, Abliz was released from Tarim Labour Camp two weeks after I was visited by the man and the woman from the People's Intermediate Court, and he returned to Ürümchi. He visited me at home the day after his arrival. I was overjoyed to see him. He had not changed a great deal – perhaps a little older, but still keeping his high spirits and enthusiasm for all things. We conversed for many hours, during which he told me that he had worked as a doctor in the labour camp and that was why he had been treated differently compared to other prisoners whose daily tasks was nothing more than long hours of hard labour work in all weather conditions. At one point Abliz escaped from the camp and on the edge of the Tarim desert he met a nomadic family who befriended him and treated him as the one of their own. After having lived with them for over a year, he suffered a heart attack one day and was unconscious for two days. Waking up, he realised the gravity of the situation that he was putting the family in and decided to return to the labour camp when he got a bit better.

He also told me of his experiences in the high security prison, where we had both spent time before our sentence. He said, 'When I was being interrogated I wanted to absolve you of any responsibility regarding the setting up of the organisation. When I told them that I was the sole person responsible for starting the organisation, the interrogator looked confused and said, "What you are saying is very strange, because Söyüngül has said the same as you. Unlike other prisoners you two are different; you do not blame others and are too eager to admit your responsibilities."'

After staying in the city for a week, Abliz left to visit his family. He later returned to Ürümchi and would visit me regularly. We would sit talking about the past and what the future would bring us. A week before our departure to Australia we said our goodbyes when he return home to get married.

The university academic committee requested to see me before my departure. I heard from them that some of my old colleagues were meeting in a room with their Kazakh friends so I went to see them as well. Arriving there I found Ahmet and Ghopur along with other Kazakh students who had been imprisoned for being members of an underground organisation. They were drinking and reviving their old friendships. Ghopur looked up from where he was sitting and simply asked how I was before continuing to look at the book he had been reading. He hadn't change much, still keeping his laid back attitude as if we had never been apart.

Ahmet simply said hello and ignored me, which was unlike the other Kazakh students who greeted me warmly and made me feel very welcome. A number of Kazakh friends looked at Ahmet and Ghopur and said, 'You should be thanking Söyüngül for destroying all the documents of your organisation which has given you the freedom today, unlike us – our documents are still in the government officials' hands and we are still fighting for our freedom from further persecution.'

I left them afterwards to go to the university office, where Mr Ghopur Réhim was waiting for me. He greeted me with a big smile and said, 'I have great news for you. Since all your troubles are now over, we'd like to confer you your doctoral degree, and hope you will now be free to seek employment without restriction. Also, the last 18 years which you've lost will be added towards your salary plan. I am very sorry for what has happened to you over the last 18 years and wish to apologise for not seeing the future like you did. You did the right thing at that time, and we were wrong for not doing anything until now. And I am deeply ashamed for having done nothing to help you. I am truly humbled by your determination to fight for our people.'

I couldn't believe what I was hearing, and my mind was in turmoil and doubt. Was I imagining what he said? I realised I wasn't as I looked into his sincere eyes. I said to him, 'There is no need to apologise, Mr Ghopur, it was difficult times. I hope that the whole nation will now wake up from the nightmare and see their future correctly.'

'Yes, you're right', he agreed with a smile. Stopping for a moment to think, he continued, 'Can't you stay here now to start a new life as the darkest years are over? It is now the time to enjoy a normal life, don't you think so?'

'If this had happened a year ago, my decision would have been different', I answered, 'But unfortunately it's a bit too late now. All the documentes have been sorted and my whole family have prepared to emigrate to Australia. We have to leave.'

'Of course. I understand you', said Mr Ghopur with a sigh.

He walked with me to the bus stop and wished me a safe journey and a bright future. He stayed there, waving me goodbye as the bus left.

Sitting on the bus, my mind was a mess as I contemplated what he had said to me. It's truly amazing how one's judgement can be changed by unexpected events of life. I thought of the incident of the broken toilet seat, which happened when Mr Ghopur was the students' disciplinary officer at the time of 'Thought Reform Movement' –

Obulqasim, a student in my year, was given a three-year prison sentence for breaking a toilet seats although he denied having been involved. A student with the last name Qasimov had claimed that he had seen Obulqasim carrying a large stone into his room, which 'must have been used to damage toilet seat'. His statement was accepted by the authorities and Mr Ghopur simply didn't investigate the matter any further. Later it was brought to his attention that two students, Sawut and Altunbeg, had been arguing over who should use the toilet first when the damage occurred.

It was later at one of the public meetings that those two admitted what had had happened. Despite their confession, Mr Ghopur failed in his duty again to correct the miscarriage of justice, as a result of which Obulqasim's education and future were ruined. It gave me mixed feelings to see Mr Ghopur's change.

On the 30th of September friends and families from near and far, including those from Chöcheck, Ghulja, and Turpan, came to say their goodbyes. Young people sat in the courtyard with musicians playing music and singing. Every room in the house was full of guests. The party had started early in the afternoon lasted throughout the night with endless laughter, songs and tears.

The following day many visitors queued outside the gate in order to get into the house. They were school friends, neighbours, colleagues and distant family members. In the afternoon, a jeep came to collect my mother and father to take them to the railway station. As they left the house and got into the jeep everyone started chanting religious texts of well being and safe journey. We followed them in buses, but that was difficult, as we returned time and time again from the courtyard into the house to say another final farewell to our loved ones and to look at our home once more. Finally with tears in our eyes we boarded the buses. One bus was filled with young people and friends singing and playing music. Our tears couldn't stop flowing as the bus took us from our motherland. I kept replaying in my mind the moment when I caught the last glimpse of our family house.

We arrived one hour before the train's departure, and everyone escorted us onto the platform. The musicians started playing songs, which was accompanied by the singing. Suddenly teachers along with groups of young children from No.5 School where Gheyshe and Sofiye worked arrived with biscuits and homemade *nan* for us to take on our journey. The platform turned into a chaotic scene as people tried to say their final goodbyes. As the train arrived we got on board in the melee of hugs and farewells. And finally, the train started to move.

It was only after settling down from the chaos of our departure did I notice the filthy condition of the train. It was overcrowded and people had to stand through their journey in the corridors. The odour was unbearable. We passed our time by talking until after midnight when we fell asleep one by one.

I woke up with a startle. It was dawn. Tengri Tagh, the Heavenly Mountains, which had followed us all the way till now, were now starting to fade away from sight. They were not saying goodbye, they were calling out for us to stop and return home. As I looked out of the window I saw the reflection of my brother's face, and the tears that were running down his cheeks.

The train seemed to be running faster now. The majestic Tengri Tagh had become pitifully miniscule and could hardly be seen, like a mother who retreats into sorrowful solitude, mourning the loss of her children. My brother and I held hands with tears falling like drops of summer rain from our eyes, as the symbol of our nation's strength and love finally disappeared.

Where is our fate taking us? What is to be our destiny? May God protect us and give us a better life. I prayed as we left the land drenched in tears.

Medical University class photo – the author with her classmate in 1962.

Wedding photo of the author's brother Sadik and his bride Saniya with the whole family in
Adelaide South Australia, in 1985.

The Author's Family Photo - with her husband, Latif, son Azat, daughter Kafiya, taken in Adelaide South Australia.

The author with her parents and two sister - childhood photo with her father, mother and her younger sister Zakiya

The Author with the translator, Rahima Mahmut,
at the International PEN Congress in Bishkek, Kyrgyzstan, October 2014.

PUBLISHER'S NOTE:

We would like to thank all those who had made financial contributions to support the publication of the book. Special thanks to Mr. Kawall Beharry, a philanthropist who is a passionate supporter of the Uyghur people's fight for freedom. We would also like to express our gratitude towards the World Uyghur Congress for their generous financial support. Above all, we are grateful to the English PEN for believing in this amazing story and awarding the translation grant, without which the publication of this remarkable memoir would not have been possible.